MAGILL'S
SURVEY
OF
WORLD
LITERATURE

MAGILL'S SURVEY OF WORLD LITERATURE

Volume 6

Spark–Zola

Indexes

Edited by
FRANK N. MAGILL

Marshall Cavendish Corporation
New York • London • Toronto • Sydney • Singapore

Published By
Marshall Cavendish Corporation
2415 Jerusalem Avenue
P.O. Box 587
North Bellmore, New York 11710
United States of America

∞ The paper used in these volumes conforms to the American National Standard for Permanence of Paper for Printed Library Materials, Z39.48-1984.

Library of Congress Cataloging-in-Publication Data
Magill's survey of world literature. Edited by Frank N. Magill.
    p. cm.
  Includes bibliographical references and index.
  1. Literature—History and criticism. 2. Literature—Stories, plots, etc. 3. Literature—Bio-bibliography. 4. Authors—Biography—Dictionaries. I. Magill, Frank Northen, 1907-
PN523.M29 1992
809—dc20
ISBN 1-85435-482-5 (set)   92-11198
ISBN 1-85435-488-4 (volume 6)   CIP

Second Printing

PRINTED IN THE UNITED STATES OF AMERICA

CONTENTS

MAGILL'S SURVEY OF WORLD LITERATURE

MAGILL'S
SURVEY
OF
WORLD
LITERATURE

MURIEL SPARK

Born: Edinburgh, Scotland
February 1, 1918

Principal Literary Achievement

A poet, critic, biographer, and dramatist, as well as a fiction writer, Spark is best known for her formal, witty novels.

Biography

Muriel Spark was born Muriel Sarah Camberg in Edinburgh, Scotland, on February 1, 1918, the daughter of Bernard Camberg, an engineer, and Sarah Elizabeth Uezzell Camberg. When Muriel was still very young, she began to write, and later, at James Gillespie's Girls' School in Edinburgh, she was labeled the school poet. Immediately after leaving school in 1937, Muriel Camberg went to Rhodesia. There, she married S. O. Spark, with whom she had a son, Robin Spark. Muriel Spark's attitude toward her life in Africa is reflected in short stories set in Africa, which show colonial society as meaningless, dull, and occasionally violent. Her attitude was doubtless colored by the fact that her marriage was failing. Because of the war, however, she was trapped in Rhodesia until 1944.

On her return to England, Spark became a writer for the propaganda branch of the British Intelligence Service. Then, for some years after the war, Spark lived in London. During this period, although she occasionally published a poem or two, her primary concern was supporting herself and her son by various jobs, including writing for a jewelry trade publication and working for a press agent. After editing the *Poetry Review* for two years, she started her own magazine, *Forum Stories and Poems*, which failed after two issues. Even though she was unable to devote full time to writing, Spark was dedicated to her craft. In fact, although she enjoyed the company of men, she had already decided that she could not be a good wife, as well as a good mother and a good writer, and therefore that another marriage was impossible.

Although she was to achieve fame through her novels, Spark's first book-length works were in other genres. While an edition of Anne Brontë, prepared jointly by Spark and the critic and poet Derek Stanford, was never published, in 1950 Spark and Stanford published an edition of essays titled *Tribute to Wordsworth* (1950). Spark's first independent critical work was *Child of Light: A Reassessment of Mary Wollstonecraft Shelley* (1951, 1987). It was followed by a collection of her own poems, *The Fanfarlo and Other Verse* (1952), and by other critical works, including that

which has received the highest acclaim, *John Masefield* (1953).

While writing her work on Masefield, Spark began to reassess the novel genre. Even though she had won a short-story contest in 1951, until this point Spark was committed to poetry, which she considered superior to fiction. Yet she now admired the narrative technique evident in Masefield's novels, as well as in his verse. Evidently she was changing her mind.

Spark was also changing her mind about religion. Although her father was Jewish and her Edinburgh school was Presbyterian, Spark did not have any religious commitment until 1953, when she became a High Church Anglican. Then, after reading the Roman Catholic theologian John Henry Newman and receiving instruction in Roman Catholicism, she was converted to that faith. Spark was received into the Roman Catholic church in 1954.

At this time, Spark was having serious physical and mental problems. Her physical difficulties were solved in part by financial aid from a number of people, which enabled her to obtain better food and much-needed medical attention; her psychological problems were eased after a period of therapy. During her stay in Kent, where she was recuperating from her illness, Spark produced her first full-length novel, *The Comforters* (1957). Its reception set the pattern for later critical reaction to her works: Even though critics praised the book, they disagreed as to how it should be interpreted. They were even more confused by her second novel, *Robinson* (1958), an allegory, which was not a success.

With *Memento Mori* (1959), Spark began a series of realistic novels. Although *Memento Mori* did not fall into the pattern of the rebellious "angry young men" who were then dominating English literature, perhaps because Spark was neither angry nor young and certainly not male, this novel was a financial success, and Spark could now become a full-time writer. The following year, she published *The Ballad of Peckham Rye* (1960) and *The Bachelors* (1960), novels that are both set in London, where she was now living.

Muriel Spark's skill in developing action through dialogue, which is evident in her novels, is also reflected in her success in dramatic works. In 1961, a number of radio plays written for the British Broadcasting Corporation were published in *Voices at Play*. The next year, her adaptation of *The Ballad of Peckham Rye* for radio won the Prix Italia, and her play *Doctors of Philosophy* (1962) was produced in London. The novel, however, remained Spark's primary interest.

While the early works had reflected her preoccupation with Catholicism, by 1961 Spark was ready to seek a reconciliation between her new faith and her Jewish heritage. That year, she spent two months in Israel doing research for a new book. A prizewinning novel, *The Mandelbaum Gate* (1965), was the result of her efforts.

After eighteen years in England, Spark felt that she needed the creative stimulus that a change of residence would provide. In 1962, she accepted the offer of an office from *The New Yorker*, which had published the novel *The Prime of Miss Jean Brodie* (1961), and for four years she spent most of her time in New York City. In 1966, however, Spark moved to Italy, where she divided her time between an apartment in

Rome and a country home in Tuscany.

Between 1968 and 1974, she published five novellas, all written in polished, economical prose, and all maintaining the viewpoint of a detached observer. The later books, however, have been more varied. In *The Takeover* (1976), a complex work about wealth, power, and crime, Spark appropriately uses a less constrained style. There are also differences in tone from one novel to another. For example, it has been noted that the mellow humor of *Loitering with Intent* (1981) is more reminiscent of her first novel than of more recent ones. Furthermore, after living in five different countries and traveling to many more, Spark was able to choose the setting of each novel from among many possibilities. All of Spark's recent works, however, continue to reflect the faith that has not wavered in four decades.

Analysis

In the fiction of Spark, one does not find the kind of passionate quest for the meaning of life so familiar in the autobiographical first novels of other authors. When she began to write novels, she was already a mature person, who had already arrived at her own certainty. Indeed, she did not publish her first novel until four years after her conversion to the Christian faith and three years after her commitment to Roman Catholicism. While her setting, her subjects, and her techniques have varied with the passage of time, the vision of reality that underlies all of her work has never changed. It is this vision that explains the many characteristics of Spark's novels that have most puzzled her critics.

As a Christian, Spark believes that, while human beings are on this earth, they live in not one world, but two, the temporal and the eternal. The theme of all of her works, then, involves the relationship between those two worlds. One must never forget that, to Spark, the purpose of life in the temporal world is to prepare for life with God in eternity. Therefore, human successes and failures must be judged rather differently than they are when the focus is on this world alone.

Spark's religious vision has an important influence on her plots, which seem to swing between the trivial and the tragic with an almost dizzying effect. For example, in *The Mandelbaum Gate*, the basic situation is as serious as that in any other adventure story set in the contemporary Middle East. Despite the warnings of people who have lived in that area for some time, the protagonist, Barbara Vaughan, a half-Jewish Englishwoman, slips into Jordan in disguise, determined to see her fiancé, and, as a result of her foolish action, places herself beyond the protection of her friends or her government. At best, she can be arrested; at worst, she may well be executed as a spy. After Barbara is hidden in a house of prostitution, however, which is also a center for spies, all sorts of improbable people begin to arrive, and, for a time, the novel becomes a comedy, indeed, almost a farce. It is difficult to know whether the author means for her readers to take the intrigue seriously or whether the story is a parody of the form in which it seems to be cast.

In the same novel, there seems to be a disproportion between the difficulties of the lovers, Harry Clegg and the indomitable Barbara, and the resolution to their problems, which is handled in an almost offhand fashion. Because Barbara is Roman Catholic, she spends a great deal of time agonizing about her liaison with Harry, who is divorced. At one point, she even offers to leave the Church in order to marry him; however, it is clear that, in reality, she will not bring herself to abandon her salvation for love. Finally, through a twist of fate or perhaps an act of Providence, it is discovered that Harry was reared a Catholic, and that therefore his non-Catholic marriage was invalid, and he can marry Barbara after all. While Barbara's spiritual torment has persisted through most of the book, the solution appears with a suddenness reminiscent of Gilbert and Sullivan. Furthermore, as a number of critics have pointed out, Spark gives the sequel only a line, stating merely that the two had a happy marriage.

Spark's abrupt changes of tone, as well as the detachment with which she treats the most tragic events, can be explained by her spiritual convictions. Although she has compassion for those who suffer in this world, Spark is also pointing out that, in God's view, the fact that Barbara and Harry are finally able to marry is a purely temporal and temporary matter. What is far more important is the struggle for Barbara's soul, which, it is suggested, would have been lost had she abandoned the Church.

Yet Spark must not be accused of simply following the party line. As interviews with her make clear, she is hardly sentimental about her coreligionists. In fact, she obviously identifies with her female protagonists, often new converts, who are appalled by narrow-minded, paranoid, and even vicious Catholics, such as Georgina Hogg in *The Comforters*, who seem determined to engulf them.

As to the Church itself, Spark has no illusions; in this world, she shows, it is often dominated by people who are more interested in attaining power over others than in embodying the principles of Christ. It is no accident that, for her fictional treatment of the Watergate scandal, *The Abbess of Crewe: A Modern Morality Tale* (1974), Spark chooses a Benedictine abbey as the setting and an assortment of nuns and priests as the conspirators. These include Alexandra, who has managed to get herself elected abbess through bugs, burglary, and slander, and Father Baudouin, a Jesuit priest who helped to organize the burglary. Even though Spark's focus is on Watergate, not on the supposed events at Crewe, it is obvious that she recognizes a parallel between political events outside the Church and those within it. As she has commented, Spark became a Catholic because she was spiritually compelled to do so, because she felt that the Church was the way of salvation, not because she felt that it or any other organization composed of human beings was perfect. The Church, too, has a secular reality and a spiritual reality. Like Dante Alighieri, Spark wishes to point out that the attainment of power within the Church in this world does not necessarily mean that one will be similarly honored in the next.

It is the sense of perspective that Spark says her faith has given her that causes her to create sinners who are appealing and intelligent and saints who seem to be fools. For example, in *The Abbess of Crewe*, the handsome Jesuit Father Maximilian, who is well informed about sin, has no moral scruples about participating in the election plot; similarly, in *The Ballad of Peckham Rye*, the charming Dougal Douglas manipulates everyone whom he meets for his own purposes, complicating and even destroying their lives. Significantly, Dougal later becomes a monk and then a writer. On the other hand, the ineffectual Freddy Hamilton of *The Mandelbaum Gate* rescues Barbara from her captors and saves her life, while the obtuse Joanna Childe of *The Girls of Slender Means* (1963) turns out to be the most courageous young woman in the May of Teck Club.

Spark's sense of perspective also explains the distance that she maintains from her characters and her willingness to make witticisms at their expense. On a spiritual level, Joanna is to be a superb creature; on a temporal level, however, she is large, humorless, and generally bewildered. Spark does not find it inappropriate to laugh at her elocution lessons or at her inability to grasp the reality of what is occurring around her. Sometimes, Spark even seems to laugh at tragedy. When the stupidest of the girls in *The Prime of Miss Jean Brodie* runs up and down dithering in a laboratory fire, Spark points out that she will later die by behaving exactly the same way in a hotel fire. Some critics have considered such comments to be not merely dispassionate but also heartless; others admire Spark's detachment and enjoy her black humor. Yet it may be that what seems shocking in Spark is, in reality, a revelation of her faith. If this world is only temporary, then the actual departure of a physical being from it is indeed not significant. From Spark's viewpoint, death is only a transition to eternity. It is this basic Christian emphasis, this insistence that everyday events are important only as they relate to the development of the eternal soul, which is essential for understanding all Spark's novels.

THE COMFORTERS

First published: 1957
Type of work: Novel

A young Catholic woman finds herself listening to the novel in which she is a character.

The Comforters, Spark's first published novel, is not only the story of the outlandish actions and interactions of a group of English eccentrics but also a novel about writing a novel. Spark later said that the reason that she wrote *The Comforters* was to see whether she could do it; with her new interest in fiction, obviously she was interested not only in writing a novel, with the usual characters and plot, but also in the process of creation itself.

At any rate, the work can be said to consist of two mysteries. One of them involves Louisa Jepp, a strong-minded old lady who seems to have a source of income of which her family is unaware. No one has worried much about it until she has a visit from her grandson, Laurence Manders, who possesses, or is possessed by, an obsessive curiosity. Laurence decides to uncover the source of her money; admittedly, her unusual collection of new friends, along with the diamonds hidden in the bakery goods, are enough to make anyone suspicious.

The second mystery involves the protagonist, Caroline Rose, who, like so many of Spark's heroines, is a high-strung young woman, given to bouts of illness, and a recent convert to Catholicism. After she has run away from a Catholic retreat center, made unbearable by the self-righteous bossiness of Georgina Hogg and by the paranoid sanctimoniousness of the others in attendance, Caroline finds herself hearing the sound of typing and of voices saying the words that have very recently appeared in Spark's novel. Naturally, she fears for her sanity and tries to find someone else who can hear what she hears. When she turns for help to her former lover, Laurence, he has two mysteries to solve.

Although the intricacies of the plot and the eccentricities of the characters in the novel produce a comic effect, *The Comforters* also has a serious theme, the exploration of Christian conduct, particularly the matter of Christian charity. This theme is introduced at the beginning of the book, when Caroline becomes so irritated with the other Catholics at the retreat house that she leaves. In contrast, both Laurence's father, Sir Edwin Manders, and his mother, Lady Manders, avoid facing such problems, Sir Edwin Manders by retreating whenever things get difficult at home, and Lady Manders by refusing to admit the possibility that there are hypocritical and evil people in the world. Clearly, what Spark is saying is that charity does not mandate blindness or sentimentality, that Christian conduct begins with a realistic look at life. It is no accident that Caroline is both the sincere convert and the accidental novelist. Like the author, Caroline is observing herself as she creates a novel and, at the same time, observing herself as she creates her own Christian life.

MEMENTO MORI

First published: 1959
Type of work: Novel

A number of elderly people are disturbed by an anonymous caller, who reminds them of a truth that they would rather ignore: that they must die.

With *Memento Mori*, her third novel, Spark abandoned the experimentation of her first two works and began to write with the sureness of one accomplished at her craft. Now, too, her efforts were being rewarded financially; it was this novel that established her as a full-time writer. The popularity of *Memento Mori* is not surprising. While, like *The Comforters*, this novel has eccentric characters, complex relationships, and puckish wit, both its subject and the direction of its plot are made clear from the very first chapter.

The subject of *Memento Mori* is death. Its characters are elderly people, who, in the course of the novel, must deal with their friends' deaths and with their own. Their attitudes are revealed by a unifying plot device: A number of them receive telephone calls from someone who says simply, "Remember you must die." What is peculiar is that none of them can agree as to the quality of the caller's voice. Ironically, at the end of the novel, although the characters who have been receiving the calls have all died, the caller has never been identified.

At the beginning of the book, Dame Lettie Colston receives one of the mysterious calls and discusses it with her brother, Godfrey Colston. Dame Lettie is not unduly bothered by the call; she has reported it to the police, and she regards it as more a nuisance than anything else, something to be put out of one's mind. As for Godfrey, he is too busy with old age to think about death. He is always irritated with his wife, Charmian Colston, a successful writer, who is intermittently confused. He is also preoccupied with his sexual needs, which are fulfilled when he sits staring at women's stocking tops and garters.

Like Godfrey, most of the characters in the novel are still clinging to life as if their time on earth will never end. When they gather for the funeral of Lisa Brooke, her relatives, friends, and former lovers are all preoccupied with their old annoyances. Dame Lettie scolds Godfrey for glaring; Janet Sidebottome snubs Lisa's rapacious housekeeper, Mrs. Pettigrew; and the amazonian Tempest Sidebottome is as angry as Dame Lettie about the impossible behavior of the poet Percy Mannering.

Unfortunately, at this gathering Dame Lettie decides that Mrs. Pettigrew would be perfect to look after Charmian. Despite Mrs. Pettigrew's machinations in regard to Lisa's estate, it never occurs to Dame Lettie or to Godfrey that, if the housekeeper were in their employ, she might be a threat to any of them. What they do not realize is that, while class and property once made them secure, age has now made them vulnerable. Simply because she is somewhat younger than they are, a person such as Mrs. Pettigrew can victimize her employers, capitalizing on Charmian's confusion and on Godfrey's sexual needs in order to seize power in the household and eventually to acquire the Colston money.

From the time that Lettie's interest in Mrs. Pettigrew is mentioned to her, Charmian's former companion, eighty-two-year-old Jean Taylor, who is now confined to a public nursing home, warns of the damage that the housekeeper can do. Jean sees all around her evidence of the way in which the elderly are treated, the patronizing flattery and the insulting tirades. Jean also sees that, like their social superiors, the old ladies in her ward spend their last days in bickering.

Only Charmian and Jean accept the approach of death with dignity. Despite Godfrey and Mrs. Pettigrew, Charmian moves to a nursing home, where she can live with the humor and grace that have always been characteristic of her. As for Jean Taylor, she has long ago decided to offer her death up to God. Therefore, she patiently endures the irritability of the other old ladies and the idiocies of the staff. When, at the end of the book, Spark describes the deaths of her various characters, it is clear that, from the vantage point of eternity, the cause of physical death is not important. What is important is to remember that everyone must die and then to spend one's days on earth in spiritual preparation for that inevitable end.

THE PRIME OF MISS JEAN BRODIE

First published: 1961
Type of work: Novel

A self-centered teacher manipulates the minds, and influences the lives, of a group of young students.

Structurally, *The Prime of Miss Jean Brodie* is one of Spark's simplest novels, focusing as it does on a single character's influence upon those who are closest to her. The protagonist is Miss Jean Brodie, a teacher at a staid Edinburgh school. At first, she seems to be a highly sympathetic character because of her passion for teaching and her independence of spirit. Instead of merely drilling her students, she tries to develop their minds. Even her bitterest enemies cannot deny the fact that the small group of girls chosen to be her intimates, "the Brodie set," seem to have a great deal of knowledge about music, art, history, political science, and current events. It would seem that these girls are indeed fortunate.

As Spark describes the gatherings of the Brodie girls, however, it becomes clear that Miss Brodie's influence is not altogether benign. She expects the few girls whom she chooses from her class to be totally loyal to her alone throughout their time in school. She ridicules the concept of team spirit, so that they will have no other attachments in their later years, when they would normally be in other groups. Furthermore, she manipulates the girls by insisting that she can perceive their real identities and by assigning roles to them based on those arrogant assumptions. Thus, Eunice Gardiner is the gymnast, Sandy Stanger, the reciter of vowels, and Rose Stanley, the sexual specialist. It is obvious that, while Miss Brodie continues to explore her own nature, her girls must depend upon her for their own development.

While Spark, in her usual detached fashion, narrates the story of Miss Jean Brodie, she provides enough clues to make it clear that she is describing a person who, while personally appealing, is actually obsessed with pride. One of these clues is Miss Brodie's admiration for the Fascists; with her insistence on blind loyalty to the flawless leader, she operates like the dictators whom she admires. Another is the fact that, while Brodie will not permit any questioning of her own authority, she considers herself to be above the rules that apply to ordinary mortals. She sees no need to observe the moral customs of her community, but she boasts to the girls about her sexual adventures, which she fictionalizes until they seem as romantic as the great love stories of history. Similarly, she scornfully repudiates the authority of her headmistress, not on a matter of principle, but simply because she refuses to bow to anyone.

Miss Brodie's admiration of excess leads her to suggest Anna Pavlova as a role model for her girls, not merely because she was a great dancer, but, perhaps more important, because of her legendary fits of temperament. As for career goals, Miss

Brodie will settle for nothing less than high drama; she wants Rose to be a famous lover and Eunice, a martyred missionary. By the end of the novel, when such talk has resulted in the death of a girl who ran away to fight in the Spanish Civil War, it is clear that Miss Brodie is, in fact, a false messiah.

Convinced that she must be stopped, one of her girls betrays Miss Brodie. Ironically, at the conclusion of the novel, her betrayer, now a cloistered nun, identifies Miss Brodie as the most important influence of her youth. One may ask whether she is emphasizing Miss Brodie's good qualities, which in the tradition of tragedy are overshadowed by her all-encompassing pride, or whether she is implying that, by experiencing a false messiah, she could find the true one.

THE GIRLS OF SLENDER MEANS

First published: 1963
Type of work: Novel

In a London hostel filled with young women, good and evil struggle for dominion.

The Girls of Slender Means illustrates Spark's belief that what may seem like trivialities are actually important events on the path to salvation or damnation. Certainly, in 1945 there is not much serious conversation at the May of Teck Club, a hostel in bombed-out London where some forty girls, mostly students and office workers of good background, can be appropriately housed. Spark can easily summarize the subjects of discourse at the club as being love and money, the latter needed to buy clothes and cosmetics in aid of the former. Except for a few such as Jane Wright, who has ambitions in the publishing business, and Joanna Childe, who, after one failed love affair, has decided to devote her life to poetry, the girls' major amusements are gossip and flirtation. The greatest success at the latter is the beautiful, self-centered Selina Redwood, who collects men of all sorts, including Nicholas Farringdon, an irresolute young man, most recently the author of a book in favor of atheism.

The title that Spark chose for this book is particularly apt. In the first sentence, she points out the obvious meaning: The story is set at a time when everyone in England had limited means. When the girls' most exciting adventure turns out to be wriggling through a bathroom window to sunbathe on the roof, however, it is clear that a slender bodily structure is indeed the means to satisfaction. Right at the point when one of the girls is stuck in the window, the comedy turns to drama. An unexploded bomb detonates, destroying the fire escapes, and when a gas main ruptures, a number of girls are trapped on the top floor. Then, of course, the slender ones can slip up to the roof, from which they can be rescued. Meanwhile, the firemen are working frantically to open a blocked-off hatch, so that the remainder can be rescued before the building collapses. At the moment that the last one, Joanna Childe, is on the ladder, the end comes, and the young woman dies in the ruins.

Less important than the matter of who lives and who dies is Spark's description of the girls' behavior during those critical minutes. For example, the slim Selina slips back into the house, not to help the others, but to rescue a prized Schiaparelli dress. On the other hand, Joanna calmly recites the appropriate psalms and waits until last to climb the ladder, as it happens, missing her own chance to escape by only a few seconds. For Nicholas, who has been on the roof throughout the rescue effort, this episode is a turning point. Inspired by Joanna's faith, he commits himself to Christianity, becomes a missionary, and later, when the survivors have returned to their everyday lives, dies a martyr's death in Haiti.

The conclusion suggests still a third interpretation of the title. Most of the girls, though they are not as evil as Selina, nevertheless are spiritually impoverished. In contrast, Joanna has so rich a faith that she is able to escape from her self. Among Spark's characters, Joanna is one of the few saints. Moreover, because it concludes with spiritual triumph both for Joanna and for Nicholas, in the context of Spark's vision, *The Girls of Slender Means* is a novel with an unequivocal happy ending.

Summary

In a time where most critics and writers limit their interest to success and failure in this world, Muriel Spark provides an interesting alternative. Like her friend and patron Graham Greene, Spark believes that it is only the spiritual reality that gives significance to temporal events.

Although the wit that enlivens her narratives may be considered a divine gift, Spark's detached tone can be explained by the long-range view dictated by her faith, which considers this world merely a testing ground for the next. Eccentric characters, preposterous plots, swift shifts between comedy and tragedy—all of these are enough like life itself to suggest that Muriel Spark's God, too, has a sense of humor.

Bibliography

Kane, Richard C. *Iris Murdoch, Muriel Spark, and John Fowles: Didactic Demons in Modern Fiction.* Rutherford, N.J.: Fairleigh Dickinson University Press, 1988.

Kemp, Peter. *Muriel Spark.* London: Paul Elek, 1974.

Massie, Alan. *Muriel Spark.* Edinburgh, Scotland: Ramsey Head Press, 1979.

Stanford, Derek. *Muriel Spark: A Biographical and Critical Study.* London: Centaur Press, 1963.

Stubbs, Patricia. *Muriel Spark.* Harlow, Essex, England: Longman for the British Council, 1973.

Whittaker, Ruth. *The Faith and Fiction of Muriel Spark.* New York: St. Martin's Press, 1982.

Rosemary M. Canfield Reisman

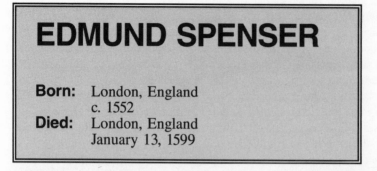

EDMUND SPENSER

Born: London, England
c. 1552
Died: London, England
January 13, 1599

Principal Literary Achievement

Spenser was the leading poet of sixteenth century England and the author of *The Faerie Queene*, the major English Renaissance epic.

Biography

Edmund Spenser achieved recognition during his lifetime as a major English poet; nevertheless, he spent twenty years of his life in Ireland, occupying a variety of positions in the colonial government. His contemporaries described him variously as the English Vergil and as a second Geoffrey Chaucer. Even so, much of what has been written about his life and accepted as biographical fact is elaborated out of Spenser's fictional works or is based on conjecture rather than evidence. Modern scholarship cannot ascertain where and when his works were written, nor can it provide any detailed knowledge of Spenser's patronage connections.

Spenser was born in London, England, around 1552, the son of John and Elizabeth Spenser. He attended the Merchant Taylor's School in London, where the headmaster was Richard Mulcaster, later well known as a humanist educator. On May 20, 1569, Spenser entered Pembroke Hall, Cambridge. He was entered as a sizar, a poor student who acted as a servant to earn his room and board.

Spenser received a B.A. in 1573 and an M.A. in 1576. His university degrees qualified him for a position in the Church, a profession that many of his classmates probably chose. He could also have become a schoolmaster, continued at the university while working toward a degree in divinity, or tried to establish himself in the household of a prominent nobleman or in the government. Those who intended to pursue a career in government usually came from families with strong connections to the court or Privy Council, and they frequently followed their university degrees with legal training from one of the Inns of Court, the four law schools in England. Spenser lacked the advantage of family connections, and there is no record of his having attended one of the Inns of Court.

By 1578, Spenser had become the secretary of the former headmaster of Pembroke College, Dr. John Young, archbishop of Rochester. Spenser later served Robert Dud-

ley, earl of Leicester, but anecdotes concerning his close relationship to Leicester and his friendship with Sir Philip Sidney, Leicester's nephew, are unlikely to be true because of the social barriers that would have existed between a mere secretary and powerful courtiers such as Leicester and Sidney. On October 27, 1579, a marriage was recorded at Westminster between Machabyas Chylde and an Edmounde Spenser, possibly the poet. References in later documents to two children, Sylvanus and Katherine, are assumed to refer to offspring from this marriage.

Some scholars have speculated that either a manuscript satire or his first published poem, *The Shepheardes Calender* (1579), got Spenser into trouble and that he was punished by being sent to Ireland, but the lack of any corroborating evidence makes this hypothesis improbable. It is more likely that Spenser's appointment as secretary to Arthur, Lord Grey of Wilton, was a mark of favor resulting from his patronage connections to Leicester and Sidney. Grey was made Lord Deputy of Ireland on August 12, 1580, and Spenser accompanied him as his secretary. Under Grey, he acted as the clerk of the Privy Council for £20 a year. He worked mainly at Dublin Castle, although he may have accompanied Grey on some of his expeditions. In March, 1581, he replaced Lodowick Bryskett as clerk of the Chancery for Faculties; in this post, his duties would have involved administering the licenses and dispensations issued under the authority of the archbishop of Dublin. Spenser may have purchased this seven-year appointment from Bryskett; in any case, since he was still employed as secretary to Lord Grey, he probably hired someone else to do the actual work.

In 1582, Lord Grey was recalled to England in disgrace; he was reported to have been too severe in his treatment of the Irish. Rather than returning with Lord Grey, however, Spenser remained in Ireland, acting as a colonial administrator. The potential economic rewards were attractive. Like many other English colonials, Spenser profited when the lands of Irish rebels were seized by the English and reallocated to loyal subjects of the Crown. In 1586, he was assigned 3,028 acres in Cork from the vast estate of the earl of Desmond, an Irish nobleman who had successfully rebelled against the Crown. In 1589, Spenser succeeded Bryskett as clerk of the Council of Munster.

Spenser may have taken possession of Kilcolman Castle and his lands in Cork in 1588, but that seems unlikely since he did not receive a lease until 1590, when he was granted a perpetual lease for £17 17s a year. Like other Englishmen who were granted such leases, he was called an "undertaker" because he had undertaken to plant a colony at Kilcolman consisting of at least twenty-four households of English settlers. Sir Walter Ralegh owned 42,000 acres around Lismore Castle, located about thirty miles from Spenser's holdings. Spenser suggests that Ralegh's encouragement prompted him to publish part 1 (books 1 to 3) of *The Faerie Queene* (1590). He dedicated the first installment of his English epic to Elizabeth I. In recognition of his achievement, on February 26, 1591, the queen awarded him an annual pension of £50.

Spenser completed the second installment (books 4 to 6) of *The Faerie Queene* in 1596, again dedicating his epic to Elizabeth I. On November 12, 1596, James VI of Scotland wrote to Elizabeth requesting that she punish Spenser for his negative portrait of James's mother, Mary, Queen of Scots. Although he was not punished, the second part of *The Faerie Queene* did not result in advancement or specific marks of royal favor. While in London in 1596, Spenser may have written *A Vewe of the Present State of Ireland*, a dialogue concerning the administration of Ireland, which, however, was not published until 1633, several decades after his death.

In 1598, Spenser was named sheriff-designate for Cork, but he may never have served as sheriff. The relations between the Irish and the colonial government were growing steadily worse. Spenser's property in Kilcolman was attacked and burned, and he took refuge with his family in the walled city of Cork. On December 9, 1598, he left for London bearing dispatches from the Munster government to the Privy Council; he delivered these messages on Christmas Eve and was paid the usual stipend of £8.

Two weeks later, on January 13, 1599, Edmund Spenser died in London. Ben Jonson later told his young friend William Drummond of Hawthornden that Spenser died for lack of bread in King Street, but this gossip occurred more than twenty years after Spenser's death. William Camden, the great Elizabethan historian, however, also reports that Spenser died in poverty, and, although modern scholars have pointed to Spenser's pension and to his having recently received a stipend of £8, the testimony of a contemporary historian must be given substantial authority. Camden has also recorded a poignant description of Spenser's funeral, which he reveals was paid for by the earl of Essex. Spenser's body was carried to Westminster Abbey by his fellow poets; they wrote elegies and threw both their verses and the pens with which they had written them into his grave.

Analysis

In 1600, Camden described Spenser as the leading poet of the age, indicating that Spenser had immediately established himself as a major poet. The body of his work differs from that of many nineteenth and twentieth century poets because each of his works is written consciously within certain literary conventions. Instead of attempting to find thematic connections among his works, each work of art needs to be assessed in relation to the earlier classical, Continental, and English works that Spenser adopted as models.

Many of Spenser's minor poems are also linked to identifiable occasions or with specific patrons: *Daphnaïda* (1591), an elegy on the death of Douglas Howard, wife of Sir Arthur Gorges, was dedicated to Helena, marchioness of Northampton, Gorges' aunt by marriage. *Prothalamion* (1596) celebrates the double wedding of two daughters of Edward Somerset, earl of Worcester, on November 8, 1596. *Fowre Hymnes* (1596) is internally dated September 1, 1596, and is dedicated to the sisters, Margaret, countess of Cumberland, and Anne, countess of Warwick.

Spenser's first major work, *The Shepheardes Calender*, a sequence of pastoral eclogues, appeared in 1579. *The Shepheardes Calender* was licensed in the Stationers' Register to Hugh Singleton on December 5, 1579, and the rights of publication were reassigned to John Harrison on October 29, 1580. Spenser is described merely as the "new poet," and his authorship seems not to have been immediately known. The authorship of the preface and glossary is attributed to an unidentified E. K., but scholars have conjectured that Spenser and his friend Gabriel Harvey were involved in preparing these commentaries on the text. The model for the typographical layout of the woodcuts, arguments, eclogues, and mottoes was the edition of Jacopo Sannazaro's *Arcadia* (1504; *Arcadia and Piscutorial Eclogues*, 1966) printed by Francesco Sansovino in Venice in 1571.

The structure of *The Shepheardes Calender* is remarkably complex. The twelve eclogues are linked to the twelve months of the calendar; they are accompanied by woodcuts, brief prose arguments, commentaries, and notes. The poem makes use of a number of genres, including love complaint, debate poem, pastoral singing match, panegyric, pastoral elegy, parable, and religious satire. Its metrical virtuosity is formidable; only January and December are in the same verse form. Judging from the number of editions printed during Spenser's life, *The Shepheardes Calender* was extremely popular with Spenser's contemporaries. New editions were printed in 1581, 1586, 1591, and 1597. The two later editions may have been printed in response to the interest generated by the publication of *The Faerie Queene* in 1590 and 1596.

The Shepheardes Calender illustrates the way in which Spenser wrote within certain conventions. He uses the framework of his classical predecessors, Theocritus and Vergil, to explore a variety of pastoral forms. Instead of expressing his personal feelings in the way that a modern poet might, Spenser consciously plays with forms and themes derived from literary tradition. He expects his readers not only to respond to his poem as a work of art in its own right but also to know how his predecessors handled the conventions of the pastoral elegy and to evaluate his work in relation to literary tradition.

Colin Clout, the central figure of *Shepheardes Calender*, is a shepherd, lover, and poet. Throughout his later works, Spenser used the name Colin Clout for his persona. Colin Clout is the central figure in *Colin Clouts Come Home Againe* (1595), and later in book 6 of *The Faerie Queene* (1596) Colin Clout again functions as a symbol of the poet-author. Even so, one cannot assume an absolute identification between Spenser and Colin Clout but should approach Colin Clout's love for Rosalind as an artful convention and pay attention to the language and images used to portray his unhappy lover.

The name Colin Clout was inspired by John Skelton's *Colyn Cloute* (1522) and carries with it connotations of lower class and rustic. In *The Shepheardes Calender*, Spenser establishes Colin as the disciple of Tityrus, who was understood to be the persona of Vergil, author of the great Roman epic, and of Chaucer. Like Tityrus, Colin (Spenser) wants to write a national epic. Technically speaking, Vergil and Chaucer are not Spenser's sources, nor is he paying tribute to their influence on his work. Using the forms and conventions that they used, he wants to write verse that will challenge comparison with that of two of his greatest predecessors.

It was not until 1590, more than a decade after the appearance of *The Shepheardes Calender*, that the first part of Spenser's greatest work, *The Faerie Queene*, appeared in print. The first three books of *The Faerie Queene* owe much to epic and romance conventions, and each one celebrates a virtue derived from Christian and classical tradition. In book 1, the Redcrosse Knight, representing the virtue of holiness, assists a fair lady, named Una (the one true faith) in freeing her parents (Adam and Eve) from the dragon (sin). Redcrosse's quest will be successful when he has conquered the dragon and restored the lost Eden.

In achieving his quest, he encounters highly complex figures such as Duessa (double or false religion, Roman Catholicism, Mary, Queen of Scots) and personifications of abstract states of mind such as Despaire. The battle between Redcrosse and the dragon in canto 11 of the first book should be read allegorically and typologically. Images of ships, seas, and sea monsters associate the dragon with the Spanish Armada, but the dragon is also sin and Satan. Typologically, Redcrosse parallels Saint George, the English fleet, and Christ.

Book 2 turns to the classical virtue of temperance, which is portrayed in the adventures of the knight Guyon. He attempts to achieve the golden mean of "nothing too much." While it is virtuous to be chaste and rational, it is a mistake to repudiate the sensual and emotional. He visits the cave of Mammon, where he is tempted not only by material wealth but also by honor. In order to prepare for his final battle against sensual intemperance, he visits the House of Alma (soul) where he learns about his own psyche and where his inner fortitude is restored. His principal opponent is Acrasia, who presides over the Bower of Bliss, a beautiful garden in which sensual beauty has become excessive and overshadows spiritual and heroic values. Guyon does not destroy Acrasia; he binds or restrains her, indicating that sensuality has its place in human nature but that it must not be allowed to control the individual.

In book 3, the narrative structure is more loosely organized, but Spenser focuses on Britomart, a female knight who embodies chastity. He interlaces the adventures of Florimell (flowers and vegetation) and Marinell (sea), Amoret (beloved) and Scudamour (shield of love), Belphoebe (beautiful Diana, Elizabeth I) and Timias (loyalty, honor, Sir Walter Ralegh), and numerous other figures with those of Britomart. Nevertheless, it is Britomart who completes the quest of freeing Amoret from the house of Busirane. No consensus has been reached concerning the precise meaning of this episode. Some critics think that Amoret needs to be freed from her own fear of sexuality or that Scudamour, her husband to be, has been too bold in his wooing of her. Yet others think that Spenser is elevating chaste married love over the adulterous conventions of medieval courtly love. Britomart's own connection with Queen Elizabeth seems clear because Britomart's marriage will create a dynasty culminating in the birth and reign of the Virgin Queen.

Spenser's *Complaints*, a collection of satires, meditations, and laments that mediate on the world's vanity and satirize social ills, were published in 1591, but some of the poems may have been written much earlier. *Complaints* was entered in the Stationers' Register on December 29, 1590, and was printed by William Ponsonby early in 1591. The collection consists of nine separate works: "The Ruines of Time,"

"The Teares of the Muses," "Virgils Gnat," "Prosopopoia: Or, Mother Hubberds Tale," "Ruines of Rome, by Bellay," "Muiopotmos: Or, The Fate of the Butterflie," "Visions of the Worlds Vanitie," "The Visions of Bellay," and "The Visions of Petrarch."

Ponsonby's statement that he collected the poems without assistance from Spenser was rejected by an earlier generation of scholars, who assumed that sixteenth century authors "saw their works through the press" and proofread each sheet shortly after it was printed. Since copyright belonged to the publisher or bookseller, authors had far less control over the publication of their work in the sixteenth century than they do presently. None of the corrections made in the text of the *Complaints* during printing would require Spenser's presence in the printing house.

One of the most intriguing poems in this collection is "Prosopopoia." Spenser uses the beast fable to describe the adventures of a fox and an ape as they travel through England exposing—and participating in—social abuses. Spenser describes "Prosopopoia" as having been written in his youth, but since no manuscript copies seem to have existed prior to the 1591 printed text, there are no substantive grounds for postulating an earlier version. The poem describes social ills, showing that a simple landowner may be fooled by greedy servants, demonstrating that an ignorant and venial priest may abuse his office and take advantage of his parishioners, and confirming that self-seeking opportunists may rise to prominence in a corrupt court. Except for interest in the topical satire in "Prosopopoia," the *Complaints* have received little attention from critics, but these meditations and satires offer readers insight into the kind of poetry that Spenser's contemporaries appreciated.

In *Colin Clouts Come Home Againe*, Spenser returned to the pastoral as a genre, but, as with "Prosopopoia," he remains engaged by the impact of court patronage on courtiers and poets. This long eclogue describes Spenser's trip to court under the auspices of Sir Walter Ralegh, offers complementary negative and positive views of the court, and pays tribute to contemporary poets and patrons.

The dedication of *Colin Clouts Come Home Againe* is addressed to Ralegh and is dated December 27, 1591, from Kilcolman. Spenser revised the poem before its publication in 1595, because in it he alludes to the death of Ferdinando Stanley, earl of Derby, on April 16, 1594. Still, the reference to Kilcolman in the title suggests that "home" for Spenser has become Ireland rather than England. In this eclogue, Spenser describes his meeting with the Shepherd of the Ocean (Ralegh) and the pleasure that they take in reading their verses to each other. He also narrates the story of his trip to the court of Cynthia (Elizabeth I). *Colin Clouts Come Home Againe* not only explores love as the subject of poetry but also examines the capacity of the court for supporting and sustaining the needs of poets. Although Cynthia herself remains an untarnished ideal, the court is far from being a congenial place for the poet.

The second part of *The Faerie Queene* was published in 1596 and, like the first part, uses the conventions of epic and romance but is more somber in tone. Book 4, which continues the action of book 3 and begins the second part, is devoted to the virtue of friendship, but included in friendship is concord, a social virtue. Book 5, the

Legend of Justice, is divided into three sections concerning English common law, the relationships among law, justice, and equity, and, finally, the application of justice to contemporary events. In this book, Spenser makes use of his own experiences as a civil servant in Ireland. He, however, seems skeptical about the degree to which justice can be understood as governing human experience.

Book 6, the Legend of Courtesy, examines chivalric values in a pastoral context. Sir Calidore falls in love with Pastorella, the fair daughter of the shepherd Meliboe, but his sojourn among the peaceful shepherds is disrupted when brigands attack the community and kidnap Pastorella. Sir Calidore rescues Pastorella as Sir Calepine saves Serena from the cannibals. The principal villain of book 6 is the Blatant Beast, who stands for slander and the misuse of language; conversely, Calidore's vision of the Graces dancing on Mount Acidale (canto 10) exemplifies poetry and the harmony of language.

Spenser died before *The Faerie Queene* was finished, but ten years after his death, an addition was made to his epic. The "Mutabilitie Cantos" include canto 6, containing 55 stanzas, canto 7, containing 59 stanzas, and canto 8, containing two stanzas. "The Mutabilitie Cantos" juxtapose a solemn inquiry into whether mutability or order controls the universe, and a comic story of the adventures of Faunus, who attempts to spy on Diana when she is bathing. These cantos were not published until they mysteriously appeared in the 1609 folio printed by Matthew Lownes, approximately a decade after Spenser's death. Since Spenser was not involved in their publication, one cannot be sure how much credence to give the printer's headnote stating that "both for Forme and Matter, [they] appear to be parcell of some following Booke of the *Faerie Queene*, under the legend of *Constancie*." They might also be a remnant of an unfinished mythological poem, but most critics have preferred to think of "The Mutabilitie Cantos" as the conclusion of *The Faerie Queene*.

THE FAERIE QUEENE

First published: Part 1, 1590; part 2, 1596
Type of work: Epic and romance

Books 1 to 3 celebrate the virtues of holiness, temperance, and chastity, while books 4 to 6 praise friendship, justice, and courtesy.

Spenser's *The Faerie Queene* was published in two parts: the first part (books 1 to 3) appeared in 1590; the second part (books 4 to 6), with which the first part was reprinted, appeared in 1596. The dedication to the 1596 edition is addressed to Elizabeth I, whom Spenser describes as the empress of England, France, Ireland, and Virginia. He adds that he is consecrating "these his labours to live with the eternitie of her fame." Although *The Faerie Queene* makes use of romance, as well as epic, conventions, Spenser intended the poem to function as an English epic, a celebration of the emerging British Empire. In his letter to Sir Walter Ralegh dated January 13, 1589, he states that the "generall end therefore of all the booke is to fashion a gentleman or noble person in vertuous and gentle discipline." Spenser also states that he will use the Aristotelian virtues as a means of organizing the themes of his epic, indicating that he will write a twelve-book epic, portraying in Arthur the twelve private moral virtues that he exercised before he was king. If this work is well received, he adds, he may continue by describing how Arthur came to embody the twelve "politick" virtues after he became king. When the second part appeared in 1596, the title page described the poem as "disposed into twelve bookes, fashioning XII morall vertues," but no suggestion is given regarding whether the moral virtues are private or public.

One of the most distinctive stylistic features of *The Faerie Queene* involves Spenser's use of allegory and typology, both of which are unfamiliar to a modern audience and have therefore often been misinterpreted. Renaissance authors inherited a tradition of reading texts allegorically from medieval writers. The method of reading Homer's works and the Bible in terms of a fourfold allegory derived from Alexandrian exegesis of these texts. According to this method of reading, anything that was not educational or useful in a text should be interpreted figuratively. No level of meaning would be taken literally. A reference to the Temple of Jerusalem, for example, would be interpreted historically as the Temple of Jerusalem, allegorically as the Church on earth, morally as the individual believer, and anagogically or mystically as the final communion of the saints in heaven.

Renaissance readers and writers think of allegory somewhat in the way that modern readers think of symbolism; meanings are concealed in the imagery and narrative. In Spenser's case, the allegory is not continuous, nor is it consistent. Elizabeth, for example, is represented by the maiden hunter Belphoebe and by Britomart, the female knight, who will marry Artegall (equal to Arthur), the knight of justice. The offspring of Britomart and Artegall will produce the Tudor dynasty culminating in Elizabeth, but in book 5 Elizabeth is also represented in Mercilla, a queenly figure who dispenses both justice and mercy.

A character or event frequently is to be interpreted on multiple levels of significance: In book 1, Redcrosse knight is the champion of the virtue holiness, but he is also the embodiment of Saint George, the patron saint of England and the defender of the one true Protestant church. Instead of trying to arrive at a specific interpretation of *The Faerie Queene*, one needs to be aware of the potential multiplicity of meanings that may be suggested in any one episode.

Interpretation of Spenser's allegory is rendered more difficult because, during the eighteenth century, the significance of the term "allegory" changed, creating confusion about what a Renaissance author intended when he wrote allegory. Instead of being used to refer to the structure of images and narrative incidents, allegory came to be used as a synonym for personification. Spenser does use personification, for example, in the monsters Error in book 1 and Lust in book 4, but under the rubric of allegory he also includes other genres such as fable, prophecy, and parable and devices such as irony (saying one thing but meaning another), hyperbole, and historical and contemporary allusions.

George Puttenham, in his *The Arte of English Poesie* (1589), makes an interesting distinction between mixed allegory, in which the poet tells the readers what the metaphor means, and full allegory, in which the poet allows the readers to determine the meaning. According to Puttenham's definition, the play *Everyman* (1508) would be considered a mixed allegory because the author reveals that Good Deeds means a Christian who follows Christ's teaching; on the other hand, William Shakespeare's *Hamlet* (c. 1600-1601) would be considered a full allegory because the character Hamlet is a specific Danish prince but can also represent Everyman. Most modern handbooks of literature reverse these classifications and would consider *Everyman* "more allegorical" than *Hamlet*.

The Faerie Queene fits Puttenham's definition of full allegory. When Spenser refers to his poem as a "dark conceit," he is alluding to the structure of images and to the narrative and rhetorical techniques in the poem, not to a structure of ideas outside it. In the letter to Ralegh, he comments: "To some, I know, this Methode will seeme displeasaunt, which had rather have good discipline delivered plainly in way of precepts, or sermoned at large, as they use, then thus clowdily enwrapped in Allegoricall devices." The allegory, for Spenser, consist of "cloudy devices," not of precepts or sermons.

Typology, another device used throughout *The Faerie Queene*, is even less familiar than allegory to modern readers. The term comes from *typos* (Greek, "to strike"). In biblical typology, a type is defined as a detail in the Old Testament that foreshadows its antitype in the New Testament. The detail may be a person (Adam, Moses, and David are all types of Christ); it may be an event (the Passover and the crossing of the Red Sea foreshadow the Redemption); or it may be an institution (the Levitical priesthood and the ritual of the old Temple are figures of the blessings of the spiritual priesthood of Christ).

In Nowell's Catechism, which every sixteenth century reader would have known, the master asks, "Why should not the Decalogue refer to the Israelites alone, because God's introduction declares: 'Hear, O Israel, I am the Lord thy God, which brought thee out of the land of Egypt, out of the House of bondage.' " The student is supposed to answer that the pharaoh of Egypt is the figure of the devil ready to oppress the Christian and that Moses' rescue of the Israelites from bodily bondage is a type of Christ's delivery of all of His faithful followers from the bondage of sin (antitype). Spenser's readers would have interpreted the battle between Redcrosse knight and the dragon in canto 11 of book 1 typologically. The imagery used to describe the three-day battle makes it clear that Redcrosse is triumphing over Satan, but the imagery also summons images of the Passion and of the harrowing of hell.

In most of Spenser's verse, including his justly acclaimed short masterpiece, *Epithalamion*, one finds him using the techniques of allegory and typology.

EPITHALAMION

First published: 1595
Type of work: Wedding poem

This work is a hymn in celebration of marriage.

Amoretti, a sonnet sequence printed with the *Epithalamion*, differs from most Petrarchan sequences because, instead of depicting the suffering of an unfulfilled lover, *Amoretti* moves from courtship to the lovers' fulfillment in marriage. The *Amoretti*, a sequence of eighty-nine sonnets, and *Epithalamion*, a verse celebration of a wedding day, were printed together by William Ponsonby in 1595, but they were entered in the Stationers' Register on November 19, 1594. Ponsonby's title page describes them as "written not long since," and they have been interpreted as documents in Spenser's biography.

Since the *Amoretti* contains references to wooing, it has been assumed that the woman addressed is Elizabeth Boyle, Spenser's second wife. If Edmund Spenser is the Spenser who married Machabyas Chylde in 1579, Machabyas had presumably died by 1591. According to numerological and astronomical analyses deriving from the sonnet sequence and wedding poem, Spenser married Elizabeth Boyle sometime between 1591 and 1594. Internal references indicate that his *Epithalamion* was probably written for his own wedding, which according to astronomical and numerological images seems to have taken place on June 11, St. Barnabas Day, possibly in 1594. The dedication to the published texts, however, does not specify a biographical link between Spenser's life and these poems. Ponsonby dedicates the poems to Sir Robart Needham, whom he thanks for having brought the poems from Ireland to England.

The term "epithalamium" derives from Greek and means literally "before the bridal chamber," but it has come to stand for many different kinds of works, including lyrics praising marriage and actual descriptions of marriage. Conventionally, the spokesman of the wedding poem is a social figure in charge of the festivities or a guest at the wedding, but Spenser varies these conventions because in his poem the bridegroom himself is the poet. His poem intermixes the conventions of the sonnet sequence and the wedding poem.

The poem has a mythological frame; both human beings and gods are wedding guests, but in stanza 10, the bride is given a *blazon*, a head-to-toe description of her beauty borrowed from the conventions of the Petrarchan sonnet. Spenser's bride is first a "mayden Queene," then her neck is like a "marble towre" and her body a "pallace fayre," but Spenser never lets the reader forget the sensuousness of the occasion. The lips of his bride are "lyke cherryes charming men to byte," her breast like a "bowle of creame uncrudded." This magnificent celebration of wedded love concludes with Spenser's prayer that his poem, "in lieu of many ornaments," will be to his wife a "goodly ornament," and that his consecration of their marriage in song will be "for short time an endlesse moniment."

Summary

On his tombstone, Edmund Spenser is described as the "prince of poets," high praise indeed for a poet who was born only about ten years before Shakespeare. His *The Faerie Queene* ranks as one of the most important national epics, and it is one of the best Renaissance efforts to preserve medieval romance while emulating the classical epics.

Bibliography

Alpers, Paul J. *The Poetry of the "Faerie Queene."* Berkeley: University of California Press, 1967.

Berger, Harry. *Revisionary Play: Studies in the Spenserian Dynamics.* Berkeley: University of California Press, 1988.

Fletcher, Angus. *The Prophetic Moment.* Chicago: University of Chicago Press, 1971.

Heninger, S. K., Jr. *Sidney and Spenser: The Poet as Maker.* University Park: Pennsylvania State University Press, 1989.

Hieatt, A. Kent. *Short Time's Endless Monument: The Symbolism of Numbers in Edmund Spenser's "Epithalamion."* New York: Columbia University Press, 1960.

Judson, Alexander C. *The Life of Edmund Spenser.* Baltimore: The Johns Hopkins University Press, 1945.

Lewis, C. S. *Spenser's Images of Life.* Edited by Alastair Fowler. New York: Cambridge University Press, 1967.

Nelson, William. *The Poetry of Edmund Spenser: A Study.* New York: Columbia University Press, 1963.

Roche, Thomas P. *The Kindly Flame: A Study of the Third and Fourth Books of Spenser's "Faerie Queene."* Princeton, N.J.: Princeton University Press, 1964.

Jean R. Brink

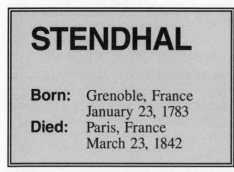

STENDHAL

Born: Grenoble, France
January 23, 1783
Died: Paris, France
March 23, 1842

Principal Literary Achievement

As well as being a brilliant depicter of the people and morals of his day, Stendhal was one of the most important innovators in the history of the novel.

Biography

Stendhal is the most widely known pseudonym of Marie-Henri Beyle. He was born in Grenoble, a provincial city in the southeast of France, on January 23, 1783. He was alive during the time of the great upheaval in French and European society brought about, in the first place, by the French Revolution and subsequently by the rise and fall of Napoleon Bonaparte. Stendhal had intimate experience with the latter phenomenon.

Grenoble was not a place where Stendhal felt at home. He had little time for its narrow outlook in matters of politics and religion, and its atmosphere was out of touch with the burgeoning spirit of liberty of the author's boyhood. Much of what Stendhal came to oppose in human affairs and behavior he initially found in his father, with whom he was severely in conflict. This antagonism was made worse by, or perhaps had its source in, the death of the novelist's mother when he was seven. In his candid and innovative, though unfinished, autobiography, *Vie de Henri Brulard* (1890, 1949; *The Life of Henry Brulard*, 1925), he details with almost embarrassing intimacy his love for his mother. This autobiography's title draws attention to Stendhal's love of pseudonyms. He is thought to have used more than two hundred pseudonyms.

In 1799, having completed his education at Grenoble, Stendhal went to Paris and enrolled in the École Polytechnique, intending to study mathematics. The attractions of the capital, however, soon militated against study, and by 1800 he had secured a commission in Napoleon's army. His duties took him to Milan, where he began a lifelong love affair with Italy. One of the four Italian words inscribed on his tomb is "Milanese," and it was in his adopted native city, finally free of the constraints of Grenoble, that he entered into the first of many ardent and arduous emotional liaisons.

His first visit to Milan lasted until 1802. In that year, he resigned his army commis-

sion and returned to Paris. For a number of years, he attempted to live an artistic life and was a frequenter of literary salons. Unable to afford the life-style that his ambitions required, he rejoined the army in 1806 and worked as a quartermaster. This position took him to Germany, Russia, and Austria. Stendhal did not see direct action, but in other respects, imaginative as well as physical, he was profoundly affected by the demands of military life. He resigned his army position in 1813 for health reasons and retired to Milan, where he remained until 1821.

These years saw Stendhal's first publications. These consisted of works of criticism and, as such, are an important introduction to his fiction (though not for their contents). The criticism takes the form of biography, Stendhal's first book being *Vie de Haydn, de Mozart, et de Métastase* (1815; *The Lives of Haydn and Mozart, with Observations on Métastase*, 1817), followed by *Histoire de la peinture de Italie* (1817). Both these works are notable for their plagiarism; yet they are also notable for their concern with style and sensibility, matters that are central to Stendhal's fiction. In addition, the biographical mode is one that his two great novels adapt and develop.

Both these works were published under the name Beyle. *Rome, Naples, et Florence en 1817* (1817, 1826; *Rome, Naples, and Florence in 1817*, 1818) was the first book of his to appear under the name Stendhal. Taken in conjunction with the biographies, it establishes the repertoire of effects upon which Stendhal's fiction was to draw. Like his biographical studies, however, Stendhal's travel works, of which there are a number, are innovative in showing how individual sensibilities may be stimulated and engaged. Travel is not only fundamental to the plot development of Stendhal's fiction but also a means of revealing the way that the world educates his protagonists.

Stendhal spent the years 1821 to 1830 in Paris, again attempting to live the artistic life. This period saw the production of such key works as *De l'amour* (1822; *Maxims of Love*, 1906) and, in the following year, *Racine et Shakespeare* (1823, part 1; 1825, part 2; *Racine and Shakespeare*, 1962), an important document in the widespread cultural debate of the day on the differences between classicism and Romanticism. It was not until 1827 that Stendhal produced his first novel, *Armance* (English translation, 1928). It was followed in 1830 by the first of his masterpieces, *Le Rouge et le noir* (*The Red and the Black*, 1898). The year 1830 also saw a revolution in France. Stendhal accepted the new regime that the so-called July Revolution had brought into power. As a result, he was appointed consul, first at Trieste, then at Civitavecchia, a posting whose gloom was relieved by its nearness to Rome. With numerous leaves of absence, mostly in Paris, where he wrote most of his other travel pieces, memoirs, and fiction, including his second great work, *La Chartreuse de Parme* (1839; *The Charterhouse of Parma*, 1895), Stendhal held this posting until his death, of apoplexy, in Paris, on March 23, 1842.

Analysis

Stendhal's prediction that his work would not be appreciated until fifty years after his death was not entirely borne out by events. In his lifetime, he won the esteem of, among others, Honoré de Balzac, the other major French novelist of the day. Yet, there is a certain amount of truth in Stendhal's forecast, not merely because his first translation into English did not occur until the later years of the nineteenth century. Translations obviously gave his work a wider audience, but the fact that they came to the attention of an international readership at a time when the criticism of fiction was becoming a more pronounced fact of cultural life led to a more influential appreciation of his distinctive artistic ambitions and accomplishments as a novelist.

It is because of its psychological interest that Stendhal's fiction is regarded so highly. That is also why it is significant that his first publications were works of criticism and of observation in a broad sense. These early works establish the bases for the kind of transition in imaginative prose that Stendhal's novels represent. Many of his concerns may be crudely reduced to his fascination with the dual, and interdependent, relationship between reason and emotion. It is from this fascination that he derives his power as a portrayer of characters. As a result, his fiction was instrumental in elevating character over story.

The shift in emphasis revealed in Stendhal's work is very much part of a larger shift in sensibility that occurred in European culture during Stendhal's apprenticeship as a writer. This transition is from the ostensible stability and sense of proportion of the predominantly neoclassical art of the eighteenth century to the Romantic art of the nineteenth century. Such a reorientation of sensibility did not occur overnight, but gradually, through a publicly perceptible process of realignment. As Stendhal himself suggests, this realignment was not necessarily exclusively revealed in the literature of the day. His most comprehensive investigation of the phenomenon, *Racine and Shakespeare*, involves great writers from other eras and praises Shakespeare for his Stendhalian spontaneity, exuberance, and vividness.

Stendhal is not merely an important analyst of the culture of his day. As his biography reveals, he was also intimately involved with the history of his times. This history, and Stendhal's experience of it, was dominated not merely by the activities of Napoleon but also by his mythic status. Napoleon was perceived by the European mind at large as the spirit of the age. To Stendhal, this spirit was dynamic, ambitious, energetic, resourceful, impassioned, and foolhardy. His response to it, as the characters of Julien Sorel in *The Red and the Black* and Fabrizzio del Dongo in *The Charterhouse of Parma* reveal, was generous. At the same time, however, it was impossible for Stendhal to identify completely with it. The youth of a Julien or Fabrizzio inspires their daring, verve, and vitality. Yet it also inspires Stendhal's most tenderly ironic critique of such qualities. His artistic ambition is to reconcile the passions of his heroes to his own dispassionate reason.

Stendhal's most important contribution to the development of the novel is his use of it to produce systematic critiques. This use not only underwrites his conception of his heroes but also shows the novel to be a means of reflecting on contemporary individuals and morals. The irony that Stendhal applies to his youthful protagonists is used much more incisively to reveal the hypocrisies, evasions, and trivialities of public life in the wake of Napoleon. It is in the figures of Julien and Fabrizzio that Stendhal expresses most cogently the philosophy that he named Beylisme. This outlook lauded the energetic, and perhaps even reckless, pursuit of happiness as the highest human calling and the animating power of all activity. Such an emphasis on individuality is a testament to the range, originality, and significance of Stendhal's writings.

THE RED AND THE BLACK

First published: *Le Rouge et le noir*, 1830 (English translation, 1898)
Type of work: Novel

This story depicts the career of a talented young man in postrevolutionary France.

Originally published in 1830, *Le Rouge et le noir* first appeared in English translation as *The Red and the Black* in 1898. Its many subsequent editions in different English translations testify to its classic status. Written in an economic and, for the most part, slyly understated style, its claim to be counted among the finest novels of the nineteenth century is undoubted.

Perhaps the only feature of *The Red and the Black* that is not entirely original is its plot. It was taken by Stendhal from a story that appeared in a newspaper, the *Gazette des Tribuneaux*, in 1827, concerning Antoine Berthet, the son of a laborer, whose career had something of the same rise and fall as that of Julien Sorel, the novel's hero. The similarity between the two cases is not merely an intriguing sidelight on the composition of *The Red and the Black*. It also speaks directly to the reality of the novel's concerns, which draw not only on the newspapers of the day but also on the recent history of France. As Julien well knows, the example of Napoleon, to which he is unwisely devoted, has made it possible for someone who is provincial, talented, and ambitious, but without social connections, to have his dreams of success realized.

Julien embodies the duality that Stendhal perceived to exist between spirit and reason. He is a lover who is also a hypocrite, a cleric who becomes a soldier, an innocent who commits a crime. He possesses a winning measure of spontaneity, verve, and daring. Yet these natural qualities are continually placed in the service of a socially inspired image of himself. It is to this image that Julien is enslaved. For all of his success, he spends much of his time unhappy, confused, and on the defensive. He wages two self-promoting campaigns, one in Verriere, the other in Paris. Though he wins a number of battles, he loses the war and becomes, like Napoleon, his idol, that war's most visible and notorious victim.

Stendhal organizes *The Red and the Black* so that his conception of duality becomes inescapable. Its overriding presence is obviously called to the reader's attention in the title. There has been much critical debate as to what "red" and "black" refer. "Red" is thought to suggest the hot-blooded vigor of the Napoleonic era. That era's conservative and small-minded aftermath, on the other hand, is said to be denoted by clerical black. Julien's career seems to confirm what his advisers imply, that the Church's uniform is the only one in which he will be able to secure the career to which his talents entitle him. A narrower reading of the color code calls attention to the political climate of the post-Napoleonic period, with red standing for republicanism and black for clerical conservatism. It is also possible to see the colors as referring exclusively to Julien. His inner life is vivid, while on the outside he seems largely colorless.

While Stendhal allows the reader to ponder the title's various possibilities, he is quite explicit in providing by other means a comprehensive sense of the dual elements in his protagonist's career. Not only does *The Red and the Black* have a two-part structure, but the stories in each of them are counterparts of one another. The natural world of Verriere, with its walks, gardens, and children, yields to the artificial world of Paris, with its salons, carriages, and callow youths. More important, Julien's affair with Madame de Renal is conducted with a ruthlessness that belies his spontaneous nature and exploits hers. The affair with Mathilde de la Mole, on the other hand, shows Julien to be the exploited one, in turn a victim of a loved one's bad faith. Thus, not only is each of Julien's two stories complementary; each provides an ironic commentary on the other. Aware of the twin force of image and reality, artifice and nature, hypocrisy and honesty, but deprived by his character of the power necessary to regulate this awareness, Julien falls afoul, not of the time but of his inability to secure his place within it.

THE CHARTERHOUSE OF PARMA

First published: *La Chartreuse de Parme*, 1839 (English translation, 1895)
Type of work: Novel

This tale describes a fateful conflict between emotional idealism and political reality, set in early nineteenth century Italy.

Stendhal's second great novel, *The Charterhouse of Parma*, was first published in Paris in 1839 and had to wait more than fifty years before appearing in an English translation in 1895. Like *The Red and the Black*, its vivid characterizations, intriguing plot, and ironical style immediately confirmed its status as one of the major achievements of the nineteenth century novel.

Almost ten years separate the original publication of *The Charterhouse of Parma* from *The Red and the Black*. The interval did not, however, produce a change in Stendhal's fictional themes or methods. Once again, the protagonist is a young man, and the environment in which he comes face to face with the world and his situation and destiny in it is one of political intrigue. Again, the protagonist's fate seems to be decided by his emotional nature, and the expression of that nature is subject to ruinous social manipulation. The larger backdrop to the novel's plot is the Napoleonic era. Yet it is used to illuminate the character of the protagonist, Fabrizzio del Dongo, and to prepare the reader for the struggle for autonomy and individuality that Fabrizzio must undergo. As in *The Red and the Black*, this struggle constitutes the bulk of the novel.

What might be referred to as the Fabrizzio narrative in *The Charterhouse of Parma* opens with a series of his misadventures in pursuit of military glory. The presentation of an ignorant, inexperienced, confused, but spirited Fabrizzio at the battle of Waterloo has long been considered not only a high point in the depiction of the individual in history but also a telling instance of the essentially modern character of Stendhal's imagination. The impetus that inspires Fabrizzio to flounder self-deceivingly in the wake of Napoleon's army, however, is the same one that guides his behavior throughout the novel. This impetus is romantic in nature. Its generous and outgoing aspects are dramatized, but with a more sensitive irony than that of *The Red and the Black*.

Fabrizzio's angelic appearance is, understandably, taken at face value by those who love him. Yet their acceptance of him is the basis of the tragic experiences that he brings their way. This acceptance places a far greater emphasis on the moral and spiritual dimension of the characters, which the remoteness of the novel's setting accentuates. The persistence with which remoteness of setting is featured throughout, ending in the charterhouse itself, and the fact that it tends to force the characters to tap their own internal resources, lends the work as a whole a distinctly operatic air, which Stendhal, the author of a biography of Italian composer Gioacchino Rossini and a lifelong lover of opera, undoubtedly cultivated.

The interest of *The Charterhouse of Parma* is at once more intimate, more desperate, and of greater human significance than that of *The Red and the Black* because the plot revolves around the inescapable nature of feeling. This orientation is embodied most substantially by the Duchess Sanseverina, who is the novel's most operatic, and most memorable, character. Through his development of the Duchess, Stendhal underlines his conception of duality. The means of doing so are quite different from those used in *The Red and the Black*. There, the focus was on ambition, mediated through the inadequacies of human society. The focus of *The Charterhouse of Parma* is love, mediated through the frailties of human nature. Fabrizzio is the most obvious embodiment of these frailties. The manner in which he embodies them, however, reveals their existence more critically in the women around him. Of these, the Duchess is the most affecting, the most compelling, and the character above all others in Stendhal's fiction who reveals this author's belief that the pursuit of happiness is ironically life's joy and tragedy.

Summary

Two novels may not seem much upon which to base an enduring reputation, even if they are as distinguished as *The Red and the Black* and *The Charterhouse of Parma*. Yet even without these two novels, Stendhal would still have a place in literary history. His place is secure not only because of the quality and interest of his other work, including his lesser known, unfinished, and inferior fiction, but also because of the precision with which the man himself felt the pulse of his time. His acuteness can be perceived in the political sophistication that suffuses his novels and his wry regard for the foibles and fashions of the day. Above all, Stendhal is noteworthy for attaining within himself the freedom to express a spirit tempered by reason, and to employ this reason without denying his emotions.

Bibliography

Adams, Robert M. *Stendhal: Notes on a Novelist.* New York: Noonday Press, 1959.

Alter, Robert, with Carol Cosman. *A Lion for Love: A Critical Biography of Stendhal.* New York: Basic Books, 1979.

Bloom, Harold, ed. *Stendhal's "The Red and the Black": Modern Critical Interpretations.* New York: Chelsea House, 1987.

Brombert, Victor, ed. *Stendhal: A Collection of Critical Essays.* Englewood Cliffs, N.J.: Prentice-Hall, 1962.

May, Gita. *Stendhal and the Age of Napoleon.* New York: Columbia University Press, 1977.

Richardson, Joanna. *Stendhal.* New York: Coward, McCann & Geoghegan, 1974.

Strickland, Geoffrey. *Stendhal: The Education of a Novelist.* Cambridge, England: Cambridge University Press, 1974.

Wood, Michael. *Stendhal.* Ithaca, N.Y.: Cornell University Press, 1971.

George O'Brien

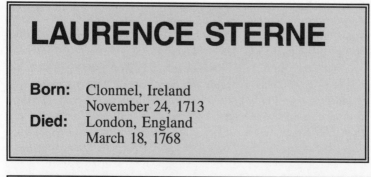

LAURENCE STERNE

Born: Clonmel, Ireland
November 24, 1713
Died: London, England
March 18, 1768

Principal Literary Achievement
As one of the prominent figures writing during the rise of the English novel,
Sterne helped explore and define its possibilities.

Biography

Laurence Sterne was born on November 24, 1713, in Clonmel, Ireland, to a respected Yorkshire family (his great-grandfather, Richard Sterne, had been archbishop of York). His father, Roger Sterne, was a young ensign, and Laurence spent his early years in towns and cities all over England and Ireland. The second of seven children, only three of whom lived to adulthood, he left at age ten for school in Halifax, England. There he was taken under the wing of his uncle Richard Sterne, a community leader who became a second father to him.

Roger Sterne squandered the family's wealth before his death in Jamaica in 1731. When Richard Sterne died the following year, Laurence, now detached from his mother, was penniless. In 1733, he entered Jesus College, Cambridge; after first working to earn the tuition for his education, he was awarded one of the Sterne scholarships established by his great-grandfather. He studied Latin, Greek, mathematics, rhetoric, and philosophy (which included geography, ethics, and the natural sciences). He admired the Greek philosopher Plato and the English thinkers John Locke and Sir Isaac Newton. Matriculating in 1735, Sterne received his degree, most likely in early 1737.

Already indebted to associates such as his lifelong friend John Hall, Sterne had few options but to go into the Church. He was admitted to the Order of Deacons and given an assistant curacy in St. Ives, an unimpressive post. For two decades, he lived a pastoral life, climbing the parochial hierarchy of Yorkshire with the help of political contacts, which included his uncle, the Archdeacon Jaques Sterne. With each post—Prebendary of Givendale, Vicar of Sutton, Commissary of the Peculiar Court of Tollerton—came increased lands and their incomes. Sterne's duties were both religious and political. He preached regularly and oversaw cases in the spiritual courts. As a rising clergyman and nephew to Jacques Sterne, he became involved in York-

shire's political life, contributing political articles to the *York Gazetteer* and publishing political pamphlets.

On March 30, 1741, Sterne married Elizabeth Lumley. A daughter, Lydia, was born on October 1, 1745, but she died the following day. A second Lydia was born on December 1, 1747; she would grow to be her father's beloved and only child. Elizabeth's health was poor, and the marriage was not happy; Sterne is known to have entertained other women during frequent visits to York. As a country parson, he read widely, played various musical instruments, liked painting and hunting, spoke mediocre French, may have participated in amateur theatrics, and farmed his land with reasonable success.

In 1758, with a staid life, a stale marriage, no hopes for more children, and an awareness of the fragility of middle age, Sterne withdrew from his parochial duties and moved to York in the hope of career advancement. When ongoing feuds with his uncle dashed his hopes, he turned to his favorite avocation, writing. In early 1759, he published a satirical pamphlet, *A Political Romance.* Aimed at political rival Dr. Francis Topham, the controversial piece was suppressed. Sterne's disappointment led him to a more ambitious project, a two-volume work of biting topical satire called *The Life and Opinions of Tristram Shandy, Gent.* (1759-1767; commonly known as *Tristram Shandy*).

The year 1759 was a tumultuous one. Sterne endured more frequent and violent attacks of the tuberculosis that eventually killed him. His wife and daughter were also ill; Elizabeth was schizophrenic and fancied herself the queen of Bohemia. Both his mother, from whom he had long been distant, and his uncle died that spring. *Tristram Shandy* was rejected by printers.

Sterne sat down to revise it, removing personal allusions, broadening the satire, and infusing the book with sentiment. He borrowed finances to publish the two volumes in late 1759. A singer named Catherine Fourmantel, with whom he was passionately infatuated, introduced the book to the influential actor David Garrick. *Tristram Shandy* was an immediate success, selling well in London and garnering both praise for its delightful wit and censure for bawdiness considered unbefitting a parson. Sterne drafted a defense against his prudish detractors, but such charges plagued him throughout his life.

Sterne was a celebrity when he rolled into London in 1760. He was the subject of biographical sketches in magazines, sat for the famed portraitist Joshua Reynolds, and was taken into the favor of the rakish Prince Edward, duke of York. *Tristram Shandy* sold out quickly, and Sterne quickly arranged for publication of two volumes of his sermons, which appeared in May as *The Sermons of Mr. Yorick* (1760, 1766).

Sterne's life was transformed. He traveled frequently between London, York, and Coxwold, where he was given a living as parson in 1760. He set to work on volumes 3 and 4 of *Tristram Shandy*, which were published in January of 1761, followed by volumes 5 and 6 the following December. Given the sensation that the novel caused, imitations and spurious editions were rampant. Sterne publicly denounced them and finally adopted the practice of personally signing all authentic copies, generally about four thousand per edition. He spent most of 1762 and 1763 in France, returning to England in 1764. Volumes 7 and 8 of *Tristram Shandy* appeared in early 1765.

Sterne passed the winter of 1765-1766 traveling through Italy and then returned to write volume 9 of *Tristram Shandy*. Amid bouts of illness, he solicited subscriptions for a book based on his travels, *A Sentimental Journey Through France and Italy* (1768; commonly called *A Sentimental Journey*). In January of 1767, he fell in love with Eliza Draper, the wife of a diplomat in India, and began a diary that would later be published as *Journal to Eliza* (1904). That autumn, Elizabeth and Lydia finally returned to York, staying with Sterne briefly before arranging to live separately under his support.

Sterne went to London in December, 1767, and *A Sentimental Journey* was published two months later. Soon after, he became seriously ill and spent his last weeks in bed surrounded by friends and supporters. He died peacefully in London on March 18, 1768, of heart failure. After his death, Lydia prepared volumes 5 through 7 of *Sermons by the Late Rev. Mr. Sterne*, published in 1769.

Analysis

Part of Sterne's allure was his capacity for self-portrayal, and the appellations of Laurence Sterne, Tristram Shandy, and Parson Yorick were, with the arrival of fame and success, interchangeable. Many a writer has produced more starkly autobiographical material, but few have so completely intertwined their real and fictional personas. Thus, while the specific "facts" of Tristram's or Yorick's existence differentiate them from their author, their personalities and tempers are completely those of Sterne. He made no effort to draw distinctions: He attributed his own sermons to Yorick and included one in *Tristram Shandy*; he listed actual dates of composition or travel in fictional narratives; and he constantly reminded his readers of his role as a storyteller. In some ways, he was, through his writing, creating the gentleman that he wished himself to be.

This intermixture of real and fictional worlds is a sign less of carelessness than of the assumptions under which Sterne worked. He wrote for a learned audience, many of whom knew him personally. He published serially or by subscription, so his work was responsive to the whims of the market. He composed quickly, and spontaneity is a trademark of his style. During the eighteenth century, the novel as a form was not highly evolved or defined, and calling *Tristram Shandy* and *A Sentimental Journey* novels by twentieth century standards is a generous use of the term. With the exception of the sermons, Sterne's work does not fit established forms but mixes mock and real autobiography, mock and real anthology, travelogue, essay, and political satire. To search for any more recognizable form is to miss the point of Sterne altogether.

Sterne's roots as a writer are in the parsonage. Grounded in classical rhetoric—the formal art of communication and persuasion—Sterne quickly became a skilled sermonist. The careful construction of argument, use of parable and example, and ability to turn a compelling phrase all carry over into his nonreligious writings. In addition, Sterne was erudite, and his familiarity with Renaissance literature and knowledge—

from military strategy to obstetrics, the doctrine of "humours," royal lineages, and archaeology—give his writing a learned, if not encyclopedic, quality.

Yet amid the erudition, Sterne never loses his humanity, most remarkably expressed in his wit, sentiment, and bawdiness. Wit was a sign of the learned eighteenth century gentleman. Clever punning was in vogue, and satire was a prime source of both entertainment and social change. The roots of Sterne's satire were political, but he was not at heart a political being. Rather, as theatrical metaphors throughout his work convey, Sterne was an entertainer: Both on paper and in court, he was a talented jester. Nothing was safe from the reach of his humor, yet it was never baldly malicious. For Sterne, whose life was marked by disappointment and frailty, laughter was a means of transcending the harshness of reality. More than entertaining others, he was, through humor, feeding his own vitality.

His quick and sharp wit, on the other hand, could easily melt into a pool of sentimentality. That, too, ennobled a gentleman, the combination of patience, empathy, earnestness, innocence, long-suffering, and extreme sensitivity exemplified best by Uncle Toby's pain on the death of a fly in *Tristram Shandy* or the various refined love affairs of the Shandys, Yorick and Sterne. The *Journal to Eliza*, which Sterne may or may not have intended to publish, takes romance and melancholy to striking extremes of pathos and humorlessness.

Finally, Sterne is celebrated for his bawdiness. Certainly, eighteenth century English sensibilities were not as prudish as their Victorian successors, but even in a society of loose tongues and swaggering rakes, indecencies were not customary from the clergy. Sterne, however, could not deny the connections between the eyes, the mind, the heart, and the sexual organs. Allusions to anatomy and desire are only thinly veiled, and they come in a characteristic spirit of good humor and honesty. His bawdiness is not gratuitous or pornographic; rather, it is integral to his vision of the world. Sterne has been criticized consistently, beginning in his own time, for lasciviousness and impropriety; at the same time, his candor, and the controversy that it arouses, has brought entertainment to millions of readers.

TRISTRAM SHANDY

First published: 1759-1767
Type of work: Novel

An easily distracted gentleman attempts to narrate the details of his life and the opinions that he has formed along the way.

The Life and Opinions of Tristram Shandy, Gent. is a long, challenging, and delightful work. Written serially over nine years, it does not exhibit unity of action or tell a single, identifiable story. Rather, it is unified by an overriding purpose—to tell the title character's life and opinions as honestly and completely as possible—and a unique style, whereby that purpose is thwarted and diverted by digressions and embellishments that grow out of the life and opinions themselves.

"Life and Opinions" was an acceptable autobiographical format for an eighteenth century gentleman. Sterne set out both to use it and to ridicule it through the character of Tristram Shandy. "Old Tristram" was the name given to a statue of a bearded beggar at the Halifax parish church from Sterne's adolescence. "Shandy" was Yorkshire slang for "odd" or "crazy." Together they suggest an offbeat character; Sterne added gentility, charm, and an incapacity for direct thought or action. Tristram is the first-person protagonist of the nine volumes of the book, and in his life and opinions he introduces an array of other characters: his pompous father Walter, his gentle Uncle Toby, the Corporal Trim, Parson Yorick, the servant Susannah, his brother Bobby, his beloved Jenny, the Widow Wadman, his friend Eugenius, and a variety of other learned gentlemen.

If *Tristram Shandy* can be said to have a plot, it has two: Walter Shandy's attempts to raise the perfect son and Uncle Toby's courtship of the Widow Wadman. Both prove unsuccessful. Their failures figure the novel's large structure, for Tristram's desire to tell his story completely also meets with failure. Underlying all the failures of the Shandy men, however, is a delight in the process of striving, be it Walter's composition of the "Tristrapaedia," by which his son will be educated, or Toby's lawn reenactment of the siege of Namur, where he received the groin wound that would ultimately precipitate his romantic failure.

Moreover, if Tristram's failure is his inability to tell a story like a straight line, it is also his triumph, for interwoven are comments, opinions, anecdotes, diagrams, and entire documents, real and fictional. Digression is the Shandean way, and the reader can expect a surprise around every corner, be it the anecdote about Corporal Le Fever or the cumbersome "Slawkenbergius' Tale." Tristram also uses unorthodox punctuation for effect, liberally litters his text with physical devices—a black page, a marble page, and even missing pages—and spontaneously devotes chapters to a variety of topics, including a "Chapter on Chapters." He directly addresses the reader, characterizing and then either castigating or pandering to him or her, thus creating an important and dynamic relationship.

Critics have debated how to classify the novel, what Sterne means by it, and whether or not he intended the cryptic last chapter, writing as he did with increasingly ill health, to mark the end of the entire work. Whatever the answers to these questions, in *Tristram Shandy* Sterne created a unique work that explores the limits of a fledgling form, the novel, and in many ways prefigures literary experiments and forms to come.

A SENTIMENTAL JOURNEY

First published: 1768
Type of work: Novel

A British parson recounts his travels and experiences in France and Italy.

Twentieth century British novelist Virginia Woolf, commenting on the style of *A Sentimental Journey Through France and Italy*, wrote:

> The very punctuation is that of speech, not writing, and brings the sound, the associations, of the speaking voice with it. The order of the ideas, their suddenness and irrelevancy, is more true to life than to literature. There is a privacy in this intercourse which allows things to slip out unreproved that would have been in doubtful taste had they been spoken in public. . . . We are as close to life as we can be.

These comments, which could apply to *Tristram Shandy* as well, underline Sterne's relationship to the stream-of-consciousness style that Woolf, Irish novelist James Joyce, and others would develop and perfect a century and a half later. Sterne did not set out to develop a style, but, in *A Sentimental Journey*, the combination of urgent delight in the flight from morality and easy familiarity with a specific readership create the immediate and intimate style that Woolf describes.

In volume 7 of *Tristram Shandy*, Tristram recounts his trip through France to escape illness; *A Sentimental Journey*, in a similar vein, is Parson Yorick's account of his travels. Sterne's book is at once a response to contemporary travel books—Tobias Smollett's had appeared two years before—that criticize the host culture and a burlesque of the Grand Tour of Europe that was a traditional part of a gentleman's education. It is also a picaresque narrative in the tradition of the Spanish writer Miguel de Cervantes' *Don Quixote de la Mancha* (1605, 1615), which Sterne greatly admired.

Sterne's Yorick goes to France and Italy seeking understanding, with a heart open to the people and the places that he visits. There are still elements of satire, especially where the upper class and artistic elite are concerned, but Sterne is gentler and mellower, and Yorick's travelogue comes directly from the heart. While *A Sentimental Journey* incorporates much material from Sterne's own travels, it is a work of imagination, dependent on extrapolation and fancification of actual experience. Yorick is a humorous and sentimental man who delights in the lives of common people and finds himself in ridiculous postures under the influence of love, lust, and infatuation. Yorick's narrative includes descriptions and catalogs of people and places, and a wide variety of travel difficulties and accidents that imbue it with humor and pathos. In the end, Yorick is cast as a "man of feeling," in true eighteenth century tradition. Sterne here brings to life *The Sermons of Mr. Yorick*, which his audience knew and loved well, and through the all-too-human observations and adventures of a sentimental journeyer, he further educates, edifies, and entertains.

Summary

In his introduction to a 1935 limited edition of *Tristram Shandy*, Christopher Morley wrote, "Perhaps *Tristram Shandy* should be read first at not over 20 years, and again at not less than 40." Whether Laurence Sterne would have agreed is questionable, but it is clear that his writing offers a dazzling combination of youthful vitality and experienced wisdom that has wide appeal. Though Sterne's contemporary reader was a certain type of eighteenth century aristocrat, Sterne's direct and intimate style speaks to many beyond that limited group and era. His humor and candor, even in more liberal-minded epochs, continue to be disarming in their simple truthfulness. Sterne is not a simple author, for much of his language and erudition is of a past world, yet for readers who approach his works as he approached life, with open heart and ravenous mind, his spirit is unmistakable.

Bibliography

Cash, Arthur H. *Laurence Sterne: The Early and Middle Years.* London: Methuen, 1975.

_____. *Laurence Sterne: The Later Years.* London: Methuen, 1986.

Fredman, Alice Green. *Diderot and Sterne.* New York: Columbia University Press, 1955.

Lanham, Richard A. *"Tristram Shandy": The Games of Pleasure.* Berkeley: University of California Press, 1973.

Moglen, Helene. *The Philosophical Irony of Laurence Sterne.* Gainesville: University Presses of Florida, 1975.

New, Melvin. *Laurence Sterne as Satirist: A Reading of "Tristram Shandy."* Gainesville: University of Florida Press, 1969.

Piper, William Bowman. *Laurence Sterne.* New York: Twayne, 1965.

Spector, Robert Donald, ed. *Essays on the Eighteenth-Century Novel.* Bloomington: Indiana University Press, 1965.

Traugott, John, ed. *Laurence Sterne: A Collection of Critical Essays.* Englewood Cliffs, N.J.: Prentice-Hall, 1968.

_____. *Tristram Shandy's World: Sterne's Philosophical Rhetoric.* Berkeley: University of California Press, 1954.

Barry Mann

ROBERT LOUIS STEVENSON

Born: Edinburgh, Scotland
November 13, 1850
Died: Apia, Upolu, Samoa
December 3, 1894

Principal Literary Achievement

Stevenson was a skillful and thoughtful literary stylist who transformed popular genres into genuine works of art.

Biography

Robert Louis Stevenson was born in Edinburgh, Scotland, on November 13, 1850, the only son of Thomas Stevenson and Margaret Balfour. His mother's family and ancestors were primarily clergymen and physicians; his father's family and ancestors were engineers. On both sides of his large extended family (both his mother and father were the youngest of thirteen children) were successful, wealthy, socially prominent professionals. His father's family, in fact, was famous in Scotland. The family firm designed and built lighthouses that had become famous landmarks, and "Stevenson" was a name to reckon with: Robert Louis' father, Thomas, and grandfather, Robert, both appear in Scotland's national portrait gallery. He was born into privilege, therefore, and was expected to carry on the tradition of a wealthy, successful professional life.

When Stevenson was an infant, his mother developed symptoms of tuberculosis, and she was an invalid for much of his first decade. After his third year, Stevenson also became sickly, plagued with fevers and fits of coughing. Eventually, he contracted what was diagnosed as tuberculosis, and much of his adult life was a scramble to stay one step ahead of the disease. He spent much of his childhood, then, as an invalid; the attitudes and habits of mind that he developed as a result meant that he was destined not to occupy the position that his family expected. He developed the eye and the attitude of the observer. He was destined to become, as it were, a perpetual tourist—a tourist of the imagination.

The day-to-day practical care of the child was given to his nanny, Allison Cunningham ("Cummy" to the family), a very pious Presbyterian who read to the invalid child for hours from the Bible and popular melodramatic literature of the day. Hers was a

"blood and thunder" religion, and young Stevenson became conscious at an early age of martyrdom, sin, and judgment. He was a precocious child with a large and unexpectedly grave vocabulary and surprisingly adult concerns about religious matters.

He did not read until he was seven, but he loved to listen to stories told to him not only by Cummy but also by his father, who would invent and recite adventurous yarns to help his son get to sleep on bad nights. By the time he was six, young Stevenson was creating his own stories and sometimes dictating them to his nanny. That is how he came to do his first important piece of "writing." One of his uncles offered a cash prize to the cousin who could write the best history of Moses. Stevenson won the prize. His second important piece of writing, and his first published work, at age sixteen, was also commissioned by his family: When Stevenson was sixteen, his father, impressed by his son's knowledge of Scottish Presbyterian history, asked him to write a history of Scotland's eighteenth century religious/political/military conflicts. The resulting pamphlet, "Pentland Rising," was paid for by his father.

His father's appreciation of Stevenson's writing ability did not, however, mean that the family expected Stevenson to become a professional writer. He was enrolled in the University of Edinburgh in 1867, when he was sixteen, with the full expectation that he would get an engineering degree and join the family firm. Stevenson was not a good student, however; he attended classes sporadically. He had developed bad study habits and a bad attitude toward academia from the constant interruptions to his schooling that his chronic illness had produced. What Stevenson did with his university time was to explore the streets and byways of Edinburgh, frequenting pubs, observing people, and taking notes in his by-now indispensible journal. He had become a tourist in his hometown—the mark of a writer.

In 1868, he met his first important mentor, Fleeming Jenkin, professor of engineering at the University of Edinburgh. Jenkin invited Stevenson to his home, which was a gathering place for artists, writers, and scholars. There, in an informal setting, Stevenson received the intellectual challenge and discipline that he had not received in the formal college classes that he had avoided. Another person important to him was Charles Baxter, a fellow student who became his lifelong friend and, eventually, literary agent.

When Stevenson finally told his father that he could not be an engineer and had to be a writer, his father made a counter suggestion: Go to law school. His father reasoned that a law degree would be a safety net if the writing did not succeed. Stevenson accepted this suggestion, pursued his studies with reasonable diligence, and was admitted to the bar in 1875. He never practiced law, however; during his law school years, he came to a parting of the ways with his father and met his second important mentor.

In January of 1873, Stevenson's father, a staunch Presbyterian, discovered that Stevenson not only had ceased to be a true-believing Presbyterian but also had lost his belief in Christianity. This discovery precipitated a debate and an estrangement that was not to be fully resolved until 1881, when the father became absorbed in the son's writing of *Treasure Island* (1883).

In the late summer of 1873, at the house of one of his cousins, Stevenson met Frances Sitwell, a thirty-two-year-old woman separated from her husband, who became his confidant and idealized love object. That relationship, by all accounts, remained platonic, in spite of Stevenson's desires. He also met Fanny Sitwell's friend Sidney Colvin, professor of fine art at the University of Cambridge and an "insider" in the world of literary publishing. Colvin, the most important influence on Stevenson's career, became Stevenson's literary and publishing mentor. He guided Stevenson into making a small name for himself in the 1870's by helping him to get his travel and opinion pieces published in literary journals.

Three years after he had met Colvin, and one year after his relationship with Fanny Sitwell had cooled, Stevenson met his future wife, Fanny Osborne, an American separated from her husband and temporarily living in France. His attraction and eventual marriage to her either annoyed or outraged Stevenson's friends and family. His mentors and friends felt that he was on the verge of making his mark on literary England, and they did not feel that Osborne was a kindred spirit; they also felt that the emotional drain of caring for an instant family (Osborne had two children) would divert energy away from literary endeavors. His family was shocked by his developing a liaison with a woman who was not yet divorced.

Stevenson pursued the liaison, however, against all objections. After Osborne had been back in California for a year, Stevenson left Scotland for California. The trip was physically punishing, and he almost died once he arrived in Monterey, where Fanny Osborne was staying. He survived, however, and in 1880 he married Fanny Osborne in San Francisco. He spent the next two months continuing to recuperate while living in an abandoned miner's cabin on Mount St. Helena, at the head of the Napa Valley.

His trip to California and his stay in the Napa Valley were watershed events; his writing matured, and he became more than a pleasant writer of travel and opinion pieces in literary journals. He became a serious observer of the duality of humankind, a serious explorer into the interior of the divided human heart. Monterey and St. Helena also provided the physical settings for *Treasure Island*, the book that established him.

Stevenson had left for California without the knowledge of his parents, indeed, without leaving them any means of contacting him. His father, however, hearing that he had fallen ill in California, had sent him money. His father, in fact, would support Stevenson and his family as long as the father lived. Stevenson's writing did not make enough money to support a family until the success of *The Strange Case of Dr. Jekyll and Mr. Hyde* (1886) in the United States earned for him a lucrative contract with Charles Scribner's Sons in 1887, the year of his father's death.

Between 1880 and 1887, his life was a continual search for a climate and a location that would ease his pain. He was susceptible to cold, damp, physical exertion, or stress, any of which could cause him to collapse with a fever or with blood filling his mouth. From 1880 to 1884, he lived mainly in rented cottages and resorts in Scotland and on the European Continent, but in 1884 his father purchased (as a present to

Fanny) a home in Bournemouth, on the southern coast of England, where Stevenson and his family lived from 1884 to 1887. Even in a resort area like Bournemouth, however, Stevenson's life was still a running battle with sickness.

In spite of his physical trials, the period 1880 to 1887 was extraordinarily productive; during that period, he wrote the principal works by which he is known today: *The Silverado Squatters: Sketches from a California Mountain* (1883), *Treasure Island* (1883), *A Child's Garden of Verses* (1885), *The Strange Case of Dr. Jekyll and Mr. Hyde* (1886), and *Kidnapped* (1886). That period also produced his most important friendship; he became friends with Henry James, the only person who fully understood him artistically.

When his father died in 1887, Stevenson used some of his inheritance to finance a sailing trip to the South Seas, still in search of a climate and location in which he could flourish physically. He finally found such a place in Samoa. It was the first place where he could engage in reasonably vigorous physical activity and not suffer days of immobilizing pain. The perpetual tourist had wandered to the ends of the earth, but he had found his home. He and his wife cleared the ground and built a home on the Samoan island of Upolu. In that home, he died of a stroke on December 3, 1894.

Analysis

Stevenson was a professional writer, in the broadest sense of that term. He was an essayist, a poet, and a writer of fiction (he even tried his hand at plays in collaboration with W. E. Henley, British poet and essayist). It is true that, until *The Strange Case of Dr. Jekyll and Mr. Hyde* took the United States by storm in 1887, he could not survive economically without his father's help. Yet his love of words and his delight in their use were strong enough that he had to write, and would have written no matter what. Writing was not only his occupation, it was his calling. This attitude means that in Stevenson's work one encounters a variety of genres and styles. It also means that technique and "manner" will be foremost; his work will manifest a certain "finish" or "polish." In his nonfiction work, this polish means that his serious themes will be very easy to digest. In his fiction and poetry, it means that his serious themes will hardly be noticed. That is both Stevenson's bane and his salvation. He survives, but in the popular imagination, not in the critical pantheon. Consequently, his books are still in print because readers are still delighted and moved by them, not because readers feel the need to discuss and analyze his works as they would the works of his contemporary, Henry James.

Stevenson was an inveterate tourist, even in his own country, so travel writing constitutes a significant part of his literary output. His first commercially published book, *An Inland Voyage* (1878), is an account of a continental canoe trip with a friend in 1876. *Edinburgh: Picturesque Notes* (1878) and *Travels with a Donkey in the Cévennes* (1879), his next two books, were also travel documents. *The Silverado Squatters*, perhaps his best writing in this genre, is an account of his "honeymoon" in the summer of 1880 with his new bride and stepson, plus assorted visitors, in an abandoned miner's cabin. This book is deceptively simple, subtly humorous, and shrewdly perceptive.

Stevenson's first novel was *Treasure Island*, serialized in *Young Folks* magazine in the fall and winter of 1881-1882 and first published in book form in 1883. Evident in this novel are the techniques and themes that dominate Stevenson's fiction. The novel is narrated in the first person in a seemingly transparent, "artless" manner. A plain person is trying to record the facts of his experience as precisely and completely as he can:

> Squire Trelawney, Dr. Livesey, and the rest of these gentlemen having asked me to write down the whole particulars about Treasure Island, from the beginning to the end, keeping nothing back but the bearings of the island, and that only because there is still treasure not yet lifted, I take up my pen in the year of grace 17—, and go back to the time when my father kept the "Admiral Benbow" inn, and the brown old seaman, with the sabre cut, first took up his lodging under our roof.

A plain beginning, except that the startling phrases "there is still treasure not yet lifted" and "with the sabre cut" provide a brief flash of the vividly colored world into which the reader is about to be seduced. This deceptive straightforwardness is a key element in all Stevenson's fiction. His first-person protagonists, plain men that they are, also end up being "hangers-on" in their own stories; there is always a minor character who becomes the focus of the reader's attention as this character becomes the focus of the narrator's attention. Jim Hawkins, narrator of *Treasure Island*, is overwhelmed by Long John Silver, the cook on his voyage; David Balfour, narrator of *Kidnapped* and its sequel, *Catriona* (1893), is overwhelmed by Alan Breck, his guide through the highlands of Scotland. In *The Strange Case of Dr. Jekyll and Mr. Hyde*, Mr. Utterson, the matter-of-fact lawyer from whose point of view the third-person narrative is told, is overwhelmed by the title characters.

These minor characters assume great importance in their stories because they are vivid mixtures of appealing and repulsive qualities. They are fascinating characters because they combine great capacity for good with great capacity for evil. This dimension raises the issue of Stevenson's dominant theme: moral ambiguity in human actions. Stevenson is a moralist, but a hard-headed moralist, not a writer of tracts. His novels provide an unflinching examination of the difficulty of either taking the right action or judging actions rightly. Alan Breck has blood on his hands, but he is a loyal and selfless friend to the narrator of *Kidnapped*. The attractive protagonist of the medieval romance *The Black Arrow* (1888) saves a minor character's life but is nevertheless bitterly reproached by that character for having been put in the life-threatening situation in the first place. Right prevails in *The Black Arrow*, but only after much destruction has made such a triumph hollow. That is the type of world found in the novels that have largely been confined to the children's literature bookshelf. The deceptive straightforwardness and "plainness" of the telling, the vividness of the incidents, the fascinating complexity of the characters' personalities—these divert all but the most careful readers from conscious consideration of the serious themes that dominate Stevenson's fiction.

A Child's Garden of Verses ranks with *Treasure Island* and *The Strange Case of Dr. Jekyll and Mr. Hyde* in long-lasting popularity. In Stevenson's poetry, as in his prose, however, "transparency" masks subtlety. A contemporary critic, quoted in J. C. Furnas' brilliant biography of Stevenson, *A Voyage to Windward* (1951), makes the point that *A Child's Garden of Verses* is

> not (as too easily supposed) a book of verse for children, but a book of verse about children. Children, of course, like many of the pieces, but essentially the poems are the disclosure of a child's mind. . . . Never was there a set of playful verses about children more completely free from mawkishness. There is no attempt to make them songs of innocence.

In his verses, as in his fiction, then, Stevenson the serious artist uses popular genres (travel writing, the adventure story, the gothic horror tale, historical romance, light verse) to exercise his considerable writing skill and flesh out his moral and philosophical values. Stevenson's advantage and disadvantage, then as now, is a skill so considerable that one revels in the telling and only with difficulty thinks about the values.

TREASURE ISLAND

First published: 1883
Type of work: Novel

In eighteenth century England, a teenaged boy entangled in a search for buried pirate treasure receives some complex lessons about trust and loyalty.

Treasure Island was first a map that Stevenson drew for the amusement of his stepson. The map proved so interesting that he created a story to go along with it, reading installments of the story to his family as he finished them. Stevenson's father, who happened to be visiting on the day of one of those readings, became so attracted to the story that he made plot suggestions, at least two of which were followed (the contents of Billy Bones's trunk and Jim Hawkins in the apple barrel).

The novel was published in serial form in a boys' magazine, *Young Folks*, and it follows the format of the standard boys' adventure novel: A boy is drawn into a fantastic, dangerous adventure, but through courage, integrity, and the help of a heroic mentor, he comes through the adventure unscathed, wiser, and more mature.

Stevenson, however, improvises on this theme. His hero, Jim Hawkins, gets hold of a map made by a famous pirate, Captain Flint, to show the location of a large treasure that Flint had buried. Hawkins enlists the aid of two adult friends to help him find the treasure. So far, Stevenson has established a plucky boy and possibly heroic mentors. The adults, however, have bad judgment in hiring crew for the voyage to Treasure Island, and there are dangerous conflicts among crew and passengers once the island is reached. Those conflicts are resolved partly by luck, partly by shrewdness, and partly by stupidity and superstition. The treasure is finally retrieved, but in a way no one had anticipated. The boy comes through the adventure unscathed, but the major villain is not brought to justice, and the boy's last words in the novel are

> Oxen and wain-ropes would not bring me back again to that accursed island; and the worst dreams that ever I have are when I hear the surf booming about its coasts, or start upright in bed, with the sharp voice of Captain Flint [the parrot of the ship's cook] still ringing in my ears: "Pieces of eight! pieces of eight!"

The story does not end, then, with the voice of newly found wisdom. Though *Treasure Island* is a standard boys' adventure on first glance, on second glance its themes and attitudes are more adult than juvenile.

Treasure Island was originally published as *The Sea Cook*, and the original title shows how big a part Long John Silver, the ship's cook, plays in the story. Jim Hawkins is the protagonist, but, as the original title suggests, Silver is perhaps the most important character in the story. He is certainly the most complex and the most fully realized character. In this, his first novel, Stevenson creates what may be his most memorable character in Long John Silver. The complexity of this character foreshadows Stevenson's techniques and concerns in most of his fiction.

KIDNAPPED

First published: 1886
Type of work: Novel

In eighteenth century Scotland, a teenage orphan who has been kidnapped escapes with the aid of a heroic fugitive, but he must survive a long chase through the Scottish highlands before he can avenge his kidnapping and gain his fortune.

Kidnapped, like *Treasure Island* before it, was serialized in *Young Folks*, the boys' magazine. It is the most Scottish of Stevenson's novels, in dialect, vocabulary, and worldview. Like *Treasure Island*, it follows the pattern of a popular genre, in this case the historical romance. Stevenson sets his story in 1751, five years after the defeat of a Scottish rebellion against the English-German King George. King George has brutally "pacified" the Scottish Highlands, and Stevenson places his protagonist, David Balfour, in conversation with a principal agent of that pacification at the moment when that agent is assassinated (the assassination is a historical fact). Those who witness the assassination suspect Balfour of complicity, and he barely escapes with his life, fleeing for weeks across the Highlands in the company and under the protection of Alan Breck, the man who was historically (and in the novel) accused of the murder.

Under the cover of orthodoxy, however, Stevenson does heretical things with the genre. Morally ambiguous characters abound. Balfour's kidnapper, a ship's captain, is an excellent seaman and dotes on his mother. David's uncle is a thoroughly unlikable character, but he suffers more than any other character in the novel. Alan Breck is a deserter and a turncoat, but he is unshakably loyal to Balfour, even at the risk of his life.

Breck and Balfour, the two principal characters, are an odd couple whose developing friendship constitutes the main business of the novel. Their relationship is made vivid and believable by Stevenson's deft hand: Balfour is provincial and stodgy, Breck is worldly-wise and extravagant, but readers can believe that they are drawn to each other because Stevenson's incidents generate the passions in each of them that inevitably make them interdependent. This concern with the niceties of a relationship is another liberty that Stevenson took with this genre.

Once again, then, Stevenson makes of a popular genre something that is more than the sum of its parts. Boys had read *Kidnapped* with fascination in *Young Folks*, but adults read it later in book form with even more fascination. Indeed, Henry James, whom some suspect of never having been a boy, believed that *Kidnapped* was the best thing that Stevenson had done.

THE STRANGE CASE OF DR. JEKYLL AND MR. HYDE

First published: 1886
Type of work: Novel

A lawyer, curious and suspicious about a nefarious character's influence on his (the lawyer's) wealthy, respectable client, finally discovers the horrible truth about their relationship.

One night, Stevenson's wife was disturbed by the movements and sounds of her sleeping husband; he seemed to be having a nightmare. She woke him. He was indeed having a nightmare, but he complained, on being awakened, that he had not come to the end of what was proving to be a fascinating tale. That morning, he rapidly wrote down the story that he had dreamed, adding an ending. When he read the tale to his wife, she was dissatisfied; she thought that it was simply a "crawler" (standard gothic horror tale) and that he should develop the moral issues inherent in the tale. He argued with her vigorously but in the end accepted her view and burned the first draft. The tale still had a strong enough hold on him, however, that he composed the second draft (the version that was published) in only three days.

Released to the public, the tale captured the public imagination and has not let go to this day. *The Strange Case of Dr. Jekyll and Mr. Hyde* made Robert Louis Stevenson a household name, and it made Stevenson's fortune. In less than a year, "Jekyll and Hyde" was an English colloquialism. In 1887, when Stevenson went to the United States, it was his notoriety from *The Strange Case of Dr. Jekyll and Mr. Hyde* that induced Charles Scribner's Sons to offer him a lucrative contract. That contract gave him his first taste of financial independence.

The story that produced such wide-ranging effects begins very quietly with a sketch of the passive, observant, tolerant Mr. Utterson, Dr. Jekyll's lawyer, the man from whose point of view this third-person narrative is told. Utterson's tolerance is being strained a little by Jekyll's curious deference to a Mr. Hyde, a man to whom Utterson takes an instant dislike. Only gradually does the intensity of the narrative increase as Utterson becomes more curious and Hyde becomes more disreputable. The story comes to a climax as Utterson helps break down a door to get at Hyde. The lawyer moves, then, from tolerance to judgment, from observer to participant; if it were not for the title of the tale, one would call Utterson the protagonist.

Following this climax is a series of letters to Utterson by a friend of Jekyll, then to Utterson from Jekyll himself; these letters, in effect, tell the story twice more from two new perspectives. These retellings clarify all remaining plot mysteries but preserve as unexplained the central mystery of the human capacity for evil. That mystery, the mystery of moral ambiguity in human judgment and action, intrigued Stevenson throughout his career.

Summary

Robert Louis Stevenson's life is a study in contrasts, if not contradictions: His parents were wealthy, but he spent the first half of his adulthood one step ahead of genteel poverty. His ancestors for three generations were pillars of the community, but he was a perpetual tourist. His family was very religious, but he became an iconoclast and an agnostic. His family made its living building lighthouses; he was to make his building imaginary worlds. In these contradictions, he rivaled the best of his complex characters. His life was an attempt to contain, and, in a sense, to live up to his own complexity. In time, however, the craftsman, the iconoclast, and the moralist became reconciled and unified, and Stevenson was still growing as an artist and as a man on the day that he died. The deeply rooted family tree flowered in Robert Louis Stevenson's short life.

Bibliography

Balfour, Graham. *The Life of Robert Louis Stevenson.* 2 vols. New York: Charles Scribner's Sons, 1901.

Calder, Jenni. *Robert Louis Stevenson: A Life Study.* New York: Oxford University Press, 1980.

Furnas, J. C. *A Voyage to Windward.* New York: William Sloane Associates, 1951.

Hammond, J. R. *A Robert Louis Stevenson Companion: A Guide to the Novels, Essays, and Short Stories.* New York: Macmillan, 1984.

James, Henry. *Henry James and Robert Louis Stevenson: A Record of Friendship and Criticism.* Edited by Janet Adam Smith. London: R. Hart-Davis, 1948.

Isaac Johnson

TOM STOPPARD

Born: Zlin, Czechoslovakia
July 3, 1937

Principal Literary Achievement

Stoppard is one of the most important and influential modern British drama-tists, praised and imitated for his ability to capture the mood and spirit of the time using references and allusions to literature ranging from Shakespeare to the present.

Biography

Tom Stoppard was born Tomas Straussler, the second son of Eugene and Martha Straussler, in Zlin, Czechoslovakia, on July 3, 1937. His father was a Jewish physician who worked for the Bata Shoe Company. In 1939, to protect the family from intern-ment when the Nazi invasion was imminent, the company transferred them to Singa-pore. There the Straussler children attended a multinational American school until the Japanese invasion of 1942 sent them fleeing to Darjeeling, India. Stoppard's father, however, remained behind and was killed; his mother married a British major, Ken-neth Stoppard, whose name the Straussler children took. In 1946 the Stoppard family moved to England and settled in the Bristol area in 1950. Stoppard was educated at Dophin School, Nottinghamshire, and Pocklington School, Yorkshire, but did not con-tinue on to a university. His knowledge of the theater and the dramatic arts is mainly self-taught. Stoppard worked as a journalist for the *Western Daily Press*, Bristol, for the next four years and then for the *Bristol Evening World* for two more years. He wrote feature articles, humor columns, and second-string drama criticism. This in-volvement with theater criticism led to a new career and is reflected in his rapier attacks on drama critics in *The Real Inspector Hound* (1968). He next became a free-lance journalist and writer. As drama critic for the *London Scene* from 1962 to 1963, he reviewed well in excess of a hundred plays. He also began writing radio and televi-sion plays, including screen versions of *A Separate Peace* (1966) and *Three Men in a Boat* (1975).

A 1964 Ford Foundation grant enabled him to stage his first play, *A Walk on the Water*, in Hamburg. He married Jose Ingle in 1965; they had two sons before their marriage dissolved in 1971. His first real success, *Rosencrantz and Guildenstern Are Dead* (1966), began as a one-act comedy in verse titled *Rosencrantz and Guilden-stern Meet King Lear*, the product of a Ford Foundation cultural picnic for promising

young playwrights. It was first produced in its present form at the 1966 Edinburgh Festival and then was booked at the National Theatre in London in 1967. The London production, which was followed by a New York production that won several awards, launched his career as a major playwright. In 1972, Stoppard married Dr. Miriam Moore-Robinson, a physician, television interviewer, and writer, and they had two sons. In the mid-1970's he directed some London productions and began writing screenplays for Hollywood. His screenplay credits include *The Romantic Englishwoman* (1975), *Despair* (1978), *The Human Factor* (1979), *Brazil* (1985), and *Billy Bathgate* (1991). Stoppard's various awards include the John Whiting Award (1967), the Prix Italia (1968), the Tony Award (1968, 1976, 1984), the New York Drama Critics Circle Award (1968, 1976, 1984), the Hamburg Shakespeare Prize (1979), the Outer Circle Award (1984), and the Drama Desk Award (1984). In addition, he received honorary degrees from the University of Bristol, Brunel University (Uxbridge, Middlesex), the University of Sussex (Brighton), Leeds University, the University of London, Kenyon College (Ohio), and York University. In 1978, he received the C.B.E. (Commander, Order of the British Empire) from the Royal Society of Literature. He settled in Iver Grove, Iver, Buckinghamshire, England.

Analysis

Stoppard is sometimes linked by critics with his near-contemporary, Harold Pinter. Both playwrights share similarities of temperament and background, though the works they produce have little in common. Stoppard and Pinter both come from immigrant families (Stoppard is, in his own phrase, a "bounced Czech"); both reject, at least in their early work, the realistic and naturalistic styles of their predecessors; both began their careers in the aftermath of the "angry young man" period stimulated by John Osborne's *Look Back in Anger* (1956). Both Pinter and Stoppard came to playwriting almost accidentally from practical non-university backgrounds, Pinter from acting and Stoppard from journalism and theater criticism. Since both men began as outsiders breaking into a clannish and traditional field of work, it is perhaps not surprising that they brought with them startlingly original points of view, perspectives from the outside that meshed smoothly with the revolution prompted by Osborne's play. With *Look Back in Anger* came a new enthusiasm for realistic working-class drama, passionate works that confronted social problems and politics. It was the end of the polite drawing-room drama of the previous era. Yet Pinter and Stoppard changed not only content but also style and approach, the former with his "theater of menace," the latter with his "high comedy of ideas."

Perhaps as a result of its originality, Stoppard's work has been difficult to classify. Most reviewers and commentators agree that he is a writer in love with language, a magician with verbal pyrotechnics who is unmatched in modern drama for the sheer exuberance of his style. Even the most untrained observer at a live production recognizes this gift in Stoppard—the words and phrases are so rapid and plentiful that a single viewing is never adequate. Beyond this linguistic agility, however, there is little agreement. Stoppard has been accused by reviewers such as John Simon and Stanley

Kauffmann of being facile, shallow, and pretentious. *Jumpers* (1972), his second major play, was particularly critized for its author's tendency to present philosophical debate on stage without integrating it into the stage action. His refusal to be serious even about figures such as Vladimir Ilich Lenin and James Joyce has been interpreted as a refusal to take his role as a writer seriously. The more academic critics of Stoppard, on the other hand, have praised his moral vision, his refusal to capitulate to relativism, and the very frivolity of his approach, which is sometimes compared to that of Oscar Wilde. His avoidance of trendy political and social subjects has sometimes been seen as integrity. Stoppard himself claims to show conflicting characters and statements on stage without taking a personal position at all—like many writers, he prefers to let his work speak for itself.

Whatever the ultimate judgment of Stoppard's seriousness or lack thereof, there can be no question about the impact of his four major plays and incidental work. He has stimulated a wide range of reaction in the theater, in academia, and in the perception of the general public. He is without question one of the most significant of modern English playwrights.

ROSENCRANTZ AND GUILDENSTERN ARE DEAD

First produced: 1966 (first published, 1967)
Type of work: Play

Rosencrantz and Guildenstern, minor characters in Shakespeare's *Hamlet*, become the main characters in an absurdist drama about the interpretation and meaning of existence.

The title *Rosencrantz and Guildenstern Are Dead* is a direct quotation from William Shakespeare's *Hamlet* (c. 1600-1601), a line delivered by the English ambassador to Horatio at the close of *Hamlet*. In Shakespeare's play it is but a minor detail, one of the many threads of the play brought to a close at the end of major events. In Stoppard's play it is of major significance, for it marks the death of the main characters. Stoppard's play depicts the "offstage lives" of Hamlet's boyhood friends Rosencrantz and Guildenstern and demonstrates how they might feel about being used as pawns who are ultimately executed with no understanding of the reason. As minor literary characters they of course have no lives apart from their roles in *Hamlet*, and this lack allows Stoppard to use them as ideal representatives of modern absurdist-existentialist protagonists—empty, "flat" characters who are uncertain of their identity and their purpose and who thus speculate endlessly about what they should do next. Their only moments of sharp definition come when the characters from *Hamlet* sweep on stage, and Rosencrantz and Guildenstern briefly speak the lines and act the parts created for them by Shakespeare. Meanwhile Hamlet, Gertrude, Claudius, and

the other members of the court go about the serious business of *Hamlet* offstage, and
"Ros" and "Guil," as they are called in Stoppard's work, are left to their own trivial
devices, such as flipping coins, arguing with the players who put on the play-within-
the-play, and alternately disagreeing and making up. Their behavior raises questions
about actors and acting and about the nature of reality: Are these characters more
"real" when engaged in the fictive role Shakespeare created for two actors to play or
when existing "on their own" outside the context of his play? Ros, Guil, and the
"Players" discuss the importance of blood, love, and rhetoric in a play and the question of role playing as reality. Ros and Guil are controlled by the action of Shakespeare's play; yet they remain under the illusion that they have choices to make and
debate whether to go home or see how events transpire and whether to go to England
with Hamlet. Inevitably, despite their fears and doubts and hesitations, they act as the
moment demands, in accordance with the Shakespearean script.

This behavior by the main characters, many critics have pointed out, is heavily
influenced by Samuel Beckett's *En attendant Godot* (pb. 1952; *Waiting for Godot*,
1954). Beckett's play is also set in a "place without visible character," as Stoppard
describes it; features two somewhat pathetic figures waiting for some outside person
to enter their lives and give them meaning; and explores issues of identity, fate, and
probability. Stoppard clearly means for his audience to recognize and enjoy this parallel with *Waiting for Godot* and to allow the resonances of one work to inform the
other. In *Waiting for Godot*, Gogo and Didi play word games to pass the time as they
wait for Godot, who apparently will come and provide a purpose for their wait. In
much the same way, Ros and Guil flip a coin endlessly as they wait for the characters
of *Hamlet* to enter and give their lives purpose. Since Ros and Guil seem "modern,"
the audience is led to consider what has happened to drama and philosophy in the period from Shakespeare's time to his or her own. The confident, eloquent, and grand
in *Hamlet* has become uncertain, banal, and trivial, with a concern not with heroes
and kings but rather with trying to make sense of anything at all. Ros and Guil question whether anyone is watching them at all—even the fact of an audience is brought
into doubt. Death is the only certainty. Because of its blend of absurdist humor,
metaphysical inquiry, and literary allusion, the play's literary and dramatic precur-
sors are often identified as T. S. Eliot and Luigi Pirandello, writers who define modernist concerns.

More than one critic has pointed out that *Rosencrantz and Guildenstern Are Dead*
is a long play in which almost nothing happens: The only real "action" is in the brief
interruptions by members of the main play and when Ros and Guil go on board ship
to travel to England to their deaths. Yet the play seems full of incident, with much coming and going, much speculation about location and time, and many time-consuming
activities such as the flipping of coins. As the first of what Stoppard calls his "high
comedies of ideas," this play, like *Hamlet*, raises questions about illusion and reality, about sanity and insanity, about what is relative and what is absolute. It has also
been termed a highly intellectual comedy, yet rather surprisingly one that has enjoyed wide popular appeal in Great Britain and in the United States and beyond. As

the work that made Stoppard's reputation, it continues to be the object of anthologies and critiques.

JUMPERS

First produced: 1972 (first published, 1972)
Type of work: Play

A retired music-hall singer married to a professor of moral philosophy is investigated for possibly shooting her husband's rival at an acrobatic exhibition.

Jumpers hinges on the absurd but very amusing idea that the members of the faculty of philosophy at a major British university are also members of an amateur acrobatic team, the "jumpers" of the title. Sir Archibald, the Vice Chancellor, a "first-rate gymnast" himself, has packed his school with gymnastically talented thinkers, a combination admitted to be unique. Stoppard's witty premise brings a dead metaphor to life through the "mental gymnastics" of Sir "Archie" and George, the professor of moral philosophy, as they argue and debate over philosophical principles and over Archie's attentions to George's wife Dotty, who is having an affair with her husband's superior. George's attention, however, is distracted by his need to prepare his side of a public debate with Duncan McFee, a rival philosopher who has enjoyed considerably more success than George. Dotty, whose state of mind seems to be just what her name implies, may have shot and killed McFee during an acrobatic exhibition in George and Dotty's apartment. Inspector Bones is the detective who comes to investigate the murder, but he is so star-struck by Dotty, a retired music-hall singer, that he is easily distracted. The comedy results in part from conversations based on incorrect assumptions (the Inspector thinks George knows of McFee's murder, but George does not) and from such farcical interplay as Inspector Bones, arriving with flowers in hand for Dotty, being met by George, his face smeared with shaving cream, a bow and arrow in hand.

The confusion does not end with the main characters; there is also a secretary who stripteases on a trapeze, a live tortoise, a dead hare, and two astronauts fighting on the moon. Yet Stoppard is able to bring a fair measure of order out of this chaos, and by the end of the play the audience has begun to accept the logic, or illogic, of this household. Stoppard makes little effort at suspending the audience's disbelief, however, for his main interest is in the long declamations by George, who continually tests the logic of his arguments for the existence of God and the absoluteness of good and evil by rehearsing them aloud. These declamations allow Stoppard to include a recitation of the logical paradoxes of the Greek philosopher Zeno, who "proved" that an arrow released from a bow can never reach its target because it must first reach a midpoint in its flight, and before that the halfway point to the first midpoint, and so on in an infinite series of midpoints that can never be crossed. The focus on philosophical and logical cruxes such as these and on an ongoing debate between relativistic ethics and philosophical absolutes makes the play intellectually challenging even as the lunatic plot amuses.

Jumpers enjoyed less success than *Rosencrantz and Guildenstern Are Dead*, with a number of reviewers complaining about the shallowness of the characters (little about Dotty is revealed, and the audience is not encouraged to care about George) and the superficiality of the plot (as in the earlier play, there are few "events" beyond what is described above). A just criticism is that the "jumpers" metaphor never really works. One reviewer notes that the practical problems of finding gymnasts who can act or actors who can jump led to a witty sideshow rather than to an integral element of the play, an integration of the sort that occurs with the *Hamlet* sections of *Rosencrantz and Guildenstern Are Dead*. Also, *Hamlet* brings with it its own credibility and seriousness, while George's maunderings seem too often the self-indulgence of a tiresome old fool, which of course he is. Yet *Jumpers* also seems very much a play of its time, with its nudity, its mocking of authority, its attempts at shocking the audience with the outrageous. The late 1960's and early 1970's were a period of wild experimentation in the theater, and Stoppard's effort seems in perfect accord with that sensibility.

TRAVESTIES

First produced: 1974 (first published, 1975)
Type of work: Play

Dadaist poet Tristan Tzara, James Joyce, and (Vladimir) Lenin become involved with one another and with the British consul in Zurich, Switzerland, in 1917.

Travesties concerns a number of possible travesties (or burlesques), including one by the author. First is the artistic philosophy of Tristan Tzara, who, like his fellow practitioners of Dada, tries to reverse all the bourgeois notions of the proper role of art and literature (Tzara "composes" a poem by cutting out all the words from a Shakespeare sonnet, putting them in a hat, and pulling them out at random). Another candidate for travesty status is James Joyce, who, his genius as a writer notwithstanding, seems to have behaved in a spiteful and money-grubbing way toward someone he might well have thanked. Lenin's travesty could well be his fleeing his scholarly pursuits in Zurich to lead a revolution that would end with the deaths of millions under Joseph Stalin. Henry Carr, the British consul in Zurich, gets involved in an undignified squabble with Joyce over some theater tickets and a pair of pants, and the case goes to court. The most likely travesty, however, may be the play itself, with Stoppard poking fun at his story, told through the point of view of an aged and confused Henry Carr, about these unlikely characters coming together in Zurich, a conservative and conventional town. This travesty, then, would be Stoppard's burlesque version of events, his focus on the grotesque in a story that is essentially true in its basic details.

Tzara, Joyce, and Lenin were all, in fact, residing in Zurich at about the same time and must have used the Zurich public library. Stoppard discovered that Joyce, on the lookout for a profit, produced an English-language version of Oscar Wilde's *The Importance of Being Earnest* (1895) and that Carr was persuaded to play the part of Algernon, with some success. Joyce and Carr had a dispute over some tickets that Carr had been given to sell and over Carr's purchase of a pair of pants to wear as part of his costume. Joyce paid Carr only ten francs, "like a tip," and the two found themselves in a Swiss court suing and countersuing, to the credit of neither. Tzara was moving in the same circles, while Lenin was using the library every day to research his book on imperialism and may well have been kept under surveillance by Carr. Stoppard interweaves these historical characters, with Tzara and Carr falling hilariously into the roles and language of *The Importance of Being Earnest* as the poet pursues Gwendolen, here Joyce's secretary, and Carr chases Cecily, now the Zurich librarian. Throughout, Lenin speaks lines Stoppard gleaned from his speeches and from various biographies and reminiscences about the Russian leader, lending a credible and serious tone to the manic romantic involvements of Carr and Joyce.

The situation allows Stoppard to compare and contrast three revolutionaries—in poetry, in the novel, and in politics—with the perhaps not surprising conclusion that there is little about which they can agree beyond the need for a revolt. Stoppard's sympathies clearly lie with Joyce's artistic practice, but he is careful to show Tzara and Lenin in sympathetic lights, allowing each to speak for himself and present his position. The related question of the proper role of art in society is explored directly or by implication in the varying philosophies of each character: Lenin's utilitarian theory, which would later become socialist realism; Tzara's goal of dumbfounding the bourgeois with perversity; and the complexities of Joyce's self-referential psychology. Yet when the tone becomes too serious Stoppard regularly resorts to parody of *The Importance of Being Earnest*, deflating the high grandeur of his world-class revolutionaries. Art is for art's sake and needs no utilitarian defense.

A final note on the staging may make Stoppard's approach clearer. In the first production of *Travesties*, in London by the Royal Shakespeare Company at the Aldwych Theatre in 1974, Henry Carr, played by the immensely talented John Wood, was initially seated at an upright piano to one side of the stage. He represented the "old" Henry Carr, who was remembering his youth in Zurich and his odd associates in 1917, and the play that followed was his distorted reverie. Wood played the piano and sang musical comedy pieces, casting the entire evening as an eccentric entertainment by a possibly senile old man. To search for "truth" within such a framing device is clearly perilous, and Stoppard's stage directions and other comments indicate that this stagy burlesque of the seriousness that follows is entirely his intention. He "squats" happily, as one commentator noted, on the fence between the popular and the academic, intriguing both sides but belonging to neither.

THE REAL THING

First produced: 1982 (first published, 1982)
Type of work: Play

Henry, a middle-aged dramatist, leaves his wife and marries again, only to face his new wife's infidelity with a younger man.

The Real Thing refers to true married love, a condition that Henry has to learn to preserve after divorcing his first wife. The play begins with a clever device, a scene between Max and Charlotte, who seem to be man and wife. Charlotte has just returned from a business trip, and Max has discovered her infidelity. When he confronts her, she walks out on him. The reader then discovers that that scene is actually from a play, "House of Cards," written by the main character of *The Real Thing*, Henry, who is in "real life" married to Charlotte. Henry is having an affair with Annie, Max's real wife, so the situation of the play-within-the-play parallels that of the main play, although with a different cast of characters. When Henry leaves Charlotte and Annie leaves Max, Henry and Annie marry and are very much in love. The story jumps forward two years, however, when Annie is acting in a provincial theater in Glasgow and is tricked into having an affair (the particular play is John Ford's *'Tis Pity Shee's a Whore*, 1633). Henry, one of the "last romantics," must avoid Max's failure to keep his marriage intact but must also find some dignity and strength that will attract Annie in spite of her guilt over committing adultery.

With this play Stoppard departs from his previous experiments in stagecraft and the avant-garde. There is no absurdist-existential empty stage, no acrobats swinging from chandeliers, no Dada poets, and no Russian revolutionaries. Instead, the audience sees the pain and suffering of a middle-aged man and his slightly younger second wife, characters who are mature, articulate, and highly sensitive to nuance. Both, in spite of their intelligence and skill with language, have made terminal mistakes in their first marriages; both have found "the real thing" in their second marriage but are unsure of how to hold on to it. Annie's affair is not dismissed cynically by Annie, Henry, or Stoppard as the price of a civilized life-style in London; this is not the clever smart-set comedy of Noël Coward. She has betrayed her husband, and both must come to terms with that dishonesty. Yet Stoppard also shows the adultery as a human event for which it is difficult simply to condemn Annie, who has been somewhat neglected by her husband and who intended no harm (she says her lover "came in under the radar"). Henry too recognizes that the harmless flirtation of everyday life, and especially of life in the theater, can lead to irreversible involvement with one small push; it is almost rude not to notice such flirtation, he says.

What is interesting about the emotional and psychological subtleties of *The Real Thing* is that they are so new to Stoppard's canon. His earlier plays were criticized as superficial, as comedies of ideas without involvement. In this play he is still exploring the existential moment and the need to create meaning and coherence but is doing so in domestic circumstances, in the interstices of everyday lives that all readers can recognize. There may be an autobiographical element in *The Real Thing*, as commentators have noted, since Stoppard was divorced and remarried, but more significantly he exhibits intense human sympathy for the pain of his characters, a sympathy absent and usually impossible in the contexts of his earlier plays.

Yet Stoppard's intellectual concerns continue in *The Real Thing*. The title, which perhaps should end in a question mark, summarizes the problem for all the characters: How can one distinguish between the bogus and the true? The "House of Cards" play-within-the-play is not real, although it initially seems to be, just as Annie's affair initially promises true love. A subplot raises the question of what true political commitment involves (a question critics have asked about Stoppard) and of what defines true generosity and gratitude. There are repetitions and echoes of earlier scenes, with some acting as mirror images of each other. In spite of the apparent radical departure from his past style, *The Real Thing* remains pure Stoppard.

Summary

Tom Stoppard's four major plays in many ways represent the times in which they were written. *Rosencrantz and Guildenstern Are Dead* is clearly in the style of Beckett's *Waiting for Godot*, a play out of the 1950's and the existential-absurdist tradition. *Jumpers* has the manic energy and outrageous non sequiturs of the swinging London of the 1960's and early 1970's. *Travesties*, although written shortly after *Jumpers*, returns to a slightly more conventional format, while *The Real Thing* is on the surface a play from a much earlier time. Yet first to last, these disparate works remain uniquely those of Stoppard, with his typical concerns for distinguishing illusion from reality, for finding one's way in a confusing and unforgiving world. Stoppard's work has the conservatism of comedy, keeping one foot firmly planted in the earthiness of the comic as if in distrust of too many abstractions, too many high-flying ideas. Finally, each play is a linguistic tour de force, inventive, sometimes lyrical, and always hypnotizing.

Bibliography

Bigsby, C. W. E. *Tom Stoppard*. London: Longman, 1976.

Billington, Michael. *Stoppard the Playwright*. London: Methuen, 1987.

Brassell, Tim. *Tom Stoppard: An Assessment*. London: Macmillan, 1983.

Cahn, Victor L. *Beyond Absurdity: The Plays of Tom Stoppard*. Madison, N.J.: Fairleigh Dickinson University Press, 1979.

Corballis, Richard. *Stoppard: The Mystery and the Clockwork*. New York: Methuen, 1984.

Delaney, Paul. *Tom Stoppard: The Moral Vision of the Major Plays*. New York: St. Martin's Press, 1990.

Jenkins, Anthony. *The Theatre of Tom Stoppard.* New York: Cambridge University Press, 1987.

Rusinko, Susan. *Tom Stoppard.* Boston: Twayne, 1986.

Sammells, Neil. *Tom Stoppard: The Artist as Critic.* New York: St. Martin's Press, 1988.

Whitaker, Thomas R. *Tom Stoppard.* London: Macmillan, 1983.

Andrew Macdonald

AUGUST STRINDBERG

Born: Stockholm, Sweden
January 22, 1849
Died: Stockholm, Sweden
May 14, 1912

Principal Literary Achievement

Strindberg was one of the leading figures in modern drama. He pioneered the drama of psychological realism and created a form of expressionistic drama that gave dramatic structure to subjective reality.

Biography

Johan August Strindberg was born in Stockholm, Sweden, on January 22, 1849, the son of Carl Oscar Strindberg, a steamship agent with an aristocratic background, and Ulrika Eleonora Norling, a domestic servant. When Strindberg was four years old, his father went bankrupt and the family, constantly on the move, lived under impoverished conditions in which food was scarce. His relationship with his parents was an ambivalent one. Though he admired his father's aristocratic heirs, he frequently saw him as a hostile force. Though he felt that his mother was violent and unreasonable, he came to see maternity as something sacred. A sensitive and anxious man, Strindberg returned to his youthful experiences for material for his works. Hunger, both physical and spiritual, became a recurrent motif in his later works. Bankruptcy came to represent not only the economic condition of his characters but also their existential condition. The class difference between his parents absorbed him in a constant analysis of class warfare; his ambivalent relationship with his mother carried over into his marriages; and the search for the mother figure became an obsessive theme running throughout all of his work.

When Strindberg was thirteen, his mother died, and his father remarried. Influenced by his mother's evangelical Pietism, Strindberg developed a scrupulous devotion to religion that eventually became transformed into a fervent skepticism. Religion, skepticism, and the quest for God would remain as focal issues in Strindberg's life and works.

In 1867, the eighteen-year-old Strindberg pursued the study of modern languages at the University of Uppsala, where he found the academic atmosphere stifling. He later became a tutor in the house of Dr. Lamm, who encouraged him to pursue medicine, but Strindberg failed his chemistry examination, left the university, and tried unsuc-

cessfully to become an actor. Acting led him to playwriting, and after writing his verse drama *Hermione* (1871), he returned to the university to engage in literary studies.

Strindberg launched his career as a dramatist when *I Rom* (1870) was produced by the Royal Dramatic Theatre. Subsequently, Strindberg received a stipend from the king. After he left the university, he became a journalist and continued to write plays. His *Mäster Olof* (pb. 1878; *Master Olof*, 1915), a historical prose drama, moved beyond the stilted form of the patriotic chronicle play. He also fell in love with Siri von Essen, a Finnish aristocrat, married to Baron Carl Gustav Wrangel. When she divorced Wrangel in 1877, Strindberg entered his first marriage. In various dramatic forms, Strindberg used the relationship between a lower-class man and an aristocratic woman while the menacing figure of the Baron became a haunting presence in his early and later works.

Strindberg became a controversial writer. *Giftas I* (1884; *Getting Married*, 1913), a collection of short stories, brought him to court on a charge of blasphemy because of sarcastic remarks about the Eucharist. Though he was acquitted, the trial put pressure on his already unstable marriage to Siri, whose acting career was constantly being interrupted. During this period, Strindberg became obsessed with the idea that a league of women was conspiring against him, he thought that his wife was trying to have him committed, and he doubted whether he was the father of his own child. Many of his delusions were fictionalized in *Le Plaidoyer d'un fou* (1893; *A Madman's Defense*, 1912), an autobiographical novel, and reappeared in his major naturalistic works: *Fadren* (1887; *The Father*, 1899), *Fröken Julie* (pb. 1888; *Miss Julie*, 1912), and *Fordringsägare* (pb. 1888; *Creditors*, 1910). Having corresponded with philosopher Friedrich Nietzsche and author Émile Zola, Strindberg began to embrace naturalism, started an experimental theater in Copenhagen in 1889, and began to acquire an international reputation.

After his divorce from Siri, Strindberg moved to Germany and joined a bohemian artists' colony. Later he met and married journalist Frieda Uhl. Again Strindberg's paranoia led to the dissolving of the marriage in 1894. That same year he went to Paris, where he experienced a psychotic breakdown known as his "Inferno" crisis. Feeling himself to be the victim of mysterious powers, he believed it necessary to read symbols and portents in everyday occurrences. After his bout with psychosis, Strindberg questioned the nature of objective truth and saw the world in terms of symbols and signs. He brought these perceptions into play in his drama *Till Damaskus, forsta delen* (pb. 1898; *To Damascus I*, 1913).

In 1901, he married actress Harriet Bosse, another career woman. Despite his feelings toward her, Strindberg's jealousy and his other delusions led to their divorce in 1904. During his last years Strindberg continued to experiment with dramatic form, collaborated with August Falck in founding the Intimate Theatre, wrote and produced a series of chamber plays, and settled in Falck's residence, called The Blue Tower. Retired and suffering from stomach cancer, Strindberg continued to be honored by torchlight parades and gala performances. The man who did battle with God and the Devil was said to have held the Bible to his chest, saying, "All is atoned for."

His role as rebel, victim, and pilgrim was played out in his life as well as in his works. He died in Stockholm on May 14, 1912.

Analysis

August Strindberg was a prolific writer. He wrote plays, short stories, novels, poems, autobiographies, literary criticism, histories, works on folklore, political tracts, studies on Chinese language and culture, treatises on chemistry, and reams of letters and journals. He is best known, however, for his work as a dramatist. His dramatic canon has an incredible range. He wrote compact one-act dramas focusing on intense conflicts between several characters as well as massive epics covering vast territories and significant lapses in time. He wrote sardonic comedies, historical dramas, fantasies based on fairy tales, family dramas portraying volatile conflicts between husbands and wives, pilgrimage plays that follow one character's odyssey through life, and symbolic dramas with ghostlike characters. Most of Strindberg's dramas are intensely autobiographical works in which characters caught in the grip of powerful forces engage in the psychological torment of themselves and others.

One recurring theme in Strindberg's dramas is the theme of sexual warfare. Since primitive times, male fantasy has projected the dual image of woman as either good mother or evil seductress, an image that Strindberg adopted. The maternal ideal for Strindberg is seen in a caring and nurturing woman, but this ideal is perverted by the Strindbergian woman's quest for power and dominance. His women are subtle destroyers of men, driving them to insanity or killing them slowly through various means of psychological torment. Even children are used as pawns in a deadly battle to the death. Laura in *The Father* drives the Captain insane and robs him of his paternal power. Julie is both repulsed by and attracted to men and always tries to exert her dominance over them. The mother in *Pelikanen* (1907; *The Pelican*, 1962) takes on a lover and drives the father to his death with her infidelity.

The male hero in Strindberg's plays is a prototype of the alienated heroes of modern drama. Caught in a world of perpetual doubt and suspicion, he finds himself a victim in a cruel world. He often experiences a paralysis of the will and is controlled by overpowering forces that consciously or unconsciously manipulate his life. In his quest for an ideal, he finds himself thwarted at every turn by the complexities of the world order. He may search hopelessly for a mother figure, as do the Captain in *The Father* and the Unknown in *To Damascus I.* He may try to break the bond of a stratified social order, as Jean does in *Miss Julie*, or he may seek for an ideal love that transcends the world of social stigmas and existential guilt. Yet no matter how hard he seeks to find a way out of his entrapment, he is left defeated and completely incapacitated.

Many critics consider Strindberg as a subjective dramatist more concerned with his own personal struggles than with social issues. Yet Strindberg is interested in class warfare. In *Miss Julie* and *Spöksonaten* (pb. 1907; *The Ghost Sonata*, 1916), he shows how flimsy is the base of aristocratic power. A miller prostitutes his wife to purchase a title from the king. Thus originates the aristocratic bloodline of *Miss Ju-*

lie. In *The Ghost Sonata*, the Colonel is a fake aristocrat who has gained his military title from an honorary position in the American volunteer service. The power structure is always questioned in Strindberg. The new monied aristocracy, of which Jean is now a part, is as shallow as the old aristocracy. Jean is like Hummel, the capitalist entrepreneur in *The Ghost Sonata* who turns out to be a vampire destroying human lives.

Strindberg also stands at the forefront of modern drama when he focuses on the theme of doubt and uncertainty in a world where truth is impossible to discern. The world of Strindberg's drama is wrapped in lies and deceptions. Fathers do not know that their children are their own. Aristocracy and birthrights are called into question. Two false witnesses determine the truth in a court of law. People are never what they seem to be, and those who try to acknowledge the truth are declared insane. Strindberg also focused on two themes that would become predominant in modern drama: the notion that reality depends on one's subjective perception and the idea that life is built on a series of illusions.

Strindberg's major drama can be classified into three major periods: his naturalistic period, his expressionistic period, and the period of his chamber plays. Discontented with the popular moralistic melodramas of his time, Strindberg created naturalistic dramas that probe the psyches of modern individuals. The motivations of his characters are complex, multiple, and usually concealed. Driven by psychological and sociological influences, his characters maintain a thin grasp on their identity and possess a fragmented sense of self. The conflict in his naturalistic dramas focuses on a few individuals battling for psychological domination. External action gives way to internal struggles in which one person subtly drives the other to his or her death in a form of psychological murder. The battle is most often played out in sexual warfare in which the woman, the weaker sex, drains the words and ideas from others and often destroys an intellectually superior male. These dramas have few characters, one setting, a short time-span, and a singular thread of action. Strindberg also called for realistic acting, a functional set with real props, subtle makeup, stage lighting, and the elimination of the intermission.

After his Inferno crisis, Strindberg moved away from naturalism to expressionism and was again at the vanguard of creating new dramatic forms. His dream plays of this period are intensely personal journeys through the mind of a central consciousness. Character in these plays becomes even more unstable and fragmented. Just as in a dream, characters, reduced to types, split, multiply, and transform themselves so that one character may be seen in many guises. Time and place change at random as one scene fades into another. The structure is episodic and similar actions recur in different forms. Dialogue varies between the cryptic and the poetic. Objects and people take on symbolic significance. In his expressionistic dream plays, Strindberg recast the medieval drama of sin and reconciliation into a modern psychodrama in which reality becomes a matter of subjective perception.

Late in his career, Strindberg experimented with a more intimate form of drama that he called chamber plays because of their resemblance to chamber music. In these plays, Strindberg returned to the short play with a small ensemble of characters. The form of the chamber play is tighter and more compressed than the expressionistic dream play. The plays are based on thematic movements rather than linear plots. They display a series of images juxtaposed and intertwined like the themes in a sonata. The plays focus on a world of discord, sin, guilt, retribution, and reconciliation. Their mood is somber and elegiac. Combining realistic scenes with grotesque symbolic images, they envelop the audience in a muted spectacle of sight and sound that borders on the surrealistic. They pave the way toward modern absurdist drama. Strindberg was a relentless experimenter who opened up new vistas for modern drama and influenced many of the great dramatists of the twentieth century.

THE FATHER

First produced: *Fadren*, 1887 (first published, 1887; English translation, 1899)
Type of work: Play

Fighting for control of her child, a wife drives her husband to insanity and death by making him doubt that he is the child's father.

The Father is often seen as a tragedy in which larger-than-life characters engage in a life-or-death struggle centered on a family conflict. Like a Greek tragedy, *The Father* has a tight plot structure, a narrow time frame of twenty-four hours, one locale, and a hint of the fatalistic forces at work behind the scenes. It has often been compared to the story of Agamemnon, who was trapped and killed by his wife Clytemnestra because he had sacrificed their daughter. *The Father* is also similar to Euripides' *The Bacchae* (c. 405 B.C.). In *The Bacchae*, Pentheus rejects the god Dionysus and his women worshipers the Maenads, only to be torn to pieces by them. In *The Father*, the Captain rejects feminine forces, both spiritual and physical. Thus, a household of women turns against him and figuratively tears him to pieces. An evil or fatalistic force seems to haunt the house. The Captain senses the web of fate that is being spun around him. Bertha hears maternal ghosts in the attic mourning over a cradle. Bertha's grandmother, who is antagonistic to her father, warns her that spirits who are ignored seek vengeance.

The Father not only examines the battle of the sexes, but questions the patriarchy, the male power structure, by casting doubts on paternity or fatherhood. The Captain wishes to assert his rights as father and husband. He tells his wife that when she married she bartered her rights in exchange for his financial support of her. Marriage, according to the societal order, is an exchange in which the woman agrees to be mastered in order to be supported. Thus, masculine law gives the father the sole right to determine the education of his child. Old Margaret, the Captain's former nursemaid, argues that a mother has only her child, whereas the father has other pursuits. The

Captain, however, insists that his burden is greater than his wife's because he is responsible for the whole family.

The Captain, a military man who surrounds himself with symbols of masculine power (military tunics, rifles, gamebags), represents the power of the patriarchy. However, the play questions the certainty of fatherhood itself. In the very first scene, the Captain tries to get one of his cavalry soldiers to accept the responsibility for impregnating one of the kitchen maids. Nojd admits to having slept with her but implies that there have been others, so that it is impossible to determine who is the father of the child. Nojd feels that it would be drudgery to support another man's child. Laura picks up this issue and notes that if fatherhood cannot be determined, how can the father have rights over the child? She says that she can prove that Bertha is not his child. The Captain, who has always held to his patriarchal privilege of passing on his soul to his child and obtaining immortality through his progeny, feels his power slipping away. The play begins to cast doubt on paternity. Johannson was forced to become the father of Old Margaret's illegitimate child when he could not be certain that he was the father. The Captain implies that the wives of both the Pastor and the Doctor were unfaithful, thus questioning their paternity. Fatherhood is called into question, and with it, masculine power. Laura turns masculine law against the Captain by having him declared certifiably insane, thereby divesting him of his power. Since he claimed mastery as provider, she will now discard him and use his provisions.

If fatherhood is being questioned, motherhood is being elevated. The Captain, rejected by his mother, makes his wife his "second mother" and surrenders his will to her like a child. He keeps his old nursemaid with him and she treats him as her "big boy." In the end, the nurse slips a straitjacket over him, pretending that she is dressing a little boy. As he is dying, he longs to lie on a mother's breast. He puts his head down on the nurse's lap, comparing her to the Virgin Mary, thus ironically replicating the Pietà, the body of Christ in Mary's arms. The play ends with Bertha coming to Laura in the semblance of an ironic Madonna. Behind the personal tragedy, *The Father* encompasses a powerful social drama.

MISS JULIE

First produced: *Fröken Julie*, 1889 (first published, 1888; English translation, 1912)
Type of work: Play

An aristocratic woman makes love to her servant and commits suicide rather than face dishonor.

Miss Julie is not simply the tragedy of an aristocratic woman with a self-destructive personality and an ambivalent feeling toward men. It is also more than a naturalistic study about a victimized woman torn apart by family strife. *Miss Julie*, a drama of paradoxes and reversals, is about the breakdown of the social order. The play begins on the celebration of Midsummer's Eve, a carnival-like festival allowing for the breakdown of social and sexual distinctions. Miss Julie, the lady of the house, would rather dance with the peasants than visit relatives with her father. Jean, her servant, is more concerned than the reckless Julie about propriety. In keeping with Midsummer's Eve, Julie wants all rank laid aside and asks Jean to take off his servant's livery. Julie and Jean then reverse roles. He drinks wine, she prefers beer; he is concerned about his reputation, she is negligent and foolhardy; he dreams of climbing, she dreams of falling.

In *Miss Julie*, aristocracy itself is a paradox. Jean fights to become a new aristocrat, but the aristocracy to which he aspires is a sham. Young ladies use foul language, their polished nails are dirty underneath, and their perfumed handkerchiefs are soiled. Miss Julie's family title was obtained when a miller let his wife sleep with the king. Thus, the aristocratic title was earned through sexual corruption. Jean's fiancée, Christine, who is not above thievery and fornication, cannot live in a house where the mistress sleeps with a servant. Jean, who realizes the hypocrisy behind aristocracy, is not beyond buying himself a bogus royal title. He cannot have Julie's noble blood (which was gained by corrupt means), yet he can make their children nobility (by purchasing a less-than-reputable title). In *Miss Julie*, the authenticity of aristocracy is questioned.

In the midst of midsummer madness, not only are class barriers falling, but gender distinctions are also becoming confused. Miss Julie's father married a common woman; yet this common woman was given control of his estate. Another reversal of roles has occurred: The commoner ruled over the aristocrat. Julie's mother also reversed gender roles and reared Julie to ride and hunt and to wear men's clothes. Furthermore, she turned the whole estate into a carnival world in which the men did the women's work and the women did the men's work. When the father reexerted his control and restored order, she burned down the estate. He was then forced to borrow her money to rebuild, thus reversing the power structure again. The same ambiguous relationship between commoner and aristocrat is played out between Jean and Julie. Julie, the woman, makes her fiancés jump over whips like trained animals and delights in having Jean kiss her shoe. She becomes the seducer while he becomes nervous about his reputation. In his bedroom, she is the one who becomes sexually aggressive while he is the one who is shocked.

Banned by the censors, *Miss Julie* was produced at a private performance in Copenhagen in 1899, was later proclaimed a revolutionary naturalistic drama, and is now one of Strindberg's most anthologized plays.

A DREAM PLAY

First produced: *Ett drömspel*, 1907 (first published, 1902; English
            translation, 1912)
Type of work: Play

   The Daughter of the Hindu god Indra comes down to earth to discover that
humanity is miserable and pitiable.

A Dream Play is an expressionistic drama built on a montage of scenes following
the journey of a central character. The Daughter of Indra is a goddess who comes
down to earth in the form of a beautiful woman to find out why humanity is so
discontent. Like Christ, she experiences the pain of being human. At first, she is
hopeful that love will conquer all, but after she listens to the anguished cries of
humanity, experiences the pain of family life, and discovers that reform will always
be stifled by the self-righteous, she can only look upon humanity with compassion.
She finally realizes that human beings are creatures who hopelessly harbor spiritual
aspirations but are held down by the weight of their fleshly existence. When she
ascends back into the heavens, she throws her shoes into the fire of purification as
she leaves a world of never-ending conflicts and contradictions.
   The play is built around the disappointments and dreams of three men: an officer,
an attorney, and a poet. The officer is a high-ranking military officer and teacher. As the
action of the play progresses, he changes from a youthful, effervescent, well-groomed
soldier to an aging, weary, unkempt derelict as he hopelessly spends a lifetime waiting for his dream lover, the opera singer Victoria. Restless and self-pitying, he is
constantly irritated by the injustice and repetitiveness of life but continues to hold on
to the romantic notion that love will cure all ills. When he rescues the Daughter of
Indra from the drudgery of domestic life and takes her to Fairhaven, a romantic paradise, he lands in Foulstrand, a modern-day inferno, where he witnesses the everlast-
ing misery of the human condition. In his constant failure to find true love, he represents disillusioned romanticism.
   The attorney is disgruntled. Through his dealings with the crimes and viciousness
of humanity, he has acquired a pale, haggard, and discolored face, along with black-
ened and bleeding hands. Denied his doctorate by the self-righteous academicians,
he becomes a Christ figure who suffers rejection because he defends the poor and the
helpless. More of a realist than the officer, he sees human beings as flawed creatures
trapped between their commitments to odious duties and their desire for life's elusive
pleasures—pleasures that always result in recriminations. He marries the Daughter of
Indra and enlightens her on the inhuman torments of living in poverty and the constant antagonisms of family life. Later, he continually reminds her of her sacred duty
to her child.

The poet is an erratic visionary who bathes in mud in order to come down from the ethereal regions of lofty thought and to immerse himself in the dirt of life. Caked with mud, he is protected from the flies. Being both idealistic and cynical, he sees through life's injustices and hypocrisies and rails against the gods. Though an earth-bound creature hampered by his bodily existence, he still reaches for spiritual rejuvenation. When those around him are abandoning hope, he realizes that human redemption will only come through suffering and death.

In *A Dream Play*, Strindberg felt that he had created a new form. That form, later termed expressionism, was adopted by the German dramatists and became a trend in modern drama.

THE GHOST SONATA

First produced: *Spöksonaten*, 1908 (first published, 1907; English translation, 1916)
Type of work: Play

A young student in search of a beautiful girl enters a house full of ghoulish characters and is surrounded by deception, guilt, and death.

In *The Ghost Sonata*, August Strindberg paints a picture of a fallen world based on illusions and deceptions, where human beings, bound together by common guilt, are condemned to suffer for their sins. Only by escaping this world can one find peace and happiness. In this world, filled with death and decay, people are not what they seem to be. Under the veneer of respectability lies corruption.

The Ghost Sonata makes use of both spatial and temporal metaphors. Strindberg sees all humanity as linked by a common network of guilt and sin; the house that the student, an idealistic young man, seeks to enter becomes a symbol for humanity and the social system. The consul, the upper class, lives on the top level; the colonel, the middle class, lives on the ground level; and the superintendent, the lower class, lives below. The poor are found outside the house clamoring at the doors.

Hummel, an old man in a wheelchair, is old enough to know all the inhabitants of the house and understands how they are linked by a chain of guilt and betrayals. The consul (upper class) has slept with the superintendent's wife (lower class); their daughter, the second generation, perpetuates the chain, for she is having an affair with the aristocrat (upper class), who is married to the consul's daughter (upper class). The aristocrat links all the classes in their sins. He has married the consul's daughter (upper class), slept with the colonel's wife (middle class), and is having an affair with the Lady in Black, the daughter of the superintendent's wife (lower class). Thus, all the generations and social classes are interconnected in a house of sin.

The play is also a journey. It begins on a sunny Sunday morning, with steamship bells announcing a voyage. The bright sunlight shines on the student's dream house.

As hidden sins are revealed and ominous pacts are planned, however, clouds appear; eventually it rains. As the student enters the house, the atmosphere becomes gloomy and claustrophobic. The mummy lives in the closest, and the ghost supper provides an eerie scene. As Hummel, who is trying to expose the inhabitants of the house, dies in a closet behind a death screen, the student symbolically invokes the light with his "Song of the Sun." The hope soon proves futile, however, as the ogre cook is persecuting the young lady and draining the nourishment from her food. Finally, the young lady, bathed in radiant light, dies as the vision of the Isle of the Dead appears. Having begun on a Sunday with a Sunday's child seeking resurrection from a night of death, the play ends in a transcendental vision of the dead. The subtle interplay of light and dark intertwines with the play's themes.

In *The Ghost Sonata*, one can see how Strindberg's work foreshadowed modern avant-garde theater. His drama is based on a series of images, not on a linear plot. Motivation is often ambiguous, and the nature of individual identity is questioned. Characters haunted by vague anxieties and grotesque visions are trapped in confined worlds where it is impossible to decipher the difference between truth and illusion. Language becomes an ineffectual means of communication, and often silence is all that is left. A relentless experimenter, Strindberg left a legacy that would influence dramatists such as Eugene O'Neill, Sean O'Casey, and Friedrich Dürrenmatt, who said, "Modern drama has come out of Strindberg: we have never gone beyond the second scene of *The Ghost Sonata.*"

Summary

August Strindberg is an influential figure in the history of modern drama. His dramas probe the psyches of alienated, confused, and disturbed characters who are crushed by social, personal, and existential pressures. He brought to the forefront of modern drama the intense struggles and inner workings of troubled sexual relationships. His dramas explore the central themes of modernism: the alienation of the individual, the subjective nature of the truth, the illusory nature of experience, and the existential struggle to create meaning in a meaningless universe. Strindberg also experimented with various dramatic forms: the tightly constructed and carefully motivated structure of naturalism, the broad, expansive form of subjective expressionism, and the mystical and evocative composition of symbolism.

Bibliography

Carlson, Harry G. *Strindberg and the Poetry of Myth.* Berkeley: University of California Press, 1982.

Stockenström, Göran, ed. *Strindberg's Dramaturgy.* Minneapolis: University of Minnesota Press, 1988.

Morgan, Margery. *August Strindberg.* Houndmills, Basingstoke, Hampshire, England: Macmillan, 1985.

Sprinchorn, Evert. *Strindberg as Dramatist.* New Haven, Conn.: Yale University Press, 1982.

Törnquist, Egil. *Strindbergian Drama: Themes and Structure.* Atlantic Highlands, N.J.: Humanities Press, 1982.

Ward, John. *The Social and Religious Plays of Strindberg.* London: Athlone Press, 1980.

Paul Rosefeldt

JONATHAN SWIFT

Born: Dublin, Ireland
November 30, 1667
Died: Dublin, Ireland
October 19, 1745

Principal Literary Achievement

Straddling the gap between ancient and modern ways of thinking, Swift gave to young and old alike new ways of viewing human life from satirical perspectives.

Biography

Jonathan Swift lived a long, active public life, though its beginning and end were cloaked in darkness. He was born on November 30, 1667, in Dublin, Ireland, to Jonathan and Abigail Erick Swift. His parents had recently moved from England to Dublin, where Swift was born a few months after his father had died. Mysteriously, he was soon separated from his mother, perhaps kidnapped and taken to England, as he later believed. Supported by an uncle, he studied at Kilkenny Grammar School and Trinity College, Dublin.

Late in 1689, he established residence at Moor Park as secretary to Sir William Temple, the man of letters and elder statesman. Temple had arranged the marriage of Princess Mary to William of Orange; their accession to the throne in 1688 inaugurated the Glorious Revolution, which brought England relative stability after the upheavals of the Puritan Revolution, the Protectorate and the Restoration. At Moor Park, a strong friendship blossomed between Swift and Esther Johnson, the "Stella" of his famous *Journal to Stella* (1766, 1768). He took the girl of eight under his tutelage, taught her how to write, and, many believe, secretly married her. They remained close friends until she died in 1728.

Swift returned briefly to Ireland in 1690, having contracted a disease of the inner ear that plagued him until death with fits of giddiness, nausea, and deafness. He soon returned to Temple's service, ever anxious to obtain preferment from his patron. In 1694, he returned to Ireland; he was ordained an Anglican priest in 1695 and took a parish near Belfast, where he was ill-received. On April 29, 1696, his proposal of marriage was declined by Jane Waring, whose counterproposal he would reject four years later.

Returning to Moor Park, Swift became embroiled in the Phalaris controversy. Scoff-

ing at the new science and philosophy then sweeping through Europe, Temple wrote an essay to champion the superiority of ancient learning over modern, foolishly citing as proof the spurious *Epistles of Phalaris* (1695). When the scholar William Wotton criticized Temple, Swift wrote *The Battle of the Books* (1704) to defend Temple and the ancients. Later, the keeper of the king's library, Richard Bentley, proved that the epistles were a fourteenth century hoax. Swift, however, had discovered his satirical powers. *A Tale of a Tub* (1704) established him as a man of letters, though it probably hindered his career in the Church.

In the decade after Temple's death in 1699, Swift held several posts in the Church of Ireland, but he visited England often on Church business or to pursue literary aims. He formed a literary circle in London with the writers Joseph Addison, Richard Steele, and Alexander Pope. During this period, Swift supported the Whig Party. His first major publication, *A Discourse of the Contests and Dissensions Between the Nobles and the Commons in Athens and Rome* (1701), defended the Whig Lords against Tory attacks led by Robert Harley, who later became Swift's close personal friend and patron. His comic wit found a fit target in the Dissenting astrologer John Partridge, whom he pilloried in the popular *Predictions for the Ensuing Year, by Isaac Bickerstaff* (1708). Swift left the Whigs in 1710 and became a Tory pamphleteer under Harley, who steadily gained ascendancy in the court of Queen Anne. Whig toleration of religious dissent troubled Swift. *An Argument Against Abolishing Christianity* (1708) and *The Sentiments of a Church of England Man* (1708) set forth his firm belief in central religious authority and intolerance of Dissenters, whom he saw as a threat to the peace of the kingdom, as well as the Church.

Swift hoped that his political connections would make him a bishop, but instead he was appointed dean of St. Patrick's Cathedral in Dublin in 1713. Ill-received, he returned to London after his installation. He found himself in a new circle, the Scriblerus Club, with the writers William Congreve, John Gay, Thomas Parnell, Pope, and Harley, who were dedicated to ridiculing false taste in learning. Swift was followed back to Ireland by a young lady, Esther Vanhomrigh (called "Vanessa" in his writings), whom he had met in London in 1707, and who had fallen desperately in love with him. Their relationship was typically perplexed, Swift playing the friendly mentor and guide, she desiring much more. Swift commemorated it in *Cadenus and Vanessa* (1726). There is no conclusive evidence to prove that Vanessa was his mistress and Stella his secret wife.

Though not an Irish patriot, strictly speaking, Swift came to abhor English domination of Ireland and to deplore the disorganization within Ireland that was both the cause and the effect of the English dominance. His *Proposal for the Universal Use of Irish Manufacture* (1720) urged Irish citizens to keep profits at home by not buying imports from England. *The Drapier's Letters to the People of Ireland* (1724-1735) stopped a scheme to debase Ireland's coinage and made Swift a national hero. Then came *Gulliver's Travels* (1726), an immediate, smashing success, and the only writing for which Swift was ever paid. He continued issuing pamphlets, among them his *Short View of the State of Ireland* (1728) and *A Modest Proposal* (1729). In the 1730's, he wrote some of his best poems, most notably *Verses on the Death of Dr. Swift* (1731), which predicts what people will say of him after he dies, and *On Poetry: A Rhapsody* (1733).

Swift's last years were darkened by senility. In March, 1742, he was ruled mentally incompetent. In September, he was paralyzed and sank into dementia until death came on October 19, 1745, in Dublin. He was buried in St. Patrick's beside Stella, "where savage indignation can no longer tear the heart," according to his epitaph.

Analysis

Swift lived through times of great change in politics, religion, and learning. Divine authority, medieval scholasticism, and Renaissance humanism were being supplanted by materialistic, mechanical, empirical skepticism, thanks largely to the work of philosophers Thomas Hobbes and John Locke and the incalculable influence of French mathematician René Descartes. Men such as Temple and Swift preferred the serene assurances of the old order based upon rational Christian humanism. They saw the acids of modernism dissolving spiritual authority and the moral values of the landed aristocracy.

From the moment of his precarious birth, Swift was in search of a place in life. Without noble ancestry, he used his talents with words to secure a high standing in society, first under Temple and later Harley, men whose snobbish and repressive instincts he affected. He maintained a stalwart faith in the Anglican establishment and despised free-thinking dissent. He scorned the new money-grubbing middle class and the follies of projectors who meant to perfect society. Yet Swift was also possessed of a diabolical imagination, and from it grew the wildly inventive satires against the very reason and order that he so devoutly defended in other writings. His mind embodied the contradictions of his age. Swift was an orthodox cleric who hated bishops, a rationalist with slight faith in reason, a believer afraid to plumb the mysteries of his faith.

Swift often hides behind a narratorial mask, a persona who poses as author, be it Isaac Bickerstaff, M. P. Drapier, or Lemuel Gulliver. The diabolical wisdom or folly is theirs, though a reader surely feels that he or she is face to face with Swift. Yet these masks must not be mistaken for Swift. Very often he is holding up a persona to ridicule, such as the dispassionate social scientist whose "Modest Proposal" would cure hunger by killing babies. Swift was emotionally incapable of the comprehensive vision of a William Blake, but Swift, too, had intellectually penetrated the contrary nature of humanity and seen through to the heart of darkness. His unblinking insight into human nature, as sane as it is said to be insane, forms the basis for his incomparable ironic satires.

The enormous body of Swift's writings displays four distinct yet overlapping personalities. First is the straightforward, plain-talking voice of common sense. Most of the pamphlets take this tack. The ideas are quite orderly, the doctrine utterly orthodox, the prose style plain and simple. He adopts this mood to attack political or religious confusion, as in his *The Drapier's Letters to the People of Ireland, A Proj-*

ect *for the Advancement of Religion* (1709), and *The Conduct of the Allies* (1711).

Second is the comic wit of roaring laughter to be found in *The Battle of the Books* and the Bickerstaff materials. Swift's *Predictions for the Ensuing Year, by Isaac Bickerstaff* poked fun at a quack astrologer and predicted that he would die on March 29. When he did not die, Swift nevertheless issued the seemingly factual *An Elegy on Mr. Patrige* (1708). Partridge's rebuttals were met with the *A Vindication of Isaac Bickerstaff* (1709). Swift had scored a hit on the pretensions of a "heavenly" pseudo-scientist who was attacking the Anglican church. London laughed long and hard at Bickerstaff's urbane barbs. Swift's comedy masks serious intent. The zany goings-on in *A Tale of a Tub*, for example, ridicule religious enthusiasm.

Third is the diabolical mode of the ironical satirist who pens *Gulliver's Travels, A Modest Proposal*, and *A Tale of a Tub*. Savage indignation lashes out at every corruption of morals or reasoning that humankind is capable of undertaking. Fancy is cut loose from all moorings to lacerate vanities and illusions. Playfully, even inconsistently, by turns this spirit may be witty and light, or coarse and vulgar, even dismally misanthropic. Swift in this humor is unmatched in English literature.

Fourth is the least familiar of Swift's personalities, the childlike personal friend. The passionless Swift shows himself in poems such as *Cadenus and Vanessa* and in his private letters to Stella to be capable of genuine tenderness and warmth. Long passages from his famous *Journal to Stella* are in baby talk, the most intimate kind of communication by which one friend engages another.

Swift was the first English writer to gauge the full force of the displacement that modernism would work upon traditional values and ways of thinking. His official self longed for institutional order, but his demonic imagination let him know that human nature could not be tamed or improved by so weak a rider as reason. As such, his disgust was enormous, and he dared to show human nature as it is. Little wonder that Swift is understood by children and often misunderstood by scholars and clerics.

GULLIVER'S TRAVELS

First published: 1726
Type of work: Travel literature

A surgeon sets out on four sea voyages that take him beyond the wildest stretch of his imagination.

Lemuel Gulliver, the title character of *Gulliver's Travels*, is a capable, brave, and educated Englishman whose unlucky adventures drive him to sickness and madness. His simple, straightforward way of telling his story suggests that he lacks the imagination to understand what he has experienced.

Gulliver is shipwrecked off the shore of Lilliput and captured by humans only six inches tall. Practical man that he is, he promises to obey their laws controlling him.

He finds Lilliput, not unlike Europe, in a state of perpetual and petty disorder. Low-heelers and High-heelers squabble over politics much as do the Whigs and Tories of Swift's day. Courtiers compete for distinctions by leaping over sticks and other such ridiculous games. Protestants and Catholics are mirrored as Big-enders and Little-enders, who cannot agree on which end of the egg should be cracked first. The war between England and France is parodied in the conflict between Lilliput and its neighbor Blefuscu. Gulliver becomes a hero by wading into the surf and carrying off the tiny Blefuscan navy. When he puts out a fire in the palace by urinating on it, he falls from favor at court and joins the Blefuscans, who help him salvage the wrecked ship in which he makes his escape.

Gulliver's next voyage takes him to Brobdingnag, the opposite of Lilliput. Proportions are reversed. People stand as tall as steeples. Gulliver is a caged pet exhibited as a freak. The queen buys him and brings him to court, where he is imperiled by the lewd curiosity of the ladies, by a dwarf who nearly drowns him in a bowl of cream, and by a monkey who almost dashes his brains out.

Yet Brobdingnagian society is a utopia, based on useful studies of poetry and history, not on metaphysics, theology, and speculative science, as in Europe. The king rules a prosperous state not torn by strife. In Brobdingnag, a law cannot be written using more than twenty-two words, and to comment on laws is a capital crime. Horrified by Gulliver's description of England's government, the king concludes that Englishmen must be "the most pernicious Race of little odious Vermin that Nature ever suffered to crawl upon the Surface of the Earth."

His third voyage, to Laputa and other islands, is the most fantastic of them all. Gulliver finds himself on the airborne island of Laputa. Its people are devoid of practicality, so lost in abstraction that servants must flap their mouths and ears with inflated bladders to keep their minds on conversations. Though bent upon music, mathematics, and astronomy, they lack reason and cannot construct walls perpendicular to the floor. The monarch is proud of his dominion over the island of Balnibari below. Any mutiny can be literally crushed by dropping Laputa upon it, smashing whole towns. Yet the monarch is reluctant to use this power for fear of cracking Laputa, and, besides, Laputians own country estates on the nether island. Swift here satirizes England's dominion over Ireland.

At the Academy of Lagado, Gulliver witnesses the absurdities of misapplied scholarship. There, the projectors experiment with building houses from the top down, making pillows out of marble, extracting sunshine from cucumbers, and the like. He visits nearby Glubbdubdrib, where the governor by sorcery summons dead persons back to life for a day. Gulliver thus meets with Alexander the Great, Homer, Aristotle, and René Descartes, who admits his philosophy is confounded conjecture. In Luggnagg, Gulliver views the ghastly spectacle of human immortality. The wretched Struldbrugs live forever, not in perpetual youth but in unending decay. From there, Gulliver makes a short trip to Japan, and thence back to England.

Gulliver leaves behind a pregnant wife to make his final journey to a land ruled by intelligent horses, called Houyhnhnms. These purely rational creatures know neither pride nor passion. Without love or lust, they procreate merely to meet a social obligation. They live in stoical calm, without government and without crime. They are served by a despised underclass of Yahoos, depraved, libidinous creatures quite unlike themselves but strongly resembling humans. Gulliver shares the Houyhnhnms' disgust and disdain for them. When a lusty Yahoo woman tries to embrace him, he is repulsed. The Houyhnhnms, however, decide that Gulliver must live as a Yahoo or else leave, so he departs on a Portuguese ship with Captain Pedro de Mendez. Still, Gulliver cannot bear the smell of the captain and crew. He shuns their civilities and tries to jump overboard. He arrives in England only under shackles. Now too proud to associate with humans, whom he sees as Yahoos, Gulliver faints when his wife kisses him, and he abandons his family to consort with horses at pasture.

Gulliver himself has become the object of the satire, for he has lost all reason and proportion. The very Houyhnhnms he so admires do him the greatest wrong, but he scorns humanity with irrational pride. Having seen him from so many different perspectives, a reader recognizes that Gulliver's weaknesses are those of humankind.

THE BATTLE OF THE BOOKS

First published: 1704
Type of work: Essay

In the library of Saint James, the modern books battle for supremacy over the ancient books.

Swift wrote *The Battle of the Books* in 1697 to buttress his beleaguered patron Sir William Temple in a controversy over the relative merits of ancient learning and modern learning. Gentlemen with old Tory money or new Whig pretensions affected a haughty disdain for the new philosophy of Descartes and the new social science of Hobbes, and their disdain affected Swift. They saw in modernism a childish self-absorption, disregard for the classics, disrespect for traditional authorities, and bad manners. Swift ridiculed the new trends by contrasting them with the sound wisdom and graceful art of the old masters.

In the library of Saint James, the modern books square off against the ancients in a mock-epic battle. Before they clash, a bee breaks through a spider's web, to the discomfiture of both. The spider chides the bee for destroying its intricate trap. Wiping off the obnoxious threads of the web, the bee spurns the spider for erecting such a petty and disgusting contrivance. Their witty sparring goes to the heart of their differing natures. The spider represents modernism; the bee, classicism. They hurl vituperous charges at each other. The bee accuses the spider of spinning everything out of his own guts, such as the regurgitated threads of its web and the venom that it injects into entangled flies. The spider accuses the bee of being no better than a thief, visiting one beautiful flower after another only to steal nectar and flee. The bee replies that the flowers are multiplied, not destroyed, by his beneficial rapine; he returns to the hive with honey and wax, thus furnishing sweetness and light.

Armed with their ink made of bitter venom, the moderns issue an ultimatum to the ancients: either abandon their glory-smitten summits of prestige or let the moderns come with their spades to level the peaks that overshadow the lower tops of modern mountains. When the ancients refuse, the moderns close ranks. The bumblings of a modern librarian have caused confusion on the shelves. René Descartes has been set beside Aristotle, Plato shoulder-to-shoulder with Thomas Hobbes, and Vergil hemmed in between the modern poets John Dryden and George Wither. The ancients are captained by Temple and Pallas Athena, goddess of wisdom. The moderns are led by Momus, god of faultfinding, who calls on the malignant deity Criticism in her cave, where she dwells with Ignorance, her father and husband; Pride, her mother; and her children, Noise, Impudence, Dullness, Vanity, Positiveness, Pedantry, and Ill-Manners. Criticism comes to the library to rally her troops, but the moderns fall into disarray. Descartes is felled by Aristotle's arrow. The poet Abraham Cowley hurls his spear at the poet Pindar, but misses. Pindar disables a dozen or so of the Cavalier poets. The modern poet Dryden swaps armor with Vergil (Dryden had translated Vergil's epic poem into English), but he finds Vergil's helmet nine times too big for him. Homer slays the modern poet John Denham. Another modern poet, John Oldham, falls to Pindar. Clearly, the ancients have carried the day, but peace talks are convened, and the matter ends inconclusively.

Swift's mockery is devastatingly effective, witty, and fun. His sarcastic jest is proven true: Some of these modern authors would have been all but forgotten were it not for Swift's record of their clash with the ancients.

A TALE OF A TUB

First published: 1704
Type of work: Essay

A diabolical wit ridicules the attempts of Christian sects to divert the attacks of materialistic science on religious faith.

A Tale of a Tub is Swift's wildest adventure in satirical humor. Speaking through a diabolical persona of his own making, he pillories the corruptions of churches and schools. The title refers to the large tub that sailors would throw overboard to divert a whale from ramming their boat. In Swift's satire, the whale is Hobbes's *Leviathan* (1651), a political monster born of Descartes' mathematical philosophy. Institutional Christianity is the ship that might be sunk in such an onslaught, and its timbers have already been loosened by schismatic factions.

The essay is an allegory of Church history. A father wills suits of clothes to his three sons, with directions that the suits never be altered. Brothers Peter, Martin, and

Jack represent Catholic, Anglican, and Puritan sects, respectively. Peter upgrades his garments with gold lace, shoulder knots, and such trappings. Martin removes the false ornamentation from his without tearing the cloth. Jack zealously rips his garment to shreds to get rid of all ornament.

This basic allegory is richly embellished with outlandish digressions, parodies, puns, quibbles, unstructured foolery, and displays of odd erudition. The diabolical narrative takes every opportunity to prick the pretensions of pedants, religious dissenters, and perfectionists whose projects try to remake human society along rational lines. Swift thought that human reason is rather weak, blown flat in fact by the merest gust of desire, and so people should behave themselves and be governed by institutions such as the Church of England. Yet his diabolical narrator weakens this myth of order and reason by showing how vulnerable the mysteries of religion are to skeptical scrutiny.

Dressed in his sactimonious vestments, Peter looks ridiculous issuing papal bulls on the superstitious doctrine that bread can be turned into mutton. The excesses of religious enthusiasts are reduced to absurdity in Jack's rantings and in a scatological satire on a sect of Æolists, who believe that wind is the essence of all things, the original cause and first principle of the universe. In their most ridiculous rite, Æolists seat themselves atop barrels that catch the wind and blow inspiration into their posteriors by means of a secret funnel. Sacred sermons are delivered by their priests in oracular belches, or bursts of internal wind.

This maniacal conception reemerges in the famous Digression on Madness. There, the modern upsurges in religion, politics, and science are diagnosed as a form of madness, caused when the brain is intoxicated by vapors arising from the lower faculties. This vapor is to the brain what tickling is to the touch. Real perceptions are disordered in a happy confusion. Thus, happiness for moderns amounts to "a perpetual Possession of being well Deceived." In the madhouse world of *A Tale of a Tub*, the modern man cut off from classical culture is lucky to be a fool among knaves, like the demonic narrator of the essay himself.

A MODEST PROPOSAL

First published: 1729
Type of work: Essay

A social scientist proposes that poor people sell their babies as food to be eaten by the rich.

Swift's *A Modest Proposal* has been called the greatest work of irony ever written. A dispassionate social scientist surveys the poverty in Ireland and structures his proposal in five parts after the classical rhetorical pattern: *exordium* (introduction), *narratio* (narrative), *confirmatio* (confirmation), *confutatio* (refutation), and *peroratio* (peroration).

The *exordium* evokes the familiar sight of female beggars followed by many children dressed in rags. The image suggests the problem of poverty, overpopulation, and hunger that the narrator proposes to solve with his "fair, cheap, and easy method" of fattening the poor babies for a year and then selling them as delicious delicacies for the tables of the rich.

In the *narratio*, the narrator coldly calculates the number of babies needed. Out of one and a half million people in Ireland, he reckons only two hundred thousand couples are breeders. Subtracting thirty thousand whose parents can afford them, and fifty thousand who die in the first year of life, and sparing twenty thousand for breeding purposes, he figures only one hundred thousand babies will be sold for slaughter each year. Instead of being a burden on families or welfare agencies, these children will contribute to the feeding and clothing of thousands of others, since their skins can also be tanned for leather.

The *confirmatio* explains the public benefits of the scheme. This meat is not seasonal and thus supplies the cyclical scarcity of fresh meat. A poor mother can clear a profit of eight shillings per child. In a land torn by religious strife, the number of Catholics would be greatly lessened. The new industry would push the gross national product higher. Parents would save, not merely eight shillings, but the far greater cost of rearing the child for years. If poor people saw a profit from pregnancy, they would be more inclined to marry and then to be more tender and caring with the family.

The narrator admits that the population would be lowered, but he thinks it should be. He scorns politicians for overlooking other solutions, such as taxing émigrés and banning imports from England. By including these proposals in the *confutatio*, Swift ironically endorses them. The narrator reminds readers that these are unwanted children who would likely rather be dead. He closes his *peroratio* by professing that he lacks self-interest: "I have no children by which I can propose to get a single penny; the youngest being nine years old, and my wife past childbearing."

Of course, Swift was saying one thing and meaning another. He means to condemn the wickedness of equating human life with monetary value. References to slavery and abortion widen the scope of this satire on the many ways in which people put a price on life. This outrageous proposal is called "modest" because it rejects the extremes of voluntary abortion before birth and euthanasia for the aged and diseased.

Summary

Readers insensitive to Jonathan Swift's ironies have dismissed him as a crazy man who hated humanity. Others have concluded that he was a humane Christian who valued human life. Upheavals in politics, religion, and learning made Swift think that the modern world was going crazy. He longed for a stable, reasonable order in society based on institutions, such as the Church, that seek to correct humanity's vanity and pride. Yet his diabolical imagination told him authority was drowning in change. Swift embodied and recorded the profound contradictions of his era better, perhaps, than any other English writer.

Bibliography

Ehrenpreis, Irvin. *Swift: The Man, His Works, and the Age.* 3 vols. Cambridge, Mass.: Harvard University Press, 1962-1983.

Quintana, Ricardo. *Swift: An Introduction.* New York: Oxford University Press, 1965.

Stathis, James J. *A Bibliography of Swift Studies, 1945-1965.* Nashville: Vanderbilt University Press, 1967.

Tuveson, Ernest Lee, ed. *Swift: A Collection of Critical Essays.* Englewood Cliffs, N.J.: Prentice-Hall, 1964.

Van Doren, Carl. *Swift.* New York: Viking Press, 1930.

Williams, Kathleen. *Swift: The Critical Heritage.* New York: Barnes & Noble Books, 1970.

John L. McLean

ALGERNON CHARLES SWINBURNE

Born: London, England
April 5, 1837
Died: Putney, England
April 10, 1909

Principal Literary Achievement

The author of varied works of verse and prose and an influential member of the intellectual circles of his time, Swinburne is best remembered for his highly personal, and intensely musical, poetic style.

Biography

Algernon Charles Swinburne was born on April 5, 1837, in London, England, to Captain (later Admiral) Charles Henry Swinburne and Lady Jane Swinburne. Much of Algernon Swinburne's early life was spent in the wild, idyllic setting of his family's estate on the Isle of Wight, where, with his brother and four sisters, he could enjoy the freedom of nature. This freedom contrasted sharply with the discipline of tutors who were to prepare the young Algernon to enter Eton at the age of twelve. All of his life, Swinburne was to suffer the effects of his unusual physique. His slight and delicate body, punctuated by a great mass of red hair, might have earned him harsh hazings in the atmosphere of the English public school had his considerable courage not allowed him to stand up to all possible tormenters. He could not escape the physical discipline of Eton, however, and, like many other schoolboys of his time, he retained a perverse desire for the floggings that were then regularly administered. Swinburne's slight physique was joined to a nervous disposition that caused him to alternate between frenzied bursts of energy and corresponding periods of depressed reverie. The same energy that allowed him to read and recite poetry for hours on end turned to violence under the influence of drink and caused Swinburne to be barred from certain households. Throughout his life, however, he retained loyal friends, whom he frequently entertained with readings in the distinctively high, singsong voice that he was said to have inherited from his mother.

Several of Swinburne's most important friendships, especially those with the poets William Morris and Dante Gabriel Rossetti, were formed during his years at Oxford. Swinburne entered Oxford in 1856, and though he never completed the examinations

for his degree, he wrote widely for undergraduate publications and began the work on the Tristan legend that would lead to his *Tristram of Lyonesse and Other Poems* (1882). Although Swinburne's study of Greek may have gotten a comparatively slow start, he had an enduring love for both French and Greek literature, on which he would draw for many of his own works.

After leaving Oxford, Swinburne settled in London near the British Museum and began work on a number of literary projects, poems, plays, and criticism. One of his contributions to *The Spectator* in 1862 introduced the poetry of Charles Baudelaire to the English reading public. Between 1862 and 1863, Swinburne shared a house in Chelsea with Rossetti, whose wife had recently died. This bachelor household received visits from many prominent men of letters but was the scene of so much riotous conduct on Swinburne's part that Rossetti finally asked him to leave.

Thus began a pattern of Swinburne's life for the next fifteen years. Unable to resist a frenzied participation in London social life, he would drive and drink himself to exhaustion, after which he would regain his health through a period of recuperation with his family. These returns home were not always voluntary. Swinburne's father, alerted by his friends as to the poet's condition, came to remove him forcibly from his lodgings, until Swinburne threatened to hide from his family if he were similarly carried off again. After a trip to France and Italy in 1863-1864, Swinburne faced one of the great disappointments of his life when, in 1865, his cousin Mary Gordon married a military officer twenty-one years her senior, with whom she went to live in Scotland. Swinburne had been extremely close to Mary and may have entertained the hope of marrying her, although there is no indication of explicit romantic involvement between them.

After the publication of his *Atalanta in Calydon* in 1865, Swinburne was to become famous for his writings. He had for some time been composing the poems that would be included in his *Poems and Ballads* (1866), but his friends advised him not to publish because of the scandalous subjects of some of the pieces. Swinburne, however, was not to be dissuaded, and, upon publication, his work was so violently attacked that the publisher promptly withdrew the balance of the edition from sale. The work was immediately reissued by another publisher. With *Songs Before Sunrise* (1871), Swinburne turned to political questions, supporting freedom in Italy. During composition of this work, he suffered a period of accidents and ill health. In July, 1868, he fainted in the reading room of the British Museum, a room from which he was subsequently to be banned.

In the fall of 1868, Swinburne traveled to France, where he shared a house in Normandy with his friend George Powell and met Guy de Maupassant, who was part of a rescue of Swinburne from drowning when the tide had swept him out to sea. Back in England, Swinburne rejoiced at the fall of Napoleon III in 1870 and was saddened by the definitive rupture of his friendship with Rossetti in 1872. During this time, he was drinking heavily and causing friends and family concern for his health.

After the death of his father in 1877, Swinburne used his inheritance to set himself up in London, where he would publish *Poems and Ballads: Second Series* (1878). Reduced to sickness by continued heavy drinking, he was finally rescued from himself by his friend Walter Theodore Watts-Dunton. With the cooperation of Swinburne's mother, Watts-Dunton took over the handling of Swinburne's financial affairs. He moved the poet into his own home, "The Pines," near Wimbledon and gradually weaned him from drinking brandy to drinking beer. By intervening as he did in the poet's life in 1879, Watts-Dunton was to give him nearly thirty tranquil years before his death.

In 1882, Rossetti died without ever resuming contact with Swinburne. Late that year, Swinburne traveled to Paris as the guest of Victor Hugo, but his enjoyment of the visit was greatly hampered by his increasing deafness. Despite his affliction, Swinburne would continue until the end of his life to declaim his poetry to avid listeners. He died on April 10, 1909, in Putney, England.

Analysis

Swinburne's lyrical virtuosity knew very few limits. Writing largely in English but occasionally in French, he could mimic the styles of a wide range of other poets. His own very personal style developed early, however, and would mark his major poems as distinctively his own. From the first publication, *Atalanta in Calydon*, that launched his literary reputation, his readers were struck by his heavy alliteration and use of rhythms quite different from traditional iambic pentameter. One of the best-known lyrics from *Atalanta in Calydon* is typical:

> When the hounds of spring are on winter's traces,
> The mother of months in meadow or plain
> Fills the shadows and windy places
> With lisp of leaves and ripple of rain.

The alternation of anapestic and iambic feet gives these lines an uneven, discordant feel, while the alliteration ("mother of months," "lisp of leaves," "ripple of rain") adds musical echoes that suggest a contrasting harmony. The verse is united as much by the choice of sounds as by the rhythms.

Apart from his unusual meter, Swinburne deliberately set out to shock his readers through his choices of subject matter. His background had exposed him to the traditions of both Catholicism and the Church of England, but Swinburne early evolved a distinctly antireligious view. His was not a calm opposition. Just as the Black Mass finds its structure in the inversion of normal ritual, Swinburne draws on religious sources to deliver a contrary message. "Dolores," one of the poems that Swinburne's friends had warned him not to publish in the first series of *Poems and Ballads*, posits a heroine clearly the opposite of the Virgin Mary. Swinburne's subtitle to the poem, "Notre Dame des Sept Douleurs," reinforces the analogy. Yet while Mary represented virtue, Dolores becomes the emblem of vice: "Seven sorrows the priests give their Virgin;/ But thy sins, which are seventy times seven,/ Seven ages would fail thee to purge in." As Mary represented chastity, Dolores is the power of female seductiveness. Of her lips, Swinburne writes, "Men touch them, and change in a trice/ The lilies and languors of virtue/ For the raptures and roses of vice." She not only sins but also tempts others to sin.

Swinburne's pervasive musicality underlines the seductiveness of "lilies and languors" and "raptures and roses" amid a continuing use of largely anapestic rhythm. Meanwhile, the flower imagery traditionally linked to Mary becomes inverted to described Dolores: "O mystical rose of the mire." For Swinburne, sin becomes an analogy to prayer: "I have passed from the outermost portal/ To the shrine where a sin is a prayer."

Despite his extensive use of Christian allusion in "Dolores," Swinburne also links his heroine to pre-Christian goddesses: "Thou wert fair in the fearless old fashion." That was the worship that Christianity destroyed: "What ailed us, O gods, to desert you/ For creeds that refuse and restrain?" Yet Swinburne predicts that Christianity will in turn "pass and their places be taken" because "the worm shall revive thee with kisses." The fusion of sexuality and death implicit as the worms give Dolores not a kiss of death but one of life reflects Swinburne's overt preference for language that would shock. Not only is Dolores repeatedly invoked as "Our Lady of Pain," a description that might be applied to Mary, but the pain is explicit and graphic: "O lips full of lust and laughter,/ Curled snakes that are fed from my breast,/ Bite hard."

Such descriptions, together with Swinburne's distinctive rhythms, struck the Victorian public as too outrageous to be taken seriously. Those amused by them, however, attempted parodies of Swinburne's verse. None of these parodies could improve on the poet's own self-parody in "Nephilidia": "From the depth of the dreamy decline of the dawn through a notable nimbus of nebulous noonshine." The extended line makes room for multiple adjectives and alliterations extended to sets of four words each so that music and description all but submerge meaning.

While Swinburne's self-mockery shows a momentary willingness to allow his music to dominate, his thought should never be submerged. Swinburne was not only widely read in both classical and modern literatures, he also drew on vast sources to create new literary composites. Nowhere is that more evident than in "Laus Veneris," another of his early *Poems and Ballads*, where he transports the classical Venus to a northern setting with the legend of Tannhäuser, the German lyric poet. The poem repeats the confrontation of Christian and pagan elements as the beauty of Venus serves to seduce a Christian knight away from his God.

The knight's story transcends his own case to echo that of humankind's seduction throughout history. Venus has already seduced "the knight Adonis" and "enticed/ All lips that now grow sad with kissing Christ." As he remains enthralled to her, the knight remembers both the pleasures of his fall ("Brief bitter bliss, one hath for a great sin") and his former status: "For I was of Christ's choosing, I God's knight,/ No blinkard heathen stumbling for scant light." While he regrets his loss of heaven, he finds with Venus another immortality because "Soul may divide from body, but not we/ One from another." Swinburne combines anew the elements of many legends to support his personal view of life just as he combined metrical devices in new ways to form his own poetic style.

AVE ATQUE VALE

First published: 1868
Type of work: Poem

Swinburne's elegy for Charles Baudelaire calls on the themes of Baudelaire's own work.

Swinburne wrote a number of elegiac poems of varying quality, but with "Ave Atque Vale," he produced one of the important elegies of English literature. Not only had Swinburne introduced Baudelaire's poetry in England with his *The Spectator* review of 1862, he also recognized in the French poet a kindred spirit. The opening lines of his elegy, "Shall I strew on thee rose or rue or laurel,/ Brother, on this that was the veil of thee?" call to Charles Baudelaire as his brother in a deep, spiritual sense.

These lines already convey the basic technique of Swinburne's poem by drawing upon the words evocative of Baudelaire himself. The allusions to flowers parallel the title of *Les Fleurs du mal* (1857, 1861, 1868; *Flowers of Evil*, 1909), and in calling Baudelaire "Brother," Swinburne echoes "Au Lecteur," Baudelaire's opening poem, where the latter addresses his reader as "mon frère." Swinburne echoes the regular rhythms of Baudelaire's verse, abandoning in this elegy his frequent anapests for iambic rhythm, though he concludes each stanza with a three-foot line that has the effect of leaving something unfinished, a feeling that one has been deprived, as Swinburne was by Baudelaire's death.

The fraternity between the two poets lay largely in their exploitation of the unconventional. Rather than fresh flowers, Swinburne suggests "Or wilt thou rather, as on earth before,/ Half-faded fiery blossoms, pale with heat/ And full of bitter summer?," flowers like the "sickly flowers" Baudelaire had cited to describe his work. This kinship of negative preoccupations reinforces their poetic vocation. Swinburne echoes the Romantic concept of the poet as seer, seeing "Fierce loves, and lovely leafbuds poisonous,/ Bare to thy subtler eye," just as Baudelaire had characterized the poet as visionary in his work.

Multiple allusions to Baudelaire's poetry follow as Swinburne speculates on what sort of existence he has found in the afterlife: "Hast thou found place at the great knees and feet/ Of some pale Titan-woman?" The image from Baudelaire's "La Géante" posits his form of paradise, while Swinburne adopts Baudelaire's vision of receding light from "Le Flambeau vivant" as an emblem of his own state: "Our dreams pursue our dead and do not find./ Still, and more swift than they, the thin flame flies." As communion with Baudelaire has now been made impossible by his death, Swinburne finds consolation in the proximity of his poems: "These I salute, these touch, these clasp and fold/ As though a hand were in my hand to hold." Yet still he remains on the "chill and solemn earth" that contrasts to the sunny, tropical land that had portrayed Baudelaire's vision of an earthly paradise.

HYMN TO PROSERPINE

First published: 1866
Type of work: Poem

Swinburne's invocation of the pagan goddess posits a victory over Christianity.

With "Hymn to Proserpine," Swinburne gives positive expression to his rebellion against conventional Christianity. The dual subtitles, "After the proclamation in Rome of the Christian faith" and "Vicisti, Galilaee," define the historical setting. The poem represents a monologue spoken by a pagan resisting the triumph of Christ. In his despair, he calls on the goddess of the underworld, "Goddess and maiden and queen, be near me now and befriend."

The antique gods that Swinburne would resurrect have dual attributes: "Yea, is not even Apollo, with hair and harpstring of gold,/ A bitter god to follow, a beautiful god to behold?" The combination of beauty with suffering coincides with Swinburne's recurring desire for punishment, but his protagonist desires neither pleasure nor pain but the sleep also associated with Proserpine. He is weary of the conflict that he sees around him because "Time and the gods are at strife." This last statement can also summarize Swinburne's feelings about his own century, a time when human progress, particulary in science, was questioning traditional religious views. Swinburne's response, conveyed through his Roman protagonist, combines a rejection of Christianity with an energetic vindication of his personal faith.

Regarding Christianity, his tone is adversarial: "Thou hast conquered, O pale Galilean; the world has grown gray from thy breath;/ We have drunken of things Lethean, and fed on the fullness of death." While Christ may have won humankind's heart for a time, the insistent theme of death undermines this triumph. Christianity depends on a belief in resurrection, but Swinburne insists that "no man under the sky lives twice, outliving his day." If death must come to all, Christ's promise will prove impossible: "Yet thy kingdom shall pass, Galilean, thy dead shall go down to thee dead."

Thus, Swinburne posits a time when people will be freed from Christianity: "I kneel not, neither adore you, but standing, look to the end." Yet in order to describe this future state, he must return to images of the past by resurrecting Proserpine as a corresponding figure to Mary: "Of the maiden thy mother men sing as a goddess with grace clad around;/ Thou art throned where another was king; where another was queen she is crowned." Proserpine's allure derives from extreme female sensuality, "Clothed round with the world's desire as with raiment." Paradoxically, given that he has just rejected eternal life, Swinburne posits the reward of those faithful to the old gods as an eternity with Proserpine "In the night where thine eyes are as moons are in heaven." The paradox is resolved, however, when it is revealed that this night is death, the oblivion, or sleep, that will obliterate strife.

Summary

At odds with the dominant culture of his day, Algernon Charles Swinburne turned to the beliefs of pagan antiquity and to kindred poets such as Baudelaire to forge a personal philosophy compatible with his desires. He expressed his views in an equally personal style dominated by alliteration and eccentric rhythms and heavy with description that emphasized female beauty and the desire for pain. While Swinburne may have deliberately exaggerated the unusual elements of his expression, it reflected a sensitive poet ill at ease in his world.

Bibliography

Cassidy, John A. *Algernon C. Swinburne*. New York: Twayne, 1964.

Chew, Samuel C. *Swinburne*. Reprint. Hamden, Conn.: Archon Books, 1966.

Fuller, Jean Overton. *Swinburne: A Critical Biography*. London: Chatto & Windus, 1968.

Gosse, Edmund. *The Life of Algernon Charles Swinburne*. New York: Macmillan, 1917.

Henderson, Philip. *Swinburne: Portrait of a Poet*. New York: Macmillan, 1974.

Nicolson, Harold. *Swinburne*. New York: Macmillan, 1926.

Riede, David G. *Swinburne: A Study of Romantic Mythmaking*. Charlottesville: University Press of Virginia, 1978.

Thomas, Donald. *Swinburne: The Poet in His World*. New York: Oxford University Press, 1979.

Walder, Anne. *Swinburne's Flowers of Evil: Baudelaire's Influence on Poems and Ballads, First Series*. Uppsala, Sweden: Uppsala University Press, 1976.

Dorothy M. Betz

JOHN MILLINGTON SYNGE

Born: Rathfarnham, Ireland
April 16, 1871
Died: Dublin, Ireland
March 24, 1909

Principal Literary Achievement

One of the most prominent Irish dramatists, Synge was a contemporary of William Butler Yeats and one of the most controversial contributors to Dublin's Abbey Theatre.

Biography

Edmund John Millington Synge was born outside Dublin, Ireland, in Rathfarnham on April 16, 1871, to John Hatch and Kathleen Traill Synge, the youngest of five children. Synge's father died within a year, and he lived most of his life with his mother, who exerted a great influence on him and is believed to have been one of the models for the strong women in his plays. Synge was ill throughout his childhood and was forced to live a reclusive life that resulted in a solitary, independent nature. At age fourteen, he read Charles Darwin's *On the Origin of Species by Means of Natural Selection* (1859), which transformed him into a confirmed naturalist who broke with his family's devout Protestantism for a private combination of aestheticism and mysticism, a quality that informs his best plays. As a boy, he had little formal schooling but later simultaneously attended Trinity College, Dublin, and the Royal Irish Academy of Music, which encouraged his decision to become a professional musician. In 1893, he left for Germany to continue his musical apprenticeship but returned to Ireland in 1894 to devote himself to a literary career, writing poetry (which he had begun composing in college) and a play in German.

In 1895, he moved to Paris and studied languages and literature at the Sorbonne. For the next seven winters, he would travel to Paris, seeking the life of a Continental writer and critic. Although he had been studying Celtic civilization and Irish, his meeting William Butler Yeats in 1896 sparked an even deeper immersion in Irish life and culture. In 1898, at Yeats's suggestion, Synge traveled to the bleak landscape of the Aran Islands off Ireland's west coast, the first of five summer visits that would permanently change the course of his artistic development and ultimately establish his place in world literature. His experiences there are rendered in *The Aran Islands* (1907), a unique account that has been described as a collection of essays, a travel

narrative, and a writer's notebook. Synge's intention was to record faithfully, yet objectively, the life that he discovered, which, despite its hard particularities, he saw as representative of the human condition. Synge then explored other remote areas of Mayo, Kerry, and the Blasket Islands, which led to a series of articles collected in *In Wicklow* (1910). A less unified volume than *The Aran Islands*, this work also reveals the writer's concern with the timeless patterns of life and nature and with the crippling poverty endured by many of his compatriots.

Between 1900 and 1901, he worked on *When the Moon Has Set* (pb. 1968), the first play that he submitted to Lady Augusta Gregory and Yeats for presentation at the Irish National Theatre but which they rejected for aesthetic and moral reasons. In 1902, he completed his two one-act plays, *Riders to the Sea* (pb. 1903) and *In the Shadow of the Glen* (1903); the latter set a precedent for the hostile reactions that greeted most of his plays. In 1905, he became a member of the board of directors of the newly created Abbey Theatre and was deeply involved in the productions of his plays. In the same year, *The Well of the Saints* was produced at the Abbey, and the next year he became engaged to the actress Molly Allgood, the inspiration for many of his poems and for the figure of Pegeen Mike in *The Playboy of the Western World* (1907). He wrote to her nearly every day, and these letters provide revealing glimpses into his love, view of nature, and artistic ambitions.

In 1907, *The Playboy of the Western World* opened to riots in the Dublin streets, and Synge found himself the object of social hysteria, notoriety he neither sought nor enjoyed. In the next year, 1908, *The Tinker's Wedding* was published; his mother died, and Synge's own health was seriously declining from Hodgkin's disease. Now severely ill, he wrote, but never fully revised, his last play, *Deirdre of the Sorrows* (1910), and was at work on the final version of *Poems and Translations* (1910) when he was admitted to a hospital. Synge died in Dublin on March 24, 1909, and was remembered by Yeats as a man "the more hated because he gave his country what it needed, an unmoved mind where there is a perpetual Last Day, a trumpeting and coming up to judgment."

Analysis

As a result of his own self-promotion, Yeats gave the impression that he molded and shaped Synge into the artist that Synge became, but as numerous scholars have pointed out, such was hardly the case. Synge came to the writing of plays and poetry with his own clearly defined set of interests and aesthetic imperatives, and while Yeats and Lady Gregory encouraged him and provided a forum in which to present his works, Synge was always an independent artist.

Synge's major concern, and the basis for his greatest literary successes, is the distinctive version of Irish-English that he developed. Like other writers in the twentieth century, he sought to demonstrate the possibilities of idiomatic language as a vehicle for expressing complex human interactions and for creating enduring aesthetic experiences. There is no question that his travels in western Ireland brought him in contact with a folk language that inspired that of his plays. His achievement, however, was not the mere incorporation of something that he found, but an artful manipulation of vocabulary, syntax, and rhythms of Irish-English.

These linguistic features are evident throughout Synge's career, with *Riders to the Sea* and *The Playboy of the Western World* representing, in different ways, the most masterful demonstrations of this style. In each of his plays, Synge depicts otherwise unprepossessing figures speaking in a rich, mesmerizing idiom that brings a sense of pageantry and splendor to the commonplace. What the plays assert as much as anything else is that language, the medium that expresses and surrounds all the characters, is perhaps their most valuable resource, without which life would be unendurable.

Closely aligned with his experiments in language is his consistent concern with the peasant class of Ireland. In many ways, such an interest would appear inconceivable for a member of the Protestant Ascendancy, yet Synge was undeniably proud of his Irish lineage, and in the peasants he saw what he regarded as the true Ireland, the last vestiges of a breed of people who had avoided the snares of civilized life and its restricting values. Synge was certainly not the first to depict the Irish peasantry in his plays. In the eighteenth century, in works written by English and Anglo-Irish playwrights, the Irish were depicted in less than flattering fashion. The term "stage Irishman" denoted a cultural stereotype, a figure full of blarney and alcohol given to hopeless malapropisms and clumsiness. Such a character came in two basic forms— a happy, besotted fool or a bumptious, irascible figure. Both versions of the stage Irishman were presented for comic effect and were broad caricatures of an imagined ethnic type.

The push for Irish independence in the nineteenth century under the nationalist leader Daniel O'Connell and the declarations of cultural independence of the Gaelic League and Irish Renaissance had elevated the peasant into a new cultural hero. As could be expected, these versions of the peasant were rife with sentimentality, and they, too, presented stereotypes.

Synge sought another alternative, and having lived among these people, he knew at first hand who they were and how complex their lives actually were. He approaches his peasants as a primitivist would, seeing in them the last remnants of a more authentic human order that the veneer of civilization has obscured. There is no question that he idealizes these figures, depicting them as mystical, wise people, yet he also reveals the hard, brutal dimensions of their existence.

One of his most ambitious experiments came in rewriting Irish myth in *Deirdre of the Sorrows*, a tale that both Yeats and Æ (George Russell) had treated in dreamy, otherworldly fashion. When his friend Stephen MacKenna first suggested that Synge devise his own version, the playwright wrote, "No drama can grow out of anything other than the fundamental realities of life which are never fantastic, are neither modern nor unmodern and, as I see them, rarely spring-dayish, or breezy or Cuchulainoid [Cuchulainn, the hero of the Ulster cycle of Irish mythology]." The kings and queens in this play are not depicted as peasants, but neither are they elevated creatures. Synge humanizes them and, in so doing, reveals his interest in the peasant as a symbol of all that is undeniably human.

In the person of the tramp, Synge found another compelling symbol. As he and other writers of his generation saw them, tramps could be equated with artists because of their solitariness and marginal position in society. Both figures were outsiders to middle-class life and therefore enjoyed a freedom from the tyrannies of social conformity. As Synge described this symbolic figure, "Man is intellectually a nomad, and all wanderers have finer intellectual and physical perceptions than men who are condemned to local habitations."

They are, furthermore, people who possess an esoteric knowledge unavailable through mainstream experiences. As many critics have pointed out, the tramp is a premier motif in Synge's work, appearing in four of his plays. Perhaps the most obvious depiction of the tinker as rogue hero appears in *In the Shadow of the Glen*, where an anonymous tramp appears and takes a dissatisfied woman away from the security of her marriage for an uncertain, but romantic, life on the road.

The theme of religious oppression is also strongly evident in Synge's work. His youthful rejection of religion, his profound suspicion of the Catholic church, which controlled the Irish people, and his own general irreligiosity surface in many plays. In *When the Moon Has Set*, a young member of the Ascendancy manages to woo his cousin away from her religious order. In *The Tinker's Wedding*, a priest agrees to marry a pair of tramps only after driving a hard bargain and then reneges on his pledge. The Saint in *The Well of the Saints* cures two blind beggars who are undone by their ugliness and the nastiness of the world. Later, after blindness returns and the Saint offers another blessing, they reject him for a life removed from religion and the blandishments of society.

In these figures, Synge depicts religion as stifling and life-denying. In every case, religion represents inflexibility and the stifling of natural impulses. As Synge saw it, religion was invariably tyrannical and repressive, and his heroes reject or escape its restrictions. Conversely, those who are devout are intimidated weaklings who have lost their humanity.

RIDERS TO THE SEA

First produced: 1904 (first published, 1903)
Type of work: Play

Living in a small rural community in western Ireland, a mother and her two daughters are forced to confront the deaths of the last men in their family.

The first of Synge's two masterworks, *Riders to the Sea* did not encourage censure or controversy when first performed, but it stands as a perfect articulation of themes and ideas that appear in later plays. Events take place entirely in a single room as two sisters, Cathleen and Nora, hide from their mother, Maurya, the news that their brother Michael, a fisherman lost at sea, has washed ashore far north of their cottage. The remaining son, Bartley, sets off to sign on with another departing fishing vessel, after Maurya fails to persuade him to stay. No sooner is Michael's death confirmed than Bartley is thrown from his horse into the sea, where he also drowns.

The complex appreciation that Synge held for nature is evident in the play; it is depicted as a grandly magisterial force that envelops and exceeds all life and human comprehensibility. It is seen as a cruel master, remorselessly taking life out of the world, leaving the destitute even more impoverished. As Maurya reveals, she has lost eight men in her life to the implacable forces of nature, and the same universal patterns that Synge detected on the Aran Islands are at play here.

The setting and characters reveal Synge's interest in peasant life, and the play offers a clear glimpse into the realities of a rural family. Details of domestic economy, farm duties, livestock trading, and fishing are presented with delicate precision. These activities, however—specific as they are to these lives—are significant for revealing a broader human condition. All people must struggle against the contingencies of their lives, and death, nature's great inevitability, visits everyone. The impulse to depict these people as quaint or noble is suppressed; instead, the raw realities of their existence are place squarely before the reader.

The harshest of these realities is the sense of doom and foreboding that hovers about the play. The sisters resist accepting Michael's death until they examine the paltry remnants recovered from the ocean. Both Maurya and the reader know that he is dead, and when confirmation arrives it comes as no surprise. Similarly, Maurya fears for Bartley, and when returning from seeing him off, she narrates a sinister vision. As Bartley rides off on a white mare, trailing a gray pony, Maurya spies Michael's ghost astride the second horse. She is convinced that it is an evil omen, and, indeed, shortly thereafter neighbors arrive with Bartley's body. She expresses her hopelessness in the play's last lines, "What more can we want than [a grave for the dead]? No man at all can be living for ever, and we must be satisfied."

Synge's wary view of religion is also subtly at play in *Riders to the Sea*. Nora tells Cathleen of the consolation that a young priest has offered, but in Synge's world God is either a phantom of the imagination or a force absent from the lives of humans. In spite of all Maurya's prayers, the well-meaning words of the priest, and the sprinkling of holy water, divinity does not prevail over the several inevitabilities of nature. Religion offers no hope and only cold comfort against the numbing pain of existence.

THE PLAYBOY OF THE WESTERN WORLD

First produced: 1907 (first published, 1907)
Type of work: Play

A young outsider, believing that he has murdered his father, visits a neighboring village, becomes a hero, and is rejected when his father unexpectedly appears.

The Playboy of the Western World is Synge's masterpiece, capturing his major themes in their most complex form. It is difficult today to discern why the play was so controversial, but the playwright managed to offend not only the repressive sexual mores examined in other plays but also the image of the peasant as a rural saint.

Christy Mahon, a lad from Kerry, is taken into a pub in Mayo, where he tells and retells, each time embellishing more elaborately, the tale of killing his father. The publican's daughter, Pegeen Mike, quickly becomes enamored of Christy, and the two pledge love. When Mahon's father abruptly appears, Christy is discredited and the same people who earlier valorized him suddenly turn against and punish him. In one of the richer ironies, Christy departs in the company of his father, leaving Pegeen to wed Shawn Keogh, a timid boy in thrall to the Church. Christy is another of Synge's nomadic heroes, one who first takes to the road without a father or a place in the world; later, he is a man who still has no home but has arrived at a firm sense of identity. He ultimately opts for a life free of Church and society and seeks a natural freedom. Christy defines tyranny, and although yearning for Pegeen's love, he settles for isolation as an alternative to conformity.

The view of the peasantry is particularly complex; they are suspicious, narrow, bigoted people who, ironically, have a remarkable sensitivity to narrative extravagance and individuality. These are not idealized figures but people in whom a passion for life is unquenchable. When Pegeen wails, "Oh my grief, I've lost him surely. I've lost the only Playboy of the Western World," she expresses her sorrow over losing a lover and the anguish of realizing that she has betrayed her best instincts and the agent of personal freedom and liberation. In Pegeen, readers will find the same paradox that Synge creates in the peasants in general—people who often realize and desire more than they accept in their lives.

In Christy, Synge presents his most developed view of the artist. He quickly develops from a backward boy into a sophisticated poet who discovers a language he never knew he had in him, a language of the imagination, which sets him apart from quotidian existence. He accepts a life of the imagination, one of complete freedom, where sensibility is raised to its highest pitch. Although decidedly idiomatic, his speech is rich in figurative tropes and densely textured. Synge artfully re-created Irish-English habits of flexible word order, elaborate turns of phrase, and rhetorical exaggeration as no other writer before him had.

Summary

While John Millington Synge has been celebrated for his voice, vision, and original contributions to the world stage, readers should keep in mind the literary task that he set for himself. Synge saw himself first and foremost as a realist, a writer rebelling against romantic conventions that he felt robbed literature of its immediacy and importance. In his preface to *The Playboy of the Western World*, he argues that "On stage one must have reality, and one must have joy; and that is why the intellectual modern drama has failed, and people have grown sick of the false joy of the musical comedy, that has been given them in place of the rich joy found only in what is superb and wild in reality." He saw himself as rebelling against the dramatic conventions of his day, and he was steadfast in his determination that drama should mirror lives as they are lived.

Bibliography

Bushrui, S. B., ed. *Sunshine and the Moon's Delight: A Centenary Tribute to J. M. Synge*. Gerrards Cross, Ireland: Colin Smythe, 1979.

Corkery, Daniel. *Synge and Anglo-Irish Literature*. Cork, Ireland: Cork University Press, 1947.

Ellis-Fermor, Una. *The Irish Dramatic Movement*. Rev. ed. London: Methuen, 1954.

Gerstenberger, Donna. *John Millington Synge*. Boston: Twayne, 1965.

_____. *John Millington Synge*. Rev. ed. Boston: Twayne, 1990.

Greene, David H., and Edward M. Stephens. *J. M. Synge, 1871-1909*. New York: Macmillan, 1961.

Grene, Nicholas. *Synge*. Totowa, N.J.: Rowman & Littlefield, 1975.

King, Mary C. *The Drama of J. M. Synge*. London: Fourth Estate, 1985.

Price, Alan. *Synge and Anglo-Irish Drama*. London: Methuen, 1961.

Saddlemyer, Ann. *J. M. Synge and Modern Comedy*. Dublin: Dolmen Press, 1965.

Skelton, Robin. *The Writings of J. M. Synge*. New York: Bobbs-Merrill, 1971.

David W. Madden

ALFRED, LORD TENNYSON

Born: Somersby, Lincolnshire, England
August 6, 1809
Died: Near Haslemere, England
October 6, 1892

Principal Literary Achievement

Tennyson achieved fame as the preeminent poet of the Victorian Age and is still considered one of the most melodious lyricists of English poetry.

Biography

Alfred Tennyson was born on August 6, 1809, in Somersby, Lincolnshire, England, where his father, the Reverend George Tennyson, was serving as rector of a church. His mother's name was Elizabeth Fytche Tennyson. Early in life he exhibited intellectual brilliance that caught his father's attention. George Tennyson arranged for his son to attend Louth Grammar School from 1815 to 1820 and gave the precocious youth private lessons thereafter. Life at home was not all serene, however, as Tennyson's father suffered from a form of mental illness that led to a serious breakdown in 1824. In fact, George Tennyson's untimely death in 1831 caused the poet to leave Cambridge without a degree so that he could help settle family affairs.

From an early age, Alfred showed an intense interest in poetry, writing verses modeled on those of James Thomson and (later) Sir Walter Scott. In the same year that he entered Trinity College, Cambridge, 1827, he and his brother published a slim volume of poetry; it was not well received by the critics. At Cambridge, Tennyson was not a good student, but he made several friendships that would figure importantly in his life. The most significant was that with Arthur Henry Hallam, a brilliant young man who was influential in Tennyson's participation in the Apostles, a famous Cambridge debating and social club. While at Cambridge, Tennyson published a second volume of poetry; it, too, was reviewed harshly.

After leaving Cambridge, Tennyson traveled with Hallam on the Continent in 1832 and published his third volume of poems. During the following year, however, Hallam, who was then engaged to Tennyson's sister, died suddenly while visiting Vienna. The death shattered Tennyson but stimulated his creative genius: During the next seventeen years, he composed more than a hundred lyrics loosely centered on his grief over the loss of Hallam; in 1850, he published these under the title *In Memoriam*. By 1837, the Tennyson family had found that it could no longer remain at Som-

ersby, and Alfred supervised the move of the clan to High Beech, Epping. He published nothing during the decade, but he worked at revising earlier poems and writing lyric and dramatic works that he would eventually publish during the latter half of the nineteenth century. In 1847, he published *The Princess*, a long narrative poem focusing on the question of women's rights and proper relations between the sexes.

Though he had fallen in love with Emily Sellwood in 1836, Tennyson was not able to marry her until 1850, the same year in which he published his elegy for Hallam. That year was a watershed in the poet's life. The poem celebrating Hallam's death became immensely popular, establishing Tennyson's reputation with the British reading public; late in that same year, upon the death of William Wordsworth, Tennyson was named poet laureate of England.

For the next four decades, Tennyson spent his professional life in service to the Crown and the British public, writing occasional poems and several major works that celebrated his country's heritage. In 1855, he published a long, complicated poem titled *Maud*, which combined his interest in the psychological dimensions of human character with his perennial desire to experiment with various forms of poetic meter. His Arthurian poem *Idylls of the King*, which appeared piecemeal between 1859 and 1885, won wide acclaim, as did collections of new lyrical and narrative verse. Profits from his work, coupled with his pension from the Crown, allowed him to provide comfortably for his family and establish himself as a respectable gentleman, though somewhat of a recluse.

In 1851, the Tennysons' first child was stillborn, but in the following year Emily gave birth to a son, whom the poet named Hallam. A second son, Lionel, was born two years later. In 1853, Tennyson moved his residence to Farringford, a country house on the Isle of Wight off the southern coast of England. In 1868, he established a second residence, Aldworth, in Haslemere. To these residences came politicians from England and abroad, writers, and tourists, paying court to the now-famous poet. He was awarded a barony by the monarchy shortly before his death.

During the 1870's and 1880's, Tennyson turned his hand to drama, completing a series of historical plays that received significant public approval. Tragedy struck the family in 1886, when his son Lionel, who had emigrated to India, died during a return voyage to his homeland. Late in 1888, Tennyson himself began to suffer from failing health. He died on October 6, 1892, near Haslemere, England—clutching a copy of works by William Shakespeare.

Analysis

An appreciation of Tennyson's achievement as an artist requires that one understand his idea of the role of the poet. For centuries, the Aristotelian idea of the poet as maker and upholder of society's best values had dominated Western thinking; but in the half century before Tennyson began writing, the notions of Romanticism, which celebrated art as self-expression and venerated the poet as rebel and social critic, had taken hold. Throughout his life, Tennyson was forced to choose between being the public artist, bent on confirming that which was best in his society, and the private mystic, attempting to explore the psychological dimensions of the human character as he experienced the vicissitudes of his own storm-tossed life.

It is not surprising, then, that one of the major themes of Tennyson's poetry is the exploration of the proper role of the poet in society. In early works such as "The Palace of Art" and "Supposed Confessions of a Second-Rate Sensitive Mind," the poet examines the alternatives that he sees for the poet: an active life struggling to right the many wrongs that he sees in the world, or a life of contemplation and the pursuit of art for art's sake, withdrawn from the fray of everyday affairs. Emblematically, in "The Lady of Shallott" he touches on the same theme. In that poem, the Lady, confined in her room, weaving her beautiful tapestry, sees the outside world only indirectly through images in her mirror; she comes to an untimely death when she abandons her safe tower to enter the world in search of the knight whose image she first discerns in her glass. Such may be the fate of the artist, the youthful Tennyson suggests. Later in his life, in poems such as "The Ancient Sage" and "Merlin and the Gleam," he adopts a more public stance, arguing that the poet is actually a prophet whose proper role is-to discover truth and bring it to humankind.

As poet laureate for more than forty years, Tennyson was frequently asked by Queen Victoria and others to write celebratory verse, and some of his work is simply "occasional" writing: writing to commemorate events, such as the marriage of the Queen's daughter to the czar of Russia. It would be wrong to dismiss all of his public writing as simply made-to-order work, however; "The Charge of the Light Brigade," prompted by gross errors of judgment in a bloody war of imperialism, aroused the indignation of the British public and helped lead to serious reforms in the military, and his "Ode on the Death of the Duke of Wellington" is one of the finest occasional pieces in the language.

Exceptionally well read and always curious about discoveries in all fields of learning, Tennyson writes frequently of contemporary controversies. His works reflect the Victorians' ongoing struggle to reconcile the advances of science, especially those involving theories of evolution, with traditional religion. While his most significant artistic work dealing with this subject is contained in the central lyrics of his great elegy *In Memoriam*, other works, especially the meditative monologue "Lucretius," structure the debate between science and religion as a central theme.

A related issue concerning the advances of science is also central to Tennyson's poetry: the value of material progress. Like many of his contemporaries, the poet was concerned with the effect of burgeoning industrialism on the quality of life for both the well-to-do and particularly the middle class and the poor. Many of his domestic idylls, narrative poems focusing on family life and often set in rural locales, explore the impact of scientific progress and advances in technology on the traditional life-styles of farmers, laborers, and other rustics. The results are sometimes poems of exceptional pathos, such as "Dora," "The Gardener's Daughter," or *Enoch Arden* (though this poem deals more centrally with issues of love and faithfulness). On occasion, however, Tennyson employs bitter satire to evoke in his readers a sense of horror at the evils of creeping materialism: His scathing portrait of the petty master in "The Northern Farmer" poems, both written much later in his life, are good examples of this style.

In an age that still revered the formal qualities of poetry and gave great concern to consistency in meter, rhyme scheme, and adherence to supposed rules of composition, Tennyson stands as something of a rebel. He was a great experimenter in verse forms, often combining different rhyme schemes, line lengths, and styles within the same work. His early education had given him a sound foundation in the classics, and much of his poetry is filled with allusions to Greek and Latin literature. A strong admirer of Vergil, Tennyson often fills his work with the sense of melancholy characteristic of the great Latin poet's work. Like his classical predecessors, Tennyson is a careful observer of nature, rendering it in meticulous descriptions that evoke the sensual qualities of the world that he sees. He is equally adept at portraying psychological states, however; poems such as *Maud* and "St. Simeon Stylites" rival the dramatic monologues of Robert Browning in their penetrating insight into the minds of characters whose psychological equilibrium is precariously balanced between sanity and madness.

A lifelong devotee of the Arthurian story, Tennyson uses the characters from this legend as subjects of numerous poems. From his early portrayals of idealists such as the maid Elaine (the heroine of his "The Lady of Shallott") and the warrior Galahad (celebrated in "Sir Galahad") to his full-length treatment of the legend in *Idylls of the King*, the poet explores the heroic qualities of knighthood. Tennyson reveals how the virtues espoused at Arthur's medieval court are relevant to the complex society of the nineteenth century. The Arthurian poems also serve as a warning about what can happen when people abandon ideals for easy pleasures or material comforts—a problem that Tennyson saw all around him in his own society.

IN MEMORIAM

First published: 1850
Type of work: Poem

> Tennyson explores his feeling of loss at the death of Arthur Henry Hallam and uses the occasion of Hallam's death to explore other contemporary issues.

In Memoriam is Tennyson's elegiac tribute to his closest friend, Arthur Henry Hallam, who died suddenly in September, 1833. Hallam's death dealt a particularly harsh blow to the poet. Almost immediately, Tennyson began attempting to capture his sense of loss and feelings of grief in brief lyrical sketches. He worked on these lyrics for seventeen years, revising and arranging them in a pattern that would give the disparate poems a central unity of purpose.

Tennyson's work follows the traditional pattern of the elegy, first established by the Greeks and appropriated by English poets such as John Milton in "Lycidas" and

Percy Bysshe Shelley in *Adonais* (1821). There is a central figure who speaks in the first person to mourn the loss of a friend; feeling that he has been left behind in a world that also is touched with this loss, the speaker examines his emotions and looks outside himself for solace. His examination of the world around him leads him to realize that, though gone, his friend is still with him in spirit; that realization gives the one who remains in the world some hope, usually for reunion in the afterlife.

Unusual among the great elegies in English, *In Memoriam* tells its story of loss and recovery through a series of interconnected lyrics, over 130 in all; each remains a self-contained unit, but the collection traces the feelings of a central character who experiences, in turn, grief, confusion, despair, personal resolution, and, finally, hope. Several critics have pointed out the similarities between Tennyson's elegy and William Shakespeare's sonnet sequence, which also carries forward a single story beneath the individual lyrics.

Though the poet employs a first-person voice in almost all the lyrics, the central speaker, or "I," of the poem should not automatically be identified with Tennyson himself. In various notes to his work, the poet cautions that he is sometimes using the speaker to represent all of humankind struggling to understand the sense of loss that has come upon it as a result of scientific discoveries that have shattered its faith in the afterlife. The speaker passes through several emotional stages: from grief and despair resulting from the immediacy and the immensity of his loss, through a period of doubt, to a state of hope based on his faith that there is a divine entity guiding humanity's destiny. The progress of the poet's feelings is marked by the three Christmas seasons celebrated in the work. During the first and second Christmases, the poet's feelings are scarred by his loss; during the third, however, he is able to rejoice in the realization that his friend, though vanished from the earth, awaits their reunion in heaven, where he has gone after fulfilling his role on earth. Hallam becomes for Tennyson a symbol of an idea that the poet and his contemporaries were slowly coming to accept and investigate: the idea of progress. By the end of his elegy, Tennyson is celebrating Hallam as the precursor of a new age that will be greater and more blessed for the world; Hallam, like Christ, is a harbinger of better times, and the poet is able to take solace in having been able to share his acquaintance and love.

The note of optimism in the final stanzas of the epilogue is reached only after the poet has agonized long over doubts about both his personal future and the future of the human race. A particularly poignant series of lyrics (ones often anthologized out of the context of the entire series) deals directly with the implications of new discoveries about evolution, and in them the speaker, comparing himself to "an infant, crying in the night," agonizes over the possibility that "nature, red in tooth and claw" is governed not by a beneficent deity but by senseless forces that serve no higher purpose.

The critic T. S. Eliot once observed that the greatness of *In Memoriam* lies not in its final message of hope, but in the quality of doubt that permeates the central lyrics. Nevertheless, the marriage that Tennyson describes in the epilogue is clearly intended to suggest the resiliency of humankind and the promise that life will continue, if not for individuals, then at least for the human race as a whole. Not only will life go on, Tennyson implies, but it will improve, and Hallam has been an early messenger of these better times. For this the poet is thankful, for he has been able to associate with one who symbolizes the great future that the world is to enjoy.

IDYLLS OF THE KING

First published: 1859-1885
Type of work: Poem

Tennyson recounts the rise and fall of the mythical King Arthur, showing how the ruler's high standards are embraced or rejected by his followers.

Idylls of the King is the culmination of Tennyson's lifelong fascination with the Arthurian legend. At an early age, the poet became taken with the story of the king who had united his country and made a perfect society, only to see it fall into ruins because of the illicit affair between his queen and his greatest knight. In several poems written when he was young, Tennyson did what may be called character sketches of Arthurian figures: the Maid of Astolat, Galahad, Guinevere, and Lancelot. Shortly after the untimely death of his friend Arthur Hallam, he composed a long narrative on the death of King Arthur; the poem was incorporated as the last of the twelve idylls that now constitute *Idylls of the King*.

Idylls of the King was published in parts between 1859 and 1885, so there has always been a question concerning the unity of the work: Should it be read as a consistent whole, considered a nineteenth century epic? Or is it a collection, in the vein of *In Memoriam*, in which individual poems suggest a thematic whole but are not intended to present a coherent story? Most critics have seen sufficient unity in the assemblage to judge that Tennyson intended his work to be taken as a single long poem, and that he consciously used various epic devices to suggest parallels with works such as Vergil's the *Aeneid* (c. 29-19 B.C.). The blank verse line, the epic similes, and other devices of phrasing and description recall John Milton's *Paradise Lost* (1667, 1674), unquestionably the most ambitious epic in English.

From his own writings about the poem, as well as from internal evidence, it is clear that Tennyson intended *Idylls of the King* to be both a commentary on contemporary society and a kind of allegory about the human spirit warring against the fleshly side of humanity's nature. Arthur is described in the epilogue of the poem as a perfect Victorian gentleman—with clear parallels to Victoria's dead husband, Prince Albert, who is celebrated by name in the dedication to *Idylls of the King* added by Tennyson after the Prince Consort's death in 1861. Throughout the Arthurian story, the poet celebrates Victorian virtues of fidelity to one's spouse—a concept not at all in keeping with the medieval concept of courtly love, wherein a knight might be in service to (and on occasion have an illicit affair with) a woman other than his wife. Further, *Idylls of the King* celebrates the importance of work over fame. In a revealing passage in the sixth idyll, "Merlin and Vivien," the aging magician, Merlin, tells the temptress that it is better to work than to seek glory, that one should revere those who perform the common duties of life. The theme is echoed by the king at the end of the eighth idyll, "The Holy Grail." When only a few of his knights return from their quest for the cup that was supposedly used by Christ at the last supper, Arthur lectures them about the devastating impact that their vain pursuit has had on the kingdom. While they were away, many necessary chores were left unattended; the king excuses his own unwillingness to seek the Grail by noting that it has been his duty to remain at home governing the land, handling the everyday tasks that befit his position. Such an attitude would have been foreign to the medieval audiences that first heard tales of Arthur and his knights, but this sentiment would have struck a sympathetic chord with Victorian readers.

In the epilogue, Tennyson also describes his hero as "Ideal manhood closed in real man" and mentions that the poem is intended to show the struggle of "sense at war with soul." The highly allegorical nature of *Idylls of the King* may be best seen in the second section, "Gareth and Lynette," in which a young hero, imbued with the ideals that Arthur preaches, fights and defeats four challengers who represent (according to an explanation provided within the poem itself) the various stages of a person's life. The message is clear: Those who live by the high ideals that Arthur promotes will rise above even death itself. The fairy tale quality of "Gareth and Lynette" is not sustained, however, as one by one even the greatest knights and ladies fail to uphold these high standards. Some, such as the villainous Tristan, openly scoff at the King's naïveté; others, such as Lancelot and Guinevere, struggle to reconcile their commitment to those ideals with the very real, physical love that they feel for each other but that they know is wrong because it violates the moral code of the kingdom.

The central theme of the poem is that devotion to such high ideals is nearly impossible in a world beset with materialism. As critic James Kincaid notes in *Tennyson's Major Poems, the Comic and Ironic Patterns* (1975), no outside force causes the downfall of Arthur's perfect society; rather, it falls from within, collapsing because the knights and ladies of the realm are unable to abide by the king's ideals. Tennyson captures the tenuous nature of Arthur's experiment with utopian living in his image of the capital city of Camelot: Gareth, on his way to meet the king for the first time, meets Merlin outside the city and asks if the spires that he sees in the mist are those of the king's capital. From them, he hears sweet music coming forth, and Merlin says that this is indeed Camelot, which is still being built: "the city is built/ To music," the seer remarks, "therefore never built at all,/ And therefore built for ever" ("Gareth and Lynette"). Like a musical composition, Arthur's kingdom relies on the harmony achieved when every player is working under the direction of a wise composer; when one chooses to play his or her own tune, the harmony is broken, and the music becomes discordant. That image, repeated throughout the remainder of the *Idylls of the King*, captures Tennyson's idea about society: Unless all work in concert with one another and follow high moral standards, civilization itself is doomed to fail.

ULYSSES

First published: 1842
Type of work: Poem

The hero of Homer's the *Odyssey* (c. 800 B.C.), living the quiet life at home after his twenty-year sojourn away from Ithaca, vows to set out again to seek new adventures.

"Ulysses" is ranked with several of Robert Browning's dramatic monologues as the best in the genre. Based on a passage in Dante Alighieri's *La divina commedia* (c. 1320; *The Divine Comedy*), the poem depicts the hero of the Trojan Wars sometime after he has returned to his native land. Ironically, the man who had lived away from his beloved wife and son for ten years before the walls of Troy, and who had then wandered the Mediterranean for ten more as a result of a curse from the gods, is now displeased with the quiet life that he finds at home. The discomfort that Ulysses feels is emblematic of the dilemma that many of Tennyson's contemporaries faced: whether to live life quietly, fulfilling one's domestic duties, or to pursue some bold adventure. For Tennyson, the poem had personal significance as well: Written shortly after the death of his close friend Arthur Henry Hallam, it was the poet's attempt to answer the question of whether to try to make a new life or to continue to wallow in his sorrow.

If one reads the poem in light of Tennyson's personal comments, then the ending suggests a strong note of optimism. After convincing himself that he should not remain at home—his son, Telemachus, is more suited to rule a land where people have no aspirations for adventure—Ulysses summons a group of mariners to sail away with him to find new adventures. There is a recognized risk in such action: "It may be that the gulfs will wash us down," he warns them, but if he and his men are fortunate, they may "touch the Happy Isles,/ And see the great Achilles that we knew." Whatever they do, they will have the satisfaction of knowing that they have done their best in struggling against the elements (and old age) to make new reputations. The ringing final line, "To strive, to seek, to find, and not to yield," becomes a battle cry for all who need support in their endeavors to make a better life.

Unfortunately, such a glib reading is not fully supported by internal evidence. The mariners whom Ulysses summons are not the same ones that sailed with him before; those men were all lost before the king returned to Ithaca. Further, his call to sail toward the west, and his remark that they may be fortunate enough to land in the Happy Isles, both suggest that this is a voyage to death. Such a reading is supported by external evidence, namely the passage from Dante on which Tennyson bases his account. Like many narrators in dramatic monologues, Tennyson's Ulysses is not to be trusted fully. His is a seductive message, a call to adventure that simultaneously encourages a flight from responsibility. How one is to determine whether Ulysses is a hero or villain is never resolved, of course; this is attributable in part to the peculiar nature of the dramatic monologue form. Readers have no external reference point from which to judge the truthfulness or sincerity of Ulysses' statements. Only a careful analysis of the substance of his request—the message beneath the compelling rhetoric—suggests that he may be seeking to abandon his responsibilities and cloak his escape in the guise of seeking further glory. The enigma may well be intentional, considering Tennyson's lifelong preoccupation with characters who are psychologically complex. There are for Tennyson two sides to every issue, and commitment to one ideal may well result in abandonment of another, equally valid one. Such is the human condition as he sees it.

LOCKSLEY HALL

First published: 1842
Type of work: Poem

A young man, rejected by his beloved for a more wealthy suitor, muses on the present state of society and has a vision of a different, better future.

"Locksley Hall" is typical of Tennyson's poetry, in that the pattern of the poem follows one characteristic of much of the poet's work. A personal experience sparks Tennyson's creative imagination, and he uses that incident as a springboard for investigating issues of greater social concern.

The biographical germ of the poem lies in Rosa Baring's rejection of Tennyson as a suitor in 1837; the poet's poor financial position made him unsuitable for her as a husband, and she rejected him in favor of a man of greater means. In "Locksley Hall," Tennyson transforms his own disappointment and grief over this rejection into a bitter analysis of the society in which materialism takes precedence over love. The speaker of the poem, a young suitor whose beloved Amy leaves him to marry a boorish man of suitable financial means, rebukes both his beloved and her new husband. His maundering attack leads him to consider the world in which true love can be dismissed so lightly, and he eventually begins to daydream about a future in which people, driven by greed, will eventually clash in world war to satisfy their insatiable materialistic appetites. In passages that border on science fiction, Tennyson describes "airy navies" engaging in battle. There is a ray of hope, however; the speaker finally sees an end to nationalistic strife, and the formation of a "Parliament of man," a worldwide federation that will eventually bring peace to warring nations. All of this is mere reverie, of course, and in the final couplets the speaker turns away bitterly from Locksley Hall, the place where he wooed his Amy unsuccessfully, and goes off to wander the world in an attempt to suffuse his bitterness.

Written in trochaic couplets, "Locksley Hall" is an excellent example of Tennyson's ability to sustain a complicated meter and rhyme scheme. Some critics have complained, however, that the jingling nature of the meter works against the serious message of the poem, the speaker's indictment of modern society. Like the best of Tennyson's poetry, "Locksley Hall" contains phrases of vivid description and lines that capture the mood of the speaker in such a way as to give his personal feelings a universal significance. The Byronic qualities of the hero of this poem, his brooding over his fate in life, and his somber portrait of the future (even when tempered by his final vision of a world at peace) suggest the darker side of Tennyson's personality; the poet seems fascinated by characters whose life experiences drive them to the brink of madness as they face frustration and disappointment in a world where money has supplanted love as the highest of human aspirations.

Summary

Alfred, Lord Tennyson's immense popularity among his contemporaries was a contributing cause to his decline in critical esteem during the first half of the twentieth century, when the reaction against Victorianism reached its height. Following the sympathetic judgment of mid-century critics such as the poet's grandson Sir Charles Tennyson and noted Victorianist Jerome H. Buckley, more recent scholars have rekindled interest in Tennyson's works and have ranked his best poems—works such as "Ulysses," "Tithonus," *In Memoriam*, and *Idylls of the King*—among the finest in the language.

Bibliography

Albright, Daniel. *Tennyson: The Muses' Tug-of-War*. Charlottesville: University Press of Virginia, 1986.

Beetz, Kirk H. *Tennyson: A Bibliography, 1827-1982*. Metuchen, N.J.: Scarecrow Press, 1984.

Ebbatson, Roger. *Tennyson*. Harmondsworth, Middlesex, England: Penguin Books, 1988.

Goslee, David. *Tennyson's Characters: Strange Faces, Other Minds*. Iowa City: University of Iowa Press, 1989.

Hair, Donald S. *Domestic and Heroic in Tennyson's Poetry*. Toronto: University of Toronto Press, 1981.

Jordan, Elaine. *Alfred Tennyson*. Cambridge, England: Cambridge University Press, 1988.

Pinion, F. B. *A Tennyson Companion*. London: Macmillan, 1984.

Sinfield, Alan. *Alfred Tennyson*. Oxford, England: Basil Blackwell, 1986.

Thomson, Alistair W. *The Poetry of Tennyson*. London: Routledge & Kegan Paul, 1986.

Tucker, Herbert F. *Tennyson and the Doom of Romanticism*. Cambridge, Mass.: Harvard University Press, 1988.

Laurence W. Mazzeno

WILLIAM MAKEPEACE THACKERAY

Born: Calcutta, India
July 18, 1811
Died: London, England
December 24, 1863

Principal Literary Achievement

More than any other writer of the nineteenth century, Thackeray presented a social history of Victorian England; *Vanity Fair* is considered to be the greatest English novel of that period.

Biography

William Makepeace Thackeray was born in Calcutta, India, on July 18, 1811, the son of Richmond Makepeace Thackeray, a collector for the East India Company, and Anne Becher Thackeray, whose ancestry could be traced back to a sixteenth century sheriff of London. His pampered life changed drastically when, after his father's death, Thackeray was sent to live with relatives in England to attend schools in South Hampton and Chiswick. His mother remained in Calcutta, married again, and did not join her son in England for four more years. This period of separation deeply affected Thackeray throughout the rest of his life.

In 1822, Thackeray continued his education at Charterhouse, a London public school. He was unhappy there and made little progress, for Charterhouse also proved to be a brutal place for the nearsighted boy who was poor at games. Thus, Thackeray's hatred of public schools and his critical view of a classical education were formed; later in life, this hostility softened somewhat. Charterhouse is featured in his writings, most notably as Grey Friars in *The Newcomes: Memoirs of a Most Respectable Family* (1853-1855).

Thackeray entered Trinity College, Cambridge, in 1829, but left only one year later to visit France. From Paris, he traveled to Germany; his happy tour there is reflected in the Pumpernickel chapters of *Vanity Fair: A Novel Without a Hero* (1847-1848). In Weimar, he met Germany's leading man of letters, Johann Wolfgang von Goethe.

Back in London, Thackeray's literary career began with his ownership of *The National Standard*, a weekly literary periodical. He was soon forced to abandon this project for financial reasons (partly because of poor investments and partly because

of his compulsive gambling). He had, however, gained a modest entrance to London's literary world and had cultivated friendships with the poets Alfred, Lord Tennyson, and Edward FitzGerald.

While at Charterhouse, Thackeray had become interested in what were to become lifelong passions—drawing and painting. With the failure of *The National Standard*, and with most of his inheritance gone, he decided to pursue these interests and went to Paris to study art. This venture proved to be unsuccessful, and to make ends meet, he became a Paris correspondent for *The Constitutional*. In 1836, Thackeray met and married Isabella Shawe. That year was also the year in which *Flore et Zephyr*, his first publication in volume form, appeared. The following year, when *The Constitutional* failed, the Thackerays returned to London, where three daughters, Anne, Jane (who died in infancy), and Harriet, were born.

Faced with the responsibility of providing for his family, Thackeray turned full-time to professional journalism, contributing to *The Times*, *The Foreign Quarterly Review*, and *The Morning Chronicle*. His work went unsigned or under such pen names as Michael Angelo Titmarsh and George Fitz-Boodle.

The next few years proved to be important ones for Thackeray. In 1840, his wife went insane and required institutionalization. Parental responsibility for his daughters was assumed by Thackeray's parents, which enabled him to pursue his writing in earnest. His most significant writings at this time appeared in *Frazer's Magazine* and *Punch*. Thackeray first caught the public's eye as one of the "Fraserians" (critics of Victorian hypocrisy and pretention) with "The Yellowplush Papers," a review of a foolish book of etiquette. This Fraserian approach is also apparent in Thackeray's short novel *Catherine: A Story* (1839-1840). Set in the eighteenth century, this tale of a murderess is based upon an actual event. It is a satirical attack upon the "Newgate School" of novelists, which glorified the lives of criminals. *Catherine* is an important work in Thackeray's career, for it marks the beginning of his fascination with the artificial life of that period. His first full-length novel, *The Luck of Barry Lyndon: A Romance of the Last Century* (1844), also had a romanticized criminal as a hero.

Literary success came slowly to Thackeray. *The Irish Sketch-Book* (1843), an entertaining personal record of a stay in Ireland, bears his signature for the first time. The "Snob Papers," issued in *Punch*, finally brought him fame. In January, 1844, *Vanity Fair*, with illustrations by the author, began to appear in monthly installments, and Thackeray had taken his place alongside other well-respected writers of the period.

Thackeray's greatest distinction was as a novelist, but he was also an essayist and lecturer. In 1851, he began lecturing on "The English Humourists," traveling the following year to America, where he was a great success. *The History of Henry Esmond, Esquire, a Colonel in the Service of Her Majesty Q. Anne* (hereinafter referred to as *Henry Esmond*), was published in three volumes in 1852 and revealed his style at its perfection—less powerful than *Vanity Fair*, but much more compassionate. In it, the author's long, platonic affair with Jane Brookfield is reproduced. *The Newcomes* was published in 1855, and a second lecture tour of the United States soon followed. This time Thackeray spoke on the "Four Georges," an indictment of the House of Hanover.

After his second American tour, Thackeray published *The Virginians: A Tale of the Last Century* (1857-1859). He became the editor of *Cornhill Magazine* in 1860 and served as such until poor health forced him to retire in 1862. His last novel, *Denis Duval*, though unfinished, appeared in *Cornhill Magazine* in 1864. Thackeray died on December 24, 1863, in London and is buried in Kensal Green Cemetery.

Analysis

Thackeray's literary significance lies in his contribution to the development of the novel. His reflections upon Victorian England through the use of an intrusive narrator became a new form of fiction, and his sprawling panoramas of eighteenth century England give the reader a psychological treatise of the times. The slow, satiric revelation of his characters and the realistic analysis of topics that other Victorian writers avoided, told in the form of a memoir by a witty, caustic observer, laid the groundwork for the psychological realism of Henry James; Thackeray's experiments with the generational form presaged the works of John Galsworthy.

Thackeray's writing can be divided into four distinct periods. The first, from 1837 to 1843, was a period in which he exercised an almost passionate vigor to point out where society had gone wrong. He places himself outside his writing through his superior attitude toward his characters, lower-class subjects whom he treats in the most disparaging manner conceivable. There is a glimmer of the Thackeray yet to come when he shifts his focus to the middle class, and when, in *The History of Samuel Titmarsh and the Great Hoggarty Diamond* (1841; later as *The Great Hoggarty Diamond*, 1848), he presents the likable Sam Titmarsh. Thackeray cast himself as Titmarsh, thereby indicating his concern about class. This concern was to dominate his writing.

Thackeray was unsure about his own place in the rigid English social system. He thus adopted a jauntily unpretentious persona in his social fictions. He developed a talent for the burlesque and began to attack other writers, ridiculing military adventure novels, satirically attacking the Newgate School, and portraying his fascination with the Europe of that time.

The years 1843 to 1848 mark a significant change in Thackeray's development as a writer. His personal involvement in his works becomes more apparent, and his association with *Punch* heightened his understanding of society's injustices. During this period, Thackeray wrote a series of short stories, *Men's Wives* (1843), that illustrate his misgivings about women and marriage. Along these same lines, he wrote several other pieces. One of particular note, "Bluebeard's Ghost," is the tale of a young widow's devotion to her dead partner; in it, Thackeray's love for Jane Brookfield and his jealousy of her fidelity to her husband are clear. The opulence of the eighteenth century, the lives of rogues, the education of gentlemen, and the presence of doting mothers blend in his best work of these middle years, *The Luck of Barry Lyndon*. Although the theme of the novel is social pretension, it is also a deliberate spoof of popular historical, crime, and romantic novels. *The Book of Snobs* (1848, 1852) is

Thackeray's classic assault on pretentiousness. His message is that the remedy for social ills is social equality.

Thackeray's first great novel, *Vanity Fair*, marks the beginning of his literary acclaim. The title, taken from John Bunyan's *The Pilgrim's Progress from This World to That Which Is to Come* (1678), and Thackeray's preface reveal the moral purpose behind his satire.

The History of Pendennis: His Fortunes and Misfortunes, His Friends and His Greatest Enemy (1848-1850) is an important book in any study of Thackeray's technique, as it presents the background for the persona who was to narrate *The Newcomes* and as it shows Thackeray's struggles with Victorian priggishness. In both *The History of Pendennis* and *The Newcomes*, Thackeray's satirical edge had disappeared. His retreat from satire was quite deliberate; he wanted to appeal instead to the hearts and souls of his reading public. In subject matter the two novels are similar: Each concerns the styles and conventions that separate people from one another. *The Newcomes*, however, illustrates better than *The History of Pendennis* the discursive style that Thackeray adopted in all of his novels—the roundabout manner of narration, the slipping back and forth in time, and the interpolations.

In 1852, Thackeray published what he considered to be his best piece of writing, *Henry Esmond*. The novel may be read on many levels, as a historical fiction, as a novel of manners, and as a romance. *The Virginians* continues the story, with Henry Esmond's grandsons, who are born in America. Of all Thackeray's novels, it is the least successful. In it, Thackeray's eighteenth century scenario has lost its appeal: The courtliness, brawling, drinking, and gambling are seen as tedious even by its chronicler. Thackeray was sick of writing novels, and he admits to this in book 1, chapter 18.

Thackeray's writings constitute a vast imaginative enterprise. For the first time, his panoramic realism gave readers of English literature a sense of living in a distinct yet diverse world. His works offer page after page of sometimes caustic, sometimes playful, sometimes serious, sometimes contemplative, and sometimes hasty observations, all written in his brilliant but seemingly discursive, careless manner, which has come to be known as Thackerayan.

VANITY FAIR

First published: 1847-1848
Type of work: Novel

In the eighteenth century, Becky Sharp ambitiously climbs her way to wealth and social position.

Vanity Fair is Thackeray's best-known work, and it established his reputation as a master of social satire. The title is taken from John Bunyan's *The Pilgrim's Progress from This World to That Which Is to Come* (1678), and it is, as Thackeray reveals in the preface, in the same manner a frankly moralistic novel. Posing as the Manager of the Performance, he reminds his readers to avoid simply passing through the emblematic *Vanity Fair* and to experience it in a "contemplative, not uncharitable frame of mind," for everyone, including the author, is a part of the fair.

Thackeray's intrusive comments serve the purpose of distancing the reader from the characters, thereby forcing the reader to judge not only the "puppets" but also himself or herself. Thus, the reader cannot feel simple approval or disapproval for any of the main figures, least of all for Becky Sharp (the best character that Thackeray ever created). Indeed, Becky is clever, underprivileged, and courageous; she is also heartless, selfish, and amoral. She takes advantage of the gentle nature of her school friend Amelia Sedley and literally stalks Amelia's brother Jos as a husband who could give her wealth and social position. In characteristic Thackerayan style, Becky's plans are foiled through no fault of her own, and Jos returns to India still a bachelor. Thus, the vicissitudes of life, over which Thackeray's characters have no control, sustain the story and propel Becky into one adventure after another.

Forced to earn an income, Becky takes a position as a governess for the household of Sir Pit Crawley. At Queen's Crawley, Thackeray begins to introduce the crowd of minor figures that populates the novel and whose purpose it is to authenticate the sprawling, wandering plot and emphasize the profuse and disorganized world in which both the characters and the readers live. The best example of these minor characters occurs in chapter 47 with the Gaunt family, which is given a history; Thackeray even describes Gaunt Square, with its statue of Lord Gaunt.

In Becky and her quest to gain entry into the rich and pretentious life of the eighteenth century upper class, Thackeray expresses his resentment against English society. Becky makes fools of the pretentiously proud Crawleys and triumphs over the aristocratic Bareacres. Her adulterous affair with Lord Steyne and her murder of Jos Sedley (if she is indeed guilty) are far less damning in the reader's eyes than her lack of motherly love. That same motherly love is Amelia Sedley's only virtue. Other than that, Amelia is absolutely vapid. Her self-indulgent devotion to her dead husband's (George Osbourne's) memory and her unworthy attitude toward Captain William Dobbin are irritating. That Thackeray focuses upon Amelia's motherly love, however, suggests Thackeray's childhood and his separation from his mother at such an early age and reveals the systematic thought that underlies all of his works.

In the end, Becky is reunited with the unsuspecting Jos, and although she cannot obtain a divorce from Rawdon Crawley, they live as man and wife. Upon Jos's suspicious death, Becky receives a considerable insurance payment and spends the rest of her life as a virtuous widow with a reputation for benevolence and generosity.

If, then, everyone is a part of the vanity fair, to condemn Becky or any of the other characters is to condemn oneself. As the puppets are put back in the box, Thackeray suggests that the best that can be expected is to possess charity toward others and to care for others as one cares for oneself. Otherwise, all is vanity.

HENRY ESMOND

First published: 1852
Type of work: Novel

Amid historical events of the late seventeenth and early eighteenth centuries, a man struggles with his love of two women.

Henry Esmond is the book that Thackeray considered to be his best piece of writing. Set in the late seventeenth and early eighteenth centuries, it presents history as Thackeray thought it should be presented. That Thackeray did not have a high opinion of the historians of his time precludes the blend of fact and fiction in this gentleman's memoir. Henry Esmond tells his own story, which is meant to be the hero's autobiography. Thackeray's blend of the relationships of private manners and historical events is characteristic of most of his other works, and the false pathos of the artificial, self-imagined hero collapses when everything is viewed from the porch of everyday life.

Henry Esmond grew up at Castlewood under the guardianship of Thomas Esmond, Viscount Castlewood. Henry was aware of some mystery concerning his birth, and he vaguely remembered living as a very young child with weavers who spoke a language other than English. When the Viscount met his death at the battle of the Boyne, young Henry was cared for by his new guardians and distant cousins, Francis and Rachel Esmond, and their children, Beatrix and Frank. Thus begins the major thematic integration of the novel: Henry's love of two women, of Rachel, the loveliest woman he had ever seen, and of Beatrix, her daughter, for whom his courtship becomes almost tedious to the reader.

Henry Esmond reflects a very personal part of Thackeray's own life. His wife, Isabella, was institutionalized for insanity in 1840, leaving him bereft of a family life, something that was very important to Thackeray. As a result of this, he became enamored of the already married Jane Brookfield, but this relationship became a drawn-out platonic affair. While he was writing *Henry Esmond*, Thackeray's love for her came to a sad crisis in September, 1851. His letters of the time indicate his painful feelings during this period, which greatly affected the tone of this "grave and sad" book.

Henry Esmond introduces Thackeray's readers to yet another Victorian fantasy world, much as *Vanity Fair* had done. First, the sexual theme begins when Henry, twelve years old, sees Rachel for the first time. He loves her as a son would, and he identifies her as his surrogate mother. As time passes, the relative ages of son and mother are reversed, and Henry becomes her "tutor"; he appears to be "older" than her, and by book 3, chapter 4, he feels as if he is her "grandfather." Thus, when Henry's love for Beatrix, who is one of the most fascinating women in all of English literature, is dead at last, the reader should not be surprised when Henry at thirty-five, marries Rachel, who is forty-three and, the reader is assured, looks younger than her own daughter.

There is something obviously Oedipal in this relationship, and Thackeray's almost reverential worship of his mother comes to the surface in *Henry Esmond*. Critics and his reading public alike were quick to sense something was amiss, and charges of incest were levied at the protagonist, Henry Esmond.

The second theme of the story is also a fantasy. When Henry discovers that he is the real Lord Castlewood, the legitimate son of the Viscount, he, out of consideration for Rachel, conceals his identity so that she and her children will not be disinherited. When the truth is finally revealed, the aristocrats who have slighted him do him homage. Even Beatrix, previously scornful of the humble Esmond's courtship, repents and considers it an honor to know him.

Henry Esmond represents, then, the culmination of middle-class wish fulfillment. Its hero is nobler than the nobles, yet he of his own volition remains a commoner. At the end, Esmond emigrates to America, thus rejecting the institutions of the aristocracy.

Summary

Although William Makepeace Thackeray is sometimes overshadowed by his contemporaries Charles Dickens and George Eliot, his works are essential in the history of the English novel. He is the master of a slow, expository style that, for range of effect, has seldom been equaled in English. His development of the intrusive narrator and his caustic realism greatly influenced writers of later generations, especially the psychological realists.

Born between that period of notable change from the Regency to the Victorian era, Thackeray composed historical pictures that provide a social history of that time. *Vanity Fair* remains his best novel, but his collected works are necessary reading for anyone who wants to understand Victorian England.

Bibliography

Auchincloss, Louis. "The Two Ages of Thackeray." In *Reflections of a Jacobite*. Boston: Houghton Mifflin, 1961.

Eliot, Charles W., ed. *The Harvard Classics: Essays, English and American*. New York: P. F. Collier & Son, 1910.

Peters, Catherine. *Thackeray's Universe: Shifting Worlds of Reality*. Boston: Faber & Faber, 1987.

Tillotson, Geoffrey. *Thackeray the Novelist*. Cambridge, England: Cambridge University Press, 1954.

Welsh, Alexander, ed. *Thackeray: A Collection of Critical Essays*. Englewood Cliffs, N.J.: Prentice-Hall, 1968.

Lela Phillips

DYLAN THOMAS

Born: Swansea, Wales
October 27, 1914
Died: New York, New York
November 9, 1953

Principal Literary Achievement

Thomas is the supreme Romantic lyricist of the English language in the twentieth century, whose love of words and their musical strength gives his poetry a rhythmic power rarely equaled in the history of literature.

Biography

Dylan Marlais Thomas was born on October 27, 1914, in the small port city of Swansea, on the South Wales coast across the Bristol Channel from Devonshire. His father, David John Thomas, was a frustrated intellectual who resented the position that he held as a local schoolmaster, which he believed was incompatible with the life of a cultivated literary gentleman. His mother, Florence Williams Thomas, was a deacon's daughter. She had no interest in literature, but she was extremely devoted to her second child, Dylan. The family lived in a relatively genteel neighborhood when Dylan was born, near the hills and rolling farm country that he was to celebrate in poems such as "Fern Hill" and "Poem in October," and within sight of the horseshoe-shaped coastline that rimmed the sea below the house. Although Thomas often felt the lure of London while living in Wales, the cultural ethos of west Wales remained one of his most important points of reference and sources of inspiration. The lyrical flow of talk in the pubs, the singing in the streets and churches, the cadences of Bible-drawn sermons spoken by local ministers who were often relatives, the feel of the rainy weather, and the look of the land all contributed to his formation as a poet.

David Thomas was determinedly agnostic, but he often recited the Bible to his son in infancy and read him to sleep with selections from the great tradition of English literature: William Shakespeare, the Romantic poets, as well as the contemporary controversial novelist D. H. Lawrence. From the start, Thomas was relatively indifferent to all forms of public education, preferring to browse in his father's extensive library, while behaving in a prankish, mischievous fashion in class. Already verbally precocious (he saw himself as a boy who "swallowed a dictionary"), he was sent to a private school and then to the local grammar school where his father was employed.

His first poems appeared in the grammar school magazine in 1925. By 1928, he

was the editor of the magazine and had begun to compile a poetry notebook that would contain in completed or rough form more than two hundred poems by 1933. As he began to think of himself as a poet, his school work deteriorated to the point that he totally failed all of his Central Welsh Board examinations and left school in 1931 to take a job with the *South Wales Daily Post* as a kind of roving reporter and general gadfly. He spent a considerable amount of time with older journalists in pubs and was introduced to the drink-drenched cultural milieu that formed the center of his social life for the remainder of his years. In 1932, he became involved with the Swansea Little Theatre as an actor and writer, and by 1933, when he left the newspaper, he was living in a style that he would essentially maintain for the rest of his life. He effectively removed any impediment to his writing, including any kind of commitment to earning a living, putting himself in the position of supplicant, which he developed into a personal skill of considerable refinement.

Thomas' disinclination to adopt "regular" hours of steady employment was as much an attempt to reserve all of his energy for writing as it was an attempt to avoid the boredom of routine and responsibility. "And Death Shall Have No Dominion" was published in the *New English Weekly* in May, 1933, his first poem to appear outside Wales, and by August of that year, he had finished twelve of the ninety poems that would eventually appear in his *Collected Poems, 1934-1952* (1952). He moved into a flat in London in November, 1934, with two friends from Wales, and the next month his first book of poetry, *18 Poems* (1934), was published jointly by the *Sunday Referee* magazine and the Parton Bookshop. It was followed by *Twenty-five Poems* in 1936, the year that he met Caitlin Macnamara, whom he married in July, 1937. Dylan and Caitlin lived with friends and relatives in England or Wales, or in their own apartment until funds ran out, their marriage turbulent and tempestuous from the start, their life together "raw, red bleeding meat," in Caitlin's words.

Thomas' second book had received favorable reviews, which helped to alleviate their financial difficulties. Thomas had also begun to deliver readings and broadcasts on the British Broadcasting Corporation (BBC), but no matter how much money was available from royalties, readings, or commissions, splurges, gifts to friends, and general carelessness placed Dylan and Caitlin in perpetual financial distress. Thomas spent most of the years during World War II traveling between London and Wales, writing scripts for the BBC and working on projects for Strand Films, eventually contributing to sixteen scripts. As the war drew to a close, Thomas and his family spent time in Blaen Cwm and New Quay, concentrating on his poetry. In a burst of poetic energy, Thomas completed "Poem in October," "Fern Hill," and "In My Craft or Sullen Art," among more than a dozen of his collected poems, his last period of relatively rapid production. Many of these appeared in *Deaths and Entrances* (1946), and James Laughlin's New Directions Press issued *Selected Writings of Dylan Thomas* (1946) in the United States later in the year.

Through the efforts of friends and patrons, Thomas was awarded a £150 traveling scholarship from the Society of Authors, and he and his family spent some time in Italy, where he was limited in his socializing by the language barrier but succeeded in writing "In Country Sleep" in Florence. He completed three film scripts in 1948 and earned more than £2,400 that year, but he had never filed a tax return and found himself in a kind of perpetual debt to the Inland Revenue for the remainder of his life. Because he could count on greater earnings from his prose work, he tended to devote more time to it, and, consequently, his poetic production was drastically slowed down. Since he had to spend a great deal of time on each work, he would produce only a few more poems, although these included "Poem on His Birthday" and "In the White Giant's Thigh," as well as his great villanelle "Do Not Go Gentle into That Good Night," written in 1951 in loving tribute to his dying father.

In hopes of overcoming his financial difficulties, Thomas made his first (of four) trips to America in 1950. His exhausting tour of the United States spawned the legend of the wild, bawdy, drunken, raving romantic delinquent, which made him a celebrity and eventually resulted in what Donald Hall calls "public suicide." Between tours, he began *Under Milk Wood* (1954), saw his *Collected Poems, 1934-1952* published to exceptional reviews, and continued his contentious relationship with Caitlin. In 1953, his body finally succumbed to years of abuse, and he died in a hospital in New York on November 9.

Analysis

In an unusually candid letter to a student who asked him how he was drawn to the "craft or sullen art" of poetry, Thomas emphasized the allure of words themselves— the "shape and shade and size and noise of words as they hummed, strummed, jigged and galloped along." Hall has called him "the maddest of word-mad young poets" and describes Thomas beginning a poem from some general idea, sense of place, or pantheistic thought and then building the poem through the sounds of words gradually arranged in the manner that satisfied his ear, as well as some deeper instinct for melody and rhythm. Caitlin Thomas recalls him struggling with single lines in his bicycle shed/studio, "balancing words, line and phrases . . . and he always did this noisily and alone in his shed, chanting and reciting, making each sound fit."

Because of his ability to write poetry that seemed drenched in word-drunk wonder, some critics have asserted that there is no substance behind the "great lyrical voice of his time." Charles Olson, whose own work depended on a tremendous concentration of mental force, commented, "He is all language, there is no man there." Olson's critique indicates the pitfalls of depending on a sensuous linguistic surface, but, although Thomas does not always succeed in going deeper, his methods of composition depended on more than the magic of words alone. In a letter that he wrote to Pamela Hansford Johnson when he was beginning to take command of the singular voice that he possessed, he suggested that a writer worked either " '*out* of words' or 'in the *direction* of them,' " as if the word was the source of the idea in the poem. In a review written in 1935, he insisted that "the word is the object," not a symbol or sign of it, and even if he complained that he was "chained by syllables," he believed that both meaning and sound are bound within language, and that it was through his uses of language that human experience could be brought into poetry. While he was not always successful in capturing the "singing light"—the song and insight inter-linked—his best poems combine a mastery of sound with his meditations on the central concerns of his life.

One of the most striking features of Thomas' poetry is the absence of any indication that it was written (with the exception of a few topical references) in the twen-tieth century. Even as Thomas took the ultimate Romantic position that his subject was himself, demanding "Man be my metaphor" and always basing his sense of the human on the "small, bone-bound island" at the center of his own universe, his treat-ment of the main themes of his art reached back toward some almost prehistoric, semi-mythic sense of universal human experience. Consequently, when he wrote about his awestruck, ecstatic delight in the presence of the infinitely appealing natural world, his perspective was similar to the rhapsodic declarations of an explorer encountering a garden of paradise. The Edenic aspects of the Welsh landscape in "Fern Hill" and "Poem in October" attest to this. Similarly, when he wrote about death as an inevita-ble presence in the midst of even the most youthful, vital moments of a person's existence, his poetry was less a function of a morbid preoccupation and more a re-flection of the same ardor that activated his love for language, the natural world, and other things that he appreciated with passion. The poems "Do Not Go Gentle into That Good Night" and "And Death Shall Have No Dominion" are expressions of his inclination to sing "like the sea" even while enchained by the inexorable passage of Time; they indicate his desire to overcome what John Tytell calls "the anguish of mutability" brought on by an awareness of Time's constant measure, to which he referred as a "running grave" always with him. The tremendous energy in poems like these, or in "The Force That Through the Green Fuse Drives the Flower," is a product of both dynamic rhythmic arrangements and Thomas' feeling that life is yet more sacred because of the inevitability of death. This kind of poem seems to have originated from a perspective prior to or beyond the era of technology.

The extreme body-consciousness and sensuality of Thomas' poetry also attest to a primal condition of apprehension. In the taut lyric "Twenty-four Years," his language bristles with the imagery of the skin, his life described as a "sensual strut," his course illuminated by the "meat-eating sun," his entrance into the world depicted as from "the groin of the natural doorway." In a letter to Johnson, Thomas wrote that what she called ugly was "nothing but the strong stressing of the physical," and that his images were drawn from "my solid and fluid world of flesh and blood." He praises John Donne's description of man as "earth of the earth" and insists that "all thoughts and actions emanate from the body." His eventual disregard for the welfare of his own body may have been as much a rebellion against limits as it was an example of wanton desecration, with his frequent references to sexual matters another illustra-tion of an interest in the fundamental facts of human biological imperatives.

The conjunction in Thomas' poetry of what Tytell calls "dense pockets of enig-matic surrealistic imagery" wrought from "a chaotic cauldron of language" with the great human themes of Time, Death, Nature, and the Skin frequently resulted in some poetic confusion. Early reviewers complained about "chaotic rhetoric" and "remarkable ineptness of technique." While some poems undoubtedly suffer from what Cid Corman calls "riddled meanings compiled in stubborn binding rhythms," it is important to recognize that the obscurity was not intentional or the product of carelessness or lack of craft. Many students have noted the evidence of the numerous work sheets that demonstrate Thomas' exhausting practice of writing a line again and again, revising and adjusting until he got what he wanted. Some poems took many months, gradually growing by a line or two added in a four-hour work session. In addition, Thomas was somewhat suspicious of what he thought of as free verse and employed both orthodox metrical patterns and a system based on syllabic count but independent of a regular stress pattern. No single system worked for him, and he eventually used what Daniel Jones calls "cadenced verse," which generally featured an alternation of weak and strong stresses, but which is much more elaborate in its juxtapositions of full rhymes, half rhymes, assonances, and alliterations.

While Thomas ultimately depended on the intricate, sensitive system of his own ear-mind-heart to create the singular, distinctive rhythmic arrangements of his best work, the various designs with which he experimented provided a point of departure, or a means of entrance, and they are a testament to his familiarity with, and dedication to, the complexity of measure in its largest sense. The strongest poems justify their form by their effectiveness and singularity; the less successful ones slide toward unintelligibility or call attention to their cleverness without transcending it. Nonetheless, in almost all of his work, Thomas' total commitment to poetry—his awareness of its possibilities, his passion for its substance—remains undeniable.

THE FORCE THAT THROUGH THE GREEN FUSE DRIVES THE FLOWER

First published: 1933
Type of work: Poem

The poet expresses his awe before the energizing forces of the cosmos and considers the interconnections between life and death.

Although Dylan Thomas was not especially eager to look back on the poems of his youth, "The Force That Through the Green Fuse Drives the Flower" was one of which he remained reasonably fond in later years. It was written in a burst of creative energy when Thomas was nineteen, possibly precipitated by the knowledge that his father had cancer and might not survive. The intensity of his feelings are captured by the propulsive power of the first line, which establishes a link between the awesome natural forces of the universe and the poetic consciousness of the young man who felt that his creative instincts were fired by the wonders of the world around him. When he declares that "the force"—a mystic surge of energy that animates and destroys—is the source of both the "green age" in which his youth glows with promise and the "wintry fever" that bends the "crooked rose," he has drawn the terms of the paradox that was to haunt him throughout his life. Even in the presence of life at its most vibrant, Thomas detected the signs of death, and the language that he uses in the poem is both destructive (dried streams, rotted roots) and fructuous (a mouth sucking life, pulsing red blood), joining the joys of passion with an anticipation of its eventual dispersal. The poet recognizes the immediacy of a moment of excitement and the realization that everything is temporary as "time has ticked a heaven round the stars."

The poem is particularly effective because both the passionate excitement and the premonition of extinction are powerfully evoked. The overwhelming rhythmic figure of the first line, typical of Thomas' ability to fashion a striking start almost impossible to extend or expand, conveys the feeling of uncontrollable motion engulfing and overpowering resistance. The poet has no choice but to submit and takes a fierce delight in his participation. Each stanza begins with a figure for this force, the third suggesting the "hand" of God, the fourth suggesting an incarnation of eternal progression. Then, the images of oblivion crowd the poet, undermining his exultation in the latent energy of the "green fuse," Thomas' symbol for the earth/ womb at the heart of creation. Blood turns to wax, the wind stirs a shroud, the clay (body) of the poet anticipates its eventual decay. The result of the juxtaposition of the dynamic and the arresting leads to a confusion that Thomas describes as an inability to say or speak ("And I am dumb"), an additional aspect of the paradox since the protestation of dumbness occurs in the poem to declare its condition. In response to the poet's proclamation of his difficulties in finding a language to describe the process of deterioration—an understandable situation since he directly experiences the life-giving component of the force but can only imagine its shattering side—a metaphysical tableau develops in the fourth stanza, which seems to suggest that some version of "Love" will ameliorate the effects of time's passage.

Since the poem is an investigation of the poet's involvement with the mysteries of existence, the language that engages these forces is more important than an explanation of their origins. The deft use of sound for emphasis, from the alliteration and repetition in the first line to the use of slant rhyme (sucks/wax/rocks; head/blood; sores/stars; womb/worm) to the rhythmic pulsation produced by the summary phrase, "And I," is evidence of Thomas' ability to make poetry that is intensely alive on the tongue and true to the emotional energy that drew it forth.

TWENTY-FOUR YEARS

First published: 1938
Type of work: Poem

The poet contemplates the inevitability of death and sets against it the eternal power of art, which animates his existence.

Because of his almost obsessive preoccupation with death, each birthday was a milestone that called for a celebration, and on several occasions, Thomas composed a poem that expresses his sense of where he stood as a man and an artist. "Twenty-four Years" is his earliest significant version of this celebratory mode, and it is full of both the exuberance of early manhood and his already familiar feeling that death was imminent. As Paul Ferris describes it, the poem is like an abrupt telegram in which a density of texture leads to a compactness that makes each line and image bristle with evocative power. The pattern of the poem is based on the oppositional tension that Thomas believed made a poem noteworthy, and the intermixture of life-enhancing and death-haunted declarations generates the tremendous energy that drives the poem (and the poet) on a journey toward "forever."

The first two lines are self-enclosed assertions of the poet's condition at the moment of creation. Thomas summarizes his life initially by epitomizing its somber qualities and stresses their importance by citing them as a constant source of sadness. Next, struggling to control his fears, he inserts as a chorus/comment the injunction to "bury the dead" so that their shade will not overwhelm everything else. There is a biblical echo in the second line as well, a suggestion that the prospect of death requires sympathy and compassion for a common human dread. Then, in a dynamic reversal of tone, Thomas matches the rhythms of the long second line with a sudden shift to the procreative, placing himself, in an echo of his birth, on the threshold of a poetic path or life-journey. In a riveting image, he sees the young poet "crouched" in a posture of readiness, prepared to leap into the light (one of his figures for creative work) of a "meat-eating sun." His location at the "groin of the natural doorway" fuses the sexual with the poetic; but the fecundity of this conception is immediately undermined by the comparison that the poet crouches "like a tailor/ Sewing a shroud"—that is, already preparing, at least subconsciously, for his demise since the light cast by the "meat-eating sun" has the potential for destruction, as well as for creation.

There follows a slight pause, although the poem does not typographically indicate its necessity. The syntax, however, compels a degree of reflective hesitancy before the poet continues his portrait. Although he is "dressed to die," his poetic life is almost arrogantly portrayed as a "sensual strut" in defiance of the aforementioned dead who "walk to the grave in labour." Thomas often uses the word "labor" to connote some kind of burden, and he is calling for a proud stride. The tone of confidence, even brashness, is continued by his claim that his "red veins" are "full of money." The poet is mocking his recognition that he would never have enough money from his poetry to live as he wished. He is also asserting that, in some utopian situation, "the elementary town," he could properly profit from his craft. The last lines of the poem extend this note of optimistic idealism. Calling his life/work an "advance," he insists that its "final direction" or ultimate goal is the time-defying, death-delaying of "forever." Whether this is a prediction, a plea, or just a series of bold words to combat his fear, the calm measure of certitude substantiates the artist's claims to be moving in the direction of eternity.

POEM IN OCTOBER

First published: 1945
Type of work: Poem

The poet seeks an appropriate arena in which to celebrate his birthday and recalls the delight that he took in the natural world as a boy.

Thomas wrote very few poems between the taut lyric of "Twenty-four Years," which marked "my birthday just arriving," and his famous celebration of what he designated his "thirtieth year to heaven"—the "Poem in October." In the intervening years of World War II, he was involved with film work in London, and he found that he was generally unable to compose poetry anywhere else but in the familiar home ground of his west Wales landscape. He began the poem in 1941, writing to his friend Vernon Watkins that the first line would be, "It was my twenty-seventh year to heaven" (using one syllable too many, as he must have sensed). He did not, however, complete it until he was again living in the cottage in Blaen Cwm, where he had written poetry since childhood.

During the summer of 1944, when he also wrote "Ceremony After a Fire Raid," "New Quay," and "Fern Hill," Thomas had reached a kind of midpoint in his life and realized that his tremendous excitement and feeling of wholeness in observation of the realm of nature might be receding beyond recollection. Both as a means of fixing this feeling permanently and as a strategy to remain in contact with one of the originating forces of his artistic passion, Thomas wrote what Donald Hall has called "a long and gorgeous rendition of weather and landscape, bird and water." What makes the poem so successful is the fact that the familiar sentiments of a very common human emotion have been placed in a form that is uniquely Thomas', and that the rhapsodic language at which Thomas excelled has rarely been as well suited to a subject.

There are two specific features of Thomas' style of composition notable in the poem. The first is his manner of constructing a frame in which details accumulate gradually while the narrative consciousness of the poet remains at a distance; then, when the full dimensions of the image have been developed, the poet's perspective on the scene is introduced. In the first stanza, Thomas follows the opening declaration ("my thirtieth year") with a series of sounds that are an invitation to the poet to join the waking world. Then, after the features of the harbor town have been recorded, Thomas gathers the poet, who has already expressed a proprietary interest by the use of the word "my" in the first and second line, into the scene in an immediate present narrative by summarizing "Myself to set foot/ that second" as he sets forth. This technique is used in many of the following stanzas, which are actually written as an extended, continuing line broken by divisions into separate subunits.

The second feature is Thomas' use of a kind of compound adjective, as in the well-known description of the seacoast as the "heron priested shore" where the "net webbed wall" marks the boundary of land and water. In later stanzas, he continues this practice with such figures as the "rain wringing wind" and a "lark full cloud" or a "blue altered sky"—the latter figure including a double-meaning recalling his lyric beginning in "Altarwise by Owl-Light."

The long rhythms of each stanza contribute to a song effect in which the interplay of rhyme, alliteration, and assonance within the line help to maintain a high energy level; each linguistic device is like a chime in a series of sonic highlights. The frequency of these sound pulses parallels the surges of excitement that the poet feels as he is overwhelmed by a display of nature's infinite variety, a phenomenon that he regards as a personal benediction, as if all he sees is a tribute to his being. "My birthday began," he starts the second stanza, as if the world is on show for him, and his description of an ascent from the harbor to the "hill's shoulder" is presented as a climb from birth through a life of "fond climates and sweet singers" toward a summit envisioned as a "wonder of summer."

The action of the poem in the first three stanzas proceeds upward beneath a "springful of larks in a rolling/ Cloud" in a journey that approximates Thomas' life before the intrusion of adult consciousness into the child's world of pure wonder. From the "parables/ Of sun light" through "twice told fields of infancy," Thomas' expressions of "the truth of his joy" as a youth are rendered with a purity of recall that places no distance between the sensation of the experience and its re-creation in the poem. Then, in a pivotal middle (fourth) stanza, there is a sudden shift as "the weather turned around." From this point, the recall of the adult is more like a review, in which the experience is seen again through the double perspective of the adult reflecting on the child's experiences. The motion now is reversed, so that the child begins to recede into memory. The focus of the second part of the poem is less a descent (for a youth, in the "sun born over and over," as Thomas puts it in "Fern Hill," there is no summit, merely the possibility of going higher). It is more an awareness now of precipitous possibilities. The goal of the adult poet is to keep the summit in sight.

The turning of the weather parallels the change of seasons from summer to autumn, indicating the passage to the poet's maturity that has occurred in the span of poetic time. There is also an added element of poignancy in the poet's recollections, because his awareness of death and time makes him even more sensitive to the temporary beauty of the natural world. The "twice told fields of infancy" relived in the double vision of the man in his thirtieth year permit the poet legitimately to claim of the boy that "his tears burned my cheeks and his heart moved in mine." The images of the poem wrought in Thomas' highly charged lyric language are a proof of this sentiment, a convincing demonstration through poetic art that "the mystery/ Sang alive/ Still." This peak of emotion is followed by a pause of reflection. The poet repeats that, amid his recapitulation of the marvelous, "the weather turned around," but that the poem itself has been the occasion for the "long dead child" to emerge and sing "burning in the sun" of a youth temporarily regained. As the poem concludes, Thomas fuses the two moments that he has celebrated, his "thirtieth year to heaven" and his "summer noon," by syntactically pulling the present and the past together. He revivifies the experience of the moment by describing the "town below . . . leaved with October blood"; the autumnal phase of the poet's life is still colored with the passion of creative action.

The final line is a universal prayer for favor and continuance from the forces of the universe. Yielding completely to the ultra-Romantic spirit of the poem, Thomas begins the last line (which is divided into a triad) with the unabashed "O" of countless effusions of feeling. His fervent wish is that his "heart's truth"—the sum of his desire as a man and a poet—will still be sufficient cause for him to "sing" (that is, to write poetry) from a position of strength and confidence ("on this high hill") when another year has passed. There is more than irony in this last wish, since Thomas often stated his fears that his days would be short. In accordance with the mood of the entire poem, he has let the "long dead child" speak at the close. Knowing quite well that he was enchained by circumstance and temperament, he could still choose, as he put it in his other great pastoral celebration of the same year, "Fern Hill," to "sing like the sea."

IN MY CRAFT OR SULLEN ART

First published: 1945
Type of work: Poem

The poet explains the conditions of composition and for whom he writes.

Along with the prologue that he wrote for the first edition of his *Collected Poems, 1934-1952* (1952), "In My Craft or Sullen Art" is a carefully designed declaration by Thomas of what he wanted the future to think of him as a poet. The conscious intent to shape his persona, however, does not betray his real convictions, though it tends to direct the reader toward certain areas of concern that he preferred to emphasize. The dual focus of the first line properly stresses the care for craft and the almost mystical connection to what Hall calls "a dark river flowing down there somewhere." Yet the use of the word "sullen" is a typically inspired choice, revealing the frustrating and unsatisfying aspects of the gift that he carried. The poem continues with the conventional Romantic emblem of the artist at work by night, his passion an antisocial one ("only the moon rages"), his energy drawn from the love/grief of humanity. It then turns abruptly to the kind of booming declaration of power that both Thomas and his audience treasured: "I labour by singing light," he proclaims. Then, in contradiction to most of the actions of his life and most of the more honest confessions of his poetry, he insists that it is not "the strut and trade of charms" that drives him, but the heart's truth that he has often celebrated. The mastery of rhythm and the powerful emphasis of careful rhyme are so seductive that the appealing message becomes the reality, although it is important to note that Thomas is actually speaking for some idealized poet as much as for himself.

The second stanza, which, like the first, is as much one long flowing line as it is separated shorter ones, continues the theme of the artist as social exile, denying an interest in political power ("the proud man") or posterity ("the towering dead"), while emphasizing again the call to poetic expression that originates in the heart's core. Using the technique of opposing forces, which he found to be one of his most successful structural devices, Thomas sets the superficial reasons for artistic endeavor in sufficiently impressive terms ("towering dead") that his ultimate commitment to "the lovers" becomes a heroic act of humanistic compassion channeled into poetic art. The relatively unselfish nature of this choice—the lovers "pay no praise or wages/ Nor heed my craft or art"—suggests the Romantic ideal of art for art's sake, which Thomas implies actually serves the interests of humanity in its support of "the lovers" since his craft/art springs from and validates the human need for love. As in the first stanza, the carefully controlled pattern of rhythmic emphasis and the sure ear for rhyme that makes its appearance inevitable instead of obligatory contribute to the seductive power of the song.

Summary

Even those writers who have strongly supported Dylan Thomas' work have had their reservations about his accomplishments. Yet the gradual recession of the legend of the wild bard into time and the postmodern regard for the possibilities of meaning in language beyond traditional conceptions of coherence have given Thomas' work an enduring appeal beyond many original estimates. His great love of language and his ear for the musical, rhythmic power of words produced a body of work that has solidified his stature in the history of English literature.

Bibliography

Brinnin, John Malcolm. *Dylan Thomas in America*. Boston: Little, Brown, 1955.
Corman, Cid. "For the Lovers (Dylan Thomas)." In *And Their Word: Essays on the*

Arts of Language. Santa Barbara, Calif.: Black Sparrow Press, 1978.

Ferris, Paul. *Dylan Thomas: A Biography*. New York: Dial Press, 1977.

Fitzgibbon, Constantine. *The Life of Dylan Thomas*. Boston: Little, Brown, 1965.

Gaston, Georg. *Dylan Thomas: A Reference Guide*. Boston: G. K. Hall, 1987.

Hall, Donald. "Dylan Thomas and Public Suicide." In *Remembering Poets: Reminiscences and Opinions*. New York: Harper & Row, 1977.

Thomas, Caitlin. *Life With Dylan Thomas*. New York: Henry Holt, 1987.

Thomas, Dylan. *Dylan Thomas: The Collected Letters*. Edited by Paul Ferris. New York: Paladin, 1987.

Tytell, John. "Dylan and Caitlin." In *Passionate Lives*. Secaucus, N.J.: Carol, 1991.

Leon Lewis

J. R. R. TOLKIEN

Born: Bloemfontein, South Africa
January 3, 1892
Died: Bournemouth, England
September 2, 1973

Principal Literary Achievement

Although popularly known as a fantasy novelist, Tolkien was also an important scholar of medieval English literature.

Biography

John Ronald Reuel Tolkien was born on January 3, 1892, in Bloemfontein, South Africa, to Arthur and Mabel Suffield Tolkien. His brother, Hilary, was born in 1894. Arthur Tolkien had emigrated to South Africa from England to head a bank and remained behind in 1895 when his family returned to England because of Ronald's health. Arthur's sudden death left the family near poverty. At first, Mrs. Tolkien lived outside Birmingham in the country, which delighted both boys, and educated the children at home. In 1900, against family tradition, she converted to Catholicism with her children. Most of Ronald's school education was at his father's old preparatory school in Birmingham, where he excelled in languages.

In November, 1904, after a year's illness, Mrs. Tolkien died from diabetes. A family friend, Father Francis Morgan, became the boys' guardian. Ronald continued to develop an interest in languages and literature. He met with school friends regularly to discuss their reading, including the Norse sagas whose spirit lies behind Tolkien's fiction. After initially failing a scholarship examination, perhaps because of his friendship with Edith Bratt, whom he later married, Tolkien won a scholarship to Exeter College, Oxford, which he entered in 1911. Morgan forcibly ended the relationship, extracting a promise from Tolkien not to see Edith until he was twenty-one.

In his first undergraduate years, he neglected Latin and Greek to study other languages, and consequently, after unimpressive examinations, he transferred to English studies. In early 1913, he was reunited with Edith, and they became engaged; she converted to Roman Catholicism. Tolkien continued his studies as World War I began, but entered military training with the University Officers' Training Corps. About the same time, he also composed some of the poetry included in *The Silmarillion* (1977). He was graduated in 1915, with first class honors in English, and a second lieutenancy. Before departing for military service in France in 1916, he married

Edith. Although uninjured, by November Tolkien had returned to England with a persistent fever. He continued to build the mythology of Middle-earth and to invent its language while convalescing. In November, 1917, the Tolkiens had their first child.

After a brief episode in Oxford contributing to *A New English Dictionary on Historical Principles* (1884-1928), in 1920 Tolkien began teaching at the University of Leeds. He and his wife had two more children while there, and Tolkien and E. V. Gordon produced the first modern edition of *Sir Gawain and the Green Knight* (1925). Later that year, he was elected professor of Anglo-Saxon at Oxford.

Tolkien's life at Oxford was that of a typical don: tutorials, lectures, committee service, and writing. It was enlivened, in the 1920's, by another child and by his friendship with C. S. Lewis. By 1926, he had accumulated a circle of friends, "The Inklings," including Lewis, who read the Icelandic sagas together. He continued to compose stories of Middle-earth and engage in serious scholarship. He was professionally active, speaking at a number of meetings, and 1936 brought acclaim for a British Academy lecture on *Beowulf* (c. sixth century).

Tolkien, Lewis, and other colleagues met regularly from the early 1930's to listen to and discuss one another's work. In 1937, Tolkien's storytelling to his children and the encouragement of his friends in The Inklings resulted in publication of *The Hobbit*, begun in 1930. In 1938, as a follow-up to *The Hobbit*, Tolkien wrote *Farmer Giles of Ham*, although, because of the war, it remained unpublished until 1949. His publishers urged him to write another Hobbit book, but the project slowly became enormous and complex, emerging as *The Lord of the Rings* (1955; includes *The Fellowship of the Ring*, 1954; *The Two Towers*, 1954; *The Return of the King*, 1955).

The war years brought professional responsibilities that delayed Tolkien's writing. Delaying him, also, were painstaking habits of revision to produce a consistent text. As he labored over *The Lord of the Rings*, he also elaborated the "invented languages" created for *The Silmarillion* as he "discovered" new races in Middle-earth. A series of obstacles, including a family move to a new residence and election as the Merton Professor of English Language and Literature, slowed his work.

Although a draft of *The Lord of the Rings* was substantially complete by 1947, misunderstandings and the publisher's reluctance to accept such a large work delayed acceptance until 1952. Allen & Unwin offered Tolkien an unusual profit-sharing arrangement; he accepted, and the first volume appeared in 1954. Reviews were generally either enthusiastic or sharply critical; sales far exceeded expectations. To his surprise, Tolkien's profits from the book enabled him to retire from teaching in 1959. Over the next few years emerged *The Adventures of Tom Bombadil* (1962), *Tree and Leaf* (1964), and *Smith of Wooton Major* (1967).

After Tolkien and his wife had spent forty-two years in Oxford, Edith's arthritis led the couple to move to Bournemouth in 1968. Tolkien continued to work on *The Silmarillion* after his wife's death in 1971, when he moved back to Merton College, Oxford, as an honorary fellow. In 1972, Queen Elizabeth named him a Commander of the Order of the British Empire, and Oxford awarded him an honorary doctorate of letters. While visiting Bournemouth in 1973, he became ill from an unsuspected ulcer, developed an infection, and died in the hospital on September 2.

Analysis

Tolkien's interest in fantasy began with his childhood curiosity about languages. Later, his professional linguistic training enabled him to create a Middle-earth in which cultural differences are significant. In the essay "On Fairy-Stories," however, he suggests what underlay this curiosity. In the traditional tales of the past, readers could explore "Faërie: the Perilous Realm itself":

> The magic of Faërie is not an end in itself, its virtue is in its operations: among these are the satisfaction of certain primordial human desires. One of these is to survey the depths of space and time. Another is . . . to hold communion with other living things. A story may thus deal with the satisfaction of these desires, with or without the operation of either machine or magic, and in proportion as it succeeds it will approach the quality and have the flavour of fairy-story.

Two key phrases, "survey the depths of space and time" and "hold communion with other living things," suggest the direction of his own fiction. He believed that imaginative participation in stories was possible only when an author invested his creation with a rich, overlaid texture of history, geography, and culture. *The Lord of the Rings* exemplifies Tolkien's intent, set as it is in a world embedded in millennia of history, enriched by an enormous variety of creatures. To borrow Tolkien's phrase, he engaged in "sub-creation":

> What really happens is that the story-maker proves a successful "sub-creator." He makes a Secondary World which your mind can enter. Inside it, what he relates is "true": it accords with the laws of that world. You therefore believe it, while you are, as it were, inside.

The true extent of Tolkien's vision lay undiscovered until the publication of *The Silmarillion*, followed by subsequent volumes of unfinished tales edited by his son Christopher. Readers glimpsed this faintly in the six appendices to *The Return of the King* (1955), which trace events in Middle-earth back several millennia.

Tolkien discusses other "primordial desires" that fantasy may satisfy: "Recovery," "Escape," and "Consolation." Because fantasy allows readers to contemplate alternatives to the present, it may offer hope for change. "Recovery,"—" 'seeing things as we are (or were) meant to see them'—as things apart from ourselves"—means recapturing the sense of wonder, dulled by familiarity, inherent in everyday life. "Escape" refers to the human need to escape threat to life and humane values. "By "Consolation," Tolkien suggests that stories that nurture communicate the hope that human suffering will end, that happy endings come unexpectedly, a "eucatastrophe," a "good disaster," providentially delivered.

This emphasis on the affective purpose of fiction separated Tolkien from contemporary stylistic experimentalists and realists. His fiction looks to the past, as is implied in an audience's "Recovery," their regaining something lost. Recapturing a sense of wonder in the natural world, reaffirming the values of human life, occur in examining a simpler age. In *The Lord of the Rings*, "progress," technology, machinery, and the destruction of nature are linked to evil. Tolkien's protagonists from another age uphold values that appear outmoded yet impart a sense of dignity, purpose, and resolve. While some readers find the heroic language and formality of epic adventures foreign, these stylistic elements seem essential to Tolkien's imaginative purposes.

Tolkien's reliance on Norse and Old English mythology may account for the novels' heroic atmosphere. The names of many locations and characters and the many "manufactured" words of his fiction are borrowed from the sagas. As an example, *The Song of the Seeress*, an anonymous tenth century Icelandic poem, contains the names of fifteen of Tolkien's characters, including Gandalf. This reliance on the Norse sagas may also explain the "unheroic" endings of the stories once victory is accomplished. In stories such as *Beowulf*, characters always seem aware of ultimate defeat in heroic conflict. Beowulf may kill Grendel, but the dragon will await him in old age.

The Hobbit and *The Lord of the Rings* are both very traditional "quest" adventures, in which an untried or uninitiated youth leaves a protected and secure environment to make a journey. The journey may lead to treasure (*The Hobbit*) or to knowledge and glory (*The Lord of the Rings*), but tests and trials await. Success depends on making correct choices and acquiring wisdom; it may lead to disillusionment, too, and reassessment of youthful ideals. The successful return home yields both honor and the need to change the society in which one grew up. Eden does not remain Eden. This mythic pattern, that of all stories from the heroic age, Tolkien makes new in his novels.

In Tolkien's novels, readers identify with one very ordinary figure, against the backdrop of heroic adventures. Tolkien's "hobbits" fulfill this function. Hobbits are intruders into the heroic world, with "little or no magic about them," cheerful, youthful, and unreflective, lacking a role in the heroic past. The victories of the heroes in the foreground, however, are impossible without the actions of the hobbits. Readers may admire the heroic Aragorn, but they identify with the struggles of Frodo. In *The Lord of the Rings*, this literally becomes two stories, as Tolkien alternates between Frodo's struggle and Aragorn's.

Tolkien's stories are surprisingly complex morally. In an age of adventure fiction, where personal decisions seem to have no moral consequences, all of his characters confront serious moral issues. Hobbits, in particular, are shown making consciously moral choices. Bilbo's decisions in *The Hobbit* lead him to reject his companions' greed, even at the cost of their friendship. Frodo's successful quest entails physical loss and ongoing pain and humility of personal failure. Good never triumphs without cost.

THE HOBBIT

First published: 1937
Type of work: Novel

A band of dwarfs, one hobbit, and one magician recover the dwarfs' treasure from a dragon.

Tolkien's *The Hobbit*, a story that has appealed to adults as well as children, provides the background to his larger work, *The Lord of the Rings*. All of these works find their place in the even larger series of stories on which Tolkien had been working from the 1920's, and which were published posthumously by his son Christopher. Tolkien peopled his stories of Middle-earth with a number of traditional fictional races, including elves, dwarfs, and trolls, as well as "orcs," goblins created by sorcery. The hobbit of the title is Bilbo Baggins, representative of a quiet, unadventurous race living in the Shire, in the west of Middle-earth. Gandalf the magician lures Bilbo, who is more adventurous than he himself thinks, into joining a group of dwarfs. They are determined to return to their home, the Lonely Mountain, kill the dragon Smaug, and recover their lost treasure and homeland. After a number of initial adventures in which Bilbo shows his resourcefulness, they are trapped in a cave by a storm in the Misty Mountains. Caught by orcs and goblins, only Gandalf's magic saves them. During their escape, Bilbo is separated from the group, knocked unconscious, and meets Gollum, a strange cave dweller. This juncture is the turning point of the story; without the help of others, Bilbo must defeat an opponent who will literally eat him if he loses. Providentially, Bilbo has found a ring that Gollum has lost, and after a riddle contest, which Bilbo wins, the hobbit can use the ring's powers of invisibility to make his escape. Eventually, Bilbo makes his way out and rejoins his companions; they continue to travel eastward. The ring proves its usefulness repeatedly on the way, as the supposedly experienced and mature dwarfs blunder into every danger they meet.

Although Tolkien plays with the elements of many serious traditional tales—magic rings, invisibility, and threatening opponents, including spiders—he creates an adventure that is generally cheerful and humorous. The ring eventually makes the protagonists' success possible, but its use often occasions comedy. With it, Bilbo, though awestruck by events, can act decisively and courageously when necessary. One element appealing to most readers is this picture of Bilbo, neglected, disregarded, literally small, and symbolically unimaginative, triumphing over hostile elves, humans, dragons, and cranky dwarfs.

His integrity and honesty also lead to his role in mediating a serious crisis between the dwarfs and their human neighbors. In the climactic scenes in the novel, Bilbo must demonstrate a maturity unseen earlier. Smaug has left the mountain, seeking revenge for Bilbo's theft of a cup. The dragon attacks and destroys a human city, Lake-Town, and is killed. When the humans who remain seek some share in the wealth—they, after all, killed the dragon—the dwarfs' greed gets the better of them. They blockade the mountain against their former friends. It is left to Bilbo to find a means of mediating peace. Unknown to the dwarfs, he has found and kept a jewel, the Arkenstone, which they have sought. Bilbo's gift of it to Gandalf and the leaders of Lake-Town forces the dwarfs to concede. This development results in a union of the allies against a powerful force of wolves and orcs. Though he is not a typical warrior, Bilbo plays his role as discoverer and mediator, very pragmatically getting done what needs doing. At the novel's end, Bilbo, now wealthy, but, more significant, imaginative and self-confident, returns to the Shire.

The Hobbit has many of the elements of a children's story, as befits its origin: a narrative persona sounding much like an adult telling a story to children, some humorous comments along the way suggesting the follies of the dwarfs, and a proper seriousness about evil. The figure of Bilbo, invisible with his ring, lurking about various castles and wastelands, and eventually in Smaug's cave, is the mischief of the sort that children enjoy. At least one element of the children's story that is retained in *The Lord of the Rings*—though most others are not—is the sense of a providential order that leads to the rescue of the companions. Twice in the novel, Gandalf and the dwarfs are in difficult straits and are rescued by giant eagles who are indebted to Gandalf. At one point, Gandalf returns opportunely to delay three trolls long enough for them to be transformed into stone by the sunrise. Elsewhere, the ring itself seems a tool provided by providence to accomplish the necessary task. Until the story's end, none of the dwarfs, Bilbo, or Gandalf is even injured. Only the final battle insists that this is a more dangerous world than Bilbo has seen before.

THE LORD OF THE RINGS

First published: *The Fellowship of the Ring*, 1954; *The Two Towers*, 1954;
The Return of the King, 1955
Type of work: Novels

Long ago, men, elves, dwarfs, hobbits, and magicians battle to destroy a magic ring and end the power of its maker.

Twenty years of continued sub-creation mark the difference in tone and design of *The Hobbit* and *The Lord of the Rings*. *The Hobbit*'s paternal narrative voice is missing, so that almost from the opening of the trilogy the reader is aware that the issues of the novel are greater.

Tolkien's trilogy has spawned dozens of multivolume quest fantasies using a medieval setting. They range from Ursula K. Le Guin's Earthsea Trilogy (1968-1973) to Stephen R. Donaldson's *Chronicles of Thomas Covenant the Unbeliever* (1977) to

Marion Zimmer Bradley's extended Darkover series (1972-1988). Each of these authors, including Tolkien, incorporates a theological element into the adventure story. Most appeal to the audience Tolkien awakened, and each has captured a share of a growing market for such fiction. Yet few succeed in the task of sub-creation. Tolkien offers readers that possibility for "communion with other living things" that he claims all humans desire, in a world in which differing races have well-documented histories, languages capable of a range of poetic expression, and differing cultural assumptions. To some extent, too, Tolkien succeeds because one can imagine life apart from adventure in Middle-earth.

The Fellowship of the Ring, like *The Hobbit*, begins in innocence. Although the Shire, Gandalf, and Bilbo reappear, almost immediately the story changes direction. Bilbo, sixty years older, surrenders the ring of invisibility to his nephew Frodo and rejoins the elves. After an interval of some years, which Tolkien compresses, Gandalf returns to announce that Frodo holds the One Ring, forged by the magician Sauron, which both empowers its wearer and tempts the wearer to exercise that power selfishly. No one can wear it safely.

Frodo, like Bilbo apparently undistinguished, unimaginative, decent, fair, and quietly stubborn, is the audience's vantage point for the story. Circumstances demand that he outgrow his hobbit isolationism, indeed, offer himself without reserve or selfishness for a whole world that he does not know. His travels take him out of the Shire and into a land utterly threatening; he is betrayed by a companion, offers forgiveness and redemption to another who betrays him, and carries a burden no good person in the novel can endure. Throughout the novel, he battles the power of the ring itself, which tempts him to use it; he also carries the burden of knowing that his success will mean that the world will change, and some of its goodness, as well as much of its evil, will diminish. In Frodo, Tolkien explores the recurring theme of substitutionary love: Some must be willing to offer their lives that others might live. His quest reverses the movement of the earlier novel; the ring, once found, must now be destroyed in the place of its forging, deep within Sauron's kingdom, Mordor.

Accompanied by several hobbits, Frodo leaves the Shire for Rivendell, acquiring along the way a human companion, the ranger Aragorn, known as Strider. Pursued, Frodo is wounded in battle before they arrive safely at Rivendell. A council representing all civilization—elves, dwarfs, humans, and hobbits—eventually agrees that the One Ring must be destroyed. That can happen only if it is returned to the place of its making, deep within Mordor. Representatives of the four kindreds agree to accompany Frodo on the journey.

A contrasting quest emerges when one of Frodo's human companions, Aragorn, declares himself the heir of the throne of Minas Tirith, the city that has opposed Mordor for millennia. As Frodo is the naïve initiate, Aragorn is the experienced warrior assuming a heroic challenge of his own. In Aragorn, Tolkien awakens Frodo and the audience to that desire "to survey the depths of space and time," for Aragorn represents a tradition and race coming from a forgotten age of the world, from the land of Numenor.

Before the first volume ends, Tolkien has succeeded in opening to Frodo and his hobbit companions an awareness of a larger world, both older and more varied than they have known. He has also suggested the capacity for growth and heroism in the unheroic, as Frodo has been wounded and has accepted the possibility of death in his willingness to take the ring to Mordor.

The Lord of the Rings is most often remembered for its scenes of adventure, particularly the heroic language of warriors confronting their foes. From the first volume onward, however, Tolkien establishes a rhythm of adventure and reflection that serves several purposes. His characters are not always journeying. In *The Fellowship of the Ring*, for example, Frodo and his companions are entertained both at Rivendell and at the secret retreat of the elves in Lothlorien. The threat of evil to destroy such places is heightened by the enjoyment and tranquillity that these places provide to their inhabitants. Tolkien undoubtedly employed such settings for this purpose, but they serve another equally important role in the narrative, as some of the film and cartoon versions of these stories make evident. *The Lord of the Rings* is not only about adventure but about preserving a world, rescuing and maintaining what is good in that world. Rivendell, Lothlorien, and the Shire are the "real world," where people live, rather than the landscape of adventure through which they travel. Moments of heightened enjoyment simply in a good meal, a song, companionship around the table or the fire, exemplify what the heroes are called upon to preserve. The filmed versions of these stories omit such moments entirely, leaving the story an extended and unrelieved battle.

The magnitude of the opposing evil forces is demonstrated first in Gandalf's apparent death in the dwarf kingdom of Moria and second in the treachery of Boromir, of Minas Tirith, who yields to the temptation of the ring and demands it from Frodo. Boromir's seduction by the desire for the power of the ring is also the first instance of an ongoing theme, which comes to dominate the action of the last half of the trilogy. Where evil does not blast goodness utterly, it may twist it or seduce it. The "fellowship" ends with Boromir's death at the hands of Sauron's orcs, who seize two of the hobbits. Frodo and his hobbit friend Sam Gamgee leave the others, attempting to make their way toward Mordor.

Tolkien himself dismissed the notion of the trilogy form, noting that readers must look to the six books of the story. Each volume contains two separate narratives, and in the two final volumes, Aragorn's story makes up books 3 and 5, while Frodo's story occupies books 4 and 6.

In *The Two Towers*, the second volume, Tolkien alternates between the two groups of now-divided companions: Aragorn, the elf Legolas, and Gimli the dwarf pursue the kidnappers of the two hobbits, while Frodo and Sam make their way toward Mordor. This journey allows Tolkien an opportunity to explore the geography of Middle-earth further and to introduce other inhabitants of Middle-earth. Other nonhuman races appear, such as the treelike Ents, who shepherd an entire forest. In *The Two Towers*, both characters confront evil from Sauron. Aragorn's confrontation with evil is conventional: He and his companions must defeat an army directed by the wizard

Saruman, allied now with Sauron. The heroic battle at Helm's Deep, the stronghold of the forces of good, is one of the most successful battle narratives Tolkien created.

The conclusion of the book pits Gandalf, returned from death, against Saruman, as Saruman attempts to win over his opponents by his persuasive gifts. The power Saruman still holds, and the depth of his betrayal, contrast with Gandalf's insight and rejection of selfishness. In book 3, Tolkien has set up very obvious tensions. Against Aragorn's and Gandalf's years of obscurity and service to others is set the treachery of the wizard Saruman, allied with Sauron to increase his own power. Paralleled as well are groups of lesser figures, such as the Rohirrim, a kingdom of horsemen whose culture seems descended from stories like *Beowulf* (c. sixth century). Having helped lead their defense, Aragorn wins the support of the Rohirrim as he moves toward Minas Tirith. By contrast, Saruman's allies, the morally and physically deformed orcs, serve him for treasure and because of fear. Their defeat and Saruman's downfall depend on the joint efforts of free humans, dwarfs, elves, magicians, and Ents.

On Frodo's journey, the power of evil is brought home repeatedly. Sauron has desolated the landscape around Mordor, and inside the "Land of Shadow," little grows but brambles. Frodo discovers the potential for evil within himself, as well, and its effects on those who serve it. One of these is Gollum, who lost the ring to Bilbo originally. In the process, Tolkien reveals that Gollum was once a hobbit, or close cousin, who through his centuries of possession of the ring has been warped and changed beyond recognition. He has shadowed Frodo since he left the Shire, seeking to reclaim the ring. Book 4 shows Frodo subduing and winning his allegiance and compassionately sparing him. Gollum guides Frodo and Mordor, though he leads Frodo into a trap as the book ends.

In *The Return of the King*, Tolkien continues his divided story, first tracing Gandalf's entrance to Minas Tirith (book 5), and the defense of that city against the enemy, then shifting to Aragorn's part in the action to relieve the city. Tolkien continues to add to his cast of characters with the defenders of Minas Tirith, among whom is Denethor, Boromir's father. He, too, has battled against Sauron, with one of the "seeing stones," the Palantir, which enable the user to become aware of actions at a distance. Sauron, however, as he has used one of the stones to seduce Saruman, so deceives Denethor that he despairs of victory. In the final battle, he commits suicide, another example of the ability of evil to spoil even those committed to good. After the victory, the heroic action draws to a climax with the anticipated final confrontation between Sauron's forces and the allies.

As the allies confront Sauron's forces for a decisive battle, Tolkien breaks off to begin book 6, tracing Frodo and Sam's journey to Mount Doom. Although brief by comparison with book 5—and necessarily brief, in that the reader is waiting for the resolution of the conflict—book 6 seems much longer. After rescuing Frodo from orcs in Mordor, Sam accompanies his master across miles of wasteland in semidarkness to reach volcanic Mount Doom. They encounter orcs moving at Sauron's command and discover the truth of the biblical proverb, "A house divided against itself cannot stand." Within Mordor, Sauron's troops bicker, attack, and murder one another. A kingdom based upon selfishness must fall. Yet, after the journey, Frodo's courage fails him. Once at Mount Doom, he claims the ring for his own. The theme of the seductiveness of power is never more fully demonstrated than when the "ordinary" individual chooses power and self-fulfillment rather than the good of others. In an entirely satisfying moment, sudden and unexpected, Gollum reappears and battles Frodo, eventually biting off finger and ring together, only to perish in the volcano. The "happy ending" out of disaster, which Tolkien calls "eucatastrophe," is both carefully prepared for and felt as entirely providential. Victory both at Minas Tirith and in the final battle occurs because "unheroic," disregarded individuals rise to the heroic challenge.

Tolkien concludes with the elegiac tone of the last episode of *Beowulf.* Aragorn's triumph renews a tradition descended from the earliest ages of the world, but he will eventually die. Frodo's destruction of the ring has both ensured victory and weakened the power that sustains the elves, so that they must depart Middle-earth. Frodo's return home with his companions is also blighted by Saruman's oppression of the Shire; even the most peaceful land in Middle-earth has suffered.

Summary

The popularity of J. R. R. Tolkien's fantasies testifies to the frustrations felt by many of his readers. Modern technological life isolates humans from nature and from one another, and diminishes the "otherness," the sense of the world as marvelous. Tolkien's response was to present a world so compellingly envisioned that both perils and marvels, joys and sorrows seem understandable and real. In the stories, as in real life, ordinary characters must make significant moral choices. In the happy endings of his stories, Tolkien responds to another felt need, the sense that no ultimate purpose exists to make human suffering meaningful.

Bibliography

Carpenter, Humphrey. *Tolkien: A Biography.* London: Allen & Unwin, 1977.

Flieger, Verlyn. *Splintered Light: Logos and Language in Tolkien's World.* Grand Rapids, Mich.: Wm. B. Eerdmans, 1983.

Helms, Randel. *Tolkien and the Silmarils.* Boston: Houghton Mifflin, 1981.

Isaacs, Neil D., and Rose A. Zimbardo, eds. *Tolkien: New Critical Perspectives.* Lexington: University Press of Kentucky, 1981.

Noel, Ruth S. *The Mythology of Middle-Earth.* Boston: Houghton Mifflin, 1977.

Rogers, Deborah Webster, and Ivor A. Rogers. *J. R. R. Tolkien.* Boston: Twayne, 1980.

Salu, Mary, and Robert T. Farrell, eds. *J. R. R. Tolkien: Scholar and Storyteller.* Ithaca, N.Y.: Cornell University Press, 1979.

Shippey, T. A. *The Road to Middle-Earth.* Boston: Houghton Mifflin, 1982.

Tyler, J. E. A. *The Tolkien Companion.* New York: St. Martin's Press, 1976.

Richard J. Sherry

LEO TOLSTOY

Born: Yasnaya Polyana, Russia
September 9, 1828
Died: Astapovo, Russia
November 20, 1910

Principal Literary Achievement

One of the greatest novelists of the nineteenth century, Tolstoy in later life became world-famous as a social and religious prophet.

Biography

Leo Tolstoy (Count Lev Nikolayevich Tolstoy) was born at his family estate, Yasnaya Polyana, about 130 miles southwest of Moscow, Russia, on September 9, 1828. His parents came from illustrious, aristocratic families accustomed to spending time at the court of the czar. His mother, Princess Marya Volkonsky, was the daughter of Prince Nikolay Volkonsky, a son of the Enlightenment, who had encouraged her to learn French and read French philosophers, particularly Jean-Jacques Rousseau. His father was Count Nikolay Tolstoy, who served in the Russian army when Napoleon I invaded Russia. Tolstoy lost both of his beloved parents by the time he was nine years old, thus ending his idyllic childhood at home. Until he was able to establish his own family at Yasnaya Polyana, Tolstoy dreamed of the lost days when his four brothers and sister lived in happiness, following the old Russian traditions. Throughout his life, his estate became an ideal in his mind.

After the death of his parents, Tolstoy lived with his aunt and attended school in Kazan. Aspiring to be a diplomat, he entered the Department of Oriental Languages at the University of Kazan; the following year, he changed his mind and entered law school. Diplomacy and law were not to be his future careers, however; instead, Tolstoy had begun writing a diary, an activity that he would continue until his death. Boris Eikhenbaum calls the diaries the laboratory in which Tolstoy perfected his writing craft and investigated moral concerns that troubled him. Tolstoy also began a rigorous reading program that included Russian classics, French novels, Charles Dickens, the New Testament, Voltaire, and his favorite, Jean-Jacques Rousseau.

Tolstoy's academic career was cut short at age nineteen, when he gained legal control of Yasnaya Polyana. Returning to the family estate, he tried to help the peasants by opening a school for children. His efforts failed because he was spending his time in debauchery. His brother, in an attempt to save him from ruin, convinced him to

accompany him to the Caucasus. Tolstoy volunteered to serve in the Russian army and was stationed in a remote Cossack village. Far from his favorite distractions—wine, women, and gambling—he devoted himself to writing and composed his first work, *Detstvo* (1852; *Childhood*, 1862), whose publication attracted the attention of the famous Russian novelists Ivan Turgenev and Fyodor Dostoevski. When the Crimean War broke out, Tolstoy fought in the Fourth Bastion at Sevastopol in 1855. Out of his wartime experiences, he wrote *Sevastopolskiye rasskazy* (1855-1856; *Sebastopol*, 1887), which depicted war in such realistic, bloody detail that Czar Alexander II gave orders that Tolstoy's life be protected.

Returning home after the Crimean War, Tolstoy found himself a military and literary hero. At Yasnaya Polyana, he tried to resume his old way of life by improving the lot of his peasants and teaching their children. He also decided that he wanted to marry and found a suitable candidate on a neighboring estate. Sophia Andreyevna Behrs (Sonya) was an eighteen-year-old girl, who, as a child, had memorized passages from Tolstoy's *Childhood* and *Otrochestvo Boyhood* (1854, 1886). They married on September 23, 1862. In the early days of his marriage, Tolstoy wrote to his Aunt Alexandra, "I didn't think it was possible to be so much in love and so happy." Yet, after the honeymoon was over, the marriage, which lasted forty-eight years and produced thirteen children, nine of whom survived, was tumultuous.

Tolstoy's greatest literary works, *Voyna i mir* (1865-1869; *War and Peace*, 1886) and *Anna Karenina* (1875-1878; English translation, 1886), were written during the first decade and a half of the marriage. Sonya proved to be a valuable partner in this enterprise. Between childbirths, she not only copied *War and Peace* seven times but also functioned as a critically astute reader.

After laboring so long on *War and Peace*, Tolstoy was near collapse by the time its serial publication was completed in 1869. His state of mind was further worsened as he began working on his next novel, *Anna Karenina*. He was distressed by the theme of the novel, the dissolution of a family, and struggled to finish the work. When the book's final installment appeared in 1878, the work as a whole met with great critical and popular acclaim. Unfortunately, Tolstoy was unable to enjoy the book's success. During this period, his beloved surrogate mother, Aunt Toinette, and two of his children died. At the age of fifty, at the height of his powers, he entered the darkest period of his life, filled with religious doubts, the fear of death, and spiritual emptiness. Fearing that he might commit suicide, he avoided guns, ropes, and knives.

Ispoved (1884; *A Confession*, 1885) documents his search through philosophy, religion, and the sciences for some answers to his spiritual malaise. He found some solace in the example of simple Russian peasants, who lived a rough, hardworking life close to nature. He also turned to Christianity and devised his own pragmatic five commandments: avoid anger, avoid lust, never take an oath, never resist evil, and love even your enemies.

In 1881, Tolstoy and his family moved to Moscow so that his children could receive a formal education. Tolstoy was deeply moved by the poverty that he saw in the slums of Moscow and attempted to ameliorate the conditions of the poor. When famine devastated Russia in 1891-1892, he organized relief efforts and established centers that fed sixteen thousand people daily. Beginning in 1880, Tolstoy devoted nearly all of his efforts to social, religious, and political causes outside literature. As he became world famous for his moral stances, disciples were drawn to Yasnaya Polyana. Sonya deeply resented these intruders, whom she called "the dark people." Sonya's dissatisfaction with her husband's withdrawal from family life increased in 1883 when Tolstoy met Vladimir Chertkov, who shared many of his social beliefs and encouraged him in publishing ventures that included producing books cheaply so that the poor could afford to buy them. The publication of "Smert Ivana Ilicha" ("The Death of Ivan Ilyich") briefly convinced Sonya that Tolstoy had not abandoned literature, thus assuring her that he would continue to provide for his family. Nevertheless, in 1891 Tolstoy renounced all the rights to his works published after 1881 and gave away all of his property to his wife and nine children. Sonya was still not satisfied and wanted more of the proceeds from his works.

Tolstoy was also contending with religious and political authorities. In *Voskreseniye* (1899; *Resurrection*, 1899), he attacked the Russian Orthodox Church and its leading official, who subsequently excommunicated Tolstoy. In a letter to Czar Nicholas II, titled "Dear Brother," Tolstoy urged reforms, warning that the Russian people were on the verge of rebellion. In "The Significance of the Russian Revolution," Tolstoy recommended that Prime Minister Pyotr Stolypin abolish the private ownership of property.

The end of Tolstoy's life was marred by the struggles of Sonya and Chertkov over his will and diaries. Wakened one night to hear his wife rifling through his papers in his study, Tolstoy decided to flee his home. He wrote his wife a letter thanking her for the forty-eight years of married life that they had shared and asking for mutual forgiveness. In his flight, pneumonia forced him to halt at the railroad station at Astapovo, Russia. He died in the stationmaster's house on November 20, 1910.

Analysis

Tolstoy displayed two distinctive attitudes toward art during his long career as a writer. During his early years, he believed that contemporary events, such as the emancipation of women and political reforms, were not the proper subject for art. In a letter to Peter Boborykin in 1865, Tolstoy claimed that art's goals are "incommensurate with social goals." Art, instead, should "force people to love life in all its innumerable, inexhaustible manifestations." Tolstoy's descriptions of Natasha at her first grand ball or Nicholas Rostov on the wolf hunt in *War and Peace* illustrate how magnificently he achieved these artistic goals. His inspiration flowed whenever he was writing about his own past and that of his family. His parents were the models for Nicholas Rostov and Marya Bolkonsky; his wife's family was the prototype for the Rostovs; his wife's sister, Tanya, became Natasha Rostov; he put himself into the characters of Pierre Bezuhkov and Prince Andrew; and Yasnaya Polyana transformed itself into Bald Hills. The past provided a buffer zone in which distant memories could be transposed into art.

He lost his detachment when he began writing *Anna Karenina*, according to Tolstoy's biographer A. N. Wilson. No longer processing past memories, he had to draw on contemporary themes, especially on his own life experiences as he lived them. This mode of operation was extremely painful; he was writing about the dissolution of a marriage in *Anna Karenina*, just as he and his wife were engaging in bitter feuds. Tolstoy believed in general that adultery was a repugnant topic with no redeeming value. In a letter to Nicholas Strakhov in 1875, Tolstoy writes, "My God, if only someone would finish *Anna Karenina* for me! It's unbearably repulsive."

After *Anna Karenina* was completed, Tolstoy turned away from fiction; no great novels would ever again issue from his pen, though he subsequently wrote some good short stories and a novel, *Resurrection*. As a sign that his creative energy was gone, Tolstoy failed to continue his saga of the Decembrists that he had begun in *War and Peace* and eventually abandoned it forever.

By the time that Tolstoy published *Chto takoye iskusstvo* (1898; *What Is Art?*, 1898), he had long entered his second period as a writer and abandoned his original conception that art should make people love life. He now believed that the artist should be socially responsible and write works that would inspire the people to live Christian lives. In *What Is Art?*, Tolstoy cites as an example his experience at a rehearsal for an opera. Observing a harried stagehand, he reflects on the downtrodden masses who must labor behind the scenes for the pleasure of the decadent bourgeoisie. He concludes that high culture and its institutions are elitist, exploit the people, and offer nothing of value to them. In contrast, art "flowing from love of God" would nourish the souls of all people.

There is much to value in Tolstoy's views, but, unfortunately, his feelings toward art tend to be totalitarian. For example, he condemns artistic works that do not fit his criteria and authors, such as the Greek tragedians, William Shakespeare, John Milton, and Dante Alighieri, of whom he does not approve. The publication of *What Is Art?* discomfited Tolstoy's European and American readers, who felt that he had become "a dragon" standing in the path of modern art.

Attempts to interpret Tolstoy's views often emphasize a perceived conflict in his nature. Edward Wasiolek in *Tolstoy's Major Fiction* (1978) argues that "Tolstoy's creative and ideational worlds are of one cloth." That is, Tolstoy in his greatest fictional works attempts to bridge the gap between the world of the flesh and the world of the spirit, not separate the two. He sought for a unifying principle that would incorporate both.

In fact, the search for a unifying principle was a common link among the great nineteenth century Russian novelists such as Dostoevski and Turgenev. Their preoccupation with the spiritual lives of their characters was attributable, in part, to their upbringing in the Orthodox Church. That they were neither Protestant nor Catholic produced in them a different conception of the novel's function. The Western churches developed under a tradition of the *disputatio*, based on the practice of medieval scholastics who debated one side of an issue and then the other. The Orthodox Church, on the other hand, urged its followers to practice the *kenotic* ideal and unquestioningly imitate the life of Christ. As a result, the forum for theological debate in Russia took place, not in its churches, where dissent was not allowed, but in the more intellectually open forum of the novel. Almost all the novels of Dostoevski and Tolstoy, for example, center on spiritual quests. While on these quests, the characters speculate on the existence of God, their place in the universe, and the right way to live. In this context, Tolstoy's novels are, as he says in his defense, exactly "what the author wished and was able to express in the form in which it is expressed."

WAR AND PEACE

First published: *Voyna i mir*, 1865-1869 (English translation, 1886)
Type of work: Novel

A young Russian nobleman searches for the meaning of life in the salons of high society and on the battlefield of Borodino during the Napoleonic wars.

War and Peace, arguably the greatest novel ever written, chronicles the alternating periods of war and peace in Russia during the first two decades of the nineteenth century. Tolstoy intended to write the story of a man returning home from exile in Siberia in 1856. The man had been a Decembrist, a member of an enlightened revolutionary movement seeking constitutional reform in Russia, before czarist forces suppressed it in December, 1825. In order to understand his hero, Tolstoy decided that he first had to write about the man's youth: thus, the story begins in July, 1805.

The reader first meets the unlikely hero, Pierre Bezukhov, at a soirée in St. Petersburg. He has just returned to live in Russia after studying abroad. Awkward, yet brash, his naïve idealism leads him into a political argument, during which he asserts his belief that Napoleon is the "greatest man in the world." After the soirée, Pierre retreats to the home of his old friend, Prince Andrew Bolkonsky, and the conversation about Napoleon continues.

Meanwhile, war talk is also in the air nearby in the Rostov household. The young son of Count Rostov, Nicholas, has decided to join the hussars, thus increasing the adoration of his cousin Sonia, who is in love with him. After a spat over Nicholas' harmless flirtation with another girl, they kiss. Observing the scene is Nicholas' impish thirteen-year-old sister, Natasha.

These early scenes of social frivolity and domestic happiness led Tolstoy in the early stages of composition to title his book, "All's Well That Ends Well." Once he reached the sections of the novel that deal with the ravages of the Napoleonic Wars, however, he became more philosophically introspective. Drawing on his own experiences during the Crimean War, Tolstoy shows how war in its wake sweeps aside individual aspirations, disturbs familial bonds and changes the destiny of nations forever. No wonder, then, that an important theme of the novel is the search for meaning in lives whose order has been completely overturned because of war.

The novel centers on Pierre's search. He is a good man who is still basically unformed. The fact that he was illegitimate underscores his uncertain sense of identity. His strength as a character is that he searches for his identity down several varied paths.

At the beginning of the novel, he explores the life of dissipation by allowing himself to fall into debauchery with wild companions. Next, he lives the life of the flesh by marrying the cold, beautiful Helene Kuragin. When she can do nothing to assuage his inner emptiness, a chance encounter with a Freemason attracts Pierre to this movement. Freemasonry, a mystical brotherhood based on the ritual and structure of medieval trade guilds, was popular in Russia at the time and appealed to intelligent men such as Pierre, who were searching for the meaning of life. Pierre eventually becomes disillusioned with his fellow Freemasons' shallow altruism.

As a last resort, he stumbles onto the battlefield of Borodino to see what war is like. Deeply upset by the carnage that he sees around him, Pierre resolves to assassinate its perpetrator, Napoleon. Believing that their destinies are linked, Pierre, in search of Napoleon, wanders around in Moscow, which is burning after the Russian army has abandoned it. Pierre is captured as an incendiary by the French, who now occupy Moscow. Spared from execution at the last moment, Pierre meditates on his fate in the company of other prisoners of war. He is particularly struck by the peasant Platon Karatáev, who is "the personification of everything Russian." Karatáev intuitively seems to know the right way to live, and Pierre wants to learn from his example.

When Karatáev dies, Pierre has a vision of a globe whose surface consists of drops of liquid:

> God is in the midst, and each drop tries to expand so as to reflect Him to the greatest extent. And it grows, merges, disappears from the surface, sinks to the depths, and again emerges. There now, Karatáev has spread out and disappeared.

Pierre's epiphany teaches him not to fear death: death is merely a reabsorption into the flow of life. Prince Andrew, mortally wounded at the battle of Borodino, discovers this same truth, unfortunately, on his deathbed:

> Everything is, everything exists, only because I love. Everything is united by it alone. Love is God, and to die means that I, a particle of love, shall return to the general and eternal source.

Besides their common philosophical beliefs, Pierre and Andrew are further linked by their relationship to Natasha, a character who intuitively experiences these notions of love. Both fall in love with her and propose marriage. Andrew and Natasha are ill suited to one another. Natasha, full of exuberant, youthful spontaneity, cannot endure the year's postponement of their marriage that Prince Andrew requests in deference to his father's wishes. They do reconcile briefly after Andrew is mortally wounded. Too late, Andrew learns to live by the heart rather than the head. His realization,

"Death is an awakening," can only remain an abstract thought, because he cannot experience it.

Pierre's compassion saves Natasha from her grief following Prince Andrew's death. They are the two characters, in particular, who have an inborn generosity and kindness of spirit. They have the capacity to forget themselves when others are in distress. At some risk to himself, Pierre saves the lives of several people during the burning of Moscow. Natasha throws the family's possessions out of the moving carts in order to transport wounded soldiers to safety. Most important, though, Pierre and Natasha save each other by marrying. Natasha, whose emotional life has been undirected toward any goal, can now focus her energies on Pierre and their children. She devotes "her whole soul, her whole being" to them. Pierre, too, finds in his home a setting in which he can live his vision of the cosmic globe.

Tolstoy ends *War and Peace* by rising above the Bezukhov's domestic scene and surveying the big picture. In the second epilogue, he asks such profound questions as the following: What does this all mean? Why did it happen? What force made people act so? He meditates on Napoleon's power and how easily his soldiers transferred their power to him. Yet, Tolstoy reminds his readers, "A tsar is the slave of history." What freedom therefore does any person possess in the face of such determinism? Tolstoy answers the question by saying that each person has two faculties: reason, which teaches humans the laws of inevitability, and consciousness, which makes them feel free. He goes on to say, "Only by uniting them do we get a clear conception of man's life." Natasha and Pierre both develop their sense of consciousness and, thus, experience freedom. The memorable moments in which they are the most free occur when they are the least aware of themselves. Their example, Tolstoy implies, demonstrates the right way to live.

ANNA KARENINA

First published: 1875-1877 (English translation, 1886)
Type of work: Novel

A married woman's love affair with another man throws her life into such disorder and despair that she kills herself.

The source of Tolstoy's next great novel, *Anna Karenina*, lies in an idea that he conveyed to his wife in 1870. He wanted to write a story about a married woman who is disgraced by a sexual scandal. He would depict her "not as culpable, but as uniquely worthy of pity." This story he knew from his own family: his only sister, Marya, had recently left her husband for an adulterous liaison with a Swedish viscount. Two years later, he saw firsthand the potential disastrous results of such a passion. One of his neighbors cast off his mistress, Anna Stepanovna Pirogova, who then threw herself under a train. Tolstoy viewed her remains afterward. Within the year, he began writing *Anna Karenina*. He was stimulated further by his reading of Alexander Pushkin's *Povesti Belkina* (1831; *The Tales of Belkin*, 1947), which he admired. He was struck by the phrase, "The guests were arriving at the country house," and began to write his story around it.

Anna Karenina begins with the oft-quoted line, "Happy families are all alike; every unhappy family is unhappy in its own way." In this novel, Tolstoy portrays both a happy and an unhappy family. The happy Constantine Levin and his wife, Kitty, resemble Pierre and Natasha Bezukhov in *War and Peace* because of their positive attitudes in the face of adversity and their compassion toward other people. Levin and Kitty's rapport is such that Levin exclaims that he does "not know where she ended and he began."

The marriage of Alexey and Anna Karenin, on the other hand, is a loveless match held in place by the dictates of society. When Anna meets the dashing officer of the guards, Alexey Vronsky, she readily abandons her husband and son for the sake of illicit passion. Far from being an ennobling force, Anna and Vronsky's love leads to chaos, ruin, and, eventually, Anna's death under the wheels of an oncoming train.

Throughout the novel, the characters of Anna and Levin are compared and contrasted. Distantly related through marriage (Anna's brother is married to Kitty's sister), they make life choices that are diametrically opposed to each other. Anna is a young, beautiful, intelligent, vital woman who inexplicably and single-mindedly chooses to destroy herself. After discovering that Anna is in love with Vronsky, Anna's husband suggests a divorce. Yet Anna rejects his offer by saying that she does not want a divorce if it is the result of "*his* generosity." Vronsky, too, is willing to accommodate her by taking her away from Moscow and marrying her, yet she once again refuses to finalize the divorce. Instead, she torments him with her possessiveness and fits of jealousy. Her last words before she throws herself under the train reflect her vindictive frame of mind against Vronsky: "I will punish him and escape from everyone and from myself."

The origins of Anna's self-destructive nature are not clear—though, in truth, Anna has what is now called an addictive personality. She demands more and more of Vronsky's love, because she can never believe that he truly cares for her. Even when he abandons his career to spend more time with her, she still cries out for more attention. Anna accurately describes the state of their interaction by saying, "My love keeps growing more passionate and egoistic, while his is waning and waning." Their relationship cannot grow in this type of environment, nor does it nourish them at all as individuals. Some critics point out that it is Anna's unbridled sexuality that corrupts her. Edward Wasiolek in *Tolstoy's Major Fiction* (1978) claims that, in Tolstoy's view, sex is "a massive intrusion on a person's being and a ruthless obliteration of the sanctity of personhood." In other words, Anna and Vronsky's sexuality interferes with their spirituality.

Though Kitty and Levin deeply love one another—Levin, in fact, believes that marriage is "the chief affair of life"—the compulsive element that characterizes Anna's sexual passion is missing in their relationship. Their love is grounded in the rural community in which they live; they work, play, love, and have babies in the midst of the active life that is occurring around them.

Levin, like Anna, experiences moments when he would like to escape from the conditions of his life. The period following the death of his brother is a particularly dark time for him. He must consciously avoid ropes and guns so that he will not be tempted to commit suicide. Tolstoy has written some of his own spiritual crisis into this description of Levin's situation. Levin achieves a measure of comfort and spir-- itual solace by simply experiencing life in the moment in which he is living it. The mowing scene shows him unconsciously living life to its fullest extent.

Later, he gains further insight from the peasant Fyodor, who advises him that a man must live "for his soul" and "not forget God." These wise words penetrate to the heart of Levin's spiritual crisis, and he resolves to transform himself. As Wasiolek points out, Tolstoy's characters, such as Pierre in *War and Peace*, come into touch with reality when they cease their efforts to "possess" it. In Tolstoy's world, the ego must be subdued in order for people to love correctly and take their place in the flow of existence. Anna fails to adjust her personality to this truth; thus, she is left wondering, "Why not put out the light?"

THE DEATH OF IVAN ILYICH

First published: "Smert Ivana Ilicha," 1886 (English translation, 1887)
Type of work: Short story

In nineteenth century Russia, a judge accidentally falls and develops a fatal illness, which forces him to contemplate death and regret the life that he has lived.

"The Death of Ivan Ilyich," one of the greatest short stories dealing with the subject of death, marked Tolstoy's return to fiction writing after his religious conversion. In 1881, his imagination was sparked when he heard the story of the death of Ivan Ilich Mechnikov, a judge of the Tula court, who expressed on his deathbed profound regret for the life that he had lived.

As in the real-life story, Tolstoy makes his Ivan Ilyich wake up to the hidden possibilities of life on his deathbed. Before then, Ilyich has lived his life thinking only of himself and his next round of pleasure. In the past, when unpleasant events occurred, such as the death of a few of his children and his wife's growing irritability, he turned away from these domestic concerns and spent time working at the office. His life continues for seventeen years in this manner, until the fateful day when he falls off a ladder while hanging drapes. He develops symptoms, a queer taste in the mouth and stomach discomfort, and, before he knows it, he is on his deathbed.

From a life built around the pursuit of pleasure and the avoidance of unpleasant reality, Ivan is suddenly catapulted into the world of sickness and death. He recalls, with irony, an old syllogism that he had learned: "Caius is a man, men are mortal, therefore Caius is mortal." Never before had he seriously contemplated his own mortality. He tortures himself with the thought, "What if in reality, all my life, my conscious life, has not been the right thing?"

The horrible truth that he indeed has failed to do the right thing transforms the remaining two hours of Ivan's life. The key to his transformation lies in his relationship to the peasant Gerasim, who does not shun the unpleasant aspects of his illness as does the rest of Ilyich's family and who treats his fatal condition matter-of-factly. Gerasim can "understand and pity him" in a compassionate and loving manner. In his final, agonizing moments, Ivan learns that he, too, can be compassionate and loving. He pities his son, who weepingly kisses his hand, and feels sorry for his despairing wife. He can die in peace, because, "In the place of death there was light."

Though Ilyich takes the last rites of the church in his final dying moments, the story is not overtly a religious parable. The story instead celebrates the virtues of pity and compassion that the simple Russian peasant knows and practices. Ilyich's fault was that, during his life, he had lived too much by his head (his surname, Golovin, suggests *golova*, the Russian word meaning "head"). The suffering that he feels in his dying moments awakens him to the suffering of the other people around him and, thus, to the brotherhood of all people. The awareness of death is what holds people together, in Tolstoy's view. Though Ilyich's new life lasts only a couple of hours, Tolstoy suggests that he is a lucky man.

Summary

Described by the Russian writer Maxim Gorky as "a whole world," Leo Tolstoy incorporated his life, the past life of his family, and the destiny of the Russian people into his art. He tried to capture the varied facets of nineteenth century Russian reality, as well as discover a unifying truth that would explain the nature of humankind's spiritual existence. In the process, he created two of the world's greatest novels, *War and Peace* and *Anna Karenina*.

Not satisfied with this accomplishment, Tolstoy in midlife abandoned art and turned his prodigious energies to social reform. He contributed to the intellectual ferment that ultimately led to the Russian Revolution, which occurred seven years after his death.

Bibliography

Bayley, John. *Tolstoy and the Novel*. London: Chatto & Windus, 1966.
Benson, Ruth C. *Women in Tolstoy: The Ideal and the Erotic*. Urbana: University of Illinois Press, 1973.
Berlin, Isaiah. *The Hedgehog and the Fox: An Essay on Tolstoy's View of History*. New York: Simon & Schuster, 1973.
Eikhenbaum, Boris. *Tolstoi in the Sixties*. Translated by Duffield White. Ann Arbor, Mich.: Ardis, 1982.

Gifford, Henry. *Tolstoy*. Oxford, England: Oxford University Press, 1982.
Rowe, William W. *Leo Tolstoy*. Boston: Twayne, 1986.
Wasiolek, Edward, ed. *Critical Essays on Tolstoy*. Boston: G. K. Hall, 1986.
_____. *Tolstoy's Major Fiction*. Chicago: University of Chicago Press, 1978.
Wilson, A. N. *Tolstoy*. New York: W. W. Norton, 1988.

Anna Lillios

ANTHONY TROLLOPE

Born: London, England
April 24, 1815
Died: London, England
December 6, 1882

Principal Literary Achievement

A popular, entertaining writer of the nineteenth century, Trollope established the novel-sequence in English fiction; his fame rests on his six Barsetshire novels.

Biography

Anthony Trollope was born in London, England, on April 24, 1815. His father, Thomas Trollope, was a well-educated barrister, but he had a difficult disposition and gradually failed in that occupation. Throughout the first twenty years of Trollope's life, his father tried many and various ways of making money, all ill-planned and mismanaged. His mother, Frances, eventually became the one who held the family together financially.

Trollope began school at Harrow at the age of seven. In his *Autobiography* (1883), one of the most widely read of English autobiographies, he writes of his schooldays as being so horrible as to be indescribable. At twelve, he was moved to his father's former school, Winchester. There, the other boys knew of the unpaid bills due the school for his education and teased and tormented him about his poverty. Trollope was sent back to Harrow as a day boy. At this time, his mother was in America to follow up on one of his father's unsuccessful money-making schemes, and he lived with his unkempt and uncouth father in a decrepit farmhouse, from which he tramped each day to sit among his smartly dressed, well-do-do classmates.

When Trollope's father went bankrupt in 1834, the family moved to Belgium, where his father died. Frances Trollope had already begun to support her family as an author. She was in her fifties when her first book was published, and when she died at eighty-three, she had written forty-one books. She was a quick, copius writer, and her son undoubtedly was influenced by her style.

Out of necessity, Trollope became a junior clerk in the General Post Office in London in 1834, a job he hated but endured for seven years. He was transferred to Ireland in 1841, and this proved to be an important turning point in his life. He was no longer working in an office under superiors who did not particularly like him. He became good at his work, made many friends, and became fond of what were later to

become lifelong hobbies, riding and hunting. While he was in Ireland, Trollope married Rose Heseltine in 1844, was promoted, and soon began to write his first novel. He set for himself the quota of completing forty pages a week, or about ten thousand words.

Trollope's literary career began with *The Macdermots of Ballycloran* (1847), but it was not until *The Warden* (1855), his fourth novel and the first of the Barsetshire series, that he began to establish the style by which he is known. Next came *Barchester Towers* (1857), *Doctor Thorne* (1858), *Framley Parsonage* (1860-1861), *The Small House at Allington* (1862-1864), and *The Last Chronicle of Barset* (1867). He considered the latter his best work.

His next series is known as the Political, or Palliser, novels, after Plantagenet Palliser, who is in all of them. This series starts with *Can You Forgive Her?* (1864) and continues with *Phineas Finn, the Irish Member* (1867-1869), *The Eustace Diamonds* (1871-1873), *Phineas Redux* (1873-1874), *The Prime Minister* (1875-1876), and *The Duke's Children* (1879-1880). The two series taken together span more than twenty years of Trollope's writing.

Trollope took pride in his diligent attitude toward his writing. He attributed the quantity of his work (forty-seven novels, several travel books, biographies, and collections of short stories and sketches) to diligent work, usually done early in the morning before he went to work at the post office. As soon as he finished one piece of writing, he began another, and he wrote even when he traveled.

In achieving such a number of works, Trollope was more concerned with quantity than with the pursuit of stylistic perfection. Thus, his adverse critics often accused him of simply meeting the popular demands of the literary market with his descriptions of the inner life of young women. Essentially, his stories are a pleasant visit to a world that is disturbed only slightly by small problems and minor disappointments.

Apart from the series of books already mentioned, the following are also important: *The Claverings* (1866-1867), *The Belton Estate* (1865-1866), *Orley Farm* (1861-1862), and *Mr. Scarborough's Family* (1882-1883). Modern critics consider Trollope's finest piece of writing to be *The Way We Live Now* (1875); it is a bitter satire on the power of speculative finance in English life. In it, Trollope anticipates England's submission to American and other foreign speculators.

In middle life, Trollope obtained all that he had yearned for as a child. He became a popular figure in London and in literary society. He was on good terms with the major writers of his time and was a particularly close friend of George Eliot. He traveled, hunted, and rode zealously, dined with his friends at his club, and enjoyed life enormously. In addition, Trollope enjoyed a happy and secure family life and was reading aloud with his family after dinner one evening when he suffered a stroke, from which he did not recover. He died a month later, on December 6, 1882, in London.

Analysis

The Barsetshire novels are regarded as Trollope's major, if not his only, significant contribution to literature. Interestingly, this viewpoint is shared by critics, literary historians, and the reading public. There are, however, many solid qualities to be found not only in this popular series but also in most of his other works.

In all of his novels, there is a vast array of characters, usually set in motion by Trollope's theme, which in each novel is simply a variation: the finely drawn English opposition of love versus property. This pleasantly complex situational novel makes for interesting reading. No problems of social significance are given serious treatment, for the chief purpose is entertainment. When Trollope did turn to more serious and often satirical fiction in later life, he focused upon English political life. Even though the Political novels are concerned with political maneuverings in upper-middle-class society and in Parliament, the focus is still on the conflicts between love and property. (Probably because of his own failure to gain a parliamentary seat in the elections of 1868, in his political novels Trollope both exaggerates and denigrates the importance of serving as a member of Parliament.)

A typical Trollope novel contains several easily identified common characteristics, and these can be readily found in the two central series he wrote, the Barsetshire novels and the Political novels. He had, first, an imaginative yet genuine concern with moral existence. This concern was his primary means of insight into his characters. Therefore, while the physical characteristics of his characters are rarely made clear, these characters are conscientiously described regarding their moral sensitivities. Trollope presents them through what they say and what they do, and also by directly commenting upon them himself.

Second, the pattern of his novels stays fairly true to form. There is no villain, and most characters are morally average, neither particularly good nor bad, not particularly exciting but not dull. Thus, readers recognize much of themselves in his books.

Third, one recognizes in Trollope's works a disregard for plot. His characters, in keeping with their average morality, lead ordinary, average lives. There are no sensational or complicated situations, no great surprises or shocking situations. Instead, his characters deal with everyday issues that test their moral sensibilities, such as the problems of poor but well-bred young women seeking a suitable husband or the proper use of church endowments.

Last, the repetition of a short phrase at brief intervals and with great exaggeration is a quality that is often seen in Trollope's works. The repetition is used most often to portray the truth of his characters' actions and to show the truth of their moral sensibilities.

Although it is easy to view Trollope's writings in a superficial manner, doing so creates a misconception of literary worth in the reader's mind. Rather, Trollope's passionate and real interest with moral existence provide for the variety and photographic accuracy of his pictures of the social life of the middle and upper-middle classes of England in the nineteenth century. In Trollope's novels, the real and the ideal meet; despite the futility of human strivings, his satire provokes laughter; and the irony of the gap between what his characters really are and what they believe themselves to be pricks the moral consciousness of his readers. His influence upon modern writers regarding the development of the novel-sequence and the use of reappearing characters cannot be overestimated.

Trollope's contradiction, then, is a simple one and can be traced back to his deprivation in childhood. He was attempting to gain literary esteem by writing novels in a world where novel writing was not held in high regard. His *Autobiography*, published posthumously, created a furor at its publication. In it, he revealed himself as a writer to whom writing was a methodical, clerical process, much as letter writing had been for him during his early days as a postal clerk. It is, ironically, even today one of the most widely read English autobiographies.

THE BARSETSHIRE NOVELS

First published: *The Warden*, 1855; *Barchester Towers*, 1857; *Doctor Thorne*, 1858; *Framley Parsonage*, 1860-1861; *The Small House at Allington*, 1862-1864; *The Last Chronicle of Barset*, 1867

Type of work: Novels

Set in the rural south of England, these six novels center on the activities of the "squirearchy" and the clergy.

Trollope's popular fame rests on his six Barsetshire novels. Taken as a whole, they are interconnected by characters who appear in more than one of them, a technique that Trollope was to use again in his second series, known as the Political novels. The Barsetshire series established the novel-sequence in English fiction.

The most famous of the Barsetshire series is *Barchester Towers*. It is typical, however, of the entire chronicle, with its fine ironic tone and pleasantly complicated situations. Though the type of plot is social satire, no problems of social significance are given serious consideration, as its chief purpose is entertainment.

The series was conceived one summer evening in Salisbury, but the settings are, for the most part, in the imaginary west-country county of Barset and its chief town, Barchester. Barchester is a compilation of the many counties Trollope visited in his position as a civil servant. Barchester's railroads and roads, its great lords and their fine castles, its squires and their parks, its towns, its parishes, and its rectors and their churches are all totally fictitious. From his careful observations and memories of his travels throughout England, however, Trollope pieced together a detailed map of Barchester. Thus, it has a totally convincing reality, based not particularly upon the geographical but rather upon Trollope's sharp insight into the moral physiognomies of his characters.

The first book of the series, *The Warden*, sets a pattern to which Trollope adhered in the later books. In *The Warden*, the focus is upon a problem concerning the proper use of church endowments. Using his vivid imagination, Trollope set in motion the issues and conflicts that surrounded the problem and how it was approached by the various people involved, people with various modes and degrees of moral sensibility.

When Trollope returned to the milieu of *The Warden* in *Barchester Towers*, he introduced a number of subplots, all related to the ecclesiastical power struggle between the new Bishop of Barchester (Bishop Proudie) and the former Bishop's son (Archdeacon Grantly). The main conflict of the novel involves both parties' intentions to preserve the integrity of the Church. In typical Trollope fashion, the irony comes forth in how the two men view themselves versus how they really are—the two clergymen are, in their own minds, fighting for the spiritual power of the Church, but they are actually fighting for power over the building, furnishings, and their clerical positions; in other words, they are fighting for the worldly things of the Church, not the spiritual.

Many other novels were written in the period during which Trollope was engaged in writing the Barsetshire series. Archdeacon Grantly and his father-in-law, however, continued to live in Trollope's imagination. He created the most solid of his male characters by blending his own personality with theirs, and in his *Autobiography* he explained the novelist's need to "live" with his characters and stressed the importance of recording change and the effects of time on them. Therefore, in *The Last Chronicle of Barset* (the book that Trollope considered his best work), the two have grown older, just as Trollope himself was growing older. The Archdeacon is the character most often described as being akin to Trollope: quick to anger but quick to forgive, generous, warmhearted, worldly. His father-in-law, who had been Warden in the first book, is portrayed at the upper limits of Trollope's moral range. He is virtuous and good, and he grows old among his family and friends. When the older man dies, it is through the mouth of the Archdeacon that Trollope expresses his estimate of both of them.

Regarding the women that he created, Trollope always referred to them as girls. He held the same notions concerning vicarious relationships with his female characters as with his male ones. For the girls whom he created, love never ran smoothly, a plot that endeared him to his readers. The confusion ensued when he brought the demands of property and social status into conflict with the power of love. The problems created by this situation involved the lovers, their families, their friends, and even their circle of acquaintants, just as it would in real life. Trollope used this plot early in the Barsetshire series and continued to use it throughout his career.

It must be noted, however, that not all Trollope's characters are likable or admirable. He was critical of himself, and through his characters one sees this personal criticism. For example, the Archdeacon's worst enemy is Mrs. Proudie, wife of the Bishop. She is one of the best-known bad-tempered women in English fiction. Even after she died (Trollope referred to her death as his having killed her), he indicated that she would still exist for him, even if as a ghost.

Barsetshire, Trollope's fictional country where the Barsetshire series is set, is as impressive as William Faulkner's Yoknapatawpha or Thomas Hardy's Wessex. The novels provide a slice of nineteenth century life, meticulously observed and entertainingly told.

Summary

Anthony Trollope attributed his success to his imagination, from which he developed an intimate knowledge of his lifelike characters. One of the most prolific of the Victorian writers and one of the most popular, he was in his own day admired as a realist; modern readers, however, tend to view his works in a more comic light, with his characters under the firm control of the writer's irony rather than simply people leading their daily lives. Regardless of how Trollope's works are viewed, they endure as classics of Victorian literature.

Bibliography

Booth, Bradford. "Trollope's *Orley Farm*: Artistry Manque." In *Victorian Literature: Modern Essays in Criticism*. Edited by Austin Wright. New York: Oxford University Press, 1961.

Chesterton, G. K. *The Victorian Age in Literature*. Notre Dame, Ind.: University of Notre Dame Press, 1963.

Daiches, David. *A Critical History of English Literature*. New York: Ronald Press Company, 1970.

Lerner, Laurence, ed. *The Victorians*. New York: Holmes & Meier, 1978.

Pope-Hennessy, James. *Anthony Trollope*. Boston: Little, Brown, 1971.

Trollope, Anthony. *The Letters of Anthony Trollope*. Edited by Bradford A. Booth. London: Oxford University Press, 1951.

Lela Phillips

TU FU

Born: perhaps Tu-ling, Shaanxi province, China
A.D. 712
Died: T'an-chou (modern Changsha, Hunan province),
China
A.D. 770

Principal Literary Achievement

Generally regarded as China's finest poet, Tu Fu is celebrated for his serious-ness of purpose, his mastery of poetic technique, and his innovations in subject matter.

Biography

Tu Fu lived during the century when China's T'ang Dynasty (A.D. 618-907) reached the peak of its political and cultural achievement and began its long decline. The pivotal event in the lives of both the poet and the dynasty was the An-Shih Rebellion, which ended the reign of Hsüan-tsung, "the Brilliant Emperor," and brought the death of many thousands of Chinese people. Its importance is fully reflected in Tu Fu's poetry; in fact, the poems that made his reputation were written after the rebellion began, when he was already in his mid-forties.

The poet was born in A.D. 712, probably in Tu-ling, a few miles south of Ch'ang-an (modern Xi'an), the imperial capital. His father's name was Tu Hsien. The family had a tradition of many generations of public service, and after some five years traveling in the south of China during his early twenties, Tu Fu returned to Ch'ang-an in 736 to attempt the examinations for imperial service. Unexpectedly, he failed, and once again he devoted himself to travel. Tu Fu wrote about these experiences many years later in "The Wanderings of My Prime."

In the early 740's, he lived in Lo-yang (Luoyang), during which time he met the poet Li Po. Tu Fu addressed several poems to Li Po, and the former clearly treasured the friendship for the rest of his life, although the two poets do not appear to have met again after their excursions of 744-745.

Tu Fu moved to Ch'ang-an in 746 and set about gaining an official position. The next year offered the opportunity of a special examination, but the corrupt first min-ister saw to it that no one was passed. Five years later, possibly as a result of three poems well received by the emperor himself, Tu Fu was again able to take the exam-ination. This time he was put on a list of those awaiting appointments, but he had to

wait a further three years before being assigned a police commissioner's post. This post he declined, and he was made adjutant in the Office of the Right Commander of the Heir Apparent's Palace Guard.

During this ten-year waiting period, Tu Fu's poetry began to show an increasing sympathy for the ordinary people of China. He had already written about the ravages of war in the famous "Song of the War Carts," and when severe rains in the autumn of 754 led to food shortages and price rises, "Sighing over the Autumn Rains" movingly tells how a little rice now required the surrender of a person's bedding. The situation was so serious that the poet had moved his family away from the capital, and joy at his new appointment was tempered by the death from hunger of his infant son, an event chronicled in "Five Hundred Words to Express My Feelings When I Went from the Capital to Feng-hsien." Yet Tu Fu's personal unhappiness was soon to be overshadowed by a national disaster, and public and private events would sit side by side in his poetry.

At the beginning of 756-757, An Lu-shan, the governor-general of the northern and northeastern border regions, captured Lo-yang and threatened the imperial capital. About ten years earlier, the emperor had taken as concubine the wife of one of his own sons. Yang Kuei-fei soon made herself effective empress, had her older sisters ennobled, and helped one of her cousins, Yang Kuo-chung, climb to the rank of highest minister of state. The unpopular Yang family was An Lu-shan's declared target, and when the emperor was forced to flee Ch'ang-an, it was the imperial troops who executed the corrupt minister, his son, and two of Lady Yang's sisters, and who finally insisted on the death of the concubine herself. Shortly thereafter, Su-tsung, the heir apparent, was proclaimed emperor and began the long process of crushing the rebellion.

Tu Fu, who had taken his family to Feng-hsien, eighty miles from Ch'ang-an, now moved them further north to Ch'iang Village and tried to join the new emperor. Yet the poet seems to have been captured by the rebels and taken to Ch'ang-an, where he stayed for about eight months, until early 757, when he managed to make his way through enemy lines to Su-tsung's headquarters. Poems such as "Moonlight Night," "Spring Prospect," "P'eng-ya Road," and "The Journey North" reflect these experiences.

Tu Fu was now appointed to a junior advisory position. He did not make a great success of this opportunity, and six months after the recovery of Ch'ang-an and Lo-yang, the poet was transferred to a minor post in Hua-chou, sixty miles from the capital. After little more than a year, he resigned and took his family to Ch'eng-tu (Chengdu, Sichuan), where he built his famous thatched hut in the spring of 760. The last decade of his life was a prolific period, and most of Tu Fu's surviving poetry comes from these years.

In Ch'eng-tu, the poet seems to have depended on the kindness of others, but after a local revolt, which forced him and his family to flee the city for almost two years, he joined the military staff of his friend Yen Wu, the new provincial governor. In early 765, after less than a year, Tu Fu resigned and moved to K'uei-chou at the west-

ern entrance to the gorges of the Yangtse River. The city prefect was extremely help-
ful, and Tu Fu probably became his unofficial secretary. By 767, the poet had two
houses and held fields and orchards, but the next year he left, possibly still thinking
of an official post in the capital. Tu Fu died in T'an-chou, China, in late 770.

Analysis

The two indigenous religions of China, Confucianism and Taoism, both hinge on
the word *Tao*, or Way, with which human beings are to seek harmony. Confucianism
tended to emphasize the social elements of the *Tao*, putting particular value on the
virtues of truthfulness, diligence, filial piety, and loyalty to government as likely to
generate harmony on earth. Taoism itself, on the other hand, was skeptical about the
possibility of illuminating the *Tao* at all, and it taught that the Way might only be
known through an inner awareness and union with the ultimate reality of all things.
Tu Fu's family history of government service generated in him a Confucian sense of
the importance of public responsibility, but as his friendship and admiration for the
Taoist poet Li Po suggest, there was a quietist streak to his character, which found
expression in frequent praise of rural life and the hermit's role. Tu Fu's sympathy
with both polarities of the Chinese value system may help to account for his enormous poetic prestige.

Until the 750's, Tu Fu did not seem to have been particularly interested in the
public world, but then he produced a number of poems on social issues, possibly in
response to a deterioration in governance. A poet would not have been regarded as
moving out of his proper sphere in writing political commentary; since Confucianism regarded government as of vital concern to the wise man, there was a long tradition of using poetry as a vehicle for social and political criticism. Tu Fu's "ballads,"
however, are unusually direct, and his engagement with political events has gained
for him the title of the "poet-historian."

One of the first of these poems was "Song of the War Carts." The opening lines
describe conscripted men going to war behind the baggage wagons, while their wives,
parents, and children stumble after them, weeping. A soldier tells how he and his
fellows, driven "like dogs or chickens," have given their blood to satisfy the emperor's expansionist ambitions. The poem has been praised for its acute sensitivity to
the ordinary person's difficulties. Tu Fu also wrote about the evils of conscription in
the three "officer" poems (759). The last of these tells of an old man who escapes
over the wall right as the recruiting officer arrives. All his sons have gone to the war,
and now even his wife and daughter-in-law are taken to cook for the army. At this
point, Tu Fu can only offer compassion since the people are being taken to defend
the empire, not expand it.

The concept of *jên*, of benevolence, charity, or good-heartedness, was the paramount Confucian virtue, and in Tu Fu's poems of the rebellion it finds frequent expression. "A Fine Lady" shows his compassion for a well-born woman. Her brothers
were killed in the rebellion, and her husband deserted her for a younger woman, so
she is now reduced to selling her pearls one by one. With an eye for compelling

detail, Tu Fu tells how she and her maid ineffectually try to cover the holes in their roof with living creepers.

Very few poets wrote about the An-Shih Rebellion, and while there were ancient precedents for such poems as "Song of the War Carts," Tu Fu was breaking new ground when he wrote about his family's experiences. "P'eng-ya Road" describes them walking through the rain and mud, their clothes wet and cold, his son eating bitter plums, and his daughter biting her father in her hunger. Eventually, they arrive at a friend's house, and the poem becomes a celebration of hospitality. Friendship is one of the traditional subjects of Chinese literature, and the drama of his family's journey and their pitiful condition makes the friend's hospitality glow all the more brightly as a moment of blessed harmony in a disordered world.

A reverence for nature is a continuing theme in Chinese verse, and many of Tu Fu's poems express a degree of unity with the natural world. In "Moonlight Night," he finds himself in harmony with his wife and children when he considers that they are looking at the same moon in Fu-chou that he sees in Ch'ang-an. In "Facing the Snow," however, he evokes tumultuous storm clouds to parallel China in rebellion. "Restless Night" anxiously represents a calm and peaceful nature as being under the same threat of war as humankind, and Tu Fu's sympathy now extends to the natural world itself.

Nature was not always bleak. "The River Village," written during the "thatched hut" period of 760-762, celebrates a secret beauty that unites all creation: the curve of the river, the swallows on the roof, the gulls in the water, his wife making a chessboard, and his sons bending needles into fish hooks. Tu Fu achieves a similar sense of oneness in "A Traveler at Night Writes His Thoughts." The poet is on a boat sailing down the Yangtse river; grasses grow on the bank, the stars are above, and the moon is reflected in the water. Bitterly, Tu Fu reflects that his poetry has not made him a name and that his life in government has not been a success. What does he resemble? A sand gull, floating between heaven and earth. This image is not one of power and authority, nor is it one of leaden impotence. The gull, or the poet, is a mediator between earth and heaven, stitching a single garment of universal harmony.

SPRING PROSPECT

Written: 757 (English translation, 1984)
Type of work: Poem

Feeling aged by the devastation of the civil war, the poet finds comfort in nature.

"Spring Prospect," Tu Fu's most famous poem, was written while he was held in Ch'ang-an and is characteristic of his verse, both in form and in subject matter. The poem seems to separate the artificial (the "nation" and the "city") and the natural ("hills and streams"), only to erase this distinction when "grass and trees" are seen flourishing in Ch'ang-an at a time of destruction. Lines 3 and 4, "feeling the times,/ flowers draw tears;/ hating separation,/ birds alarm the heart," are willfully ambiguous. Burton Watson, the translator, has given the flavor of the original by using dangling participles. Who is the implied subject of "feeling" or of "hating"? Is it the poet or the flowers and birds? Is nature sympathizing with humanity and the poet? And are the flowers crying over the political situation, or the birds suffering because Tu Fu and his family are apart? On the other hand, the lines can be taken to mean that the poet is weeping on the flowers, symbols of beauty and renewal, while the birds' songs stoke his emotional anguish. Thus, the poetry weaves humanity and nature together into one fabric.

The "beacon fires" of line 5, "Beacon fires three months running," were used by the Chinese to maintain contact between garrisons; they would be lit at regular times to indicate that all was well. In the poem, their use for three months shows how long the emergency has lasted. The final two lines focus on the poet, but he refuses to take himself too seriously: He is losing so much hair that soon there will not be enough in the topknot for him to pin on his hat, and it will fall off. This wry, self-deprecating humor is typical of Tu Fu.

The poem in Chinese consists of eight lines of five words each, a form called *lüshih*, or regulated verse. It was one of a group of forms known as "modern style," which developed after the fifth century A.D. and could be written with either seven or five syllables to the line—Chinese words normally have only one syllable. Tu Fu is particularly admired for his mastery of this very strict form. There were precise rules for verbal and tonal parallelism in the second and third pairs of lines, and the translation preserves most of these antitheses, as indicated for example, in lines 3 and 4: "feeling"/"hating"; "the times" (political and personal dislocation)/"separation"; "flowers"/"birds"; "draw"/"alarm"; "tears"/"heart."

THE JOURNEY NORTH

Written: 757 (English translation, 1973)
Type of work: Poem

Tu Fu describes his journey across a devastated land to visit his impoverished wife and children.

In "The Journey North," Tu Fu has received formal permission from the emperor to make a visit to his wife and children, but the poet wonders how important he should consider his family at a time when "the whole universe is suffering fearsome wounds." In this state of confusion and anxiety, he begins his phantasmagoric journey through a devastated and depopulated countryside. There is temporary respite when he comes to the mountains—"Here retired pursuits could be enjoyed." Yet the world calls him back, and he must cross an old battlefield at night, the moonlight illuminating white bones.

The poet's homecoming is a widely praised passage. He finds his wife and children in patched clothes; his spoiled son is now barefoot and pale, and Tu Fu himself falls sick and takes to his bed. At this point, he realizes that he has some cosmetics and silk in his bag, and the children take immediate pleasure in the makeup, playing at being grown-ups. The poet can temporarily forget the trials of life in the pleasure of being with his children.

After these three dozen lines of domestic realism, the poem returns to its initial mode, and Tu Fu turns to speculating on the outcome of the rebellion. He says that he believes that the "demonic atmosphere will soon break," that the empire is, after all, built on firm foundations.

The poem is striking for its mixture of the domestic and the high political. The "shifting style," with its abrupt changes of mood and topic, is characteristic of Tu Fu and sets him apart from his contemporaries. He is quite happy to let the personal stand beside the public and to unify the two in the space of a poem, although his sense of himself as a potentially public figure, and sometimes as a mildly absurd one, constantly draws him back to earth.

Summary

The horrors of the mid-century An-Shih Rebellion elicited in Tu Fu the supreme Confucian value of compassion for his fellow human beings. Parallel to his strong awareness of the everyday world and his sense of public responsibility was an urge to experience the unity of humanity and the natural world. Yet the physical destruction and dislocation that he saw around him made it hard for the poet to see nature as harmonious, although occasionally he was able to transcend his own troubles and those of his country.

Bibliography

Cooper, Arthur, comp. *Li Po and Tu Fu: Poems Selected and Translated with an Introduction and Notes*. Harmondsworth, Middlesex, England: Penguin, 1973.

Davis, A. R. *Tu Fu*. New York: Twayne, 1971.

Feng Yuean-chuen. *A Short History of Classical Chinese Literature*. Translated by Yang Hsien-Yi and Gladys Yang. Hong Kong: Joint Publishing, 1983.

Hawkes, David. *A Little Primer of Tu Fu*. Oxford, England: Clarendon Press, 1967.

Hung, William. *Tu Fu: China's Greatest Poet*. Cambridge, Mass.: Harvard University Press, 1952.

Lin, Shuen-fu, and Stephen Owen, eds. *The Vitality of the Lyric Voice: Shih Poetry from the Late Han to the T'ang*. Princeton, N.J.: Princeton University Press, 1986.

Liu Wu-chi. *An Introduction to Chinese Literature*. Bloomington: Indiana University Press, 1966.

Owen, Stephen. "Tu Fu." In *The Great Age of Chinese Poetry: The High T'ang*. New

Haven, Conn.: Yale University Press, 1981.

Watson, Burton. *Chinese Lyricism: Shih Poetry from the Second to the Twelfth Century, with Translations*. New York: Columbia University Press.

_____. *The Columbia Book of Chinese Poetry: From Early Times to the Thirteenth Century*. New York: Columbia University Press, 1984.

William Atkinson

IVAN TURGENEV

Born: Orel, Russia
November 9, 1818
Died: Bougival, France
September 3, 1883

Principal Literary Achievement

Among major Russian writers in the nineteenth century, Turgenev was the one most assimilated into the culture of Western Europe, where he was admired and widely read.

Biography

Ivan Sergeyevich Turgenev was born in Orel, Russia, on November 9, 1818. His mother, Varvara Petrovna Lutovinov, was a cruel and malicious woman of great wealth. His father, Sergey Turgenev, six years younger than his mother, was a handsome and charming cavalry officer who was descended from an old and distinguished but relatively impoverished family. Turgenev's parents became acquainted when his father visited Spasskoye, Varvara's estate, looking to buy horses for military use. Sergey Turgenev married Varvara Petrovna Lutovinov to save his family from financial ruin. Until he died in 1834, he was regularly unfaithful to his cruel but adoring wife.

In fairness to Turgenev's mother, it must be noted that she had an unhappy childhood. She was all but ignored by her own mother, then abused by her drunken stepfather, then sequestered by the uncle with whom she sought refuge. On the other hand, there is evidence that brutality was hereditary with the Lutovinovs. They seem to have acquired their great wealth by heavy-handed methods. None of this cruelty toward people passed to Turgenev, who grew up to be an excitable but gentle and compassionate man.

In spite of her character, or perhaps because of it, Varvara Petrovna exerted a strong influence on her son. She encouraged Turgenev's education with a view toward seeing him become an important state official. Turgenev studied first at the University of Moscow, then at St. Petersburg, and then in 1838 he left for Berlin to complete his training. This westerly movement during the course of his education may be seen as a metaphor for Turgenev's thinking, which inclined steadily in the direction of European liberalism and away from the formula of "autocracy, orthodoxy, and nationalism" which expressed the regime of Czar Nicholas I (1825-1855).

Two things happened in 1843 that were important to Turgenev for the rest of his

life. He published, at his own expense, a narrative poem, *Parasha* (1843), and in doing so more or less recognized (much to his mother's displeasure) that literature was to be his vocation. Then, in autumn of that year, he met the famous singer Pauline Garcia Viardot and fell in love with her almost immediately. Pauline was married to a theater manager twenty years her senior. Her husband tolerated her admirers, whom she attracted by her beautiful voice and strong character. She was not especially pretty and might be thought of as a benign version of Turgenev's mother. In any case, Turgenev formed an attachment to her that lasted until his death forty years later. The exact nature of the relationship is not clear. Though Turgenev and Pauline Viardot may briefly have been lovers, they seem for the most part to have shared romantic friendship, and Turgenev eventually came to be recognized as a curious appendage to the Viardot family, close to wife, husband, and children alike. (The Viardots also reared Turgenev's illegitimate daughter, Paulinette, born to him and one of his mother's serfs.)

Turgenev's literary fame may be dated from *Zapiski okhotnika* (1852; *Russian Life in the Interior*, 1855; better known as *A Sportsman's Sketches* (1932), a collection of short pieces that express a highly sympathetic but unsentimental view of the Russian peasantry, who until emancipation in 1861 were largely serfs. Turgenev hated the institution of serfdom (he freed his own serfs when he inherited property upon his mother's death in 1850), and his book is thought to have had something to do with ending that wretched system. *A Sportsman's Sketches* appeared in the same year as Turgenev's laudatory article on Nikolai Gogol, who had recently died in disgrace (from the government's point of view) for writing satiric portraits of Russian life. Turgenev was arrested, briefly imprisoned, and then exiled to Spasskoye for his praise of Gogol; the authorities regarded him with suspicion until things eased at the beginning of the reign of Czar Alexander II. It was during this exile that Turgenev wrote "Mumu," one of his most famous stories. Based on an incident involving Turgenev's mother and one of her serfs, it tells the story of a deaf-mute servant who is forced by his mistress to destroy his beloved pet dog.

Mesyats v derevne (1855; *A Month in the Country*, 1924), Turgenev's play suggesting illicit love relations, was finally licensed for publication in 1855. Then, in 1856, Turgenev published *Rudin* (1856; *Dmitri Roudine*, 1873; better known as *Rudin*, 1947), and he might be thought of as having now entered his major phase. *Dvoryanskoye gnezdo* (1859; *Liza*, 1869; also published as *A Nobleman's Nest*, 1869; better known as *A House of Gentlefolk*, 1894), appeared in 1859. *Pervaya lyubov* (1860; *First Love*, 1884), a short story in which a boy falls in love with his father's mistress," appeared a year later. Turgenev acknowledged that this story was close to his own experience and that the picture given of the father strongly resembled his own father. These works were followed by *Nakanune* (1860; *On the Eve*, 1871), *Ottsy i deti* (1862; *Fathers and Sons*, 1867), *Dym* (1867; *Smoke*, 1868), *Stepnoi Korol Lir* (1870; *A Lear of the Steppes*, 1872), *Veshniye vody* (1872; *Spring Floods*, 1874; better known as *The Torrents of Spring*, 1897), and *Nov* (1877; *Virgin Soil*, 1877). Most of these short novels present the reader with members of the Russian gentry who are somewhat likable but also ineffectual. More often than not, love relationships are frustrated or futile or both. There are elements of humor, but as with Anton Chekhov, the famous Russian writer in the generation after Turgenev, the humor is touched with sadness.

Turgenev settled with the Viardots at Baden-Baden, Germany, in 1863. In 1875, he bought jointly with the Viardots an estate at Bougival, near Paris. He enjoyed a wide literary acquaintance and considerable fame. His health began to fail in 1882. Cancer of the spine caused him great pain before he died on September 3, 1883, in Bougival, attended in his last illness by Pauline Viardot.

Analysis

Nineteenth century Russia was divided by a cultural debate between Slavophiles and Westerners. Slavophiles were conservatives who tended to regret the effort of Peter the Great to impose the culture and technology of Western Europe on his people. They believed that Russia was different from the West and superior in that difference. Westerners were liberals who were deeply troubled, if not simply contemptuous, of autocratic repression, which they saw most obviously displayed by the serf system, which effectively made chattels of the peasant class. They favored a reordering of Russian society that would liberate the serfs and establish a constitutional monarchy, if not a people's democracy. In this debate, Turgenev sided with the Westerners.

His position and how he expressed it in his art were not readily apparent except for his obvious dislike of serfdom. Turgenev's inclination to a moderate view may be related to the paradoxes in his character. He was a tall, well-made, handsome man who was generally harmless in his relations with women; he seems not to have had much passion in his life despite his attachment to Pauline Viardot. He was a very gentle person who loved shooting game birds. He lived in Western Europe much of the time but almost always wrote of his homeland and native people. Because he saw many sides to life, he could not create stories that would satisfy zealots. He could not divide the world into bad people and good people, but this did not keep him from believing that Russia would be made better by liberal reform.

In January, 1860, Turgenev published the essay "Gamlet i Don Kikhot" ("Hamlet and Don Quixote") in the *Contemporary Review*. He expresses the thought that the world comprises passive, introspective, ineffectual Hamlets and active, energetic, outward-looking Don Quixotes. He suggested that the Russian problem was too many Hamlets and not enough Don Quixotes, that something in the national character kept Russia from realizing its potential, but it is tempting to see these observations as Turgenev's unwitting revelation of himself. Whether he was consciously dominated by strong women throughout most of his life is a question to be debated but never finally answered. That he wrote fictions that included irresolute men who are perhaps not strong enough for the women whom they desire seems obvious.

In fact, most of Turgenev's novel-length works are studies in character (which tends to encourage a psychoanalytical approach in reading them critically). It does well to remember that Turgenev also wrote plays, for his stories contain more drama than adventure. People gather in a parlor or garden and talk to one another. Characters enter and exit the scene. Then some of the characters move to another location where the same pattern is repeated, with new characters added to replace those who have been left behind. This pattern repeats until the reader reaches the end of things, which is usually a failed love relationship (*A House of Gentlefolk, The Torrents of Spring*) or a death (*On the Eve, A Lear of the Steppes*) or both (*Fathers and Sons*).

What gives Turgenev's stories their interest is the clarity with which he presents his characters and the subtlety of detail by which he makes them individuals. When Turgenev began a novel, he constructed biographies of his characters and became intimately familiar with them. By this method, he was able to create convincing portraits of that part of Russian society in which he lived, particularly the Russian gentry who, it seemed to him, were becoming increasingly irrelevant as the world changed. His novels make clear that he was aware of the larger world and that he had opinions about it, but the people who drew his attention were those who did not quite fit, who were superfluous. The thought that members of Russia's leisured class were largely superfluous had been around since the time of Alexander Pushkin's verse novel *Evgeny Onegin* (1825-1833; *Eugene Onegin*, 1881).

Excepting *A Sportsman's Sketches* and *First Love*, most of Turgenev's fiction employs a third-person narrative voice, which takes the reader into thoughts and feelings of a multiplicity of characters. This technique also promotes impressionistic description of the external world, the look of characters and the Russian landscape that they inhabit. For that matter, Turgenev's first-person narratives are effectively descriptive, but when the story is given by a person within the action itself, nothing more comprehensive than the awareness of that single figure may be included. The author is bound by the narrative vehicle and denied the power of selection that sometimes makes great art.

The point to be made is that Turgenev was an artist. His novels and short stories are frequently cited as examples of the "art" of fiction. Seeing as he did the complexities of life, Turgenev did not incline to a single vision of the human condition that would have given him status as a thinker, but he ranks high among writers of his time for the artistry with which he created his fiction.

A SPORTSMAN'S SKETCHES

First published: *Zapiski okhotnika*, 1852 (English translation, 1855)
Type of work: Short stories

Hunting for game birds in the Russian countryside, a member of the gentry has repeated encounters with the humble, frequently mistreated peasant class.

A Sportman's Sketches effectively describes the stories that constitute the collection. They do not always express concentration of elements toward the resolution of a clearly defined plot that readers associate with modern short stories. In one of the most famous pieces, "Bezhin Meadow," the sportsman-narrator loses his way while hunting. At dusk, he stumbles into a camp of peasant boys who have brought horses out to graze in the cool night air. He sits among them, listens to their ghost stories, and leaves them at dawn with a sharpened sense of them as individuals rather than faceless members of the peasant class.

In "Yermolai and the Miller's Wife," the sportsman-narrator hunts with a serf named Yermolai, who seems to have a clandestine relationship with Arina, the miller's wife. Only toward the end of this sketch does Arina's story materialize. She was taken to St. Petersburg to be maid to her master's wife. When she fell in love with Petrushka, the footman, and asked for permission to marry him, she angered her mistress (who would not tolerate the inconvenience that a married servant might entail) and was banished to the countryside, where she now lives in a loveless marriage, dependent on Yermolai for the little happiness that she has.

For all of his sympathy with the peasants, Turgenev is faithful to the realities of the world that he depicts. In "The Singers," the sportsman wanders into a desolate village where two peasants are about to engage in a singing contest at the local tavern. When the singing begins, the contestants prove by their efforts that beauty can be found even in the voice of a simple peasant, but when the sportsman passes the tavern again at evening, everyone is drunk. In "Biryuk," the forester Biryuk is harsh with the luckless peasant that he has caught cutting a tree before he finally lets him off, but Biryuk, a handsome, vigorous man, has had his own bad luck, for his wife ran away with a traveling peddler. One of Turgenev's finest stories, "A Living Relic," was not added to *A Sportsman's Sketches* until 1874. Seeking shelter from a rainstorm, the sportsman enters a rude hut where he encounters Lukerya, once the most beautiful servant on his family's estate. Yet shortly before she was to be married, Lukerya injured herself in a fall, and for seven years she has wasted away toward death, patiently and devoutly submitting to her bitter fate.

When *A Sportsman's Sketches* appeared in 1852, Nicholas I was still czar of Russia, and direct criticism of his regime was not permitted. Turgenev's "sketches" were perhaps as effective as anything in their time in bringing the plight of Russia's underclass to the attention of a literate public.

FATHERS AND SONS

First published: *Ottsy i deti*, 1862 (English translation, 1867)
Type of work: Novel

Evgeny Bazarov, a nihilistic disciple of scientific materialism, dies after cutting himself at a carelessly performed autopsy.

Fathers and Sons is probably Turgenev's most famous work. It addresses ideas of the period more directly than most of his other works and creates debate over these ideas as a conflict of generations. The novel's story is simple enough. Arkady brings his friend Evgeny Bazarov home with him at the end of his university studies. Home is a country estate occupied by Arkady's father, Nikolai Petrovich (who is a widower), his uncle Pavel Petrovich, Fenichka (a young woman living under Nikolai's protection) and Mitya, the son whom Fenichka has borne to Nikolai. Nikolai considers himself a progressive; Pavel cultivates the manner of an English aristocrat. Conflict develops when these middle-aged men enter into discussion with Bazarov, who rejects all authority but the evidence of scientific materialism and regards art with amused contempt.

Presently, Arkady and Bazarov pay a visit to town. They meet Sitnikov and Kukshin, a foolish young man and woman who pose as radical intellectuals. Then, at a Governor's Ball, they meet a young widow, Anna Sergeyevna Odintsov, and her younger sister Katya. Arkady and Bazarov are both smitten by Madame Odintsov and visit her at her country estate. When Bazarov declares his passion to Madame Odintsov, he is rejected. He then takes Arkady to visit his parents, traditionalists who belong to the modest gentry. Bazarov is an only child, deeply loved by his gentle, countrified parents.

After a time, Bazarov and Arkady revisit the Kirsanov estate, where Bazarov and Pavel Petrovich fight a nonfatal duel over a misunderstanding about Fenichka. Bazarov and Arkady visit Odintsov again, and now it is clear that Arkady is attracted not by Anna Sergeyevna but by her sister, Katya, a pretty but conventional (and marriageable) young woman.

Bazarov returns to his parents. He assists his father, a retired army doctor, in medical proceedings. One day, he participates in an autopsy on a man who has died of typhus. He cuts his finger, neglects to disinfect the cut, and dies of typhus. As the novel concludes, Arkady and his father unite with Katya and Fenichka in a double wedding.

Fathers and Sons caused controversy in Russia at the time of its appearance. Conservatives thought Turgenev was too sympathetic toward Bazarov. Radicals thought that he was not sympathetic enough and resented Bazarov's dying while his friend Arkady settled into the conventional happiness of marriage and life on his father's estate. Turgenev claimed sympathy with his ill-fated hero, declaring that he agreed with Bazarov on everything but his view of art. Yet it is difficult not to see that Bazarov is a half-willing suicide, and this leads the reader to question whether Bazarov himself does not recognize that, without love, which is hardly an element of scientific materialism, life is a dreary business.

Summary

Ivan Turgenev demonstrated that Russian literature could be written and judged by the standards that obtained in Western Europe. If he was not as profound a thinker as his contemporaries Fyodor Dostoevski and Leo Tolstoy, he was as great an artist and, in his own way, as perceptive concerning the difficulties of the human condition. His novels and stories are not ponderous things to read. He moved easily in literary circles in France and England and even attracted attention from the American novelist Henry James, who wrote an essay expressing admiration for Turgenev's craftsmanship. Turgenev is still read more than one hundred years after his death.

Bibliography

Costlow, Jane T. *Worlds Within Worlds: The Novels of Ivan Turgenev*. Princeton, N.J.: Princeton University Press, 1990.

Lowe, David, ed. *Critical Essays on Ivan Turgenev*. Boston: G. K. Hall, 1988.

Magarshack, David. *Turgenev: A Life*. London: Faber & Faber, 1954.

Moser, Charles A. *Ivan Turgenev*. New York: Columbia University Press, 1972.

Pahomov, George S. *In Earthbound Flight: Romanticism in Turgenev*. Clifton, N.J.: Kingston Press, 1985.

Pritchett, V. S. *The Gentle Barbarian*. New York: Random House, 1977.

Schapiro, Leonard. *Turgenev*. New York: Random House, 1978.

Seeley, Frank P. *Turgenev: A Reading of His Fiction*. Cambridge, England: Cambridge University Press, 1991.

John Higby

MARIO VARGAS LLOSA

Born: Arequipa, Peru
March 28, 1936

Principal Literary Achievement
Vargas Llosa is extensively recognized for his prose fiction; his plays and critical essays are also noteworthy.

Biography

Jorge Mario Pedro Vargas Llosa was born in Arequipa, Peru, on March 28, 1936, the son of Ernesto Vargas Maldonado and Dora Llosa Ureta. In 1946, his parents sent him to a parochial school, the life of which he portrayed in *Los cachorros* (1967; *The Cubs*, in *The Cubs and Other Stories*, 1979), a short novel. His father, alarmed at Mario's desire to become a writer, decided to enroll him in the Leoncio Prado, a Peruvian government military boarding school, which he attended from 1950 to 1952. At this institution, he was exposed to a brutal reality that marked him to the core. Vargas Llosa transposed his experiences in the Leoncio Prado in his novel *La ciudad y los perros* (1963; *The Time of the Hero*, 1966), the publication of which provoked a serious official reaction in Peru. After his two years in the Leoncio Prado, Vargas Llosa completed high school in Piura, where he instigated student unrest and a strike that later served as the basis for his short story "Los jefes" ("The Leaders"). This short narrative won for him the Leopoldo Alas Prize in Spain. In addition, in Piura he wrote his first play, "La huída del Inca" ("The Flight of the Inca").

In 1953, Vargas Llosa enrolled in the School of Law at San Marcos University in Lima. He became an advocate of socialist causes while studying at San Marcos, although communist ideology turned out to be disappointing to him. In 1955, when he was nineteen years old, he married Julia Urquidi, one of his uncle's sisters-in-law. The economic pressures brought about by his marriage were magnificently re-created in his novel *La tía Julia y el escribidor* (1977; *Aunt Julia and the Scriptwriter*, 1982).

By 1957, Vargas Llosa's short stories were appearing in journals and newspapers, and he was the editor of several literary journals. In 1958, his short narrative "El desafio" ("The Challenge") won first place in a competition sponsored by the French journal *La Revue française*, and he traveled to Paris. At this time, he also traveled through the Peruvian Amazon jungle along the upper Marañón river, which gave him culture shock but made him appreciate the inhabitants of that remote area. His second novel, *La casa verde* (1966; *The Green House*, 1968), and *El hablador* (1987;

The Storyteller, 1989) reflect the observations made during this and another expedition to the jungle in 1964.

In 1958, he obtained a scholarship to the University of Madrid, Spain. He devoted his doctoral dissertation to a study on Gabriel García Márquez, an outstanding Latin American writer of his generation, who would win the Nobel Prize in Literature in 1982. After finishing his studies in Madrid, he moved to Paris and requested another scholarship from Peru, which was denied. Nevertheless, he began to work for the French radio-television network, which allowed him the opportunity to come in contact with other prominent Latin American authors such as Julio Cortázar and Jorge Luis Borges from Argentina, Alejo Carpentier from Cuba, Miguel Ángel Asturias, a Nobel laureate from Guatemala, and Carlos Fuentes from Mexico. At this time in his life, he began a self-imposed exile that would last until 1974.

In 1963, Vargas Llosa divorced his wife, Julia Urquidi, and the following year married his cousin Patricia Llosa. In 1965, he was invited to Cuba to judge the literary competition sponsored by the journal *Casa de las Américas* and became a member of the editorial board. After the birth of his first son, Alvaro, in 1966, he and his family moved from Paris to London, where he taught literature at Queen Mary College. In 1967, he traveled to Caracas to receive the Rómulo Gallegos award for his novel *The Green House*. As his reputation grew, he traveled worldwide and began to participate in the International PEN Club (the Association of Poets, Playwrights, Editors, Essayists, and Novelists), of which he became president in 1976. His second son, Gonzalo, was born in 1967, a year that he spent lecturing in Western Europe, the Soviet Union, and the United States. That year he was also writer-in-residence at Washington State University, where he began to review his voluminous novel *Conversación en la catedral* (1969; *Conversation in the Cathedral*, 1975). In 1969, he taught at the University of Puerto Rico at Rio Piedras, and in 1970 he established his residence in Barcelona, Spain.

The decade of the 1970's was a prolific one for Vargas Llosa. In 1971, he published his critical essays *García Márquez: Historia de un deicidio* and *Historia secreta de una novela*. In addition, his fourth novel, *Pantaleón y las visitadoras* (1973; *Captain Pantoja and the Special Service*, 1978), was published in a first edition of one hundred thousand copies and was successfully adapted to the cinema. *Aunt Julia and the Scriptwriter*, which originally appeared in 1977, was also adapted to the cinema. In 1975, he produced another acclaimed volume of critical essays, *La orgía perpetua: Flaubert y "Madame Bovary"* (*The Perpetual Orgy: Flaubert and "Madame Bovary,"* 1986). In the late 1970's, several journals dedicated issues to the study of his works, and in 1977 the University of Oklahoma dedicated to him its Sixth Oklahoma Conference on Writers of the Hispanic World.

His novel *La guerra del fin del mundo* appeared in 1981 (*The War of the End of the World*, 1984). Vargas Llosa also sustained a keen interest in the theater. His two-act play *La señorita de Tacna* (*The Young Lady from Tacna*, 1990), which opened in Buenos Aires and in Lima in 1981, was awarded the Annual Argentine Prize of Literary Criticism. In 1983, his play *Kathie y el hipopótamo* (*Kathie and the Hippopot-*

amus, 1990) was equally successful. In 1988, his book *Elogio de la madrastra* (*In Praise of the Stepmother*, 1990) was enthusiastically received. He sought the presidency of Peru in 1989, but he was defeated.

Analysis

Vargas Llosa is considered a prodigy among the Latin American authors who emerged during the so-called literary boom of the early 1960's. His love affair with literature and writing began very early. He recalls the pleasure that he found in reading the adventures of Tom Sawyer, Sinbad the Sailor, and other stories. During his adolescence, he immersed himself in the French novel. He learned through his readings the characteristics of modern fiction and began to assess the effects of narrative techniques. In addition, his readings introduced him to the works of Henry Miller, James Joyce, Ernest Hemingway, Marcel Proust, André Malraux, Jorge Luis Borges, and William Faulkner.

An overview of Vargas Llosa's works provides an insight into his narrative techniques and themes. In his first novel, *The Time of the Hero*, which is the story of a young cadet, Vargas Llosa's cinematographic techniques, multiple character point of view, disturbed chronology, and incorporation of taboo language achieve the portrayal of the marginalized sectors of society. The military academy Leoncio Prado, where the novel takes place, became a fictional microcosm of Peruvian society and its ills.

By the time this book was published in 1963, Varga Llosa had become concerned with the role of the writer in society. This preoccupation became evident in a speech, "Social Commitment and the Latin American Writer," that he delivered at the conference held in his honor at the University of Oklahoma in 1977. In this speech, he stated the difference between Latin American writers and writers from Western Europe and the United States. In order to fulfill their mission, the former must rigorously uphold their artistic values and their originality to enrich the language and the culture of their countries. On the other hand, Latin American writers must also assume a social responsibility.

His social preoccupations, along with his craftsmanship, were also evident in his second novel, *The Green House*. It is a complex novel developed through five different plot lines, which takes place simultaneously in two Peruvian locales. Although *The Green House* seems to be a structural puzzle that the reader must solve, the themes of frustration and victimization are evident. Individuals are abused for economic gain or for religious reasons.

The victimization of an entire generation through political oppression is the main theme of the next novel, *Conversation in the Cathedral*. This work provides a panoramic view of Peruvian society during the dictatorship of General Manuel Udria from 1948 until 1956. The reader becomes aware that the brutality of this regime spread through all of Peru. Technically speaking, this novel presents on a larger scale some of the stylistic and structural characteristics of Vargas Llosa's previous novels. The plot development appears fragmented and the characters' relationships become at times extremely complex. Yet the theme that emerges constitutes an indictment against political regimes that bring about social depravity.

Vargas Llosa demonstrates new thematic and stylistic trends with the publication of *Captain Pantoja and the Special Service* and *Aunt Julia and the Scriptwriter*. These works exhibit a simpler plot development than prior works. In *Captain Pantoja and the Special Service*, Varga Llosa satirizes the Peruvian army and ridicules the members of a religious cult. Pantoja, a man endowed with maniacal organizational skills, is charged with the secret task of creating a squad of prostitutes to visit the military posts located in the jungle. He carries out his job with such dedication that he becomes entangled in a web of absurd adventures that produce hilarious results. Although this novel is a light, comic narrative, it contains a serious theme, the social evils of any sort of fanaticism.

The War of the End of the World is a historical novel that narrates an upheaval in the backlands of Brazil in the nineteenth century. As in other works by Vargas Llosa, the reader finds two main settings in this novel: Bahia, a coastal city, and Canudos, a religious community. The argument arises among the conservative peasant masses, Bahia's urban politicians and Rio de Janeiro's central government. This dispute rapidly acquires the proportions of a civil war of catastrophic consequences. Using cinematographic techniques such as close-ups, Vargas Llosa makes the reader aware of the horrors of war. Moreover, the writer emphasizes the lethal consequences of all ideological fanaticism.

In some of Vargas Llosa's later works appears yet another preoccupation, an insistent inquiring into the nature of writing. The author investigates the process of writing, the creation of fiction, and the difference between a real writer and a scribbler. Some works included in this category are *Aunt Julia and the Scriptwriter*, *¿Quién mató a Palomino Molero?* (1986; *Who Killed Palomino Molero?*, 1987), *Historia de Mayta* (1984; *The Real Life of Alejandro Mayta*, 1986), and even *The Storyteller*. In *The Real Life of Alejandro Mayta*, there is the presence of a writer-narrator who announces that he is going to reconstruct the unknown or ignored story of the Peruvian leftist revolutionary Alejandro Mayta. He states that it will be a fictional story, but one that will carry the truth of fiction. Moreover, as the writer begins to produce Mayta's story, he reflects on the question of bringing about changes in Peruvian society through revolutionary means. In turns out that Mayta is an insignificant individual who never was able to launch his revolution. At the end of the novel, the apparent underlying theme is intimately related to the production of fiction and the nature of fiction itself.

A new theme appears in Vargas Llosa's novel *In Praise of the Stepmother*, for in it the reader is confronted with the presence of evil in innocence and the difficulties of utopias. It narrates the story of a man who thinks that he has a perfect grip on life until his wicked child seduces his stepmother. This book has some of the characteristics of *Aunt Julia and the Scriptwriter* and *The Storyteller*, for it presents two clearly noticeable textual divisions.

In sum, the novels of Vargas Llosa move gradually from extremely complex structures to simpler works with substantial themes that are more appealing to the general public.

AUNT JULIA AND THE SCRIPTWRITER

First published: *La tía Julia y el escribidor*, 1977 (English translation, 1982)
Type of work: Novel

An eighteen-year-old boy struggling to become a writer marries his uncle's sister-in-law, who is twelve years his senior.

Aunt Julia and the Scriptwriter has become one of Vargas Llosa's most popular novels and has been adapted for film under the title *Tune in Tomorrow* (1990). Like other novels by this author, this narrative presents two definite textual portions narrating two different types of stories. The first story depicts the autobiographical account of the narrator's love affair with his aunt by marriage, Julia. This relationship causes an uproar in the narrator's family, for Julia is not only a distant relative but also a divorcée from Bolivia who is twelve years older than the narrator. Hence, the lovers must elope.

The second textual track contains segments of soap operas composed supposedly by Pedro Camacho, the scriptwriter that figures in the title of the novel. Camacho, a machinelike writer of radio soap operas, eventually overloads his memory and has a nervous breakdown, bringing catastrophic consequences to his works. His characters become entangled in different stories, and situations become chaotic, culminating in apocalyptic tragedies in which the characters expire en masse.

Vargas Llosa's skillfulness becomes evident when he occasionally brings together those two different tracks. These points of contact occur when the narrator's personal affairs begin to acquire the characteristics of Camacho's melodramatic sagas and also when people around the narrator bring up the occurrences in Camacho's stories. The two evident tracks touch each other in this manner. Nevertheless, in between those two plot lines there lies the story of the narrator, who is desperately struggling to become a successful writer. He is searching for ways to achieve realism in fiction. When he urgently needs funds to sustain his relationship with Julia, he engages in a frantic writing activity that his friend Javier calls prostituting one's pen. Javier means that the narrator is producing book reviews and articles for mere profit. The narrator finds this type of writing disgusting, too. On the other hand, when he writes a short narrative, he eagerly shares it with Javier and Julia. Unfortunately, they consistently find his stories unrealistic.

Although Camacho is very successful, the narrator dislikes his style. The scriptwriter's work is a type of wholesale writing to be sent over the air waves for the masses to enjoy. The narrator, however, cannot help but admire Camacho's tenacity and his fanatical dedication to his work. In the final chapter of the novel, the reader knows that the narrator has finally found the kind of writing for which he longs. Nevertheless, one sees Camacho reduced to a disgraceful state. He has turned into a simple gopher for a sensationalist newspaper. Thus, the roles of the narrator and of Camacho are reversed in terms of success and productivity. *Aunt Julia and the Scriptwriter* constitutes an artistic and humorous novel. In it, Vargas Llosa disguises one of his major themes, the inner workings of creative writing.

THE STORYTELLER

First published: *El hablador*, 1987 (English translation, 1989)
Type of work: Novel

An autobiographical narrator tells the story of a Jewish friend who becomes a storyteller among the Machiguenga Indians of the Peruvian jungle.

Varga Llosa initiates *The Storyteller* with the presence of an author-narrator who, while strolling the streets of Florence, sees an exhibit of photographs depicting Peruvian Indians. He notices that one of the photographs shows what he believes to be a Machiguenga storyteller surrounded by his listeners. This encounter prompts him to recall a journey to the upper Marañón River in the Peruvian jungle and his keen interest in the Machiguenga Indians. At the same time, the photographs unleash memories of his Jewish friend Saúl Zurata at San Marcos University, who was well versed in the ways of the Machiguenga.

In the second chapter, the story leaps to the past so that the reader becomes acquainted with Zurata, who, from the beginning, appears to be a specially marked individual. He bears an enormous wine-colored birthmark that covers the entire right side of his face and that earns him the nickname Mascarita (Little Mask). Although he is apparently not bothered by unkind comments on his external appearance, and although he seems open and uncomplicated, the reader suspects that he secretly harbors feelings of alienation. One comes to this conclusion when the narrator points out Zurata's singular affinity for Franz Kafka's writings, especially "The Metamorphosis," which he knows by heart. This short story by Kafka centers on Gregor Samsa, a character who is so alienated from his world that one morning he wakes up and discovers that he has turned into an enormous, repugnant insect.

After the presentation of Zurata, the novel presents two well-defined textural divisions. Chapters that present the narrator's relationship with Zurata alternate with chapters in which a Machiguenga storyteller is the sole narrative voice.

The storyteller's discourse depicts the way of life of the Machiguenga, including their rituals, cosmogony, and system of beliefs. One of the most noteworthy accomplishments of Vargas Llosa in these portions of the novel is the creation of the Machiguenga speech. It is a mythic narrative style of soothing simplicity that seems to flow forever, joining one story to the next without noticeable pauses. The reader sees the Machiguenga always walking, always moving toward a more secure spot near a river. The author-narrator, who derives great pleasure from probing his Jewish friend about his knowledge of ethnology, is deeply disappointed when, on accepting a scholarship to Spain, he loses contact with Zurata, who seems to disappear into thin air. A missionary mentions having heard the unending discourse of a Machiguenga storyteller, which prompts the author-narrator to want to know more about this person. This storyteller is an albino with an immense wine-colored birthmark on the right side of his face, which reveals to the reader that the Machiguenga storyteller is Zurata. In addition, the reader finds the storyteller identifying himself as Gregor-Tasurinchi and narrating a horrifying experience; he dreams that he has turned into an enormous, repugnant insect.

Summary

Mario Vargas Llosa is one of the most prominent and prolific writers of the literary "boom" in Latin America. His works demonstrate that he has successfully developed a great variety of themes. Social injustice, political oppression that brings about societal decadence, the abuse of human beings, the creative act of writing, the dangers of fanaticism and of utopias, and the intrinsic value found in primitive cultures are some of his major preoccupations. He sees the mission of the Latin American writer as one of a spiritual nature, through which life may become better for all.

Bibliography

Castro-Klaren, Sara. *Mario Vargas Llosa*. Columbia: University of South Carolina Press, 1990.

Díez, Luis A. *Mario Vargas Llosa's Pursuit of the Total Novel: A Study of Style and Technique in Relation to Moral Intention*. Cuernavaca, Mexico: CIDOC, 1970.

Geisdorfer-Feal, Rosemary. *Novel Lives: The Fictional Autobiographies of Guillermo Cabrera Infante and Mario Vargas Llosa*. Chapel Hill: University of North Carolina, Department of Romance Languages, 1986.

Gerdes, Dick. *Mario Vargas Llosa*. Boston: Twayne, 1985.

Harss, Luis, and Barbara Dohmann. *Into the Mainstream*. New York: Harper & Row, 1967.

Lewis, Marvin A. *From Lima to Leticia: The Peruvian Novels of Mario Vargas Llosa*. Lanham, Md.: University Press of America, 1983.

Rossman, Charles, and Alan Warren Friedman, eds. *Mario Vargas Llosa: A Collection of Critical Essays*. Austin: University of Texas Press, 1978.

Williams, Raymond L. *Mario Vargas Llosa*. New York: Frederick Ungar, 1986.

Cida S. Chase

LOPE DE VEGA CARPIO

Born: Madrid, Spain
November 25, 1562
Died: Madrid, Spain
August 27, 1635

Principal Literary Achievement

Lope de Vega Carpio is recognized as both the most prodigious writer of Spanish letters and the creator of the Spanish national theater.

Biography

Lope Félix de Vega Carpio was born in Madrid, Spain, on November 25, 1562, the son of Félix de Vega Carpio and Francisca Fernández Flores. By the age of five, and before he could write, Lope de Vega Carpio was already bargaining with schoolmates to copy his verses for him; at thirteen, he wrote his first *comedia* (comic play), *El verdadero amante* (pb. 1620; the true lover). At the Universities of Alcalá and Salamanca, Lope de Vega Carpio began translating Latin poetry and concentrating on his own literary endeavors. Both parents died when he was a young man. Yet he maintained his parents' passion for living, particularly his father's inclination toward amorous adventures, which structured his life-style and career.

In the early 1580's, Vega Carpio, now strongly attracted to the world of the theater, met the daughter of a well-known theater figure, Elena Osorio, with whom he established a love relationship that lasted many years. Elena's father, however, eventually opposed the relationship and forbade his daughter from seeing the young, aspiring dramatist. Consequently, Vega Carpio wrote several vicious attacks on the Osorio family and was brought to court for his defamations. Only twenty-six years old, he was sentenced to exile from the court for eight years and from the kingdom for two years.

During Vega Carpio's years in exile, he married by proxy Isabel de Urbina and immediately went to fight for the invincible Spanish Armada. During this time, he wrote the twenty-canto poem *La hermosura de Angélica* (1602; the beauty of Angélica). After Spain's defeat against England, Vega Carpio returned to Valencia in eastern Spain, where a popular dramatic school was flourishing. Between 1588 and 1591, he wrote many *romances* (octosyllabic, assonant verse) and *comedias*, which he sent to Gaspar de Porres, his agent in Madrid. It is during these years that he acquired national fame and earned the nickname "fénix de los ingenios" ("phoenix of

the witty"). In 1590, his exile completed, he returned to Toledo, a city fifty miles south of Madrid, and was employed as secretary to the duke of Alba. He maintained this position for five years, during which time he wrote *La Arcadia* (1598), a pastoral novel that deals with the theme of love. In 1594, his first wife died in childbirth. Four years later, he married Juana de Guardo, with whom he had three children. Shortly after this marriage, he returned to Madrid to be closer to the theater. There, he met another important female figure, Micaela de Luján. Although still married to Juana, Vega Carpio lived with Micaela and with her had seven children. She is present in many of his poems under the pseudonym Camila Lucinda. Around 1608, however, her name disappeared from his work.

In 1605, Vega Carpio began his employment with the duke of Sessa, for whom he was secretary for twenty-six years. He established an intimate correspondence with the duke, twenty years his junior. Throughout their exchange of letters, Vega Carpio revealed many intimate details about his life and relationships. A few years later, he wrote his serious study on dramatic principles, *El arte nuevo de hacer comedias en este tiempo* (1609; *The New Art of Writing Plays*, 1914), which shaped the characteristics of seventeenth century Spanish drama.

The years between 1610 and 1613 are considered to be the happiest of Vega Carpio's life. *Fuenteovejuna* (1619; *The Sheep-Well*, 1936); *El acero de Madrid* (pb. 1618; *Madrid Steel*, 1935), and *El perro del hortelano* (pb. 1618; *The Gardener's Dog*, 1903) are all proof of his superior dramatic creations of this time period. His wife Juana died in childbirth in 1614, however, and he fell into an intense depression that led him to take up monastic orders. Shortly after turning to the priesthood, he met Marta de Nevares Santoyo, a married woman with whom he became passionately involved. Her presence is apparent in many of his poems. He wrote about her in his poetry as Amarilis. They were happy together for more than ten years, but in 1632, Marta, blind and insane, died at the age of forty. It was at this time of his life that Vega Carpio produced his famous tragedy, *El castigo sin venganza* (pb. 1635; *Justice Without Revenge*, 1936). He also published *La Dorotea* (1632), a largely autobiographical work written in both prose and verse.

In the last year of his life, Vega Carpio regularly repented for his errors. The last work that he ever created, *Égloga a Claudio* (1637; eclogue to Claudio), focused on a self-critical yet nostalgic reflection on his life. He recorded that he had written more than one hundred plays, each within a twenty-four-hour period, and that the total number ascended to fifteen hundred. At the age of seventy-three, after a life overflowing with adventure and emotional trauma, Vega Carpio passed away on August 27, 1635, in Madrid.

Analysis

While Vega Carpio's genius extends to all literary genres, he is most recognized as a dramatist. One of his main achievements was to bring all the diverse elements of preceding Spanish theater together and unify them under a few basic guidelines. Although he had been writing plays since the 1570's, it was not until 1609 that he published his poem of practical guidelines for dramatists, *The New Art of Writing Plays*. In this work, he stresses unity of action in a three-act play written in polymetric verse. Whether a comedy, tragedy, or tragicomedy, the drama should have one *gracioso*, a witty servant, either male or female, who parodies the actions and lines of the main characters and who delights the audience with puns and anecdotes. He also states that language should be appropriate to the individual characters and that verse should be appropriate to the scene that it describes. Suspense, however, is important; the audience should not know the ending until the ending. Vega Carpio's major theme, honor, is usually revealed through a conflict between the court and the town, between new Christians and old Christians, or within love triangles. For him, the most important part of the play was the audience's enjoyment, but, at the same time, he never disregarded the didactic importance of his plays. These specifications remained the defining elements of Spanish theater well into the eighteenth century.

After Vega Carpio's death, his protégé, Juan Pérez de Montalbán, attributed 1,800 *comedias* and more than 400 *autos sacramentales*, one-act plays with a religious theme, to his master. Since the 1960's, however, most critics accept that there are 314 plays that are definitely by him and some 187 that may be his.

Vega Carpio's dramatic works can be divided into various categories: plays of *capa y espada* (cloak and sword), which deal with an intriguing love affair usually ending in marriage, religious and mythological plays, and those based on another literary work or a historical event. The cloak-and-sword plays are characterized by a plot that includes jealous lovers, a woman who is covered up or disguised in some way, and some sort of duel. Some examples of this type of drama are *La dama boba* (pb. 1617; *The Lady Nit-Wit*, 1958), *Madrid Steel*, and *Las bizarrías de Belisa* (pb. 1637).

The most celebrated of this group of plays, however, is *The Gardener's Dog*. In this play, he deals with the conflict between honor and love. Doña Diana, the countess of Belflor, falls in love with her secretary, the commoner Teodoro, who does not know his heritage. Her dilemma is a real, modern-day one because the code of honor does not allow the different economic classes to intermarry. She is, like the dog in the proverb that forms the play's title, "the gardener's dog who neither eats nor stops eating." Teodoro's servant, Tristán, convinces everyone but Diana that his master is a real count. Yet Teodoro, disgraced by the lie, insists that he must leave Diana. She immediately responds that his sense of honor proves his nobility, and, thus, they can marry, and he can become a real count. With spectacular characterization and intrigue, Vega Carpio addresses the conventions of modern day honor. He insinuates that because honor, in the sense of public reputation, is satisfied by the lies of Teodoro, then the whole concept of honor is a sham.

Vega Carpio's religious plays were important in teaching Christian principles to seventeenth century Spain. Besides the Church and public storytellers, plays were the only way for the commoners, almost all of them illiterate, to learn about the Bible. He created many plays that dramatized incidents from the Old Testament. His interpretation of the Book of *Esther*, *La hermosa Ester* (pb. 1610; beautiful Esther), is perhaps his most beautiful biblical drama. Stories from the New Testament were strictly supervised by the Church and limited to those dealing with Christ as an infant; it was considered indecent to portray Christ's adult life in the playhouses. Vega Carpio wrote numerous biblical *comedias*, as well as *comedias de santos*, dramas that interpreted the life of a saint. The mythological plays, written for the court, included spectacular visual effects that the regular playhouses could never have afforded.

Vega Carpio also enjoyed basing his plays on historical events. In this way, history itself would serve a didactic end in the theater. One of his earlier dark tragedies, *El duque de Viseo* (pb. 1615; the duke of Viseo) is based on Portuguese history and deals with the difficulty of administering justice. *The Sheep-Well* is based on an actual fifteenth century uprising. A villainous commander abuses his villagers to such an extent that they finally revolt and kill him. When the monarch tries to extort evidence of the guilty party, the village unites, and the whole community takes the blame. Finally, they are pardoned by the king. Vega Carpio brings to the stage the themes of justice, loyalty, and harmony within the state.

PERIBÁÑEZ

First published: *Peribáñez y el comendador de Ocaña*, 1614 (English
translation, 1936)
Type of work: Play

In a farming town, a newlywed couple represents the ideals of love and honor by overcoming the obstacles that the lustful commander presents to them.

Peribáñez typifies Vega Carpio's ideas of the necessary ingredients for a successful drama and is truly one of Spain's greatest plays. In this three-act *comedia*, Peribáñez, a young farmer, and his bride, Casilda, confront the local commander of Ocaña, their town, in his attacks against their love and honor. The play opens with the wedding scene of the young couple and includes some beautiful verse between the newlyweds proclaiming their love for each other and their individual expectations of their marriage. The day is cursed, however, when the young and noble commander of Ocaña suffers a terrible fall from his horse. Peribáñez and Casilda offer their home to the commander so that he may recover from his accident. When he finally regains consciousness, he sets his eyes on the beautiful bride and immediately falls in love with her. The commander decides that he will stop at nothing to fulfill his desires for Casilda. He plots to bribe the couple with gifts of mules and earrings in hopes of winning their trust and taking advantage of Casilda. The rest of the first act deals with the young lovers' trip to Toledo, where the king of Spain is celebrating the summer festival, and how the commander follows them there and secretly hires an artist to paint a portrait of the woman whom he so strongly desires. In these descriptions of the wedding and the festivals, Lope de Vega vividly describes the houses and the dresses that the women wear and, in this way, offers the reader a rich description of the local colors and customs.

In the second act, the overlord, with the help of his two servants, gains entrance to Casilda's house when Peribáñez is away on business. Casilda, however, rejects his propositions using lines from a famous ballad: "far more do I care for Peribáñez in that brown cape of his than for the Commander in his embroidered one." For Casilda, love outweighs wealth and riches. Yet the commander does not take lightly to her scorn. He swears that he will, in the end, have her: "Well, even though you cost me my property, my honor, my blood and my life, I am going to overcome your disdain, I intend to conquer your resistance." As with most cape-and-sword dramas, the hero discovers the stain of his honor and tries to recuperate his loss. Peribáñez is in Toledo when he discovers the portrait of his wife in the house of a local artist and deduces the commander's real motives. He quickly returns to Ocaña, fully trusting his wife but unsure of how to deal with the commander. In this act, the conflict is fully revealed, and, as the curtain falls, the audience postulates the outcome of the play.

At the beginning of the last act, the commander decides to knight Peribáñez and put him in command of a squadron of soldiers fighting the Moors. His reasons, of course, are selfish. As the army leaves, Peribáñez and one of the soldiers, Belardo, reflect on life. It has been suggested that Belardo represents Vega Carpio himself as he discusses life, gardening, and the sacristy. In this last act, Vega Carpio integrates historical figures and events into the drama that connect the themes of honor, love, and justice portrayed on the stage to the audience's real world.

That night, Peribáñez secretly returns and awaits the uninvited guest in the bedroom. When the commander enters, Peribáñez runs his sword through him and then kills two others for being traitors to his household. King Henry III hears the story of a commoner slaying a nobleman and immediately offers a reward to bring the guilty man to court for execution. Peribáñez turns himself in and begs that the king listen to his story. The just king grants him the favor, Peribáñez explains, and the king both pardons and praises him for upholding his honor. The curtain closes as the king and queen reward the loving couple for upholding love and honor in the face of conflict.

JUSTICE WITHOUT REVENGE

First published: *El castigo sin venganza*, 1635 (English translation, 1936)
Type of work: Play

In this tragedy, Vega Carpio exposes the moral hypocrisies underlying the lifestyle of the nobles and shows how "honor" can cruelly govern and instigate unjust paradoxes.

Justice Without Revenge, one of Vega Carpio's last works, is an ironic tragedy based on a short novel written about a historical fact. In this drama, there are three protagonists: the womanizing duke of Ferrara, his illegitimate son, Count Federico, and the young noblewoman, Casandra, whom the duke marries for legal reasons. In the beginning of the play, Vega Carpio develops the relationship between the characters. In contrast to *Peribáñez*, in which the charming heroes win the approval of a just monarch, the protagonists of this drama do not represent upstanding citizens. Yet in spite of their antiheroics, the audience does, to some extent, sympathize with their decisions and actions. The duke regularly frequents the local whorehouses but knows that he has to marry and beget a legitimate heir for his estate. He has little interest, however, in remaining faithful to his young, attractive bride. Federico, his illegitimate son, whom the duke sincerely loves, is selfishly concerned about his hereditary position and has little patience for his father's amorous adventures. Upon seeing his future stepmother, whom he rescues in a stagecoach accident, he falls instantly in love with her. Casandra reciprocates these feelings, although, at the same time, she accepts her commitment to her future husband, and the two lovers suffer the anguish of not being able to express their love openly.

In act 2, Vega Carpio develops the moral positions of each of the characters. The two young lovers resist their feelings even though the duke continues his nightly adventures with the local prostitutes. Unexpectedly, the duke is called to fight in the religious wars. Federico and Casandra are left alone, and in beautiful and powerful verses they openly admit the intense love that they feel toward one another. This explosive scene is the climax of the love that Federico and Casandra feel for one another. The audience is torn between sympathizing with the two victims or rejecting them because they do not maintain their family honor.

In act 3, the duke returns from the wars a reformed man, vowing to be faithful to his wife. At this point, Vega Carpio aggrandizes the duke and tries to make him a worthy central figure. Upon his arrival, the duke receives an anonymous letter explaining the truth, technically incest, between his wife and his son. He suddenly realizes his own guilt for what has happened and decides to act, not as vengeful father or husband, but as supreme justice. He punishes his son and wife, although violently, without revenge. First, the duke tricks his son into killing Casandra, who is bound and gagged in a sack. Then, he accuses Federico of killing the duchess for fear of losing his inheritance and sentences him to death. The duke is condemned to live his life knowing that he has killed the one whom he loves most, his son. In this tragedy, Vega Carpio presents a somber conflict between love and honor, the hypocrisy that surrounds them both and the pain that is suffered from their clashing.

Summary

Ezra Pound said that Lope de Vega Carpio was like ten brilliant minds inhabiting one body, and that any attempts to enclose him into any formula would be like trying to make one pair of boots fit a centipede. He lived an adventurous, amorous life, reflected in his prose and poetry. His fame within the Spanish theater is unprecedented. His diversity of themes, spontaneity and naturalness of dramatic characters, concern for the audience's enjoyment, and innovations of seventeenth century theater define him as one of the greatest dramatists of the Western world.

Bibliography

Flores, Angel. *Spanish Drama*. New York: Bantam Books, 1962.

Fox, Dian. *Refiguring the Hero, from Peasant to Noble on Lope de Vega and Calderón*. University Park: Pennsylvania State University Press, 1991.

Hayes, Francis C. *Lope de Vega*. New York: Twayne, 1967.

Parker, A. A. *The Approach to the Spanish Drama of the Golden Age*. London: Hispanic and Luso-Brazilian Councils, 1957.

Rennert, Hugo Albert. *The Life of Lope de Vega, 1562-1635*. New York: G. E. Stechert, 1937.

—————. *The Spanish Stage in the Time of Lope de Vega*. New York: Hispanic Society of America, 1909.

Underhill, John Garrett. *Four Plays by Lope de Vega*. New York: Charles Scribner's Sons, 1936.

Carolyn A. Nadeau

VERGIL

Born: Andes (near Mantua), Italy
October 15, 70 B.C.
Died: Brundisium (Brindisi), Italy
September 21, 19 B.C.

Principal Literary Achievement

Vergil, through the pastorals of his youth and the epic of his maturity, created verse which, while Greek in its inspiration, specifically reflects the sophistication of Augustan Rome.

Biography

As is the case with many ancient writers who achieved wide popularity in their lifetimes, much of the vast amount of biographical material written about Publius Vergilius Maro during or immediately after his lifetime is unreliable. From the outset of his career, the Roman poet whom readers popularly identify as Vergil (or Virgil) was the poet most associated with the patriotism of the Pax Romana (the worldwide Roman Peace) of the emperor Augustus. Furthermore, Vergil's poems went almost immediately into the school curriculum; they became the means by which generations of children learned literary Latin, and the Italy that these works portray became an idealized rendering of that under Augustus. Their creator quickly assumed the stature of patriot-poet, and his poems acquired mystical interpretations tied to Rome's desinty.

Vergil was born on October 15, 70 B.C., in Andes, a countrified region near the town of Mantua, in Italy. His background appears fixed in the respectable but not particularly wealthy middle class. That is clear from the solid education that he received at Cremona and Rome. Particularly useful in establishing his family's relatively modest circumstances is the fact that Vergil's education lacked the philosophical component of study at Athens. By contrast, Vergil's poet-contemporary Horace (68 B.C.-8 B.C.) had enjoyed this advantage. It is also certain that the region of Vergil's birth underwent a dramatic shift in its political allegiance during the first century B.C. Though part of Cisalpine Gaul was Romanized, it was not until 49 B.C. that the residents of Mantua received the rights of Roman citizenship. Thus, it was not until he had reached the age of twenty-one that Vergil could properly consider himself a fully enfranchised Roman.

Previously, instability and violence had filled Italy. Lucius Sergius Catilina (Cati-

line), the insurrectionist exposed in Cicero's Catilinarian orations, died fighting against Roman legions; Vergil would have been seven years old at the time. The civil war between Julius Caesar and Gnaeus Pompeius (Pompey), riots in Rome, Caesar's assassination on the Ides of March (44 B.C.), and the civil war between Caesar's heir Octavian (who assumed the title "Augustus" in 27 B.C.) and Marcus Antonius meant that war filled twenty-nine of Vergil's fifty-one years. All of these factors plus Augustus' professed determination to create an environment congenial for artists and the flowering of Roman culture could only have led the young Vergil to recognize the special ties that he had with Augustus' vision of Rome and, at least initially, to work toward its realization.

It appears that Vergil's father had been a potter or perhaps a day laborer. Ancient sources testify that Vergil's mother, Maggia Pollia, was of the lower landed gentry and that her family in some way employed the man whom she would marry, but this is essentially speculation. Similarly, the name of Vergil's mother appears in medieval testimonies as support for belief in the magical powers of Vergil's work, the poet's own name etymologized as from *virga* ("wand"). That accounts for the corruption "Virgil," familiar as the spelling one finds in many modern texts.

Vergil pursued his higher studies in forensics, though he was without gifts in oratory, and tradition has it that he argued only one case at the bar. Convinced that a future in the courts was impossible for him, Vergil began higher studies in Greek literature with Epidius and in Epicurean philosophy (the vogue at the time because of Lucretius). Around this time, 41 B.C., former soldiers of Antony armed with senatorial approval claimed a number of farms in Cisalpine Gaul, Vergil's among them. The commissioners Gallus, Varus, and Pollio recommended that Vergil petition the young Octavius, and this action saved the family farm. Vergil immortalizes this kindness in *Eclogue* 1 of the *Eclogues* (43-37 B.C.; English translation, 1575; also known as the *Bucolics*).

Still, it appears that the emperor's intervention did not reduce the threat to Vergil's life or that of his father. Roving bands of former soldiers, frustrated at not having obtained the lands promised them, ranged the countryside in search of the peasants who rightly held these lands, and this threat caused Vergil and his father to flee south. For a time, father and son resided with Vergil's tutor Siro, then in a villa near Nola and at Naples. It was there that Vergil composed his four-book poem on farming known as the *Georgics* (c. 37-29 B.C.; English translation, 1589).

Vergil's pastorals brought him to the attention of Augustus, as Octavius now styled himself. Augustus had a definite vision of Rome as a sophisticated, urbanized empire that derived its strength from its ancient origins and sturdy peasantry. The *Eclogues* and *Georgics* made Vergil the poet most qualified, in the emperor's view, to treat the legend of Aeneas' search for "New Troy" in Italy after the Trojan War. Clearly, Augustus hoped for an epic poem in Latin hexameters corresponding to the *Iliad* (eighth century B.C.; first codified early second century B.C.; English translation, 1616) and *Odyssey* (eighth century B.C.; first codified early second century B.C.; English translation, 1616) of Homer; it was, of course, the magnificent *Aeneid* (c. 29-19 B.C.;

English translation, 1553) that he ultimately received.

Augustus almost never did receive the *Aeneid*. Vergil repeatedly delayed in complying when the emperor requested to hear sections of the work in progress. To what degree it was complete when Vergil had returned ill from his tour of Asia Minor is a moot question. He had, it is certain, asked that the unrevised manuscript of the *Aeneid* be burned should he be unable to complete its revision. Just as sure is that Vergil, whose health had always been delicate, contracted fever at Megara (capital of Megaris, a district of Greece on the isthmus of Corinth) and that his health deteriorated rapidly upon reaching Italy at Brundisium (the modern Brindisi). On his deathbed at Brundisium, Vergil again requested that his poem be destroyed, since he remained dissatisfied with its degree of revision. Vergil died on September 21, 19 B.C. Tradition has it that Augustus' intervention alone saved the *Aeneid* and that the emperor commissioned Varius and Tucca with its final editing. This process took approximately two years, and thus it was that in 17 B.C. Latin literature produced the most eloquent tribute to Roman glory ever written.

Analysis

Vergil's deathbed request that the unfinished *Aeneid* be destroyed is an example of one characteristic of his style: insistence upon perfection. He considered this essential to achieve the civilized, cosmopolitan elegance that characterizes all of his verse. Such urbanity appears even in Vergil's pastorals. The four books of the *Georgics*, for example, took seven years for him to complete. Based on the total number of 2,188 lines, this would mean an average of about one verse per day. Indeed, Aulus Gellius, the second century commentator on assorted literary matters, reproduces a remark attributed to Vergil that he licked his verses into shape the way a mother bear does her cubs.

This slowness toward final form springs partly from Vergil's perfectionism, but even more from the poet's need to reflect a Romanized version of Greek forms. It was Vergil's fate to work in poetic forms in which Greek poets cast an overwhelming shadow, even in the genres of Latin literature: Theocritus and Hesiod in pastoral, and, of course, Homer in epic. To avoid being called a mere Roman imitator of these Greek masters and to push the Latin language to its limits in order to accommodate the style that he felt appropriate to Augustan Rome, Vergil had to proceed slowly.

Some, even among contemporary critics, are content to describe Vergilian poetry as Latin imitation of Greek models, but that is a convenient dismissal of the specifically Italian character that all Vergil's poetry attains. The shepherds of his *Eclogues* have Greek names; their love affairs and concerns resemble those of the characters in the *Idyls* (third century B.C.) of Theocritus, but the countryside that they describe is indisputably that of Tuscany and the Campagna. The ten poems that comprise the *Eclogues* are clearly the collection upon which Vergil worked to hone his specifically Roman style. To be overly concerned with their order of composition overlooks the fact that Vergil privileged the unity of larger finished products over any single constituent. Thus, although four (2, 3, 7, 8) reflect the Theocritean debt that Vergil obviously felt he owed, two others (5, 10) describe a specifically Roman and notably Augustan world. The remainder (1, 4, 6, 9) are least Theocritean of all and are arguably the finest of the entire collection. In their final arrangement, they form a reciprocal pattern. Briefly stated, this pattern yields the themes of recovered land, lost love, and Augustan greatness. The collection evokes the Caesar element in eclogue 5, foreshadowed in the climax of eclogue 1 (the imperial generosity that restores rightful ownership) and 4 (which predicts a second golden age heralded by young Augustus). Topical references sprinkled throughout the work (Asinius Pollio and Vergil's rival poets Bavius and Maevius) extend the contemporary Augustan tone Vergil sought.

Escaping the poetic tastes of the poetic generation that preceded his own was another task that Vergil faced. These extended in two directions: the erotic verse of Caius Valerius Catullus and, to some extent, the philosophic poetry of Titus Lucretius Carus. One difficulty simply lay in creating a taste for the specifically Roman poetry that Vergil wrote. Augustus' political program assisted that to some degree, as did imperial subventions to the circle of poets in which Vergil functioned. The enormous financial resources of Gaius Gilnius Maecenas added to Vergil's financial security, for Vergil was primary among a group of poets supported by this wealthy Roman. Developing a literature that simultaneously glorified Roman origins yet looked toward greatness as the empire's destiny became paramount for the Maecenas group, and no poet, not even Quintus Horatius Flaccus (Horace) or Publius Ovidius Naso (Ovid), both of whom also received such subventions, could satisfy these goals as completely as Vergil.

Specifically, Roman concerns emerge even more boldly in the *Georgics*, a four-book didactic poem on agriculture. This work follows the *Eclogues* by eight years and reflects Vergil's maturity as a poet. It owes a nominal debt to Hesiod's *Works and Days* (c. 700 B.C.) or to Nicander's *Georgika* (c. 100 B.C.), but it is not in any sense Hellenic. Vergil's *Georgics* is not an exercise in virtuosic treatment of prosaic subject matter, nor is Vergil (like Lucretius) trying to make difficult subject matter easy, nor does Vergil expect Roman farmers to use the advice that it gives as a practical guide to farming. The *Georgics*, like the *Eclogues*, rather represents concerns central to human life in Augustan Rome. It provides a clear set of moral values, which extend to respect for tools and the work itself, a religious justification for the work of farming, a calendar that specifically relates to the growing seasons of Italy and the varied forms of agriculture one finds there, including a substantial final section on beekeeping. As with the *Eclogues*, there is a clear Augustan message. Hard work and diligent application wrings fertility from infertility, life from death. This remains the work of all farmers at all times, but the *Georgics* casts it in terms of a theodicy for the Golden Age of Augustus. A clear cosmic sympathy watches over Italy under Augustus; given the application of its people, labor yields justice and prosperity.

It is precisely this destiny that favored creation of Augustan Rome, and Vergil develops the theme even further in his *Aeneid*. *Fatum* (fate) through *labor* (work) tempered by *dolor* (sorrow and grief) and *pietas* (piety and humility) led Aeneas to lay aside personal desires for the sake of establishing a "New Troy" at Lavinium in Italy.

It would take nearly half a millennium, but the race formed from an amalgam of Trojan and native Italic elements would give rise to that of Romulus. From Romulus and the Roman kings would spring the Roman republic and, ultimately, the empire established by Augustus.

As with both the *Eclogues* and *Georgics*, there is also a debt to Greek poetry; obviously, the *Aeneid* owes its inspiration to Homer's *Iliad* and *Odyssey*. Characteristically, however, the similarity is structural rather than aesthetic. The *Aeneid* is less than half the length of either of Homer's poems. Vergil has arranged its books to recall first the wanderings of Odysseus (*Aeneid* 1-6), then a new war at Lavinium (*Aeneid* 7-12), which corresponds to the Trojan War as described in the *Iliad*. Thus, rather than concealing the literary past upon which the *Aeneid* depends, Vergil effectively flaunts it, making it underscore the thesis of the poem itself: that the past and its difficulties are essential to build the new order of his own present, that of Augustan Rome.

Vergilian epic, despite these similarities, thus differs markedly from that of Homer. Vergil's is urban, national epic. Critics unfavorably inclined sometimes call it Augustan propaganda, but even if this is so it is also great art and Roman poetry at its highest level of development. One measure of its greatness is the fact that, like Homeric poetry, its style was imitated in a series of works attributed to Vergil. These poems, collectively called the *Appendix Vergiliana* (A.D. first century) but actually the work of an inferior subsequent imitator, reveal not only the profound effect that Vergil had on Roman poetry but also, by contrast, the superiority of the master.

ECLOGUES

First published: 43-37 B.C. (English translation, 1575)
Type of work: Pastoral poetry

The ten pastorals of this collection successfully translate the settings, characters, and thoughts of their Greek counterparts to a frame of reference specifically that of Augustan Rome.

The *Eclogues* is a remarkable achievement of Vergil's late twenties and shows that the poet, even at this early age, intended to develop a style distinct from those of his Greek and Roman predecessors. The ten-poem collection falls into three major categories. *Eclogues* 2, 3, 7, and 8 are the most Theocritean; the rustic characters that they present have Greek names (Corydon, Amoebaeus, Damon, Alphesiboeus), and the situations that the poems describe find their counterparts in the works of Theocritus. *Eclogues* 1, 4, 6, and 9 are specifically non-Theocritean; these poems deal with matters particularly significant to life in Augustan Rome (exile revoked, respect for right of ownership, arrival of a new Golden Age, warnings of the passing of this Golden Age, doubts for the future). The collection turns on *Eclogues* 5 and 10, the two Daphnis poems; Daphnis represents Caesar in the first of these, and the poet Gallus becomes Daphnis in the second. The clear result of this arrangement is to introduce Augustan reference into what had been the timeless environment of pastoral. The characters thus acquire a tendency toward introspection and a degree of psychological development unmatched by Theocritus.

Augustan time is always present in Vergil's pastoral world, yet it remains unobtrusive primarily because of the reciprocal pattern of arrangement that Vergil follows. Eclogue 1, for example, finds its parallel poem in *Eclogue* 9. In *Eclogue* 1, the content Tityrus explains his happy state of mind to Meliboeus by noting that a god restored his farm. While never leaving the bucolic environment, one imagines the change of scene that takes Tityrus to Rome and an encounter with the young emperor. Vergil never uses the names Octavian, Caesar, or Augustus, yet the automatically generous response of an emperor concerned for his subjects makes the identity of the *iuvenis* (young man) whom Tityrus sees at Rome unmistakable. *Eclogue* 9 answers *Eclogue* 1; both poems refer obliquely to the land seizures of 41 B.C., though the ninth pastoral creates a somewhat discordant note. There, a distraught Moeris tells Lycidas that he is about to undertake a similar journey to petition for restoration of his land. This poem specifically recalls the Tityrus poem and implies that Octavian's ascension to the throne has not automatically eliminated treachery. It is impossible to say what intervened in Vergil's life to produce this changed mood, but the realism that this poem introduces adds an element that had never appeared in pre-Vergilian pastoral.

Such reciprocity allows grouping of the collection into two major categories. *Eclogues* 1 to 5 present essentially conciliatory Augustan situations; *Eclogues* 6 to 10 qualify comparable situations. Thus, while *Eclogue* 2 asserts the triumph of reason over essentially unworthy love, *Eclogue* 8 answers by presenting Daphnis bound in the spell of an unworthy love whose consequence is death. *Eclogue* 3 describes a crude and abusive singing contest that ends in peaceful nondecision; its answer, in *Eclogue* 7, presents a similar contest in which the mild Corydon defeats the harsh Thyrsis. *Eclogue* 4, interpreted during the Middle Ages as the "Messianic Eclogue," predicts the coming of a new golden age under Octavian (again without use of the emperor's name); *Eclogue* 6 notes the passing of these hopes into a series of unnatural loves and changes in form. Like *Eclogue* 9, it implies the transitory nature of happiness and contentment as part of the human condition. Even Octavian cannot alter this essential fact of life. *Eclogue* 5 presents the death and transfiguration of Daphnis, a poetic masque for Octavian; its answer is *Eclogue* 10. There, Gallus wastes away for unrequited love of Lycoris, who has run off with an unnamed soldier. The final effect of these poetic answers is to privilege the historical to the timeless situation and the realistic outcome to the ideal.

GEORGICS

First published: c. 37-29 B.C. (English translation, 1589)
Type of work: Didactic poetry

The *Georgics* represents both a continuation of Vergil's Augustan program and a departure from pastoral verse in favor of didactic verse.

The *Georgics* is didactic verse, purportedly instructing readers on matters relating to agriculture. As such, it nominally springs from the tradition established by Hesiod in the seventh century B.C. Though its subject provides a rural setting, the *Georgics* is assuredly not pastoral poetry. Similarly, though its structure is more complex than that of the *Eclogues*, there is no exalted theme, nor indeed is there any sustained narrative at all. What the *Georgics* essentially represents is evidence of a mature creative mind, one capable of writing about humble subjects in an elegant way that particularly reflects Augustan Rome.

Though not a narrative, the *Georgics* is a coherent work, one essentially independent of literary predecessors. On one level, the poem is Vergil's response to his patron Maecenas' request for a work that heralds the dignity of Roman agriculture. On another level, however, the *Georgics* reflects Vergil's own wish for the rehabilitation of rural Italy from the anarchy, decay, and neglect that followed the civil wars. Obviously, it is only superficially a guide to farming; there is little in it that a farmer would not have already learned from experience, and it is difficult to imagine even the most cosmopolitan Augustan farmer consulting it as a manual.

Essentially, the *Georgics* is a virtuosic work of art arranged in four books of verse. Like the *Eclogues*, it follows a pattern of reciprocal contrasts; these are four in number, between books 1 and 2, 3 and 4, 1 and 3 and 2 and 4, and 1 and 2 and 3 and 4. Book 1 outlines the farmer's continual struggle with inanimate nature. The farmer cares for tools as a warrior does weapons, enters the field to do battle with nature, works by the calendar as does a soldier on expedition, and contends with nature's extremes as with an enemy. Moreover, Jupiter has deliberately made life hard so that humanity might discover civilization. Book 2 answers 1 in the sense that it enumerates the rewards of nature once ordered. Trees and vines yield their fruit in due course and in appropriate varieties. Sound produce yields healthy livestock, and the varied landscapes of Italy, exemplified by Tuscany, Mantua, and Capua, contribute to this harmony.

Book 3 continues the theme through a discussion of the relationship of love and death. Large and small animals mate, and this fertility contrasts with the pestilence represented by weeds, thieves, snakes, diseases, and plague. This book suddenly shifts the emphasis to animate nature, and while never quite personifying the animals that it presents, nevertheless allows understanding of the love-death process in human terms. It finds its reciprocity in book 4, the major section on beekeeping with which the *Georgics* concludes. In one sense, the fourth book mirrors the entire structure of the poem (and the cycle of farming) since it moves from location of the hive to encouraging the swarming needed for reproduction, to harvesting, to regeneration (resurrection) of the bee.

Vergil's *Georgics* maintains the indefinite outcome that characterizes the *Eclogues*. Essentially, the farmer fights a continuing battle against the deteriorating nature of things. Though the farmer may do all that is possible to ensure a favorable outcome to his work, nature remains a variable that can destroy all efforts. Augustan Rome provides the best hope for success, but it requires the efforts of all concerned and does not in itself provide automatic solutions.

AENEID

First published: c. 29-19 B.C. (English translation, 1553)
Type of work: Epic poem

The *Aeneid* shows the full development of its author's talent, brilliantly extending the range of Latin literature and providing noble ancient origins for Augustan Rome.

It is impossible to gauge the seriousness of the dying Vergil's request that his *Aeneid* be burned upon his death. Despite the dramatic command of Augustus to spare it from the flames, it is difficult to imagine that any of Vergil's contemporaries would have taken it upon themselves to destroy what promised to be the most extraordinary poem ever written in Latin, and that is precisely what those who knew the work in progress realized it to be. It is more likely that Vergil's request stemmed from the almost manic pessimism that one notes as counterpoint in both the *Eclogues* and *Georgics*. Such resolution through a minor key produces great art, however, and Vergil knew that no poetic form yields more easily to an indeterminate conclusion than epic. The *Aeneid*, despite the difficulties inherent in its composition, thus offered Vergil the surest possibility for ultimate development of his talent.

In one sense, the *Aeneid* obviously depends upon Homer's *Iliad* and *Odyssey* for its very creation. Echoes and lines parallel to those of Homer abound within it. Nevertheless, Vergil's purpose and the nature of the verse itself are altogether different, for Vergil's is urban poetry reflecting the Trojan War myths from a Trojan (and consequently Roman, rather than Greek) point of view. Rather than conceal his use of Homer, Vergil's use of the Homeric legacy supports a major part of his thesis: that the present draws from the past and that the quality of what was determines the worth of what is.

Typical Vergilian reciprocity appears in the structure of the *Aeneid*. Its first six books are effectively an Odyssean series of adventures that take Aeneas and the Trojans from their destroyed city to Dido's North African city of Carthage and ultimately to the Underworld's Italian entrance at Cumae, near Naples. *Aeneid* 1 to 6 are Odyssean only in the sense that the adventures externally parallel those of Odysseus. Aeneas, unlike Odysseus, has responsibility for the collective destiny of his nation, and Vergil consistently distinguishes between his hero's personal preference and what *fatum* (fate) requires him to do. Hence, Aeneas must flee Troy, though he would have preferred to die there. Fate, through the instrumentality of the storm conjured by joint request of Juno (to delay *fatum*) and Aeneas' mother, Venus (to provide rest for her son), casts Aeneas upon Dido's shore. Venus mercilessly causes the flame of passion to grow in Dido, using the young queen as an instrument to ensure that Aeneas may pursue his destiny to found an Italian Troy. The flames that destroyed Troy thus resolve themselves into the flames of passion that ultimately cause Dido's suicide and find final expression in the flames of her funeral pyre. Again, Aeneas must lay aside his obligations toward Dido for the larger obligation that he owes the Trojan people.

Fatum thus governs all: the *furor* (anger) that Aeneas must direct at those who would impede founding of a new Troy at Lavinium in Italy; the *labor* (work), the struggle to escape and reach the site of the new city; *dolor* (grief), the suffering that requires decisions for the collective well being; *pietas* (piety), the humility needed to accept what fate decrees. All of these elements bring Aeneas to his Underworld meeting with the shade of his father Anchises in *Aeneid* 6. It is there that Aeneas beholds a procession of as yet unborn heroes important to the destiny of a city to rise in the remote future. Aeneas knows nothing of Rome and no more of the heroes important to its history, yet he knows that what he witnesses is in some way important. Augustus himself appears among these unborn heroes, and his connection with Aeneas (if ever doubted) becomes explicit in this scene.

Aeneid 7 to 12 looks toward Trojan establishment of Lavinium, the city that must rise if Rome itself is ever to rise. These are the Iliadic books since they describe a second Trojan War with the Trojans cast as invaders of the Italian city on the site fated for Trojan habitation. Lavinia, daughter of King Latinus, thus has a role that corresponds to that of Helen in the Trojan War. Aeneas is destined to marry Lavinia to begin amalgamation of the Trojan and native italic peoples, but Lavinia is already promised to the Rutulian warrior Turnus. Since Turnus is hardly committed to this marriage agreement, war might have been avoided had it not been for Juno's longstanding anger against the Trojans. The fury that she causes provokes violence that spreads across the countryside, and the Trojan War in Italy begins in earnest.

Preparations for the war allow Vergil to establish the antiquity of the peoples of Italy. Aeneas, for example, journeys north on the Tiber to the Etruscan city then known as Pallanteum, but which is located at the site of what would one day be Rome, the city of Romulus. *Aeneid* 8 takes the reader through Pallanteum, which even then has landmarks familiar to an imperial Roman. Evander, King of Pallanteum, concludes an alliance with Aeneas and gives him men, as well as his own son Pallas, a protégé whose counterpart in the *Iliad* is Patroclus.

Back at Lavinium, Ascanius (the young son of Aeneas, now called Iulus to establish his identification with the Julio-Claudian emperors) distinguishes himself in the fight against the Latins and their allies. A renegade Etruscan king named Mezentius has allied himself and his son Lausus with the Latins. Cast out by his own city of Caere, Mezentius has found refuge with King Latinus and now fights against his own people. This villain paradoxically acquires the reader's sympathy upon the death of Lausus, killed when he interposes himself between his father and the advancing Aeneas. Despite Mezentius' contemptible deeds as king of Caere, and though he hates the gods, Mezentius is still a father, and Lausus has shown him due filial *pietas*. When Mezentius dies immediately thereafter, also at Aeneas' hands, his death assumes a tragic aspect; such is Vergil's skill for the dramatic that he can make pitiable even the death of a villain.

The death of Pallas at Turnus' hands clearly corresponds to Aeneas' killing of Lausus, and Vergil presents both deaths sympathetically. Obviously, Vergil avoids setting what would have been a more logical contest between young warriors, that of Iulus and Lausus. That is clearly because Iulus, called Ascanius in *Aeneid* 1 to 6, represents the link between Troy past and the new incarnation of that city in Italy. When Iulus distinguishes himself on the battlefield, he does so against uniformly undeveloped personalities in order to allow him alone to hold the central position in the narrative. Accordingly, Iulus remains unscarred by his battlefield contests, almost but not quite succeeding in encountering Turnus.

Meeting Turnus on the battlefield is Aeneas' fate, and Aeneas enters the fray in much the same state of mind as had Achilles in the *Iliad* following the death of Patroclus. The final question that faces Aeneas once he has the Rutulian Turnus at bay is whether to administer the death stroke. He decides to do so as soon as he sees that Turnus wears the belt that he had stripped from young Pallas upon killing him. Thus, the *Aeneid* ends in the middle of events, as is characteristic of epic poetry, but also with the element of qualification that characterizes all Vergil's works.

Summary

It has become fashionable to declare that Vergil is less of an Augustan patriot-poet than generations have believed. Clearly, there is a dark side to the Italian pastoral landscape of the *Eclogues*, a sense that the struggle against nature is essentially a holding action in the *Georgics*, and a feeling that Aeneas is capable of acting less than nobly in the *Aeneid*. None of this, however, detracts from Vergil as an urbane, sophisticated poet, very much a man of his own times and a poet capable of far greater intricacy of thought and poetic figure than even the Greek masters who inspired him. Indeed, Vergil's greatest gift is his ability to echo Homer, Hesiod, and Theocritus (and, among the Roman poets, Quintus Ennius and Titus Lucretius Carus) without in any sense imitating them. Vergil's skill in doing so through settings in which his own Augustan Rome serves as counterpoint is a measure of his greatness.

Bibliography

Bailey, Cyril. *Religion in Virgil*. New York: Barnes & Noble Books, 1969.

Camps, W. A. *An Introduction to Vergil's "Aeneid."* Oxford, England: Oxford University Press, 1969.

Commager, Steele, ed. *Virgil: A Collection of Critical Essays*. Englewood Cliffs, N.J.: Prentice-Hall, 1966.

Conte, Gian Biagio. *The Rhetoric of Imitation: Genre and Poetic Memory in Virgil and Other Latin Poets*. Ithaca, N.Y.: Cornell University Press, 1986.

DiCesare, Mario A. *The Altar and the City: A Reading of Vergil's "Aeneid."* New York: Columbia University Press, 1974.

Highet, Gilbert. *The Speeches in Vergil's "Aeneid."* Princeton, N.J.: Princeton University Press, 1972.

Johnson, W. R. *Darkness Visible: A Study in Vergil's "Aeneid."* Berkeley: University of California Press, 1976.

Knight, W. F. Jackson. *Roman Vergil*. New York: Penguin Books, 1969.

Otis, Brooks. *Virgil: A Study in Civilized Poetry*. Oxford, England: Clarendon Press, 1964.

Pöshl, Viktor. *The Art of Vergil*. Translated by Gerda Seligson. Ann Arbor: University of Michigan Press, 1962.

Robert J. Forman

PAUL VERLAINE

Born: Metz, France
March 30, 1844
Died: Paris, France
January 8, 1896

Principal Literary Achievement

Verlaine's greatest works are brief lyrics that speak with unparalleled metrical and rhetorical elegance of delicate longings and tender-hued nature.

Biography

Paul Marie Verlaine was born in Metz, France, on March 30, 1844. His father, Captain Nicolas-Auguste Verlaine, was a gruff, brusque, career military man. His mother, Elisa, had been longing for a child. She had had three miscarriages before Paul, her only child, was born. She lavished affection on him, and, in consequence, he became strongly attached to her. His early lack of independence is indicated by the fact that, when he was sent to school at age nine, he ran back home on the first day and had to be coaxed to return with sweets and sweet words. Eventually he adjusted to the school regime, going first to the Institution Landry (in Paris, to which the family had moved) and then graduating to the Lycée Bonaparte in 1855. While still in school, he acquired the adult vices of drinking and visiting prostitutes.

At this point, his indulgences did not deflect his life from a straight course. After graduating, he obtained a civil service job in Paris and began getting involved with the group of Parnassian poets. This group, while continuing the themes of Romanticism, advocated greater refinements in poetic technique. Two years after entering the work world, Verlaine published his first book, *Poèmes saturniens* (1866), in which he hewed closely to the Parnassian style. His life continued on its uneven keel; he maintained his government job and his attendance at artistic salons, while also continuing his nights of drink and debauch that now often involved him in drunken violence. In three more years, he produced *Fêtes galantes* (1869; *Gallant Parties*, 1912). In this book of poems, he avoided the touches of derivativeness visible in his previous work and, drawing on eighteenth century painting, created a luminescent fantasy world of delicate emotion and discourse.

Perhaps attempting to arrest the course of his dissipation, Verlaine now became engaged to a young girl, Mathilde Mauté, who came from a good family. Thinking of their coming union, Verlaine composed a set of lovely pictures of connubial bliss in

verse, published as *La Bonne Chanson* (1870). These poems delightfully anticipated their marriage, but, once they were married, in August, 1870, he stopped writing.

His ardor, accustomed to feeding on dreams, cooled quickly after the nuptials, while the marriage was little helped by the dislocations attendant on France's explosive political situation. The country had entered an ill-considered war with Prussia, and, after humiliating defeat in the field, the starved and oppressed people in Paris overthrew the city government and established the revolutionary Paris Commune. Verlaine took a post in the Commune and then, when it was overthrown in turn with fire and sword in June, 1871, fled with his wife to his mother's relatives in the country. Verlaine and his wife returned to Paris after the summer, where their marriage met its final blow, the entrance of the sixteen-year-old Arthur Rimbaud (the young prodigy who revolutionized French poetry while still in his teens). Rimbaud, who had read Verlaine's books, wrote to introduce himself and to ask for money to come to Paris from the provinces. As a calling card, he included a sheaf of astonishing poems. Verlaine forwarded him the necessary funds, and Rimbaud came to town, where he quickly proceeded to estrange Verlaine from his friends by his bad manners and obnoxious behavior and to wreck Verlaine's marriage by leading the older poet into a maze of alcohol and homosexual dalliance. (Verlaine's homosexual leanings had never emerged openly until this time.)

The distraught wife, now with an infant son, George, born on October 30, 1871, demanded that her husband choose between her and Rimbaud. Though there was a brief reconciliation in the family, eventually Verlaine chose the young genius. The pair decamped for a vagabond tour of Belgium and England. During this period, Verlaine composed his most celebrated book, *Romances sans paroles* (1874; *Romances Without Words*, 1921). Rimbaud was no charmer as a companion, having about the same regard for love and friendship as he did for poetic tradition. He grew tired of the older man and told him that he was leaving him. Having sacrificed his wife and reputation for Rimbaud, Verlaine lost his temper and tried to kill Rimbaud. He shot and wounded the young poet, resulting in Verlaine's arrest and imprisonment for almost a year and a half. In prison, he worked on his last major work, the book of poems *Sagesse* (1881). In it, he recorded a sincere religious awakening in movingly simple Christian verse.

Unfortunately, his newfound virtue would not long outlast the enforced celibacy and sobriety of prison. He emerged from penal servitude in January, 1875, to find that he was no longer welcome in Paris. His work was rejected, by those who had once welcomed it, as that of a reprobate. For the next five years, he worked as a teacher in the French provinces and in England. He befriended a student, Lucien Létinois, with whom he maintained a cautiously platonic alliance. In 1880, the two took over a French farm, but years later their venture went bankrupt, and the pair returned to Paris.

There, surprisingly, the tide had turned. A new generation of poets, less squeamish about his scandalous behavior, had come to admire the technical precision and delicate moodiness of his poetry. The acclaim at first meant little to him, for his friend

Létinois had died of typhoid in 1883. He would live for quite a few more years, now lionized and writing a considerable amount, too, while he continued his drinking and other bad habits; but the spark of inspiration was only very occasionally flickering. He died in Paris on January 8, 1896, in a ménage with an aging prostitute.

Analysis

Verlaine's reputation is not as high as it once was, and this is largely because his poetry lacks the depth of that of his greatest contemporaries. Poets such as Charles Baudelaire and Stéphane Mallarmé were nearly as technically proficient as Verlaine, but they had thought deeply about life and the relation of poetry to life in a way that Verlaine had not. Rimbaud, contrastingly, was less technically skilled than Verlaine, but Rimbaud's lack of emphasis on poetic form followed from a principled and logically consistent rejection of much of tradition, also indicative of serious thought.

Yet, there was a disarming feature of Verlaine. He both acknowledged his shallowness and defended himself by arguing that a kind of mistiness in thought was necessary to convey the type of limpidity for which he strove in his writing. In "L'Art poétique," published in the volume *Jadis et naguère* (1884), he wrote, "De la musique avant toute chose" ("Music before all things"), and stated that it is best to accomplish that by creating verse "où l'Indécis au Précis se joint" ("where the undefined and precise join"). In other words, to capture an ineffable mood it is necessary to have an underlying structure of thought that is itself rather vague and incomplete. It is hard to argue with his advice, especially since his work is preeminent in French literature in being able to convey delicate, illusive feelings.

It is important to be aware of how he speaks of a combination of the precise and imprecise, for it is not merely by the use of vague words that he creates his moods—his effects cannot be achieved so easily. He combines vagueness and concreteness in precisely the right measure. In "Il faut, voyez-vous, nous pardonner les choses" ("You see, we have to learn to pardon all"), his method of combination can be seen. (This poem, like many of his poems, takes its title from its first line.) The speaker is asking for forgiveness, and he wishes that he and the listener could return to their childish innocence. Exactly what is to be forgiven is left tremulously vague; yet, at the right moment, a concrete image is introduced, a description of frightened little girls who feel enormously guilty for a minor lapse. This image gives the speaker's suit a poignance based in reality, though still a reality only analogically related to his continuingly unclear original sins.

Three other traits help Verlaine in his quest for distinct indistinctness: musicality, conversational tone, and natural imagery. The verbal music, which he put before all things, was that of an easy lilt and a graceful chiming of vowels and consonants that gave his verse a prettiness that few other poets have matched. In poems such as "Chanson d'automne" ("Song of Autumn") and "Il pleure dans mon coeur" ("It is crying in my heart"), the easy grace of the lines creates a melody that connects sympathetically to the tremulous passages of a weary sadness.

At the same time, adding to the poetry's weight and thus balancing its tendency toward evanescence, is a conversational tone that conceals the artistry of the work by creating the sense of listening to a relaxed monologue. Thus, Verlaine may open a poem with an unaffected statement such as "Tournez, tournez, bons chevaux de bois" ("Turn, turn wooden horses"—carousel horses), or with a casual request, as in "Écoutez la chanson bien douce" ("Listen to the sweet song"). In order to embody this tone, Verlaine made a number of innovations and reemphases in the rather strict conventions of French verse. For one, against the more strident practices of Romanticism, he preferred weak rhymes, ones that called less attention to themselves. He broke with the tradition of having a caesura, a brief pause of sense and sound at the middle of the typical twelve-syllable line. Moreover, he worked less with the preferred twelve-count line than with shorter measures and particularly, unusually, ones of odd-numbered syllables, from five to thirteen. He also practiced enjambment (*rejet* in French), that is, the method of not ending a clause and sense unit at the line's end but carrying it over to the following line. None of these alterations in standard procedures was made as a technical experiment, but each was done to deemphasize the rigidity and formality of verse (factors that proclaimed, "this is a poem") in favor of naturalness.

This naturalness, too, helped toward the necessary vagueness, which would have been harder to reach within the tougher shell of stricter methods. Verlaine also conveyed this prized quality by choosing to portray nature in its filmy moods. He begins his celebrated "En Sourdine" ("Muted") by describing a wooded glade, "Calmes dans le demi-jour/ Que les branches hautes font" ("Calmly in the twilight/ Created by the upper boughs"). "L'Heure du berger" ("Dusk") begins "La lune est rouge au brumeux horizon;/ Dans un brouillard qui danse" ("The moon is red along the smoking horizon;/ In a shifting mist"). In each case, a shuttered half-light and the incompletely discerned shapes of foliage or of the sun draw the reader into a web of a twilight world in which formless emotions appear.

More specifically, what were the emotions of which the poet sang? It might be said that Verlaine's feelings are not those of the will, such as hatred and passionate desire, but those of passivity, such as nostalgia, regret, and unrequited longing. Thus, in "Mon rêve familier" ("My familiar dream"), he dreams, literally, of a nameless woman who understands him, saying of her, "Est-elle brune, blond, ou rousse—Je l'ignore" ("Is she brunette, blond, or redheaded?—I do not know"). Perhaps even more representative is a passage in "It is crying in my heart." There, the speaker experiences a piercing yet unaccountable ache in his heart. He concludes, not by diagnosing the feeling's cause, but by finding, "C'est bien la pire peine/ De ne savoir pourquoi . . . Mon coeur a tant de piene" ("It is by far the worst pain/ Not knowing why . . . My heart has such pain"). These lines evoke the immediacy of Verlaine's verse, his ability to make the reader feel the keenness of an emotion whose exact dimensions, such as the dream-woman's hair color, are withheld.

It is paradoxical, in the end, that a man whose emotional life was filled with above-average turmoil and turbulence should be found to have his chief excellence as a poet in the portrayal of moods that lack contour and are nearly indecipherable.

GREEN

First published: 1874 (English translation, 1921)
Type of work: Poem

The speaker presents a beautiful woman with gifts, his relation to her growing gradually more intimate and more mysterious.

"Green," written in the period of Verlaine's escapades with Rimbaud, can be read as the recording of an impulse toward reconciliation with his wife. It is a complex piece of three four-line stanzas, in which each phrase both fills in more details of the speaker's immediate relation to the woman being addressed and, simultaneously, shrouds further in mystery the couple's ultimate connection.

The poem can also be read, in terms of literary history, as an interesting play with the tradition of the harsh mistress. The male Romantic poets, following a convention dating to the Middle Ages, often portrayed unnaturally cruel lovers, who remorselessly broke the hearts of the tortured but loyal lyricists. Verlaine unveils two variations on this motif. First, while the traditional poet's torments as he described them were undeserved, the speaker in "Green" seems to have some unspecified trespass on his conscience and, so, cannot avoid his sense that rejection by the addressed woman would be richly merited. Second, there is no evidence in the poem, as there would be in the typical Romantic lament, that the addressee is actually disdainful. It is only that the poet, possibly misled by guilt, anticipates that she will be. Thus, in the poem's opening, the speaker offers her a beautiful plait of flowers, fruits, and sprays (including, as an afterthought, his heart); he then pleads that she not break the offering and cast it aside: "Ne le déchirez pas avec vos deux mains blanches" ("Do not break it with your two white hands"). Such cruelty, however, seems more in the poet's mind than in reality, since, as it happens, she does not spurn the peace offering and will allow even greater liberties later.

In the first stanza, all that is clear is that the speaker has come in from the garden. The second quatrain suggests that the speaker has been on a long journey, which, complexly, can be seen as endearing him to the woman, as he is weary and pitiably cold with the morning dew; but it may also estrange him somewhat from the listening woman, whom he may have deserted in some sense. Whatever the mix of these elements, he has advanced enough in her estimation—each stanza notes the speaker's greater physical proximity to the woman—to request that he might lay himself at her feet.

In the last stanza, their bodies move still closer. Verlaine confesses to the reader that she has kissed him, as if in her joy at his recovery from absence, and then, trading on this intimacy, begs that he might lay his head on her breast.

Two interesting points about relationships appear at the end. The speaker remains a pleader. No matter what ground he has crossed in reviving their old feelings, he is still as unsure and abject as he had been at the outset. Verlaine's view of the game of love seems to be that every conquest of a degree of intimacy leads the conqueror merely to another field with a new series of hurdles blocking communion. The second point is that the ending reveals that the speaker's desired haven is rest on a maternal bosom. The loved woman, who is young, merges back toward the mother and does so very naturally since the connection suggested up until the end has been loving but not erotic. Without negating the originally portrayed situation between adult man and woman, this return delicately indicates how such scenes, whether of reconciliation or tidy closeness, may be lit from within by evergreen reminiscences of childhood passions.

MY GOD SAID TO ME

First published: "Mon Dieu m'a dit," 1881 (English translation, 1948)
Type of work: Poem

Jesus asks for the addressee's love, citing His sufferings on Golgotha as reasons to embrace His cause.

"My God Said to Me" shows interesting variations on earlier Verlaine themes. Many poems in *Romances sans paroles* (1874; *Romances Without Words,* 1921) are in the form of a plea, the speaker begging an imagined listener for some favor, some tenderness. In Verlaine's sequence of ten religious sonnets, of which "My God Said to Me" is the first, appearing in *Sagesse* (1881), the volume following *Romances Without Words*, it is God who is doing the praying. Jesus Christ is begging the listener, who is presumably Verlaine, since he claimed that these poems marked his religious conversion, to love Him.

Another daring departure from Verlaine's customary style found in this poem is that the emotion felt is presented in a blunt, raw way, which contrasts markedly with the ineffability of emotion that reigns in most of his pieces. It is as if, where Verlaine finds humans to be inexhaustibly vague in their moods, he is compelled to portray God as knowing His own mind. Thus, in the first line, Jesus states forthrightly, "Il faut m'aimer" ("It is necessary to love Me"—addressing the listener).

In keeping with Verlaine's emphasis on sensation over thought, what God brings forth to motivate the listener to become a Christian are not reasons but wounds. Jesus stands, as it were, in front of the poet as He did before Doubting Thomas and has him examine His pierced side and torn heart.

There is, however, more than show-and-tell to this poem. It is a sonnet, a fourteen-line poem with five rhythmic units per line. Sonnets have been known for compressed arguments that lead to something of a twist in the concluding thought. Verlaine accepts this tradition, though the argument that he presents is rather startling. He has

Jesus pass beyond listing His afflictions to state that the world is primarily a place of the flesh and that, therefore, suffering is what counts above all things. It is the type of argument that would certainly strike a sensualist such as Verlaine. The poem's ending twist is that, to drive the argument's point home, Jesus says that His own sufferings are very much like Verlaine's own. He tells the poet, "N'ai-je pas sangloté ton angoisse suprême?" ("Have not I sobbed in your supreme anguish?") The line can be taken to indicate either that Jesus' tortures have been as bad as the poet's or that Jesus has somehow been suffering Verlaine's troubles in His own flesh.

Certainly, in one sense, the ending smacks of the writer's self-importance, as if God had to prove that He had suffered as much as Verlaine. Yet, in the context of the whole poem, that is only one example of the poem's most remarkable feature: the intimacy of the appeal from Jesus to a sinner. The Son of God frames His pleas to the bent of the listener and loses no dignity in so doing.

Summary

If the world had nothing but major poets, there would be a surfeit of grand statements on such themes as love and death, but important lesser matters would be forgotten. A minor poet, such as Paul Verlaine, is not a bad poet. A bad poet is hackneyed or overtaxed by projects beyond his or her capacity. A minor poet has accurately gauged his or her own skills and creates estimable work of less than earthshaking proportion. Verlaine described a world of reflected light, half-hearted moods, and undrawn connections. With all the craft at his command, he built a diaphanous, yet richly inscribed, tissue of verse.

Bibliography

Adam, Antoine. *The Art of Paul Verlaine*. Translated by Carl Morse. New York: New York University Press, 1963.
Carter A. E. *Verlaine*. New York: Twayne, 1971.
_____. *Verlaine: A Study in Parallels*. Toronto: University of Toronto Press, 1961.
Richardson, Joanna. *Verlaine: A Biography*. New York: Viking, 1971.
Stephan, Philip. *Paul Verlaine and the Decadence, 1882-90*. Manchester, England: Manchester University Press, 1974.

James Feast

JULES VERNE

Born: Nantes, France
February 8, 1828
Died: Amiens, France
March 24, 1905

Principal Literary Achievement

Admired as a writer for young people, Verne created adventure stories that form a part of contemporary myth.

Biography

Jules Verne was born on February 8, 1828, the eldest son of a lawyer in the provincial port of Nantes, France. His education was typical of that of a middle-class nineteenth century family, since his parents intended for him to take over his father's legal office. According to family legend, Verne was a good student, but he entertained daydreams of adventure, leading to an attempt at the age of eleven to run away to sea. As the eldest son, Verne consented to attend law school despite a lack of interest in the subject, while his younger brother Paul was allowed to follow the more exciting career of captain in the merchant marine.

Family legend also attributes to Verne a childhood love for a cousin. In order to get Jules out of the way during her engagement, he was sent to Paris to continue his studies. While in the capital, Verne became close to the popular novelist Alexandre Dumas and frequented literary and theatrical groups. He was soon trying his hand at vaudeville as well as tragedy.

Although he had successfully completed his law degree in 1848, Verne refused to return to Nantes. He began to publish in the journal *Musée des familles*. In Parisian salons, he met explorers and scientists and began to use what he could learn from them for his stories.

In 1856, Verne met Honorine de Viane, a young widow with two daughters. Her brother was a financial agent, and Verne decided that that line of work would be the ideal way for him to earn a living while writing. Verne married Honorine in 1857; his only child, a son, Michel, was born in 1861. The following year, Verne met the publisher P. J. Hetzel, who was especially interested in books for youngsters. In 1863, Hetzel published Verne's first novel, *Cinque Semaines en ballon* (1863; *Five Weeks in a Balloon*, 1876). The success of the book owed something to the exploit of the balloonist Nadar the same year. Verne continued to publish both serially, in the *Musée*

des familles, and in volume form and published *Voyage au centre de la terre* (1864; *A Journey to the Center of the Earth*, 1872). The following year, he signed a contract with Hetzel, according to which he agreed to furnish three volumes a year for three thousand francs each. This arrangement gradually allowed him to abandon all other work and devote himself to writing.

In 1867, Verne went to New York aboard the steamer *Great Eastern*. This trip furnished the material for *Une Ville flottante* (1871; *A Floating City*, 1876). He was working at the same time on what was to become *Vingt mille lieues sous les mers* (1869-1870; *Twenty Thousand Leagues Under the Sea*, 1873), as well as *Autour de la lune* (1870; *From the Earth to the Moon . . . and a Trip Around It*, 1873). Throughout his life, Verne would be correcting the proofs of one book while composing another and often taking notes for a third. His fertile imagination presented him with more ideas than he had time to commit to paper. The following year, he bought his first sailboat, the *St. Michel*, and signed a more favorable contract with Hetzel.

In 1870, Verne received the cross of the Légion d'Honneur.

Honorine and her children found refuge in Amiens during the Franco-Prussian War. Verne was horrified by the rebel-backed Paris Commune. His political opinions would always be moderate. After the war, he decided to move to Amiens, but the Parisian social scene did not agree with him. *Le Tour du monde en quatre-vingts jours* (1873; *Around the World in Eighty Days*, 1873), published serially, was a huge success, and the volume that appeared in 1872 sold 108,000 copies. It was to be Verne's best-selling work.

Verne's son, Michel, was a source of considerable worry as the author continued to produce book after book. Because some of Verne's books were being translated into Russian, they had to be read by diplomats before publication in an effort to avoid any misunderstanding. The sales of his books permitted him to buy a yacht and to sail around the Mediterranean, but his son's conduct continued to worry him. Michel's debts were significant and, at the age of eighteen, he demanded his independence in order to marry an actress. This marriage did not last long, and soon Michel eloped with a pianist who was also a minor. Verne would be obliged to support his son and his family for a long time.

Verne lived in a very comfortable, upper-middle-class manner in the provincial town of Amiens. In 1866, however, he was obliged to sell his yacht, the upkeep of which had become too expensive. In the same year, he had an unfortunate accident. His nephew Gaston, the son of his brother Paul, shot him in the foot during a fit of temporary insanity. Verne would never recover completely from the wound. Shortly after this accident, his publisher, Hetzel, died, and, although Verne continued working for the same house under the direction of Hetzel's son, his relationship with the successor was not what he had known with the father.

In spite of increasing health problems and lesser financial success, Verne continued to produce book after book. In 1905, acute diabetes was discovered, and Verne died soon after, on March 24, in Amiens, surrounded by his family. His productivity was such that posthumous novels would appear until 1914.

Analysis

Verne was drawn to the sea and the life of adventure from an early age, yet his biography is remarkably prosaic. Aside from a trip to Scandinavia and one to America, he spent most of his life in the provincial French town of Amiens. It is true that he owned a sailboat as soon as he could afford to buy one, exchanged it for a larger one, and finally purchased a yacht, but his travels were limited to the Mediterranean coastline. Verne was an adventurer of the mind.

In 1863, when *Five Weeks in a Balloon* first appeared, Verne was an immediate success and was especially recognized as the creator of a radically new type of novel. Under the name of science fiction, works resembling those of Verne would continue to fascinate readers of all ages. His fertile imagination continued to furnish more ideas for novels than he could complete. His success, however, was not entirely attributable to the novelty of the genre. Verne's ideas correspond to the ideology of the second half of the twentieth century. Since antiquity, literature had exploited the voyage as a theme, but Verne's concern for scientific knowledge made his voyages educational as well as exciting. The curiosity that led to exploration and invention during Verne's lifetime also provided an enthusiastic reading public.

The continuing popularity of the stories and their successful adaptation in motion pictures demonstrate that, beyond the scientific apparatus, which now appears dated, Verne's novels appeal through their mythological structures. The epic struggle against evil, the voyage as initiation, and the unfathomable mystery of Captain Nemo still fascinate readers.

A JOURNEY TO THE CENTER OF THE EARTH

First published: *Voyage au centre de la terre*, 1864 (English translation, 1872)
Type of work: Novel

Upon discovering a coded parchment, Harry, his uncle Professor Hardwigg, and their Icelandic guide, Hans, find a volcanic crater that leads them into the bowels of the earth.

Like the greater number of Verne's works, *A Journey to the Center of the Earth* is a novelistic description of scientific phenomena. This third of Verne's works is geological and paleontological. The different geological strata of the earth, its minerals, the formation of the planet, and the different hypotheses concerning its core are reviewed. At the same time, the structure of the work calls upon the archetypal descent of the hero into the underworld.

Verne's characters are conscious that their scientific goals echo those of humanity. Mister Fridriksson, their Icelandic host, who converses with the hero Harry in Latin,

bids them farewell with "this verse that Virgil seems to have written for us: 'Et qua-
cumque viam dederit fortuna, sequamur' " ("And whichsoever way thou goest, may
fortune follow"). Verne knew that others had written of the descent into the underworld, usually as a pretext to criticize society on the surface of the planet, without
any scientific pretensions. His motivation is otherwise: explore scientific data and
imagine an adventure story.

The story is told by one of its protagonists, the student Harry, a lover of geology.
Verne seems to voice his opinion when the narrator proclaims the scientific validity
of the expedition:

> No mineralogists had ever found themselves placed in such a marvelous position to
> study nature in all her real and naked beauty. The sounding rod, a mere machine, could
> not bring to the surface of the earth the objects of value for the study of its internal
> structure, which we were about to see with our own eyes, to touch with our own hands.

The characters of the novel are limited to the three of the expedition. Harry's cousin
and fiancée, Gretchen, is reduced to the figure of the knight's lady who sends him off
on his mission and welcomes him home, a hero, at the conclusion of the adventure.
Harry's youthful imagination, his concern with practical details such as eating and
sleeping, contrast sharply with the stereotype of the universal scientist represented by
his fanatical uncle, who is unable to imagine danger and is motivated only by scientific curiosity. The third member of the crew, the Icelandic guide Hans, never speaks.
He represents instinct, has no interest in the discoveries and, apparently, no fear in
the face of dangers. He finds water, constructs a raft, and repeatedly saves the scientists' lives, all for three dollars a week.

A precise date is given at the beginning of the work situating the story in the
reader's near past, and at one point the use of the journal or log kept by Harry during
the crossing of an interior sea allows the story to be told in the present tense. All of
this contributes to the realism of the narration. The cause of realism is served by the
didactic side of the work as well: Lists of equipment and scientific instruments for
the venture are given; the trip is a lesson in geology and paleontology. Once the expedition reaches the interior sea, however, geological references become rare. Now the
voyage seems to allow the explorers to discover humanity's past. Verne's heroes are
fascinated by the mystery of humanity's origins. The eternal question of the source of
life was accentuated in the nineteenth century by the controversy that followed publication of the theories of naturalists Charles Darwin and Jean-Baptiste Lamarck.

Once on the interior sea, Harry's scientific hypotheses blend with symbolism. The
fantastic appeal of electricity at the time explains Verne's use of it to illumine the
Central Sea:

> The illuminating power in this subterranean region, from its trembling and flickering
> character, its clear dry whiteness, the very slight elevation of its temperature, its great
> superiority to that of the moon, was evidently electric; something in the nature of the
> aurora borealis, only that its phenomena were constant, and able to light up the whole
> of the ocean cavern.

More and more, Harry reveals his impressions of being "imprisoned," of the "awful grandeur" of the scene: "Imagination, not description, can give an idea of the splendor and vastness of the cave." The discovery, first of fossils, then of bones, then of living prehistoric creatures, and finally of a humanoid giant allow for many narrow escapes: "The fact was that my journey into the interior of the earth was rapidly changing all preconceived notions, and day by day preparing me for the marvelous."

When at last their way seems blocked, the travelers do not hesitate to open the earth with explosives. In doing so, they provoke a volcanic eruption that rather miraculously restores them to the surface of the earth, not in Iceland, whence they began their journey, but in an island of the Mediterranean.

TWENTY THOUSAND LEAGUES UNDER THE SEA

First published: *Vingt mille lieues sous les mers*, 1869-1870 (English translation, 1873)
Type of work: Novel

Shipwrecked, Professor Aronnax, his servant Consul, and a sailor, Ned Land, are taken aboard the submarine of the mysterious Captain Nemo.

In *Twenty Thousand Leagues Under the Sea*, Verne created a character, Captain Nemo, who would continue to haunt the imagination of generations to come in the manner of Homer's hero, from whom Nemo took his name. In the *Odyssey* (c. 800 B.C.), Ulysses calls himself Nemo, or "No one," in order to hide his identity from the Cyclops. Verne's unknown renegade, making war on injustice, has likewise become a myth.

The best known of Verne's works was also the one that took the longest to find its way into print. It is certain that the author was working on a story tentatively titled "Voyage Under the Waters" in 1865. After his exploration of the air in *Five Weeks in a Balloon* and his *A Journey to the Center of the Earth*, it was logical that Verne would pursue his pedagogical mission by exploring the bottom of the sea.

This novel, though, was to be different from the others. Verne was very excited about the creation of a hero entirely cut off from the earth and humanity. His publisher, Hetzel, on the other hand, was very uneasy about Nemo. Verne refused to explain who his captain was and what his past had been. Letters show that the author would have liked to have made Nemo a Pole, oppressed by Russia. For commercial reasons, this was impossible, as Verne's books were translated into Russian. The violence of Nemo's hatred of his enemies, and his cruel sinking of ships, given with many hair-raising details, worried Hetzel, but Verne was adamant in preserving the hero driven by hatred.

As is usual with Verne, the motivation in the novel is a double one: scientific, with the description of the submarine vessel and the underwater world that the submarine allows the heroes to explore, and entertaining, with an unprecedented series of adventures to be encountered. Professor Aronnax is fascinated by the marvels of submarine geology and biology, which he can study in his fantastic underwater laboratory, the *Nautilus*. Ned Land, on the other hand, is a simple sailor, a natural man; his name, Land, makes him incapable of remaining at sea. He remains indifferent to everything except the loss of liberty that Nemo has inflicted upon his "guests."

The story is told by Aronnax, who is capable of understanding both points of view. He comes to admire and pity the genius Captain Nemo, while agreeing with Land that it is impossible to remain with him for the rest of his natural life.

The narrator, Aronnax, is often conscious that his story is an incredible one. In the space of ten months aboard the submarine, he travels twenty thousand leagues—that is, a trip around the world, under the seas. The journal form, which allows the tale to be told in the present tense and makes for considerable suspense as well as an illusion of reality, is used throughout. Many details contribute to the realism of the story: dates, the names of ships encountered, maps on which the itinerary of the *Nautilus* is traced. Historical references to the American Civil War and the revolt of Crete add to the impression of reality. Probably the most impressive aspect of the narration is the quantity of scientific data given. Interminable lists of submarine plants, shells, and animals serve to present a scientific alibi for the adventure story.

When the story opens, the *Nautilus* has seldom been sighted but has given rise to a legend that there is a new sort of sea monster in the oceans. When Professor Aronnax agrees to leave his museum and set sail, it is to hunt the monster. Verne has thus given his novel the appearance of an epic adventure. When the narrator discovers the mechanical nature of the submarine, the mythic side of the story does not come to an end. The *Nautilus* is powered by electricity, a phenomenon that remained mysterious enough at the time to allow Verne to play on the fantastic possibilities that it might offer.

Nemo's courage, his intelligence, and his determination excite the admiration of the narrator. Yet when Nemo dreams while improvising on his pipe organ, Aronnax admits that the captain remains essentially a mystery to him. It is the figure of Nemo, at his organ, towering over humanity after having declared war on it, understood by no one, which continues to fascinate generations of readers.

Summary

Science-fiction writer Ray Bradbury once declared himself "a son of Jules Verne." If the nineteenth century French writer of educational works for young people can be considered a founder of the science-fiction novel, it is not attributable simply to his interest in the techniques and discoveries being made in his own time. There is something timeless about Verne's novels. Like the best science-fiction works, they call upon mythological structures. The voyage, whether it be around the world, to the moon, to the center of the earth, or under the sea, is first of all a quest for the self. All Verne's journeys are initiations, which permit his hero to come to a greater self-awareness.

Bibliography

Chesneaux, Jean. *The Political and Social Ideas of Jules Verne.* Translated by Thomas Wikeley. London: Thames and Hudson, 1972.

Costello, Peter. *Jules Verne: Inventor of Science Fiction.* New York: Charles Scribner's Sons, 1978.

Evans, I. O. *Jules Verne and His Work.* London: Arco Publications, 1965.

Martin, Andrew. *The Knowledge of Ignorance: From Genesis to Jules Verne.* Cambridge, England: Cambridge University Press, 1985.

Waltz, George H. *Jules Verne: The Biography of an Imagination.* New York: Henry Holt, 1943.

Nancy Blake

VOLTAIRE

Born: Paris, France
November 21, 1694
Died: Paris, France
May 30, 1778

Principal Literary Achievement

Voltaire is one of the principal literary and intellectual figures of eighteenth century Europe; few writers have played such an important social role in their century.

Biography

François-Marie Arouet ("Voltaire"), though born a fragile child on the twenty-first day of November, 1694, in Paris, the capital of France, was destined to have a long and tumultuous literary life. So great was his influence during the eighteenth century that historians speak of the Century of Voltaire. Few deny that he possessed a brilliant mind that both understood and moved the literary and political events of the time.

The young Arouet received little formal education before the age of nine, when he was sent to the Jesuit College of Louis-le-Grand. He had, however, been taken under the wing of his deist godfather, the Abbé de Châteauneuf, who was the chief cause—much to his father's chagrin—of Arouet's early introduction into the freethinking Society of the Temple. In this circle, ideas were debated, libertine literature read, and religious dogma examined. He remained under the official care of the Jesuits until, at the age of seventeen, he came home to a father (his mother had died when he was seven) who insisted that his son study law.

After some futile attempts to follow his father's wishes, Arouet began the dangerous activity of writing libelous verse. Composing lampoons against the current French government eventually cost him eleven months in the infamous prison of the old regime, the Bastille. Never one to idle away his time, while imprisoned he began his epic poem *La Henriade* (1728; *Henriade*, 1732) and revised his play *Œdipe* (1718; *Oedipus*, 1761). Released from the Bastille on April 11, 1718, he exited with a new name that he had completely invented, Voltaire. During the ensuing years, the young Voltaire remained ever restless, accepting secret diplomatic missions, courting noble ladies, and always writing with intensity. In December, 1721, his father died, leaving him a considerable inheritance. It was soon augmented with a pension by a forgiving

regent. His plays appeared on the stage; his tragedy *Mariamne* (1724; English translation, 1761) was particularly successful.

Though an earlier bout with smallpox caused him to be seriously ill, an event soon took place that marked him more deeply. At the end of 1725, while attending a social gathering in Paris, Voltaire believed that he had been insulted by a nobleman, the Chevalier de Rohan. Not able to hold his sharp tongue, Voltaire challenged the chevalier to a duel; Rohan declined. Eighteenth century French justice, weighted entirely on the side of privilege and nobility, did not wince when the bourgeois Voltaire was later soundly beaten by Rohan's lackeys.

It was Voltaire who remained confined to the Bastille for two weeks. Upon his release, and at his own request, he departed immediately for England for three years. Voltaire had received a political lesson that he would not soon forget. The old regime could not, however, have chosen a more energetic, intelligent, and prolific enemy with which to cross sword with pen.

In 1726, Voltaire left France known as a gifted poet and playwright. Three years later he returned, one of the foremost writers and thinkers of his time. Literature and patronage had brought him wealth and many friends in England—the Walpoles, First Viscount Bolingbroke, Sarah Marlborough, and Alexander Pope. Voltaire had also come into contact with English institutions, parliament, commerce, religion, science, and literature (notably William Shakespeare). All of this was to have a profound influence in forming the philosopher who would champion the cause of moderation and tolerance to the rest of the world. Voltaire's *Letters Concerning the English Nation* (1733) captures the atmosphere of these years and the opinion of the English about their own customs and institutions. While in England, he had also worked on his play *Brutus* (1730; English translation, 1761) and on *Histoire de Charles XII* (1731; *The History of Charles XII*, 1732).

Voltaire returned to France with an even deeper conviction and clearer vision of his own intellectual place among those who would question religious authority and social injustice. His plays *Ériphyle* (1732) and *Zaïre* (1732; English translation, 1736) were acted on the stage, the latter with much success. In his long poem *Le Temple du goût* (1733; *The Temple of Taste*, 1734) Voltaire praised progress and wrote a biting satire of his literary contemporary, Jean-Jacques Rousseau.

The following year, *Letters Concerning the English Nation* was condemned by the French censor; all copies were seized, and a warrant was issued against the author. Voltaire took refuge in the independent duchy of Lorraine with Mme Émilie du Châtelet (well known in the eighteenth century for her scientific ability) in her famous château of Cirey. There, Voltaire and Mme du Châtelet lived a somewhat idyllic existence, often receiving important guests and conducting their own scientific experiments in Mme du Châtelet's well-equipped laboratory. Voltaire gave his time to the writing of social history, composing much of his great study of universal history, *Essai sur les mœurs* (1756, 1763; *The General History and State of Europe*, 1754, 1759) and *Le Siècle de Louis XIV* (1751; *The Age of Louis XIV*, 1752).

During his long sojourn at Cirey, two important plays were completed, *Mahomet*

Voltaire

2037

(1742; *Mahomet the Prophet*, 1744) and *Mérope* (1743; English translation, 1744, 1749), along with his philosophical tale *Zadig: Ou, La Destinée, histoire orientale* (1748; originally as *Memnon: Histoire orientale*, 1747; *Zadig: Or, The Book of Fate*, 1749). Voltaire and Mme du Châtelet took full advantage of the sizable fortune that the former had accumulated (through both shrewd investments and literary publications) by holding private performances in their own theater and enjoying all the other luxuries that the eighteenth century had to offer.

With the sudden death of Mme du Châtelet in September, 1749, a grief-stricken Voltaire accepted an invitation by Frederick the Great of Prussia to visit Berlin even though the relationship between the two men had become strained. For some time before Mme du Châtelet's death, Voltaire had regained favor with the French government (becoming historian to Louis XV in 1745) and had again attempted to reside in Paris. He simply, however, could not be comfortable in a city where he still felt threatened by those who reigned. Thus, on June 15, 1751, he left Paris for Berlin and the princely court of Frederick.

Frederick had wooed Voltaire to his palace in hopes of presiding over lofty and philosophical discussions on political and social theories. For a time, both great men, if not always in agreement, seemed to have tolerated one another. As always, Voltaire's pen moved lightly across blank pages, finishing such well-known works as his tale *Le Micromégas* (1752; *Micromegas*, 1753). Yet, in spite of Frederick's generosity toward Voltaire and the latter's privileged place at the monarch's table, it was quite impossible for the two temperamental men to get along. The break between them was bitter, and again Voltaire was forced to depart hastily.

His first residence was near Geneva, in a country house he named Les Délices. His *Poème sur le désastre de Lisbonne* (1756; *Poem on the Lisbon Earthquake*, 1764) was published during this period. Though having a comfortable home, Voltaire sought to acquire something even more grand; he did this by his purchase of the nearby château Ferney. Henceforth, he became known as the patriarch of Ferney. It was there that the "enlightened lord," surrounded by his niece (Mlle Denis), friends, and villagers, would pass the last years of his life. Voltaire, now driven more than ever by an intense will to create and participate in every aspect of daily life surrounding the château of Ferney, wrote his philosophical tales *Candide: Ou, L'Optimisme* (1759; *Candide: Or, All for the Best*, 1759) and *L'Ingénu* (1767; *The Pupil of Nature*, 1771; also as *Ingenuous*, 1961), his philosophical pieces *Traité sur la tolérance* (1763; *A Treatise on Religious Toleration*, 1764) and *Dictionnaire philosophique portatif* (1764; *A Philosophical Dictionary for the Pocket*, 1765; also as *Philosophical Dictionary*, 1945). While engaging in correspondence with almost all the principal literary and political figures of his day, he found time to build a watch factory, a stocking factory, and a tannery. Nor did he hesitate to come to the defense of citizens whose rights had not been respected.

Voltaire's final triumph came ironically, in Paris—the city that had so often rejected him. In Paris, the French Academy and all Parisian society received him with much fanfare and rejoicing. He attended several Academy meetings (on one occasion embracing Benjamin Franklin), went to the premiere of his play *Irène* on March 16, 1778, and then, exhausted by fatigue, emotion, and stimulation, died in Paris at the age of eighty-three on May 30, 1778. He had returned to the city to receive his laurels and, eventually, to be buried among other French heroes in the Pantheon.

Analysis

Very early in his life, Voltaire gained a reputation as the outstanding poet and playwright of his time. Yet although his poetry and plays earned for him fame and considerable sums of money, most are now seldom read or performed. *Henriade*, his one serious epic poem, is considered heavy reading. Some of Voltaire's poetry, however—especially pieces such as *Le Mondain* (1736; *The Man of the World*, 1764) and *Poem on the Lisbon Earthquake*—has survived the test of time. His best poetry presents his philosophical ideas in the critical, often satirical, and epigrammatic style that is so characteristic of almost all of his writing. *The Man of the World* and *Poem on the Lisbon Earthquake* were vehicles for Voltaire's ideas—ideas that summarized the principal intellectual currents of the eighteenth century, the age of the Enlightenment.

Voltaire held firmly to the idea that reason, human intelligence, was the cure for all ills. He employed reason as a weapon in his attack against the social and political abuses of the old regime, as well as its religious intolerance. In *The Man of the World*, he stressed the importance of economic progress and the right of individuals to enjoy the luxuries and pleasures that modern society had begun to produce. In *Poem on the Lisbon Earthquake*, written just after the terrible earthquake (1755) in Lisbon, Portugal, which killed some thirty thousand people, Voltaire questioned the philosophical optimism of the famous German thinker Gottfried Wilhelm Leibniz and the English poet and essayist Alexander Pope. He soundly rejected the notion that "all is well" here on earth and that one should accept Divine benevolence as an explanation for all that befalls humans.

Voltaire's concern for the individual's place on earth, the role that humans play in making their own history, was also apparent in the approach that he took in writing *The Age of Louis XIV* and *The General History and State of Europe*. In both these works, Voltaire broke new ground in the serious writing of social history. He very carefully documented his many volumes, often using unedited texts or securing eyewitness accounts. Even today, his *The Age of Louis XIV* is considered an interesting history of the French king.

From one of Voltaire's earlier works, *Letters Concerning the English Nation*, to one of his later works, the *Philosophical Dictionary*, he continued to define and spread far and wide his ideas on liberty, politics, religion, and literature. His *Letters Concerning the English Nation*, the principal literary result of Voltaire's three-year stay in England, had a profound influence when first published on the Continent. "The first bomb launched against the old regime" is the way the well-known French literary historian Gustave Lanson summarized the impact that piece had on France. In much the same style as that of a modern journalist, Voltaire presented ideas and information on English society in clear, direct, and often cutting prose. Readers of his day had little difficulty in understanding that Voltaire was drawing direct comparisons—always to the detriment of the old regime—between the societies of England and France.

While living in England, he wrote especially on the religious and political liberties enjoyed by English citizens. In short "letters," published in his book *Letters Concerning the British Nation*, he described the many religious sects (Quakers, Anglicans, Presbyterians, and Unitarians, for example) that tolerated one another and avoided religious persecution. In another letter, this one on the English Parliament, Voltaire underscored the limitations that English government placed on its monarchy; the same restrictions on kings did not exist on the Continent, and Voltaire made a point to highlight the differences in the two political systems. The last letter of the volume, and also the most controversial of its time, was an attack on the religious pessimism of the Jansenist writer Blaise Pascal. Voltaire, concerned with worldly pleasures, refused to accept Pascal's position that humans were fundamentally mean and condemned to be unhappy while on earth.

These themes are continued and elaborated upon in the *Philosophical Dictionary*. Short, caustic, satirical entries titled "tolerance," "torture," and "tyranny" in the *Philosophical Dictionary* are typical in style and content of so much of Voltaire's writings. In these pieces, Voltaire denounces the folly of humanity's intolerance, the despotism of unlimited political powers, and the excesses of religious fervor. The image that finally emerges in these works is that of a mature and measured writer, a writer who has completely mastered his craft. Also appearing in these works is the definition most widely applied to the term "humanist." Voltaire, perhaps more than any other modern Western writer, defined and summarized European humanism and human emergence from the age of despotic religious and political authority. His impious expression *Écraser l'infâme* (to crush the infamous) became one of the slogans of the eighteenth century. It was not so much directed against religion or even the Church of Rome as against those people (enemies of Voltaire) who used religion to justify literary censorship and their own misuse of authority.

The themes of social justice, religious tolerance, and the acceptance of the relative nature of an imperfect world were the central subjects of Voltaire's philosophical tales. Even though he expressed disdain for novels or short stories as a genre, it is these works that are most often read today. Beginning with *Zadig*, he finished some twenty-five philosophical tales. As with all of his tales, *Zadig* was meant to be entertaining without any regard for verisimilitude or the likelihood that so many adventures, or misadventures, could really befall his heroes and heroines. Voltaire never missed the chance to impart a message or to use literary entertainment as a means of propaganda. Zadig, the hero of the tale, tries in vain to understand rationally why some humans are happy and others are not. In the end, having become ruler of oriental Babylon, he opts to reign wisely in his own kingdom in order to establish peace for his subjects. Zadig (unlike the French monarchy) became the enlightened sovereign, giving his people abundance and glory.

The tale *Micromegas* was written while Voltaire was at the château of Cirey with Mme du Châtelet, and her scientific influence on Voltaire was evident. Micromegas, an intergalactic traveler, has more than one brush with the principal scientific theories of the age. Voltaire took the opportunity to ridicule the prestigious French Academy of Sciences for still adhering to Cartesian astronomy (named after René Descartes, the French philosopher and mathematician) and ignoring the explanations posited by Sir Isaac Newton (the English scientist, mathematician, and philosopher). Ridicule and exaggeration were at once part of Voltaire's style and philosophical message. Exaggeration in *Micromegas* took the form of actual physical size: While visiting different planets of the universe, Micromegas is alternately viewed as a giant and a lilliputian. Voltaire meant to underscore the importance of maintaining an open mind and of avoiding a slavish devotion to one's own perspective.

Candide, the most widely known of all Voltaire's works, is the philosophical tale of young Candide's fall from paradise (the château Thunder-ten-tronckh) and of his sojourns from Europe to Latin America and finally to Constantinople. Voltaire had recently arrived at his last home, the château of Ferney, and he was still shocked by the number of lives that had been lost in the huge 1755 earthquake in Lisbon. *Candide* became his angriest cry against those who would explain away both natural and human-made disasters by appealing to Providence. Voltaire's prose was never more sarcastic and ironic in its condemnation of war, dogmatism, and intolerance than in this tale, which takes its readers from the torture chambers of the Portuguese inquisition to the golden streets of Eldorado and, finally, to the simple garden cultivated by Candide and his beloved Cunegonde.

ZADIG

First published: 1747 (originally published as *Memnon*, 1747; English
              translation, 1749)
Type of work: Philosophical tale

Zadig, a wise and just man, seeks the definition of happiness in a chaotic and capricious world.

Zadig, Voltaire's first published philosophical tale, was written at a time when the author was finally receiving official recognition for his many literary accomplishments. In 1745, Monsieur Arouet de Voltaire received a court appointment from the king of France, Louis XV. As Royal Historiographer and later Ordinary Gentleman of the King's Bedchamber, Voltaire moved easily through the long galleries of the royal palace of Versailles. A close look at courtly pettiness, intrigues, and plotting served only to reinforce Voltaire's already low estimation of palace royalty and boot-licking government officials. This time was also the period when Voltaire's long love affair with Mme de Châtelet was ending. She had chosen a younger man over him, and for a time Voltaire was in a jealous rage.

Zadig, a tale set in eighteenth century Persia, reflects both the personal circumstances of Voltaire and the more profound philosophical questions concerning the nature of free will and happiness. Voltaire asks the same question on almost every page of the story: Can an honest and wise person lead a happy life in a world filled with liars, scoundrels, and cheats? In a story with a very thin plot, the reader follows the intelligent and kind Zadig through his travels among dishonest, deceitful, and cruel people who attempt to do him harm at every turn. First married to one of the most noble, desirable, and beautiful women of all Babylon, Zadig, to his great dismay, learns that his wife is unfaithful. Having been disappointed by an aristocratic woman, a woman from the court, he next turns to a woman chosen among the people. Again he has no luck: She also proves to be lacking in true love for Zadig.

Though a person of bourgeois origin, Zadig so distinguishes himself for his intelligence among the citizens of Babylon that he comes to the notice of the king and queen. Zadig's name is mentioned as one of the persons deserving of a prize that King Moabdar intends to give to his subject who has performed the most generous action during the year. With no attempt at disguising his ironic allusion to life in the French royal court of the eighteenth century, Voltaire has King Moabdar grant the most wonderful prize in all Asia (a golden goblet studded with precious stones) to Zadig, because he is the only one who has not spoken ill of a disgraced government minister who had incurred the king's wrath.

Zadig, in complete favor with King Moabdar and Queen Astarte, assumes the heavy responsibilities of prime minister. His every act at court demonstrates the subtlety of his genius and the goodness of his soul. Ogled by women and praised by all in the kingdom for his fairness in settling long-standing disputes, Zadig appears to enjoy all the good fortune that fate could possibly bestow on him. He even succeeds in arranging a truce between two religious sects that have quarreled for fifteen hundred years over which foot—left or right—one should first use to enter the holy temples.

In spite of all the rewards and praise Zadig receives as prime minister, he continues to reflect upon the precariousness of his own good fortune and the tricks that life has played on him in the past. As prime minister, Zadig believes the laws of Persia must be applied evenly to protect the innocent. Still, these laws are not able to quell the fanaticism and ridiculous quarrels that seem to presage the fall of Babylon. As if to underscore the validity of Zadig's personal and political fears, Voltaire has Zadig fall hopelessly in love with the wife of the jealous king, the beautiful and sensuous Queen Astarte. Then, because of war and competing factions within the country, all Persia is thrown into social and economic chaos. The reader of Voltaire's tale cannot miss the striking similarities, first between Voltaire's own romantic adventures and those of Zadig, and then between France's dismal political condition and that of Persia. Voltaire, of course, makes little attempt at accurately describing the Middle East; his purpose is instead to explore the human condition, the questions of human freedom and determination, and to attack the political stupidities and excesses of his own country, France.

The wise and just Zadig is forced to flee for his life from Babylon. He seeks asylum in Egypt. During his flight, he reflects upon humankind: "He pictured men as they really are, insects devouring each other on a little patch of mud." Though he remains a champion of light and reason, he encounters only brutality and prospering scoundrels on his voyage. After rescuing a woman from a savage beating by her husband, he is condemned to be sold as a slave. On another occasion, he persuades the women of Arabia that there is no reason to practice the custom of burning themselves on their husbands' funeral pyres; for this, he incurs the enduring wrath of the priests, who collect the women's jewelry from the ashes. Wherever he travels—from Egypt to Arabia to the Isle of Serendib and back to Persia—Zadig gives wise and excellent counsel and saves women, men, and even kingdoms from disaster. He, however, can neither find personal happiness (he still yearns for the beautiful Astarte) nor understand why dishonest and corrupt people appear to prosper. The ways of Providence remain a deep and disheartening mystery to him.

While spending time with a prosperous brigand chief, Zadig learns that King Moabdar has been killed and that confusion reigns in Babylon. Arbogad, the brigand, repeats to Zadig that he (Arbogad) is the happiest of men, and he exhorts Zadig to follow his example. Zadig declines the offer to associate himself with one of the richest thieves of the East. He leaves the robber's castle, plunged more deeply than ever in his mournful reflections about the sadness of life. He is grief-stricken to think that Astarte may have perished in the riots of Babylon.

On the road back to Babylon, Zadig sees a lady on the bank of a little stream. As he approaches, he notices that she is tracing, with a small stick, a name in the fine sand. To his astonishment, the name he reads is his own: Zadig. The lady is Astarte herself, the woman whom he adores and for whom he has returned to Babylon. Zadig, filled with joy, throws himself at her feet asking, "Can it be true? Immortal powers that preside over the destinies of frail mortals, do you give me back Astarte?" Chance has reunited the two lovers. Both recount their misadventures, and Zadig tells Astarte by what accident he happened to be walking along the banks of the little stream.

Although together again, Zadig and Astarte must yet undergo a number of trials and adventures before finally becoming the monarchs of Babylon. Zadig is obliged to participate in a medieval joust and to solve a number of riddles proposed by the Magi of the city. Before taking part in the knightly tournament, however, Zadig happens upon a hermit who speaks to him of fate, justice, and ethics and then proceeds to burn a home and murder a young man. The hermit fantastically transforms himself into the angel Jesrad and tells an astonished and angered Zadig that all on earth is meant to be and that events transpire as they must; what appears to be chance is not, and Zadig should go on his way to Babylon.

Voltaire ends his tale in both an ambiguous and a positive fashion: Zadig, as a mere human, cannot hope to understand why Providence acts in certain ways. Zadig could not know that a treasure is buried under the burned home or that the young man, if allowed to live, would kill his aunt in a year's time and Zadig in two. In his story, Voltaire leaves unanswered the recurrent metaphysical questions asked by Zadig, questions about the nature of free will and the existence of evil in a universe created by a supreme Being. Yet in an obvious optimistic conclusion to his tale, Voltaire describes the just Zadig and the intelligent and beautiful Astarte presiding over the peaceful and bountiful kingdom of Persia. In his philosophical tale *Candide* (1759), written some twelve years later, both Voltaire's narrative tone (in *Zadig* only mildly satirical for Voltaire) and his views on metaphysical optimism and Providence would change dramatically. From an enlightened kingdom in Persia to the small garden plot of *Candide*, the journey is long and discouraging.

CANDIDE

First published: 1759 (English translation, 1759)
Type of work: Philosophical tale

Through a long series of misadventures and catastrophes, Candide searches for his beloved Cunegonde.

Candide is Voltaire's most widely known work and one of the most widely read pieces of literature written in the French language. Voltaire invented the philosophical tale as a means to convey his own ideas and, at the same time, entertain his readers with satirical wit and ironic innuendo. Candide (the name refers to purity and frankness) is the tale's main character. He embodies the philosophical idea of optimism that Voltaire intends to oppose.

As the story begins, Candide is forced to leave Wesphalia because he has been caught kissing the baron's daughter, the beautiful Cunegonde. Candide is driven from the splendid castle of the Baron Thunder-ten-tronckh, where Doctor Pangloss has been Candide's tutor and has taught him that all is well in this "best of all possible worlds." Little time passes before the naïve Candide finds himself conscripted into the Bulgarian army. As a soldier, he witnesses firsthand the terrible atrocities of war. Escaping to Holland, he miraculously encounters Pangloss, who is himself in a pitiful physical state. From the ever-optimistic philosopher, Candide learns that his former home in Germany has been burned to the ground and that all of those inside have been massacred by the advancing Bulgarian army.

Voltaire continues to narrate his story with a cascade of adventures. He nonetheless keeps close to the principal reason for telling his tale: discrediting the metaphysical idea that all that happens on earth has been determined by Providence and therefore must be judged as being for the good of humankind. Pangloss, who has lost part of his nose and one eye to syphilis, continues to insist that all is going well in spite of overwhelming adversity. Candide and Pangloss travel to Lisbon, where they arrive just in time to experience the famous earthquake of 1755. Not only are they caught in Portugal during this natural disaster but they also become embroiled in the Inquisition. Only by the reappearance and intervention of Cunegonde is Candide saved (Pangloss is a presumed victim of the Inquisition). In rescuing Cunegonde, however, Candide must kill an Israelite and the Grand Inquisitor.

Candide, Cunegonde, and an old woman (the daughter of Pope Urban X) flee to South America. Even there, they are tracked by the agents of the Inquisition; Candide and Cunegonde must separate or risk being burned at the stake. Candide takes refuge in Paraguay, the kingdom of the Jesuits, where "Los Padres have everything and the people have nothing." Candide comes upon Cunegonde's brother among the Jesuit leaders. They quarrel because Candide, in spite of his humble origins, insists on marrying the young baron's sister. Candide wounds him, apparently mortally, and again takes flight with his valet and companion Cacambo.

Throughout all the journeys of Candide, who next discovers Eldorado (the city of gold and precious jewels), Voltaire delights in attacking the excesses of humankind— from the brutality of wars to the ignoble institution of the Inquisition. In order to emphasize tolerance and moderation, Voltaire presents characters that are immediately identified as representing extreme philosophical positions: Pangloss (who reappears at the end of the story in Constantinople) holds tenaciously to an absurd optimism, and Martin (Candide's companion on his trip back to Europe and on to Constantinople) affirms with equal stubbornness that there is little virtue and happiness in a world filled with evil.

While in Venice, Candide learns that his once-beautiful Cunegonde is now washing dishes on a riverbank for a prince in Turkey. From Cacambo, he hears that Cunegonde has even grown ugly and ill-tempered. Still, being an honorable man, Candide intends to marry Mlle Cunegonde, and he sets off immediately for the Turkish city. While en route, he finds Pangloss and Cunegonde's brother (resuscitated) among the galley slaves on the Turkish boat. Candide still possesses some of the diamonds that he carried away from Eldorado and is able to buy his friends' freedom. As chance would have it, all the characters of this tale end up living together on a small vegetable farm somewhere on the outskirts of Constantinople. Candide's money is exhausted, Cunegonde grows more unendurable, Cacambo curses his fate as a vegetable seller, Pangloss despairs because he is not teaching in a good German university, and Martin persists in seeing humankind caught in either the throes of distress or the doldrums of lethargy. Candide does not agree, but he no longer asserts anything. Instead of arguing metaphysical and moral questions, he heeds the advice of an old man who tells him, "work keeps at bay three great evils: boredom, vice and need." From this lesson, Candide concludes "that we should cultivate our gardens." In the end, the little farm yields well, and all eat candied citrons and pistachios. Voltaire ends the tale, on a note of neither pessimism nor optimism, with his characters working and living in peace together.

Summary

The philosophical tales of Voltaire stand as a tribute to both Voltaire's ability as a writer and storyteller and his genius in summarizing the principal philosophical and political questions of the eighteenth century. After more than two hundred years, *Zadig* and *Candide* remain entertaining pieces of reading because of their author's sardonic intelligence and crystalline prose. In many respects, Voltaire remains today what he was for his own century: a popularizer and disseminator of ideas. The Voltairien spirit, with its quick and bright outbursts of wit, continues to attack the modern scourges of intolerance, fanaticism, and injustice.

Bibliography

Ayer, A. J. *Voltaire*. New York: Random House, 1986.

Besterman, Theodore. *Voltaire*. Chicago: University of Chicago Press, 1969.

Bottiglia, William F., ed. *Voltaire: A Collection of Critical Essays*. Englewood Cliffs, N.J.: Prentice-Hall, 1968.

Gay, Peter. *Voltaire's Politics*. New Haven, Conn.: Yale University Press, 1988.

Ricardo, Ilona, and Peyton Richter. *Voltaire*. Boston: Twayne, 1980.

Voltaire. *The Portable Voltaire*. Edited and with an introduction by Ben Ray Redman. New York: Viking Press, 1963.

Waldinger, Renee, ed. *Approaches to Teaching Voltaire's "Candide."* New York: Modern Language Association of America, 1987.

James Gaasch

DEREK WALCOTT

Born: Castries, St. Lucia, West Indies
January 23, 1930

Principal Literary Achievement
Walcott is widely regarded as not only the finest Caribbean poet but also one of the finest English language poets of his generation.

Biography

On January 23, 1930, Derek Alton Walcott and his twin brother, Roderick Alton Walcott, were born to Warwick and Alix Walcott on the Caribbean island of St. Lucia, in the West Indies. In addition to his twin brother, he had one older sister, Pamela. Walcott was born into a Methodist family, while most of his neighbors were Catholic, the legacy of long French colonial rule. In April of 1931, Walcott's father, clerk of the First District Court, died, leaving Alix Walcott, the headmistress of the Methodist Infant Day School, to rear the children. With two white grandfathers and his family's economic and religious status, Walcott was caught between races and classes.

Four influences shaped his aesthetic growth: his formal English education, his talent as a painter, the life of the island itself, and his religious background. His colonial education was thorough, including Greek and Latin and the essential European masterpieces. Following his father's talents, Walcott was as interested in painting as in literature. His mentor, the local painter Harry Simmons, recognized that Walcott's talents as a writer surpassed his talents as a painter and guided him through the transition from painting to poetry. His poems are replete with the language and actions of fishers and peasants, as well as the acute observations of the natural world. His religious background also served to train him for the craft of poetry, and, as he asserts in an interview in *The Paris Review,* "I have never separated the writing of poetry from prayer. I have grown up believing it is a vocation, a religious vocation."

When Walcott was fourteen, his first poem was published in a newspaper. Four years later, in 1948, he sold his privately printed *Twenty-five Poems* (1948) on the streets to repay his mother, who had provided for printing costs. In 1950, his first significant play, *Henri Christophe: A Chronicle,* was produced by the St. Lucia Arts Guild. The play's subject was Henri Christophe, who, with Toussaint-Louverture and Jean-Jacques Dessalines, led the only successful slave revolt in the Caribbean, resulting in the creation of the nation of Haiti. In this same year, Walcott, on a British Co-

lonial Development Scholarship, left for the University of the West Indies in Jamaica. In 1951, his play *Harry Dernier: A Play for Radio Production* and his *Poems* were published. After receiving his B.A. in 1953, he moved to Trinidad, where he worked as a book reviewer, journalist, and art critic, while continuing his work as a playwright and poet. In 1954, Walcott's play *The Sea at Dauphin* was produced. Also that year, he married Faye Althea Moston (they were divorced in 1959). In 1957, he received a Rockefeller Fellowship, which took him in 1958 to New York City, where *Drums and Colours* (1958) was performed for the First Parliament of the West Indies.

In 1959, Walcott founded the Trinidad Theatre Workshop, and his play *Malcochon: Or, Six in the Rain* was produced. The year after receiving the Guinness Award for Poetry in 1961, Walcott's collection of poems *In a Green Night: Poems, 1948-1960* (1962) was published, bringing him international attention. In 1962, he married Margaret Maillard. The 1960's saw the publication of *Selected Poems* (1964), *The Castaway and Other Poems* (1965), and *The Gulf and Other Poems* (1969). In each of these volumes, Walcott's poetry continues to move from the more stilted and conventional language of *In a Green Night* to such distinct lyrics as "Coral," "The Swamp," "The Gulf," and "Crusoe's Journal." These poems show Walcott not controlled by technique but controlling technique to fully express his vision.

By the mid-1960's, Walcott had become a frequent traveler to North America to oversee the production of his plays and to teach. His most important play, *Dream on Monkey Mountain,* premiered in Toronto in 1967; it was awarded an Obie in 1971. Its central character, Makak, is a figure of not only one repressed by a slave society but also one who expresses the primal connections between the peasant or folk culture and the landscape.

Walcott's book-length autobiographical poem, *Another Life* (1973), demonstrates how he connects his life, his art, and the ocean. Divided into twenty-three chapters, the poem is a retrospective view of his process of becoming an artist, his growing political awareness and disenchantment, the loss of innocence, and the ever presence of the sea. In 1976, *Sea Grapes* was published, followed three years later by *The Star-Apple Kingdom* (1979). In these volumes of poetry, his understanding of the Caribbean is the most lyrical. With his 1981 collection of poems, *The Fortunate Traveller,* his sense of the division between North America and the Caribbean, of being displaced and unempowered because of his rootlessness, creates an ironic cast to his identity as a "fortunate traveller."

Walcott's training as a painter merges with his 1984 collection of poems, *Midsummer.* In this fifty-four poem sequence, Walcott traces a year from summer to summer. His *Collected Poems, 1948-1984* appeared in 1986, followed in the next year by *The Arkansas Testament* (1987). This collection, like *The Fortunate Traveller,* is divided between the Caribbean and elsewhere; as in that earlier volume, Walcott explores his identity as an outsider, as well as the conditions of a collapsing empire. Walcott's second book-length poem, *Omeros,* was published in 1990. The title, the Greek name for Homer, invokes the web of connections with which Walcott has worked throughout his career. It overlays a variety of personas and histories, most centrally Achille, a fisherman who sets out on a quest for self-identity. Through Achille, various layers of history are enfolded, including classical, Caribbean, and literary; in him also exists the history of the exile, the one who must test boundaries in order to establish identity. Achille is prefigured in Walcott's earlier work, particularly in the persona of Shabine in "The Schooner *Flight*" (from *The Star-Apple Kingdom*) and the autobiographical voice in *Another Life*.

Walcott's later plays include *The Charlatan* (1974), *O Babylon!* (1976), *Remembrance* (1978), *The Isle Is Full of Noises* (1982), and *Beef, No Chicken* (1981). His interest in drama informs his poetry. Many of his poems are constructed in the form of a dramatic monologue, where the poem's voice is a fully conceived dramatic persona. In 1981, Walcott received the prestigious MacArthur Fellowship and in 1988, the Queen's Medal for Poetry. He continued to divide his time between Boston (teaching at Boston University), St. Lucia, and Trinidad.

Analysis

The Russian-born poet Joseph Brodsky has written, in regard to Walcott's work, that "Poets' real biographies are like those of birds, almost identical—their real data are in the way they sound. A poet's biography is in his vowels and sibilants, in his meters, rhymes and metaphors." If this is true, then Walcott's biography is indeed a rich and varied one, for he is a master of metaphor, image, meter, and rhyme. Walcott's technical abilities are not the source of his power as a poet; rather, his power lies in the full realization of language in its historic, cathartic, and revelatory condition. Walcott's major themes are time, ocean, and language. Each of these is linked to the others in inextricable ways. Time implies not only history but also the measured beat of poetry. That leads to language, which of course is history, memory, poetry, and creation. The ocean throughout Walcott's work provides life and sustenance; the ocean is also history, for that is what both Shabine of "The Schooner *Flight*" and Achille of *Omeros* discover in their oceanic quests. The ocean holds memory and life; as such, it is also language.

All of these concerns hinge on identity. In "Names," from his collection *Sea Grapes,* Walcott opens with "My race began as the sea began,/ with no nouns and with no horizon." Walcott consistently investigates his status as not only a colonial but also a colonial of African descent. His race—that hybrid that Shabine defines as, "I have Dutch, nigger, and English in me,/ and either I'm nobody, or I'm a nation"—is new, and thus the poet occupies the position of Adam or Orpheus. The combination of scorn and self-assurance that typifies Shabine is not present in the first section of "Names." Instead, the section ends with despair, the poet is reduced to the condition of an indifferent castaway whose identity is lost. Walcott extends this condition of endless denial, from the colonial to everyone, as at the end of the poem "Greece," from *The Fortunate Traveller,* where the speaker is forced to begin again, to rename creation and sound a new language.

Also in "Names," Walcott alludes to the middle passage, that nightmarish journey across the Atlantic and the culminating diaspora of the slave auctions. This history informs "Names" and much of Walcott's work. One's name and one's family were discarded and new names were imposed. Walcott identifies this diaspora as a deep historical sense of exile, where one is driven into the solitariness of the self.

In his early poem, "A Far Cry from Africa," Walcott poses the question of how to choose between his African heritage and the language of his poetry and of his colonial history and tradition. Furthermore, he asks how he could live if he did turn his back on Africa. These questions reveal the difficult balance that he faces as a poet who, by circumstance, belongs to differing and exclusive traditions. If the poem "Names" poses the question of self-identity, this poem questions the identity of the historical self. To live in the world, Walcott argues, a poet must address the conditions of his or her history. This mandate is especially true for the colonial who is defined by so many disparate histories.

Walcott continually attempts this process through his use of metaphors and images of the natural world. This persistent necessity to name and to provide metaphors for phenomena, and therefore extend the process of naming by drawing similarity out of difference, is found throughout Walcott's work. Metaphor attempts to uncover and generate the truth or essence about phenomena. Metaphor works against the force of oblivion. The terms that colonial powers use to describe the people and ecology of their colonies—marginal, unimportant, provisional—indicate the force of oblivion against which Walcott struggles. By persistently drawing his Antillian archipelago into metaphoric relationship with the Greek archipelago and all the implied foundations of Western culture, Walcott is able to provide a history and importance to the Antillian world.

The natural world constantly seeks to overrun the possibility of identity, as in these lines from *Another Life,* "growths hidden in green darkness, forests/ of history thickening with amnesia." Walcott's poetry reflects the lushness of his childhood landscapes. This lushness of image corresponds to the division between the body and intellect that he both expresses and criticizes. Yet what his profoundly painterly eye realizes is the misunderstanding of this tropic lushness. The northern, metropolitan vision is portrayed by him as creating stereotypes of the Caribbean world and its people: The Caribbean becomes a tourist's Eden and a place of fitful revolutions. Walcott's poetic responsibility is to create images that rescue his landscape and history from the distortions of stereotype, since those stereotypes serve to deny identity. Walcott transforms his European tradition and education into that of the reality of his geography, as in the poem's concluding lines, "Then, in the door light: not Nike loosening her sandal,/ but a girl slapping sand from her foot, one hand on the frame." In this Caribbean world of sea and light, and extraordinary lushness counterbalanced by centuries of poverty, Walcott recognizes the potential—or rather, the beginnings— of a new world.

CODICIL

First published: 1965
Type of work: Poem

Walcott argues that language and life are inextricable; to change one, the other must change.

"Codicil," which appeared in his 1965 *The Castaway and Other Poems,* is an autobiographical poem of thirty lines composed in varied stanzaic forms. The poem is a meditation on identity. Its title, referring to an addendum to a will, implies an awareness of mortality; thus, the poet takes account of himself. The poem's tone is both angry, reflecting some of his earlier work such as "A Far Cry from Africa," and exhausted or dispirited, forecasting the mood of many of his poems in *The Fortunate Traveller* and *The Arkansas Testament.* Walcott was a journalist during the early 1960's, and this poem reflects the sense of frustration that most writers feel when faced with dividing their language into two styles, "one a hack's hired prose, I earn/ my exile." The poet's exile is his exile from poetry. Later, this exile will become a self-imposed exile from the Caribbean.

The poet is weary, exhausted by the world's cares and demands, as well as his past failures. The poet states in the seventh line that "To change your language you must change your life." The most significant line of the poem, this line serves to challenge his position and to reveal the direct relationship between one's language and the quality of one's life. The growth of a poet's voice demands a continual change and self-examination of one's language and life. The line implies that one constitutes his or her world through language: Language defines reality.

The poem continues with images of inescapability—"Waves tire of horizon and return"—and physical decay. On this moonlit beach in Tobago, the poet considers that once he thought love for the country was enough. The country is both nation and poetry; in each case, the poet sees nepotism and corruption. Walcott argues that writers, like colonial clerks, "root like dogs/ for scraps of favor" from the masters, particularly the European hierarchy.

The poem shifts from this outwardly directed anger and social critique to a self-critique. Middle-aged and self-critical, the poet literally enacts "Peer Gynt's riddle," where, in Henrik Ibsen's play *Peer Gynt* (1867; English translation, 1892), Gynt likens the layers of an onion to his own character and finds nothing at the core. The poet scornfully admits that the "hack's hired prose" has dulled him and that "At heart there's nothing." The world's familiarity has inured the poet to violence. Although the flesh or the body is on fire with anger, the poet no longer fears "that furnace mouth of earth" or "that kiln or ashpit of the sun" nor the passage of time, "clouding, unclouding sickle moon." Although consumed by rage, directed both inwardly and toward the political world, this rage is expressed by indifference. The final line, "All its indifference is a different rage," suggests nihilism. The only other line that is set apart like this final line, however, formulates the means of change: "To change your language you must change your life."

THE SCHOONER *FLIGHT*

First published: 1979
Type of work: Poem

In this long dramatic monologue, Shabine tells of his voyage across the Caribbean and into history, dream, and myth.

"The Schooner *Flight*" appears in Walcott's *The Star-Apple Kingdom* (1979). The poem is perhaps his most celebrated persona poem, as well as one of his most accomplished longer poems. Nearly five hundred lines long, the poem is divided into eleven sections of varying length. The poem's main speaker and central figure is Shabine, who describes himself in the first section as "just a red nigger who love the sea . . . I have Dutch, nigger, and English in me,/ and either I'm nobody, or I'm a nation." This description fits Walcott who, although of African descent, is also of English and Dutch ancestry. What Shabine underscores is the complex mix that defines an individual in a colonial society and defines the society itself. Nicknamed by his society, Shabine becomes an Everyman.

In this persona poem, Walcott creates a figure who is compelled to tell his story. In many ways, *The Rime of the Ancient Mariner* (1798), by the English romantic poet Samuel Taylor Coleridge, is a precedent for Walcott's poem. Both are dramatic monologues narrated by one who has ventured into the ocean and has undergone a transforming experience. Coleridge's poem, however, explores the Mariner's transgressions against nature, whereas Walcott's Shabine confronts history. Shabine is also an Odysseus. Like the *Odyssey* (c. 800 B.C.), the poem traces Shabine's journey from island to island in the Caribbean sea.

The first section, "Adios, Carenage," is rich in image and detail of the island that Shabine leaves. Disgusted with the corrupt postcolonial politics, Shabine leaves on what is a quest of purification. The second section, "Raptures of the Deep," describes Shabine's past as a smuggler double-crossed by his employer, a corrupt official. Shabine then describes in phantasmagorical detail his work as a salvage diver. In the rapturous descriptions of the sea, Shabine reveals the enchantment that the sea has cast over him.

In both sections, Shabine is torn between the sea and his lover, Maria Concepcion. To stay with his lover is to remain confined to the island and not explore the ocean, which is the realm of potentiality and poetic imagination. At the end of the second section, in the throes of the rapture of the deep, Shabine sees God in the form of a harpooned grouper and hears a voice telling him to leave Maria. In the third section, "Shabine Leaves the Republic," Shabine's disgust with the politics of the Caribbean deepens, as does his despair over Maria.

The fourth section, "The *Flight*, Passing Blanchisseuse," is a short but lyrical section describing a beach, "bare of all but light," seen from the schooner, as night approaches, "dark hands start pulling in the seine/ of the dark sea, deep, deep inland." This passage is typical of Walcott's ability to create metaphors that work on a variety of levels: visual imagery, rhythmic melody, and juxtaposition of disparate phenomena. The image of the night being compared to the work of fishermen pulling in the seine net, itself a metaphor for the sea, creates a brief narrative or myth. The fifth section, "Shabine Encounters the Middle Passage," describes a hallucinatory vision of "a rustling forest of ships/ with sails dry like paper." On the decks of these ghostly ships, he sees all the great admirals and hears the orders shouted to his ghostly counterparts. At the end of this section, he passes the slave ships, from a variety of nations, and knows that sequestered below their decks are his forebears, who cannot hear his shouts.

The sixth section, "The Sailor Sings Back to the Casuarinas," is an Orphic moment in the poem, where Shabine questions the nature of names. That, of course, is a central theme in the poem, beginning with the history of Shabine's own name, the pun on Maria Concepcion's name, and Shabine's rhetorical question upon seeing the slave ships in the fifth section, "Who knows/ who his grandfather is, much less his name?" Looking at the graceful, wind-bent gray pines known variously as cedars, cypresses, and casuarinas, Shabine reflects that "we live like our names and you would have/ to be colonial to know the difference,/ to know the pain of history words contain." Shabine reveals the full irony of such a homily when he quotes, " 'if we live like the names our masters please,/ by careful mimicry might become men.' "

"The *Flight* Anchors in Castries Harbor," the seventh section, introduces Shabine as poet. The next section, "Fight with the Crew," depicts the crew mocking Shabine's poetry and his fight to regain possession of his poetry notebook. Again, it is another manifestation of Shabine's struggle to define himself. The ninth section, "Maria Concepcion and the Book of Dreams," continues Shabine's quest; this leg of his journey takes him from St. Lucia to Dominica. The section begins describing the illusion of progress, which prompts Shabine's historical memories and imagination to fuse in a vision of an escaping Carib running through the tropical forest. The section then turns to a vision of Maria Concepcion's "Book of Dreams," which prophesies an apocalyptic storm. This vision empowers Shabine, who states with almost biblical force, "I shall scatter your lives like a handful of sand,/ I who have no weapon but poetry and/ the lances of palms and the sea's shining shield!"

The prophesied storm arrives in the tenth section, "Out of the Depths." With the passage of the storm and the ensuing calm comes dispensation. In the eleventh and final section, "After the Storm," Shabine has a vision of Maria marrying the ocean and drifting away. She has been figuratively swept away by the storm. Shabine transforms this loss into a form of spiritual compensation. After that moment, Shabine wants nothing, as he has attained a sense of wholeness or union with nature. The poem asserts a lyrical unity, where voice and creation are one: "Shabine sang to you from the depths of the sea."

THE FORTUNATE TRAVELLER

First published: 1981
Type of work: Poem

The poem is a meditation on the twentieth century's cataclysmic history.

"The Fortunate Traveller," the title poem of a volume of Walcott's poetry, is divided into 4 sections and is 208 lines long. Dedicated to the American writer and philosopher Susan Sontag, best known for her analyses of culture, as in *Illness as Metaphor* (1978), the poem is in many ways a catalog of the failures of civilization to be humane. The narrator of the poem is indeed the ironic "fortunate traveller," a play on the English satirist Thomas Nashe's picaresque tale, *The Unfortunate Traveller: Or, The Life of Jack Wilton* (1594). Walcott's traveler, like Nashe's, is an emissary between powers. Furthermore, Walcott has created in this persona someone of ambivalence and moral relativity; while able to recognize the horrors of the Nazi concentration camps, the narrator is indifferent to the poverty of the Third World. In his indifference, he becomes an immoral fortune seeker and an emissary of famine.

The opening lines of the poem immediately convey the physical and spiritual decay of Europe, which describes Walcott's ambivalence with the industrialized West. The first section describes the narrator's double-crossing of two officials from an impoverished country. The narrator becomes an incarnation of famine. He carries a briefcase that is likened to "a small coffin." Throughout this section of the poem, images of despoliation occur: A jet is likened to a weevil in a "cloud of flour," and governmental bureaucrats are "roaches/ riddling the state cabinets, entering the dark holes/ of power, carapaced in topcoats." The narrator has no mercy; he goes to Bristol to be paid "Iscariot's salary, patron saint of spies./ I thought, who cares how many million starve?" In the concluding stanza of this section, the narrator sees in the genuflecting officials with whom he has dealt the repetition of previous corrupt orders stretching back historically to the conquest of Florida by Juan Ponce de León and apocalyptically to the locust plagues in the Bible.

In the second section of the poem, the narrator confronts the poverty of a church service in St. Lucia conducted by a frail and disreputable priest. Walcott juxtaposes this image to that of Albert Schweitzer, the medical missionary in Africa, at his harmonium. Walcott then allows the music, beginning with the choristers in St. Lucia, continuing with Schweitzer, to carry "to the pluming chimneys" of the Nazi death camps. The allusion to *Lebensraum*, or space required for life, refers to the geopolitical theory used by the Nazis to justify their territorial expansion, which implicitly applies to the European and North American control of the Third World. The poem then argues that "the heart of darkness is not Africa" but "the white center of the holocaust." The second section concludes with the argument that, if God is so indifferent to His creation, then one should now write "After Dachau," not *anno domini.*

The third section continues to develop this morally terrifying character, who argues for keeping the hungry ignorant and deceived by the false promises of religion, so that like lice they will "swarm to the tree of life." The argument concludes that "we cared less for one human face/ than for the scrolls in Alexandria's ashes." That is the "ordinary secret" of inhumanity that the narrator reveals. The narrator sees in European civilization a failure of compassion; he is able to recognize it because of his own moral indifference.

In the final section, the narrator's double-crossing is discovered. The final two stanzas become prophetic and serve to reinforce the poem's epigram from Revelation. The hypocrisy of the industrialized, postcolonial world is inscribed in this prophecy: "the weevil will make a sahara of Kansas,/ the ant shall devour Russia." This poem is one of Walcott's strongest condemnations of the industrialized world powers.

I ONCE GAVE MY DAUGHTERS, SEPARATELY, TWO CONCH SHELLS . . .

First published: 1984
Type of work: Poem

This is a lyric meditation on writing, continuity, memory, and love.

This untitled poem is the fiftieth poem in a sequence of fifty-four poems that constitute the midsummer to midsummer movement in the collection *Midsummer* (1984). It invokes Walcott's central themes of language, exile, and art. Yet, to these the theme of love must be added. In this poem, as in so many of his other poems, the image of the ocean is primary. In the poem's twenty-three lines, Walcott moves from a memory of two conch shells that he gave to his daughters to the poetry that he wrote when he was the age of his daughter Elizabeth to his mature poetry. The poem then shifts to a memory of his father and the irony of his name. The poem concludes with a layering of movements, each reflecting the others.

As with all the poems in this collection, the poem's lines are long, often containing more than fourteen syllables. Such long lines allow for rumination, the overall tone or mood of this poem. The poet speaks directly to the reader, offering both confession and a sense of thinking aloud. The long lines also suggest an inclusiveness that may approximate prose. Most central, however, is their mnemonic quality.

The poem begins with conch shells "dived from the reef, or sold on the beach": gifts from the sea. In their "wet/ pink palates are the soundless singing of angels." The term "palates" is a homophone for the painter's palette; thus, Walcott has combined the angelic sound of the sea, part of the mouth that allows for speech and poetry, and painting. He recommences the poem, linking himself with his daughter, not through a gift but through remembering what he did at her age. This memory forces a realization of his distance from youth.

He reflects on his poetry, stating that his poems "aren't linked to any tradition/ like a mossed cairn," but that each poem belongs to the collective memory and unconscious, as well as to the world's collective history. His poems belong to the sea insofar as they are also natural processes. He relinquishes his poems to the sea or the collective memory. Walcott asks of the poems to let him enter them as his "father, who did watercolors,/ entered his work," becoming "one of his shadows,/ wavering and faint in the midsummer sunlight." Walcott asks that his works contain a shadow of his presence, thereby providing a stay against oblivion. He sees his grandfather, who named Walcott's father, Warwick, after Warwickshire, inscribing the continuity of the memory of one's origins in a name.

"Ironies are moving," Walcott writes, and then immediately translates that emotion into physical action:

> Now, when I rewrite a line,
> or sketch on the fast-drying paper the coconut fronds
> that he did so faintly, my daughters' hands move in mine.
> Conches move over the sea-floor. I used to move
> my father's grave from the blackened Anglican headstones
> in Castries to where I could love both at once—
> the sea and his absence. Youth is stronger than fiction.

In these final lines of the poem, Walcott draws together all the strands of the poem's images. Though the poem strikes an elegiac tone, it also seeks an affirmation in the very act of writing. Although the final sentence of the poem suggests *carpe diem*, it should be understood ironically for both youth and youth's sense of immortality passing.

Summary

Who inherits language and what powers come from that language and the circumstances of its inheritance? Derek Walcott's poetry and drama consistently address and explore this question. His use of image, metaphor, persona, rhyme, and meter are all marked by technical distinction. While the effects may falter in individual poems—metaphors that finally overreach, for example—the demands made upon language to sing are fully present. His themes of exile, language, art, memory, and love necessitate his rigorous brilliance. Finally, his sense of landscape, particularly of the Caribbean and the sea, inform his language.

Bibliography

Baugh, Edward. *Derek Walcott: Memory as Vision*. London: Longman, 1978.

Breslin, Paul. "'I Met History Once, but He Ain't Recognize Me': The Poetry of Derek Walcott." *TriQuarterly* 68 (Winter, 1987): 168-183.

Brodsky, Joseph. "The Sound of the Tide." In *Less than One: Selected Essays.* New York: Farrar, Straus & Giroux, 1986.

Dove, Rita. "'Either I'm Nobody, or I'm a Nation.'" *Parnassus* 14, no. 1 (1987): 49-76.

Hamner, Robert D. *Derek Walcott.* Boston: Twayne, 1981.

McCorkle, James. "Re-Mapping the New World: The Recent Poetry of Derek Walcott." *Ariel: A Review of International English Literature* 17 (April, 1986): 3-14.

Mason, David. "Derek Walcott: Poet of the New World." *Literary Review: An International Journal of Contemporary Writing* 29 (Spring, 1986): 269-275.

Ramke, Bin. "'Your words Is English, Is a different tree': On Derek Walcott." *Denver Quarterly* 23 (Fall, 1988): 90-99.

Wyke, Clement H. "'Divided to the Vein': Patterns of Tormented Ambivalence in Walcott's *The Fortunate Traveller.*" *Ariel: A Review of International English Literature* 20 (July, 1989): 55-71.

James McCorkle

EVELYN WAUGH

Born: London, England
October 28, 1903
Died: Combe Florey, Somerset, England
April 10, 1966

Principal Literary Achievement

Waugh, associated early in his career with the "bright young people" of the 1920's and 1930's, became the foremost satirist of his day and a principal critic of secular twentieth century society.

Biography

Evelyn Arthur St. John Waugh was born in London, England, on October 28, 1903, the second son of Arthur Waugh, author and managing director of the publishing firm of Chapman and Hall, and Catherine Charlotte Raban. Evelyn Waugh was five years younger than his brother, Alec Raban Waugh, who would also become a professional writer. The boys grew up in the London suburb of Hampstead, with Evelyn feeling very much overshadowed by his gregarious, good-natured, athletic brother. Evelyn's writings, his correspondence, and anecdotal evidence clearly document a sibling rivalry that existed, on his part, for the rest of his life, while the elder brother appears to have harbored no such feelings whatsoever. After having been acknowledged for many years as a more eminent writer than his brother, Evelyn still bristled when an article suggested that Alec had sold more books than he.

Evelyn's father and brother had attended Sherborne School, but Alec had been dismissed following a sexual misadventure. He then made matters worse, from the Sherborne point of view, by publishing *The Loom of Youth* (1917), a sensational exposé of public school life. Interestingly, Alec Waugh would go on to write more than forty books but would not duplicate the success of this first novel until the publication of *Island in the Sun* (1956). At any rate, his explosion onto the literary scene made it impossible for his younger brother to attend Sherborne. Evelyn Waugh attended Lancing College, one of the less fashionable public schools, before going up to the University of Oxford, where he had gained a scholarship to Hertford College.

At Oxford, Waugh became a member of a set of intellectual and aesthetic dandies, several of whom would also have noteworthy literary careers. He dined and drank and enjoyed Oxford society enormously, while reading history in a desultory fashion. As a result, he left the university in 1924 with a modest third-class degree. Waugh tried

several vocations before finally turning to the profession of his father and brother. He studied art, to which he was strongly attracted, and cabinetmaking—he would later say that he considered himself a craftsman who made books as another person might make furniture. He taught briefly at two obscure public schools and was profoundly unhappy as a schoolmaster—so unhappy, in fact, that he attempted to drown himself in the ocean. His suicide attempt, however, ended as ludicrously as a scene from one of his novels when he was stung by a jellyfish and forced to return, smarting, to the shore. His ineffective schoolteaching, though, did give him material for his first novel.

In the autumn of 1927, Waugh met and began to court Evelyn Gardner. The two were soon married on the strength of Waugh's literary prospects. His first two books appeared in 1928. The first, *Rossetti: His Life and Works*, a study of the Pre-Raphaelite poet-painter and his circle, was a commercial failure. The second, *Decline and Fall*, was a madcap novel in the spirit of Voltaire's *Candide* (1759). It spoofed Oxford, the public schools, and the penal system, which the novel's hero likens to an English public school. The novel pleased both the critics and the public, and Waugh's literary career was launched. His personal life, on the other hand, was in ruins.

After only two years of marriage, She-Evelyn, as his wife was called, left Waugh for another man. *Vile Bodies* (1930), Waugh's second novel, satirized the "bright young things" of London society. He and his wife had been very much a part of that frenetic, irresponsible way of life, and the novel was an ironic commentary on his own psychological devastation. Thereafter, the majority of his novels prominently featured unfaithful wives, indicating that he never really recovered from She-Evelyn's desertion. Waugh's two wildly comic novels had contained little-noticed religious themes, and in September, 1930, he was received into the Roman Catholic church.

For the next seven years, Waugh traveled compulsively and had no fixed residence. He visited the Mediterranean, Africa, and South America. These wanderings did not grant him peace of mind, but they did give him material for three travel books, *Labels: A Mediterranean Journey* (1930), *Remote People* (1931), and *Ninety-Two Days* (1934), and for his next two novels, *Black Mischief* (1932) and *A Handful of Dust* (1934). In 1935, he returned to Africa as a war correspondent, subsequently publishing *Waugh in Abyssinia* (1936), whose punning title he neither chose nor liked. Out of that experience grew another comic novel, *Scoop* (1938).

In 1937, however, Waugh's personal life had taken a turn for the better. After a long and anxious wait for a papal annulment of his first marriage, he was finally free to marry Laura Herbert. She was Catholic, shy, much younger than Waugh; their marriage of almost thirty years produced six children. Still, within a few years, Waugh was off again, this time as a result of World War II. After much difficulty because of his age, he wangled a commission and served in combat on Crete and later as liaison to communist partisans in Yugoslavia. His novels from the war years are *Work Suspended* and *Put Out More Flags*, both published in 1942, and *Brideshead Revisited* (1945, 1959), written while its author was on leave from active service. The latter has a romantic and nostalgic quality not found in the earlier novels; it quickly became Waugh's most popular book, especially in the United States.

Waugh believed that in entering the alliance with the Soviet Union his country had sold her honor to win the war. He found the postwar period just as disillusioning; the ascendancy of the Labour Party, with what he perceived to be its pandering to class grievances, convinced him that Britain had become just another crude, secular modern state. His novels from the decade following the war reflect a deep pessimism: *Scott-King's Modern Europe* (1947), *The Loved One* (1948), *Helena* (1950), and *Love Among the Ruins: A Romance of the Near Future* (1953). *The Loved One* is ironically enlivened by a grotesque but hilarious representation of the California funeral industry. *Helena* is of some interest as his only historical novel.

Waugh set himself up as a country squire, first at Piers Court, Stinchcombe, in Gloucestershire, and later at Combe Florey in Somerset. *The Ordeal of Gilbert Pinfold: A Conversation Piece* (1957) is an autobiographical novel based upon a psychotic episode he experienced during this period. In 1959, he published *The Life of the Right Reverend Ronald Knox*, his second biography of a Catholic subject; the first had been the prizewinning *Edmund Campion* (1935). His career as a novelist concluded with his war trilogy, *Men at Arms* (1952), *Officers and Gentlemen* (1955), and *The End of the Battle* (1961; also known as *Unconditional Surrender*). *Basil Seal Rides Again: Or, The Rake's Regress* (1963) is a slight novella, of interest primarily as Waugh's last work of fiction.

The aging Waugh had become profoundly depressed over the changes in the Roman Catholic church flowing from Vatican Council II. His death at Combe Florey from a massive heart attack occurred on April 10, 1966. Appropriately, he died on Easter Sunday, shortly after returning home from a traditional Latin mass.

Analysis

From the 1940's until his death, Evelyn Waugh infuriated left-wing critics on both sides of the Atlantic and seemed to delight in doing so. These critics found his religious views superstitious, his social views obsolete, his political views reactionary, and his views on black-white relations racist.

Waugh's early novels were almost universally praised, while critical opinion on the novels of his maturity has been seriously divided. Although much of the adverse criticism since the hostile reception accorded *Black Mischief* was clearly unwarranted, it could not be attributed entirely to a left-wing animus. A number of influential critics, foremost among them Edmund Wilson, lauded the early novels but condemned the later ones as betraying the promise first shown. So great is the division among Waugh's critics that what some describe as growth in the later novels, others call decay. Wilson and others were quite distressed by the contrast between the elegantly witty prose of the early novels and the progressive Catholicism, medievalism, and romanticism of the later works. Waugh's style did change over time, although he showed that he could, at will, recapture the manner of his first novels whenever he chose.

That Waugh's literary reputation has endured is remarkable, considering how greatly at odds he was with most of his fellow writers, leading literary critics, and influential academics. He certainly put an immense strain upon the objectivity of the socially conscious critic when he stated during the Spanish Civil War that if he were a Spaniard, he would be fighting for General Franco; when he expressed an open admiration for the Italian dictator Benito Mussolini; when he made no attempt to disguise his distaste for the working class; when, in one of his novels, he pictured African soldiers eating their new boots and otherwise behaving in a primitive manner, at a time when many felt all humane Britons ought to be asking forgiveness for their colonial behavior; and when he launched Swiftian attacks upon anything that smacked of socialism or progressivism. Some critics (most notably Edmund Wilson and J. B. Priestley) responded by writing, in effect, that no one with such absurd notions could possibly author good books. Wilson had praised the early novels, even to the point of judging Waugh to be the greatest comic writer in the English language since George Bernard Shaw. *Brideshead Revisited*, however, the first of the Catholic novels, dismayed him. The pervasive Roman Catholicism of the novel apparently bothered many other critics of secular persuasion.

Waugh's well-documented snobbery and tendency toward disagreeable behavior must also have taxed the fair-mindedness of his contemporaries. His diaries, which began appearing in expurgated installments in 1973, give ample evidence of the unattractive, even ugly, aspects of his personality. America and Americans were generally dealt with contemptuously in his work. Waugh's best-known novella, *The Loved One*, is a savage satire on those aspects of Southern California society he found most false, tawdry, and dehumanizing. Little wonder that the arrogant, peremptory, and generally nasty protagonist of Kingsley Amis' *One Fat Englishman* (1963)—a British novelist on an American lecture tour—was immediately labeled a portrait of Evelyn Waugh.

An ambitious effort to denote the characteristic features of Waugh's art and to trace their evolution through the body of his fiction is that of William J. Cook, Jr. Cook attempts to account for Waugh's change in technique by carefully examining the persona of the protagonist in each novel. These altered personas, he argues, are the key to the difference between the "early" and "late" novels. *Decline and Fall* and *Vile Bodies* employ the objective point of view. In *A Handful of Dust*, the narrator-persona and the protagonist-persona become more closely identified. Waugh's experimentation with first-person narrative in *Brideshead Revisited* is, therefore, extremely important. Finally, the identification between the narrator-persona and the protagonist-persona is complete in *The Ordeal of Gilbert Pinfold* and the war trilogy *Sword of·Honour* (1965; includes *Men at Arms, Officers and Gentlemen*, and *The End of the Battle*).

Waugh was a writer obsessed with technique. Virtually everyone with whom he discussed his work, in interviews and in correspondence, has testified to the meticulousness with which he chose both the language and the incidents of his books. For such a writer, the movement of the narrative point of view, over a period of some thirty years, from the objective, through the first person, to the limited third person, reveals much about Waugh's development as an artist and about the degree of his engagement with the world he described in his fiction.

Many writers pass through phases or periods of change. Yet few literary careers have a division as pronounced as Waugh's. Was it the Catholicism, medievalism, and romanticism of the postwar novels, or was it the altered personas, the new techniques and stylistic tendencies that led Edmund Wilson to believe Waugh had strayed over a precipice? A contrary view is put forward by the perceptive critic James F. Carens, who believes that the "second stage" of Waugh's career, ushered in by *Brideshead Revisited* and leading inevitably to the war trilogy, produced his most satisfying satire. In the novels dating from 1945 to 1961, he successfully exposes folly while introducing positive values absent from the early books. Are the novels of Waugh's middle years the blighting of early promise, or are they his crowning achievement? The question poses extreme alternatives, but they are appropriately extreme. Waugh consistently evoked extreme responses, both as an artist and as a man.

VILE BODIES

First published; 1930
Type of work: Novel

The "bright young people" of the postwar generation lead frenetic, chaotic, and absurd lives.

Adam Fenwick-Symes, the protagonist of *Vile Bodies*, is in a sense a man of the world: a novelist, recently returned from Paris, and one of the "bright young people." Yet he is passive, an antihero like so many other Waugh protagonists. Things simply happen to him as he drifts through the novel.

When the young novelist disembarks following a perfectly awful Channel crossing, an overzealous British customs officer leafs through the just-completed manuscript of his autobiography, determines it is too lubricious for native consumption, and seizes it on the spot. His action causes Adam to breach his contract with his publisher. Adam is then forced to sign a new one that commits him to virtual bondage. Because he has no money, he is unable to marry his fiancée, Nina Blount. The remainder of the novel is highly episodic; what plot movement there is emanates from two rather mild conflicts: establishment disapproval of the younger generation and Adam's desultory quest for the means to marry Nina.

In *Vile Bodies* the narrator frequently becomes a sort of camera's eye that cuts from scene to scene, revealing dialogue and external behavior only. Since the narrator, during these montage passages, does not go inside the minds of any of the characters, he appears more distant than does the narrator of Waugh's first novel, *Decline and Fall*. Two themes that appeared in the first novel—and which would be addressed with increasing seriousness in the novels to follow—are treated in a broadly comic fashion. These are the modern perversion of Christianity and the destruction of the stately homes of England.

The action of the novel occurs largely during the Christmas season (November 10 to Christmas Day) in the "near future," as the author points out in his foreword. The first cleric to appear is Father Rothschild, S.J. This ubiquitous Jesuit possesses in profusion those qualities that most excite British prejudice: He is a plotter in international affairs; he knows everything about everybody, even the location of the prime minister's love nest in Shepheard's Hotel; and he is a member of a wealthy banking family, thus exuding the double menace of wily Jesuit and crafty Jewish financier. Another ecclesiastic, a rector, plays a small comic role as Colonel Blount's neighbor and reluctant chauffeur. The novel also features the making of a bogus film of the life of John Wesley at Doubting Hall, known to the locals as "Doubting All."

The embodiment of "modern" religion in the novel is the rum-drinking revivalist, Mrs. Melrose Ape. She is clearly a caricature of Aimee Semple McPherson and is one of the few characters in the novel whose models can be definitely identified. The lesbian Mrs. Ape is accompanied by a band of angels, who carry their wings in violin cases and sing her famous hymn "There ain't no flies on the Lamb of God." During the revival in Britain, two of her angels, Chastity and Divine Discontent, are ironically proselytized away from the proselytizer by the Latin American Entertainment Company, a white-slavery ring.

A Mr. Isaacs of the Wonderfilm Company of Great Britain demeans Doubting Hall at the behest of the dotty Colonel Blount. In the film made there, John Wesley is wounded in a duel, is nursed back to health by his lover, Selina, Countess of Huntingdon, and later, in America, is rescued from Red Indians by the same Lady Huntingdon disguised as a cowboy.

The degradation of religion and the great house, bulwarks of a once-healthy England, is portrayed against a background of neurotic merrymaking. The escapades of the "bright young people" often end in disaster, several times in death. These deaths elicit no sympathy from the reader, not because the reader (or Waugh) is a monster, but because these characters are. They are grotesqueries, to whom cruel and terrible things indeed happen. Yet they are like circus performers called out by the ringmaster, Evelyn Waugh, to run through their paces. Their various acts may contain a latent tragedy, but it is well disguised behind the gaudy costumes and painted faces.

A HANDFUL OF DUST

First published: 1934
Type of work: Novel

A cuckolded husband leaves England to recover his ideal world but meets a terrible fate in the South American jungle.

Waugh's "new" style, which is so closely associated with *Brideshead Revisited* (1945), was actually introduced in *A Handful of Dust*. This novel contains familiar elements, the most obvious of these being the victim as hero. The reader's perception of the tone, or spirit, of the earlier novels is largely determined by a lack of identification with their protagonists. Adam Fenwick-Symes, for example, is a cardboard figure whose passivity is thoroughly appropriate to the world of *Vile Bodies*, a world in which there is a crazy inconsequence to everything, including infidelity, financial ruin, and even violent death. The things that happen to Tony Last in *A Handful of Dust* will not be unfamiliar to the reader of the earlier novels. Yet whereas Adam is a farcical figure, Tony is a tragic one.

Tony Last loves his ancestral home, Hetton. Each bedroom at Hetton features a brass bedstead and a frieze of Gothic text. Each is named from Sir Thomas Malory's *Le Morte d'Arthur* (1485). Tony has slept in Morgan le Fay since leaving the night nursery, and his wife, Brenda, sleeps in Guinevere (a fitting bedchamber for the adulteress she is to become). Tony eventually loses Brenda to John Beaver, a despicable nonentity from London. His loss of Brenda is not amusing, as is Adam's loss of Nina, but poignant. In *A Handful of Dust*, identification exists between the narrator-persona and the protagonist-persona. Thus, Tony engages the reader in a way that Adam never does.

Tony loves churchgoing. Every Sunday he sits in the family pew, and he reads the lessons on Christmas Day and Harvest Thanksgiving. Yet his religious practice, though not a sham, is merely a part of the venerable Hetton tradition, a refuge-within-a-refuge from the modern world. He is humane, but not Christian. Tony is secular man at his best: kindly, loving, selfless. Yet when his wife abandons him and his son, John Andrew, is kicked to death by a horse, Tony's fine qualities cannot save him (in fact, they make him an easier prey for the predators surrounding him). He has, moreover, no faith by which to save himself.

An amusing representative of this empty Anglicanism is the Reverend Tendril, who adds his own touch of fantasy to divine services. He composed his sermons during his many years in India. They were addressed to the congregation at the garrison chapel, and he has made no attempt to accommodate them to his altered circumstances. They are, therefore, studded with references to the Queen Empress and to home and loved ones far away. These sermons in no way trouble his parishioners, who do not expect the things said in church to have any application to their own lives.

In his misery, Tony is led by the strange Dr. Messinger on a search for a lost city in the Brazilian jungle. The expedition ends disastrously. Dr. Messinger is drowned, and Tony, ravaged by malaria, falls into the hands of Mr. Todd, a mad half-breed. As Tony daily reads Charles Dickens to his illiterate host, he comes to realize with increasing horror that he is a prisoner. Mr. Todd will never let him go. He must spend the rest of his life reading Dickens to a madman in the middle of the jungle.

Now the scene switches to England again, and the narrative is quickly concluded. Tony is declared dead. Brenda, whom Beaver has long since abandoned, marries Jock, Tony's old friend. Tony's poor relations inherit Hetton and turn it into a fox farm. All that remains of Tony Last is his monument, bearing the simple (and ironic) epithet "Explorer" for this least adventurous of Englishmen.

BRIDESHEAD REVISITED

First published: 1945
Type of work: Novel

A young painter falls under the spell of glamorous aristocratic family members and becomes enmeshed in their tragedy.

Brideshead Revisited first appeared in a limited edition in December, 1944 (Waugh often published small, sometimes specially engraved and illustrated limited editions for his friends). The regular edition followed in May of the next year. For fifteen years, Waugh had been acquiring a faithful but not a huge audience. *Brideshead Revisited* made him a best-selling author for the first time. It also alienated a number of critics.

To some, like Edmund Wilson, the richness of the language is the novel's chief sin, causing it to tend throughout toward romanticism and sentimentalism. For others, the structure of the novel is at fault. James F. Carens argues that too much of the novel is devoted to the Oxford period and too little to Charles Ryder's love affair with Julia Flyte. For still others, the protagonist himself is the chief problem. Ryder is a snob who seems clearly lacking in generosity of spirit. Moreover, Waugh, so these critics argue, compounds his difficulties by choosing Ryder as his narrator. So strong is the suggestion, even if it be erroneous, that the first-person narrator is a mouthpiece for the author, that for the first time Waugh was personally identified with his unsympathetic hero.

The novel is a framed story. It begins with a prologue and ends with an epilogue, both set in wartime England. The flashback, which is the bulk of the novel, constitutes "The Sacred and Profane Memories of Captain Charles Ryder" (the subtitle). This flashback is divided into two books: "Et in Arcadia Ego," which deals largely with Ryder's Oxford years, and "A Twitch upon the Thread," which chronicles the working of the divine will upon the Marchmain family and, through them, upon Ryder.

As the novel begins, Ryder, a thirty-nine-year-old captain of infantry, is transferred, along with his battalion, to a new camp. The troops arrive in the middle of the night, and Ryder does not realize until the next morning that he has returned to Brideshead, once the elegant country home of the Marchmains. As he looks out over the familiar vista, the nostalgic memories that make up the novel proper are triggered.

In book 1, set in the Oxford of the 1920's, Ryder meets and becomes infatuated with charming, irresponsible Sebastian Flyte, second son of Lord and Lady Marchmain. Lord Marchmain has been separated from his wife for many years and lives with his mistress in Venice. Sebastian takes Ryder to Brideshead to meet the rest of his family: Lady Marchmain, beautiful and enigmatic; Brideshead (Bridey), heir to his father's title, as stolid as Sebastian is animated; Julia, with whom Ryder will eventually fall in love; and Cordelia, the youngest child, devout in a natural, unaffected way. The Marchmains are a Catholic family, and *Brideshead Revisited* is often called a Catholic novel. Sebastian is attempting to escape the demands of his religion through drink and is rapidly becoming a hopeless alcoholic. Julia is rebelling by marrying Rex Mottram, a Canadian adventurer and wheeler-dealer. This far-from-ideal family is a curious device if, as some have charged, Waugh's novel is a Catholic apologia.

In book 2, Ryder becomes an architectural artist; he paints the great houses of England, often just ahead of their dismemberment or destruction. Thus, two of Waugh's recurring motifs, the artist-as-hero and the great house, come together in the character of the protagonist. Ryder marries Celia Mulcaster, whom very quickly he cannot abide. He is glad to learn that she is unfaithful, for he is then free to dislike her. Ryder and Julia encounter each other on an Atlantic voyage and become lovers. Lady Marchmain has died, and Lord Marchmain returns to Brideshead to die. His deathbed conversion (in a scene roundly condemned by some critics) profoundly affects Julia. The smoldering coals of her Catholicism are fanned into a raging blaze. She breaks off her affair with Ryder and declares that she will remain married to the loathsome Rex.

In the epilogue, Ryder never states but strongly implies that he has become a Catholic. He enters Brideshead's art-nouveau chapel to find a lamp burning before the altar there. Although he has lost most of what he desired in life, for the convert Ryder, the faith, to him both ancient and new, lives on.

SWORD OF HONOUR

First published: 1965; includes *Men at Arms*, 1952; *Officers and Gentlemen*, 1955; *The End of the Battle*, 1961 (also known as *Unconditional Surrender*)

Type of work: Novel

This trilogy recounts the wartime experiences of Guy Crouchback, another of Waugh's maimed romantics.

Sword of Honour is both a general title for Waugh's World War II trilogy and the specific name of a streamlined, one-volume collection of the novels appearing toward the end of the author's career. Waugh did some cutting here and there and eliminated a few minor characters, but none of the three novels are substantially altered in the *Sword of Honour* edition.

The trilogy may or may not be Waugh's best work; certainly it is his most ambitious. His heavily plotted story charts the moral deterioration of the West and the spiritual growth of his hero, ironically concurrent developments. He deftly "modulates" (a favorite term among critics of the trilogy) the tones of irony, satire, farce, and tragedy against a naturalistic background. Furthermore, most of *Sword of Honour* was written during Waugh's fifties when, according to his biographers, his health was failing and he was becoming progressively more disheartened, depressed, and lethargic. To him, Nazi Germany had been defeated at the cost of British honor; his country was rapidly becoming a thoroughly agnostic, materialistic, socialistic state; and, most horrifying of all, the Holy Mother Church that he had embraced in 1930 was, only twenty-five years later, admitting liberalizations (to Waugh, corruptions) and accommodating itself to the society that it ought to be resisting with all its might.

Men at Arms introduces the protagonist, Guy Crouchback, a familiar Waugh character type. Following his divorce, Guy has spent eight empty years at Castello Crouchback in Santa Dulcina, Italy. His wife, Virginia (like so many of her fictional predecessors), is a shallow, amoral woman who left her husband for another man. After the Russian-German alliance, Guy returns to England seeking a commission. In opposing the hateful combination of Nazism and Communism, he feels he is taking up arms against the Modern Age. Before leaving Italy, Guy visits the tomb of Sir Roger of Waybroke, an English knight who was shipwrecked near Santa Dulcina while on his way to the Second Crusade. Guy runs his finger along the sword atop the knight's effigy and swears to take up Sir Roger's unfulfilled quest. Sir Roger's is the first "Sword of Honour." Waugh will introduce, with bitter irony, a second sword in the final novel. Because of his age, thirty-six, Guy experiences difficulty in gaining his commission, but he finally finds a place with the Royal Corps of Halberdiers. Guy loves the army and this venerable unit. His first real shock is the discovery that the British military would welcome the breakup of the Russian-German alliance, thinking only of the diminished odds against them, not of Guy's romantic crusade.

Guy soon meets the two major comic characters of the book. Apthorpe is a slightly absurd junior officer of Guy's age. Brigadier Ben Ritchie-Hook is a war lover who has lost one eye and most of his right hand during a lifetime of "biffing" whatever enemies he could find. *Men at Arms* is the most comic of the three novels largely because of a protracted conflict over Apthorpe's thunderbox, his personal chemical toilet, acquired during his African days. Ritchie-Hook discovers its existence, covets it, and launches a wildly funny guerrilla campaign designed to secure it for himself. Apthorpe's ludicrous death at the end of *Men at Arms* is reminiscent of several deaths from the early novels. After Apthorpe suffers a recurrence of jungle fever, Guy smuggles a bottle of whisky into his hospital room. Apthorpe later consumes the entire bottle, suffers a violent reaction, and dies.

The tone of *Officers and Gentlemen* darkens markedly, especially in the disastrous battle for Crete (in which Waugh himself fought with distinction). Two more crucial characters are featured: Trimmer, a lazy, incompetent probationary officer, who appears briefly in *Men at Arms*, and Corporal-Major Ludovic, an effete man with disconcerting pink eyes and no documented past.

Trimmer is a man of many names. He was Gustave during his career as a hairdresser on ocean liners. He is the fabricated hero of an inconsequential and totally mismanaged operation called Popgun. As such, he is sent on a morale-boosting tour of Britain in the guise of Captain Alistair McTavish; he occasionally promotes himself to Major McTavish. In Glasgow, he meets Virginia, whose hair he once did on the *Aquitania*. They have a brief affair, and he leaves her carrying his child. The Ministry of Information finally determines there are too many Scots heroes. McTavish becomes Trimmer once more and is returned to active service. He promptly deserts and is never heard from again.

Ludovic has been likened to one of Henry James's evil-minded servants. Beneath his inscrutable façade, he is a hard and crafty man. When, on Crete, the Brigade Major breaks down under fire and becomes a liability to the men of his command, Ludovic kills him. He is the embodiment of the British army's ignoble retreat to the sea, a rout in which the men are killing their officers and taking their uniforms and vehicles. Later, Ludovic murders a sapper Captain in order to claim his place in the getaway boat. He mistakenly believes that Guy has knowledge of these murders and, during the balance of the trilogy, he grows increasingly paranoid from fear that Guy will one day expose him.

Unconditional Surrender was published under the title *The End of the Battle* in the United States. It covers the last years of the war and the period immediately following. Disillusionment is piled upon disillusionment. Guy, now an intelligence officer, is posted to Yugoslavia, where he recognizes Premier Tito's war effort as primarily a means to defeat the royalists and his other rivals and communize the country. The British blithely hand their former Serbian allies over to the Communists to be shot. Ritchie-Hook turns up in Yugoslavia as an observer but throws his life away in a bogus partisan attack. The happy warrior's death is appropriate since the modern world has no use for those of his ilk.

In London, Sir Ralph Brompton, a sinister politician and Ludovic's former homosexual lover, is loading the British military mission to Yugoslavia with Communists. In terrible contrast to Sir Roger's sword, the Sword of Stalingrad, the loathsome symbol of Britain's alliance with atheism and totalitarianism, is displayed in splendor in Westminster Abbey. In Guy's private life, interesting developments have preceded his departure for Yugoslavia. Virginia, after failing to find a suitable abortionist in war-torn London, decides to have Trimmer's child. Guy, who as a Catholic believes that his marriage to Virginia—now divorced from her most recent husband—has never truly ended, feels obligated to marry her again. She has the baby, legally Guy's, and leaves it in the country. She is later killed by a "doodle" bomb in the final days of the war.

After the war, the tortured and reclusive Ludovic moves to Italy, even masochistically purchasing the Castello Crouchback. He becomes the best-selling author of *The Death Wish*, an extravagantly romantic novel that most critics take to be a satiric version of Waugh's own *Brideshead Revisited*. Guy returns to Broome, his country home, and marries Domenica, the tomboy daughter of friends. Virginia's son is christened Gervase, the noblest name in the Crouchback line, and Guy unselfishly wills the family name and all that goes with it to the son of Trimmer.

Of the two titles, *Unconditional Surrender* and *The End of the Battle*, the first is clearly the more successful artistically. As well as referring to the surrender of the Axis Powers, it hints at Britain's surrender to expediency in order to win the war. Finally, it suggests that Guy's final, selfless act in the trilogy is a surrender to the Divine Will.

Summary

Evelyn Waugh's earliest novels were received, and praised, as farces and amusing romps. His essential seriousness of purpose was ignored or misunderstood. He was long viewed as a talented entertainer whose language and syntax were flawless, whose plots were delightfully inventive. As the body of his work grew and as he reiterated his theme of the spiritual emptiness of modern life, however, critics were forced to take note. Eventually, to those who shared his view of humanity's fallen nature, who shared his passions and his fears, he became much more than an entertainer. He became a kind of witty Jeremiah, prophesying the end of grace, both divine and earthly, from behind a mask of scornful laughter.

Bibliography

Carens, James F. *The Satiric Art of Evelyn Waugh*. Seattle: University of Washington Press, 1966.

Carpenter, Humphrey. *The Brideshead Generation: Evelyn Waugh and His Friends*. Boston: Houghton Mifflin, 1990.

Cook, William J., Jr. *Masks, Modes, and Morals: The Art of Evelyn Waugh*. Rutherford, N.J.: Fairleigh Dickinson University Press, 1971.

Crabbe, Katharyn W. *Evelyn Waugh*. New York: Continuum, 1988.

Greenblatt, Stephen J. *Three Modern Satirists: Waugh, Orwell, and Huxley*. New Haven, Conn.: Yale University Press, 1965.

Heath, Jeffrey. *The Picturesque Prison: Evelyn Waugh and His Writing*. Kingston, Ontario: McGill-Queen's University Press, 1982.

Phillips, Gene D. *Evelyn Waugh's Officers, Gentlemen, and Rogues: The Fact Behind His Fiction*. Chicago: Nelson-Hall, 1975.

Pryce-Jones, David, ed. *Evelyn Waugh and His World*. Boston: Little, Brown, 1973.

Stopp, Frederick J. *Evelyn Waugh: Portrait of an Artist*. Boston: Little, Brown, 1958.

Sykes, Christopher. *Evelyn Waugh: A Biography*. Boston: Little, Brown, 1975.

Patrick Adcock

H.G. WELLS

Born: Bromley, Kent, England
September 21, 1866
Died: London, England
August 13, 1946

Principal Literary Achievement

Still read for his lively, provocative scientific romances, Wells is also recognized for the strength of his best realistic fiction and for a temperament that helped shape and predict modern life.

Biography

Herbert George Wells was born in Bromley, Kent, England, on September 21, 1866, the third son of Joseph and Sarah Neal Wells. In rather mean surroundings (Wells later called it "a suburb of the damnedest"), Sarah struggled to rear her son, returning to her employment as a lady's maid after her unreliable husband (who was first a gardener and then a professional club cricketer) abandoned the family. Giving Wells the rudiments of an education—teaching him the alphabet and borrowing books from the public library—Sarah took employment with the Fetherstonhaugh family at Up Park, Sussex. These circumstances—growing up poor among the wealthy, observing at close hand the disparity between social classes, and striving to acquire independence by dint of his formidable intellect and energy—were to mark Wells for the rest of his life, informing all of his writing and accounting for his drive to dominate the age in which he lived.

At fourteen, Wells was apprenticed to a draper at Windsor, a humiliating, menial occupation for a young man whose imagination had been stimulated by reading works such as Nathaniel Hawthorne's *The House of the Seven Gables* (1851), Eugène Sue's *Les Mystères de Paris* (1842-1843; *The Mysteries of Paris*, 1843-1846), and Jonathan Swift's *Gulliver's Travels* (1726). At a very early age, Wells had developed a mind that transcended his immediate reality and conceived of other worlds on a scale much grander than his position in life permitted.

Soon discharged from the draper's shop as unfit, Wells became a teacher; he returned to his mother at Up Park, then became a chemist's (pharmacist's) assistant before submitting once more to an apprenticeship in a draper's shop. At seventeen, he broke once and for all with the world of commerce, becoming a teacher at Midhurst, studying Plato, geology, physiology, chemistry, and mathematics, attending London

Normal School of Science, and coming under the influence of T. H. Huxley, one of the great champions of Charles Darwin and nineteenth century science.

A desultory student, Wells began writing the sketches that would become his first science-fiction stories and fell in love with his cousin, Isabel, marrying her in 1891. After a brief bout with tuberculosis and the writing of two scientific textbooks, Wells left his first wife for Amy Catherine Robbins ("Jane"), whom he would later marry even while initiating a lifelong series of romantic relationships with women who would figure (slightly disguised) in several of his novels.

Wells's first major success, *The Time Machine: An Invention* (1895), showed that his forte was fantasy: an adventure story that appealed to the late Victorian interest in scientific experiment and in the isolated, lonely heroes of science who challenged their contemporaries' stodgy ideas about the nature of society and of the universe. Quickly becoming a best-selling author of such works as *The Invisible Man: A Grotesque Romance* (1897) and *The War of the Worlds* (1898), Wells transformed himself into a public figure, taking an interest in radical politics and joining the Fabian socialists for a brief period. He embarked on a series of what he called "discussion novels"—*Marriage* (1912), *The Passionate Friends* (1913), *The Wife of Sir Isaac Harman* (1914)—designed to raise the issue of relations between men and women in the light of feminism and the scientific advancements of his age. Wells pursued and attracted powerful and intelligent women—first Amber Reeves, the young daughter of prominent Fabian socialists, and then Rebecca West, the newest and freshest personality among the suffragists.

At the same time, in *Mankind in the Making* (1903), *A Modern Utopia* (1905), and later books and articles, Wells pursued a career as journalist, historian, and philosopher, arguing for a form of international government and recognition of human rights that would transcend the aggressive relationships of nation states. Many of his speculations about world wars, atomic theory, and other developments in the future proved prophetic.

Wells continued to write novels to the end of his career, producing in 1917 perhaps his last great novel, *Mr. Britling Sees It Through*, a sensitive, moving acount of World War I and its aftermath in England. He became less interested in fiction, satirizing Henry James's religious devotion to the novel in *Boon* (1915). Increasingly, Wells turned his attention to world history, producing *The Outline of History: Being a Plain History of Life and Mankind* (1920), and to propagandistic works. Wells's wife died in 1928, and his later years were beset by an increasing frustration with his flagging physical and imaginative powers. He died on August 13, 1946, in London.

Wells produced 114 volumes in his lifetime. Only a handful of novels are still read today, with his scientific romances winning new generations of readers. Much of his other work is still of interest to social and literary historians, who must take him into account in their appraisals of the late Victorian and Edwardian periods.

Analysis

In all of his work, Wells prided himself on his opposition to the status quo. He became attracted to people of science because they proved to be the most capable of thinking beyond their times, of imagining other ages and forms of society. He delighted in twitting the stolid attitudes of the late Victorians and Edwardians, showing a London laid waste by a Martian invasion, a populace agog at the machinations of an invisible man, and a community outraged by the heroine's seduction of an older man in *Ann Veronica: A Modern Love Story* (1909), a book that hardly concealed the fact that it was based on his scandalous liaison with Amber Reeves.

Powerfully influenced by the ideas of Darwin—as they had been interpreted and disseminated by Wells's teacher, T. H. Huxley—Wells sought to show the direction in which history was headed. He clearly foresaw that feminism would triumph, in the sense that women would eventually enjoy an equal relationship with men. He anticipated the world of atomic weapons and the mass destruction of cities, of total war that would respect no enclaves of humanity. He was, in many respects, a pessimist, and yet he continued to hope that somehow humanity would see its folly before it was too late.

Through his imagination and reason, Wells indefatigably created fiction and philosophical treatises aimed at stimulating and teaching the world to think ahead. The planet itself, he believed, was threatened—perhaps by invasions of aliens, perhaps by its own blindness to its self-destructive potential.

The Darwinian idea of evolution, however, suggested to Wells that human beings could, in fact, trace the outline of history and encompass it so that something approaching a world government might be possible. His task was to unite the individual with the cosmic, to imbue the culture with a universal consciousness commensurate with the immensity of the world's maturation.

Thus, the scientific romances and the realistic novels are but different sides of Wells's comprehensive attack on provinciality and his plea for an enlarged human understanding that would overthrow the conventions of polite society. He found that England wanted to be jarred; it needed to perceive itself as under threat from above and outside itself. *In the Days of the Comet* (1906), for example, he described a Europe very much on the eve of the destruction that it visited upon itself in 1914, the start of World War I. In *The World Set Free: A Story of Mankind* (1914), he prophesied an atomic war in 1958. In *The Shape of Things to Come: The Ultimate Resolution* (1933), he accurately described an air attack on London in 1940.

In *Tono-Bungay* (1908), Wells drew upon his own childhood at Up Park to show how the class structure and capitalistic growth actually abetted each other and produced a world that demeaned individuals even while promising them great wealth and prestige. In *Marriage*, Geoffrey Trafford, a promising scientist, finds himself trapped in his marriage to the forceful Majorie Pope, who gradually draws him into the petty, materialistic middle-class life that derails his once bright career. In *The Passionate Friends*, Lady Mary, the daughter of an earl, forsakes her true love, Stephen Stratton (a commoner), for an arranged marriage that brings her into the world of politics, wealth, and power, only to realize, too late, that she has made a tragedy of their lives.

Wells did not believe, however, that either literature or science provided a panacea.

Wells's scientists are often arrogant and authoritarian, so sure of their superiority and of the rightness of their inventions and insights that they run roughshod over humanity, literally mowing down people in the street (as the invisible man does) or sadly recognizing (too late) the limitations of their innovations (as the inventor of the time machine does). By the same token, Wells had little patience with progenitors of literary modernism—novelists such as Henry James, who made of literature a precious institution dangerously separated from the masses. Wells detested the introverted, self-absorbed quality of James's fiction, preferring a view of the world of letters far more extroverted and in closer touch with the reading public.

If Wells opted to appeal to the largest possible audience, in both his fiction and nonfiction, it was because he forthrightly wanted to shape minds, to call attention to evil and to suggest possible solutions, warning people as a modern prophet who saw no necessary contradiction between art and education and between literature and entertainment. He scorned all forms of snobbery in society and in the literary circles of his time. What he did not realize, however, was that his strenuous efforts to win and influence minds would take a terrible toll on his own prose, so that he gradually settled for quantity over quality, producing masses of words that might overwhelm but not necessarily persuade his readers. He became accustomed to looking for immediate results; consequently, one Wells volume had to be quickly succeeded by another to sustain the public clamor. In such a torrent of words, faith in the power of the word diminished, the right word, the appropriate word, that Wells ultimately could not find once he had determined to overthrow the fastidious, finicky approach to language favored by James and his modernist successors.

THE TIME MACHINE

First published: 1895
Type of work: Novel

A time traveler gives his account of his visit to the year A.D. 802,701 and then mysteriously disappears on other travels.

The Time Machine begins with a dinner party, in which the inventor of a time machine explains to his disbelieving guests the principles on which his invention is based. This scene is a quintessential one in stories by Wells, in which an original mind finds itself checked by an audience that is taken aback by daring and ingenuity. The time traveler persists, however, gradually making his auditors reconsider their basic premises, even if they do not concede that it is possible to travel through time.

Although Wells rarely bothered to construct elaborate scientific justifications for his romances, the inventor's speech can still seem convincing to the nonmathematician. Much of the book is cast in the inventor's first-person narration, in which he recounts to his friends the results of his journey through time.

In the far distant future, the time traveler (he is never given a name) lands among a small, delicate, and timid people, the Eloi, who live on fruit. Their environment seems benign, yet they are afraid of the dark, huddling against the appearance of another people, the Morlocks, who the time traveler gradually discovers are the subterranean masters of this future world. The Morlocks are the meat eaters, feeding on the Eloi but otherwise staying below ground in deep shafts, which the time traveler must explore in pursuit of his time machine, the Morlocks having carried it away.

Much of the novel concerns the time traveler's horrifying discovery of this divided world. It gradually becomes apparent that the novel is more than an adventure story, more than a book about the wonders of scientific speculation; it is also a parable about the oppressed, about the ultimate kind of society stratified by class, by those who have and those who do not. Quite explicitly, near the end of the novel, the time traveler speculates that this is where history is headed: toward this bifurcation of humanity, this division of the powerful and the powerless, in which humanity will literally construct a society that feeds upon itself.

After effecting a narrow escape (the time traveler locates his machine and beats off the Morlocks), he travels to a more distant future, a land where all trace of humanity has disappeared and where the earth is inhabited by large monsters and plants. As in his earlier adventure, the confident scientist is confronted with a future that belies contemporary faith in perfectibility, in the power of science to give humanity control over its environment. He returns to the present a chastened, exhausted man.

The time traveler's tale is greeted with enormous skepticism, except for one of his friends, who conveys the time traveler's story and who witnesses the time traveler's departure for an unknown destination. The novel ends with no sign of the time traveler, no assurance that he will return, and with the cautionary word that human beings must act as if they can still positively affect the future. It is an extraordinarily grim forecast, a foreboding glimpse of both the power and the limitations of science and of Wells's own doubts over whether the new discoveries of science would, in the long run, prove beneficial. Much of the novel's drama comes from the first-person, eyewitness account and from the time traveler's total immersion in another world, making the assumptions of his own present terrifyingly inadequate.

THE INVISIBLE MAN

First published: 1897
Type of work: Novel

An isolated researcher discovers how to make himself invisible and determines to dominate the world, becoming a menace to society who must be destroyed.

The Invisible Man is about a lone researcher, Griffin, whose discovery of invisibility alienates him from his fellowman. At first, Griffin merely wants to be left alone, taking a room in a boardinghouse and secluding himself with his apparatus. In the midst of ignorant, prying people, he is a figure of some sympathy and mystery. As his means of support diminishes, however, he feels no compunction about stealing from others, viewing his crimes as a necessary way of continuing his research for a way of reversing his invisibility.

Growing more and more irritable because of the curious who try to discover the purpose of this strange man swathed in bandages, Griffin arrogantly throws people out of his room, and finally he is forced to leave his room, setting off on a cross-country rampage that leads to injury or death for those who get in his way.

Griffin eventually takes refuge in the home of an acquaintance, Dr. Kemp, and confides to Kemp his plans to establish a reign of terror based on his discovery of invisibility. Having lost all sense of humanity, Griffin does not see the impact of his words on Kemp, who promises not to betray Griffin but who almost immediately decides that he cannot allow Griffin to carry out his plans. Summoning the police, Kemp puts his own life in jeopardy, but he survives and an exhausted, irrational Griffin is eventually subdued and killed.

Obviously a portrait of the amoral scientist, *The Invisible Man* demonstrates Wells's affection for the common individual and his criticism of modern scientists who forget the purpose of their discoveries and believe that they can legislate the quality of existence for others. The early part of the novel, when Griffin's motivations and his invisibility are not yet discovered, is the best, for there is much humor and tension built up around the subsidiary characters who come into contact with him.

Wells is less successful in providing Griffin with a convincing account of his discovery of invisibility, and it is somewhat improbable that a man of Griffin's intellect should completely ignore the practical consequences of traveling around England in January in the nude—the only way to preserve his invisibility. On the other hand, the invention of invisibility is a powerful metaphor standing for precisely that aspect of science—its inaccessibility to the populace—that makes modern science seem at once so impressive and so potentially malign.

Perhaps only a man as antisocial as Griffin could conceive of a scheme that would put him so at odds with his fellow human beings and present him with the opportunity of totally dominating them. Wells rightly foresees in this novel and in others the way in which science sometimes proves to be the perfect instrument of the totalitarian mind.

THE WAR OF THE WORLDS

First published: 1898
Type of work: Novel

The Martians invade England, immobilizing the society but then succumbing to the bacteria that have long since vanished from their own planet.

In *The War of the Worlds*, the Martians invade England, landing in ten cylinders at twenty-four-hour intervals, terrorizing the countryside and devastating the heart of London. It is perhaps the most plausible of Wells's romances, for at the time it was thought that Mars might be inhabitable and that it was far older than the earth. It could well serve, then, as the site of beings who antedate humanity.

The Martians are much more highly developed than humans, but as the narrator discovers, they have landed on Earth to use it as a feeding ground. The Martians are wormlike creatures with bulging eyes and sixteen long, sensitive tentacles projecting from their mouths. They suck living blood. They arrive in huge, spiderlike engines, smothering cities with black smoke and defeating the opposition with heat rays not unlike lasers that can disintegrate artillery.

The Martians succeed where the invisible man failed in establishing a reign of terror, and much of the novel concerns their relentless, apparently invincible progress across the country. There is much less characterization in *The War of the Worlds* than in Wells's other science fiction. Rather, the novel is intent on describing the mass hysteria such an invasion would stimulate and on showing how unprepared civilization is for the onslaught of forces from another world.

Wells is particularly hard on a vicar who takes refuge with the unnamed narrator, as if to suggest the usual comforts of religion, especially organized religion, are to little avail in a truly otherworldly event. The vicar is reduced to a state of abject terror, mouthing Christian pieties and proclaiming the day of judgment. In a half-starved, delirious state, he ventures toward the Martians before the narrator can stop him and is killed.

The concrete descriptions of London and of the damage wreaked upon it by the Martians enhance the verisimilitude of the narrative as the narrator struggles to survive and retain his presence of mind. Although he comes across another character who vows to carry on the fight, human expressions of defiance seem more pathetic than encouraging. It is astonishing how quickly civilization seems morally and physically bankrupted by the invasion.

There is little comfort in the denouement of the novel. The Martians succumb to the environment, having no antibodies to cope with bacteria that attack and destroy their nervous systems. Otherwise, they might very well have succeeded in destroying civilization. The narrator gradually comes to realize that the Martians are dying when he hears their awful, moaning shrieks.

Reviews of *The War of the Worlds* noted that the novel had the gripping quality of a firsthand newspaper dispatch, a dramatic presentation of bulletins as the Martians conduct their relentless advance, instilling terror, physically and mentally immobilizing the population. Part of the excitement stems from closely following the narrator's narrow escapes and his piecing together of what has happened in the city.

The Martian invasion provides Wells with a scenario for commenting on the organization of modern life. The mass of humanity is treated as just that: a mass, a mob of largely undifferentiated human beings who trample upon each other and cannot organize a common defense. They are as weak as the Elois who are dominated by the Morlocks, as unconscious of worlds larger than themselves as are the Sussex inhabitants who peer curiously at the invisible man.

The Martians, the time traveler, the invisible man—for all their differences—function as devices for upsetting human complacency. Wells deeply distrusted human self-satisfaction and what he regarded as a typically English contentment with life as it is—as though life had always been that way and would continue so. Wells believed the contrary, that modern life would be a series of disruptions and that the twentieth century would see apocalyptic changes, perhaps initiated by science, but probably exacerbated by human ignorance, greed, and smugness. Humanity might, as in *The War of the Worlds*, be able to escape the worst fate Wells could imagine for it, but it could not count on such a conclusion.

TONO-BUNGAY

First published: 1908
Type of work: Novel

Tono-Bungay is one of Wells's most realistic novels, and his use of a first-person narrator and his criticism of contemporary British society align this work with his romances and his journalism.

In *Tono-Bungay*, George Ponderovo has decided to tell his life history in the form of a novel. He has grown up in Bladesover, a great country estate, which he describes as a metaphor for the state of English society. As a boy, George sees the world of the wealthy through the eyes of the servants, a comic collection of men and women whose stultifying conversation mirrors the rigidity and unimaginativeness of their plight. Drawing on his memories of Up Park, Wells portrays these lower-class characters with affection, although he shows that the clichés they find so comforting are precisely what prevent them from appreciating life to the fullest.

George's own feelings, as those of a servant's boy, are kept on a tight rein, but he is liberated from the life below the stairs by Beatrice Normandy, a beautiful young lady of the house who demands that George be allowed to play with her. Exhilarated by her attention, George is gradually able to express himself and to develop a strong sense of his own worth, but then he is banished from Bladesover when he gets into a fight with her half brother.

After a series of misadventures resembling Wells's own youth, George finds refuge with his Uncle Edward Ponderovo, an ebullient country chemist who dreams of huge commercial success. Unfortunately, Uncle Edward's first foray in the stock market is a dismal failure, and George discovers that his mother's small but essential fund of savings has also been depleted by his uncle's speculations.

Nursing a grudge against his uncle, George turns to science, studying for a university degree and falling in love with a young woman, Marion, who refuses to marry him until he has a steady, adequate yearly income. Suddenly, George is summoned by his uncle, who has made a smashing success with Tono-Bungay, a patent medicine that promises rejuvenation. At first, George balks at his uncle's plea that he needs George to run the new company, for George knows that the product is bogus, kept afloat by aggressive advertising and not by an inherent positive property. He is troubled by what he sees as modern life's tendency to market goods of no intrinsic value, products that contribute nothing substantial to the economy or to the health of the country. Yet, he is smitten with Marion and sees that, by the management of his uncle's affairs, he will have the income that will convince her to marry him.

Accepting his uncle's offer, George turns his mind to business, fashioning a company that becomes one of the leading enterprises of the time, expanding into lines of new products and remedies (extolling the magical properties of various brands of soaps, for example). George marries but is dissatisfied, realizing that his wife is dull and conventional and does not share his romantic, sexual drives. Disgusted with both his marriage and his business, George turn to affairs with other women and to scientific experiments, concentrating on efforts to develop an airplane.

What troubles George is the growing commercialism of society—not only his uncle's blindness to the sham involved in marketing his products but also his wife's mercantile mentality. She wants the comforts of life, but she has no passion. George concludes that he has bought himself a wife, one who would not consent to marriage until he raised his offer, telling her that he would be earning five hundred pounds a year, a two-hundred-pound increase over the amount she said would be necessary for their married life.

At this point, Beatrice Normandy reenters George's life. They have not seen each other since George's banishment from Bladesover. Both of them realize that they have always loved each other, although Beatrice is engaged to an older, wealthy upper-class man. Although they become lovers, Beatrice refuses to marry George (now divorced from his wife), and he supposes it is because of his class origins and his business. He eventually learns to accept the fact that she is (by her own account) a selfish woman whom he would not be able to please in marriage. She has grown accustomed to her imperious, privileged life, and George, who has lost most of his fortune in his uncle's sudden crash, would never be able to satisfy her.

Tono-Bungay is one of Wells's finest novels because it contains such rich characters and astute social analysis. George's desire to be distinguished, his craving for money, and his yearning for a place in society epitomize the development of modern life. By writing his autobiography, he is simultaneously showing how the modern self develops, encounters the categories of class and capitalism, and thrives or fails by the canons of a society based on the exploitation of human desire. The products that his Uncle Ponderovo markets as a way to renew the self are simply the material manifestation of George's aspirations. George knows that these aspirations are romantic, that they are not rooted in reality, and yet he can fool himself as easily as his uncle fools his customers.

At the same time, there is a reckoning for Tono-Bungay and for Edward and George

Ponderovo. A society cannot stand only on self-promotion, Wells implies. Edward never faces this fact. He is always the genial uncle, the innocent who is so at one with the principle of self-aggrandizement that he never suffers George's self-critical doubts. Consequently, he becomes a victim of his own enterprise. On the other hand, George's yearning to fly expresses his realization that society, the status quo, cannot gratify his highest aspirations. He must find a way to transcend his time. As such, he is the archetypal Wells character, attempting to fulfill himself by going beyond himself, traveling through time and space to a greater world that will yield a greater self, an identity that has truly shed the limitations of class and culture.

Summary

In his fiction and nonfiction, H. G. Wells dreamed of a future that would fundamentally change the conditions of the present. He was fascinated by the scientific and technological developments of his time; he explored politics and business, looking for the roots of self and society. He used his formidable intellect and imagination to lay bare the faults of his age, and he created characters who strove against but often succumbed to the temptations of the emerging capitalist and corporate culture. He often despaired that humanity would find a way to express its highest potential, yet his own prodigious output argued for the value of an inquiring mind, unfazed by obstacles and resolved on accomplishing a revolution in the consciousness of one's contemporaries.

Bibliography

Batchelor, John. *H. G. Wells.* Cambridge, England: Cambridge University Press, 1985.
Belgion, Montgomery, *H. G. Wells.* London: Longmans, Green, 1953.
Bergonzi, Bernard, ed. *H. G. Wells: A Collection of Critical Essays.* Englewood Cliffs, N.J.: Prentice-Hall, 1976.
Costa, Richard Hauer. *H. G. Wells.* Rev. ed. Boston: Twayne, 1985.
Huntington, John, ed. *Critical Essays on H. G. Wells.* Boston: G. K. Hall, 1991.
MacKenzie, Norman, and Jeanne MacKenzie. *The Life of H. G. Wells: The Time Traveller.* Rev. ed. London: The Hogarth Press, 1987.
Parrinder, Patrick, ed. *H. G. Wells: The Critical Heritage.* London: Routledge & Kegan Paul, 1972.
Raknem, Ingvald. *H. G. Wells and His Critics.* New York: Hillary House, 1962.
Smith, David C. *H. G. Wells.* New Haven, Conn.: Yale University Press, 1986.
Young, Kenneth. *H. G. Wells.* Harlow, England: Longman Group, 1974.

Carl Rollyson

ELIE WIESEL

Born: Sighet, Romania
September 30, 1928

Principal Literary Achievement

A Jewish survivor of Auschwitz, Wiesel has written more than thirty books—including *Night*, his classic memoir—and is widely acknowledged as one of the most important writers to emerge from the Holocaust.

Biography

The journey that took Elie Wiesel through the Holocaust, the systematic destruction of nearly six million Jews by Nazi Germany during World War II, began in his native Romania, in Sighet, where he was born on September 30, 1928. Reared in a religious home, Wiesel was the third child and only son born to his parents, Shlomo and Sarah Feig Wiesel. Sighet, his hometown, was in the northern area of a region known as Transylvania. Sighet's residents at that time included some ten thousand Jews, about 40 percent of the population, and most of them were religiously Orthodox.

Sighet's Jews were subjected to Hungary's anti-Jewish policies, which included socioeconomic discrimination and deprivation of basic civil rights. Wiesel's father, a shopkeeper in Sighet, was jailed for a time because he helped rescue Polish Jews who had found their way to Hungary. Nevertheless, the young Wiesel's worlds of study, faith, and Jewish tradition remained relatively undisturbed until the Germans occupied the territory of their faltering Hungarian allies in March, 1944. Within a few weeks, the Jews of Sighet were ghettoized and then deported to Auschwitz in four transports between May 16 and May 22. Weisel survived the shattering experiences of that German death camp and went on to write about them in his classic memoir *Un di Velt hot geshvign* (1956; and the world remained silent). His older sisters, Hilda and Beatrice, also escaped death during the Holocaust, but Wiesel's mother, father, and little sister, Tzipora, did not.

Liberated from Buchenwald on April 11, 1945, Wiesel was assisted by French relief agencies and eventually established residence in Paris. With French as his adopted language, he plunged into literature and philosophy at the Sorbonne from 1948 to 1951. Unable to complete all of his university study because he had to support himself, Wiesel found employment as a journalist. Writing for Israeli, French, and American newspapers, he took assignments that sent him to Israel and then to New York in 1956 to cover the United Nations. He became a U.S. citizen in 1963.

During the first postwar decade, writing of more than a scholarly or journalistic kind had been on Wiesel's mind. Yet he had vowed to be silent about his Holocaust experiences for ten years, and thus it was only in 1956 that he published his first book. Written in Yiddish, *Un di Velt hot geshvign* was an eight-hundred-page account of his life in Auschwitz. Two years later, he pared the manuscript to little more than a hundred pages, translated the book into French, and published it as *La Nuit* (1958; *Night*, 1960). This memoir is the best-known work of his many writings and certainly the place to begin for any reader unacquainted with them.

More than thirty of Wiesel's books have been published since *Night* appeared. None of the others focuses so explicitly on the Holocaust, but that event shadows every word that he writes, and thus all of his subsequent books are built around *Night's* testimony. Wiesel followed *Night* with two short novels, *L'Aube* (1960; *Dawn*, 1961) and *Le Jour* (1961; *The Accident*, 1962). His fiction became longer and more complex with *La Ville de la chance* (1962; *The Town Beyond the Wall*, 1964) and *Les Portes de la forêt* (1964; *The Gates of the Forest*, 1966). By 1965, he was winning book awards such as the French Prix Rivarol and the National Jewish Book Council Literary Award.

In the year after he published *Le Mendiant de Jérusalem* (1968; *A Beggar in Jerusalem*, 1970), one of his most brilliant novels, Wiesel married Marion Rose, a native of Vienna and also a survivor of the Holocaust. She began doing the English translations of Wiesel's writing, which were done originally in French. In 1972, Wiesel was appointed distinguished professor in the department of Jewish studies at City College of the City University of New York, a position that he held until 1976, when he became Andrew Mellon Professor in the Humanities at Boston University.

Also in 1972, Wiesel published one of his best-loved books, *Célébration Hassidique* (1972; *Souls on Fire*, 1972). In this book and several others that he has written subsequently, Wiesel uses his post-Holocaust perspective to retell the stories of teachers who led a pre-Holocaust tradition of Jewish spirituality known as Hasidism. Especially strong in Eastern Europe, Hasidism influenced Wiesel's town and family. Many followers of this tradition perished in the Holocaust. Wiesel strives to keep the memory of them and their Hasidic tradition alive.

Awarded honorary degrees by Wesleyan University (1979), Brandeis University (1980), and Yale University (1981), to name only a few, plus literary prizes such as France's 1980 Prix Livre-Inter (for *Testament d'un poète juif assassiné*, 1980; *The Testament*, 1981), Wiesel accepted new responsibilities when President Jimmy Carter appointed him to chair the United States Holocaust Memorial Council, which is charged to honor the dead, remember the past, and educate for the future. He served in this position from 1980 to 1986. During this period, his prolific writing continued, as did his long-standing commitment to humanitarian causes.

Wiesel's writings are repeated protests against injustice. Buttressing his words with deeds, Wiesel has spent much of his life protesting on behalf of oppressed people and interceding with world leaders to help those in need. His words and deeds alike were distinctively recognized in ceremonies held in Oslo, Norway, in December, 1986, when he received the Nobel Peace Prize. He used his Nobel Prize to establish The Elie Wiesel Foundation for Humanity, to support educational efforts aimed at reducing hatred and the destructive conflict that it produces. Such themes continue to be dominant in books such as his novel *Le Crépuscule, au loin* (1987; *Twilight*, 1988) and *Sages and Dreamers: Biblical, Talmudic, and Hasidic Portraits and Legends* (1991), the latter based on lectures that Wiesel has given for many years in New York.

Analysis

"I never intended to be a philosopher," insists Wiesel. "The only role I sought was that of witness. I believed that, having survived by chance, I was duty-bound to give meaning to my survival, to justify each moment of my life." Many optimistic assumptions about the innate goodness of human nature, humanity's moral progress, and even love itself were incinerated at Auschwitz. Yet Wiesel, the survivor, testifies that despair is not the answer. His writings sustain the plea that death deserves no more victories and that evil should never have the last word.

"The Holocaust," writes Wiesel, "demands interrogation and calls everything into question. Traditional ideas and acquired values, philosophical systems and social theories—all must be revised in the shadow of Birkenau." Birkenau was the killing center at Auschwitz, and Wiesel finds its shadow putting everything to the test. Whatever the traditional ideas and acquired values that have existed, whatever the philosophical systems and social theories that human minds have produced, they were too late or too inadequate to prevent Auschwitz, or, worse, they helped pave the way to that place. The Holocaust, insists Wiesel, shows that how people think and act needs revision in the face of those facts, unless one wishes to continue the same blindness that produced the darkness of *Night*. The needed revisions, of course, do not guarantee a better outcome. Yet failure to use the Holocaust to call all of humankind into question diminishes chances to mend the world.

"The questions," contends Wiesel, "remain questions." He does not place his greatest confidence in answers. Answers—especially when they take the form of philosophical or theological systems—make him suspicious. No matter how hard people try to resolve the most important issues, questions remain, and rightly so. Typically, however, the human propensity may be to quest for certainty. Wiesel's urging is to resist that temptation, especially when it aims to settle things that ought to remain unsettled and unsettling. If answers aim to settle things, their ironic, even tragic, outcome is that they often produce disagreement, division, and death. Hence, Wiesel wants questions to be forever fundamental.

Wiesel's point is not that responses to questions are simply wrong. They have their place and can be essential. Nevertheless, questions deserve lasting priority because they invite continuing inquiry, further dialogue, shared wonder, and openness. Resisting final solutions, these ingredients can create friendship in ways that answers never can. "And yet—and yet. This," says Wiesel, "is the key expression in my work." Always suspicious of answers but never failing for questions, Wiesel structures problems not simply for their own sake but to inquire, "What is the next step?" Reaching an apparent conclusion, he moves forward. Such forms of thought reject easy paths in favor of hard ones.

Wiesel's "and yet—and yet" affirms that it is more important to seek than to find, more important to question than to answer, more important to travel than to arrive. The point is that it can be dangerous to believe what one wants to believe, deceptive to find things too clear, just as it is dishonest not to strive to bring them into focus. Even the endings to Wiesel's stories resist leaving his readers with fixed conclusions. Instead, he wants his readers to feel his "and yet—and yet," which provides hope that people may keep moving to choose life and not to end it. In short, Wiesel seeks the understanding that lives in friendship—understanding that includes tentativeness and fallibility, comprehension that looks for error and revises judgment when error is found, and recognition that knowing is not a matter of final conviction but of continuing dialogue.

Wiesel urges his readers not to draw hasty or final conclusions. Rather his emphasis is on exploration and inquiry. It might be objected that such an outlook tends to encourage indecision and even indifference. One of Wiesel's most significant contributions, however, runs in precisely the opposite direction. His perspective on understanding and on morality is of one piece. Thus, his writings emphasize that dialogue leads not to indecision but to an informed decisiveness. Tentativeness becomes protest when unjustified conviction asserts itself. Openness results not in indifference but in the loyalty of which friendship is made and on which it depends.

"[P]assivity and indifference and neutrality," adds Wiesel, "always favor the killer, not the victim." He will never fully understand the world's killers. To do so would be to legitimize them by showing that they were part of a perfectly rational scheme. Although for very different reasons, he will not fully understand their victims, either; the victims' silent screams call into question every account of their dying that presents itself as a final solution. Yet Wiesel insists that understanding should be no less elusive where indifference prevails. Too often, indifference exists among those who could make a difference, as it can characterize those who stand between killers and victims but aid the former against the latter by doing too little, too late.

NIGHT

First published: *Un di Velt hot geshvign*, 1956; *La Nuit*, 1958 (English translation, 1960)

Type of work: Memoir

Wiesel describes his teenage experiences in Auschwitz and Buchenwald, where he endured the Holocaust in 1944-1945.

At the beginning of *Night*, Wiesel introduces someone he met toward the end of 1941. His name was Moshe, and he became one of the boy's teachers. They discussed religious topics, and one day they talked about prayer. Wiesel asked Moshe why he prayed, and his teacher replied that he prayed for strength to ask God the right questions. Later, the Hungarian police deported Moshe from Sighet, Wiesel's hometown, because he was a foreigner. His destination was Poland and death at the hands of the Germans, but somehow Moshe escaped and found his way back to Sighet. The Jews of Sighet did not believe his tale of destruction.

Although the Holocaust was raging all around them, the Hungarian Jews were not decimated until 1944. Their lives began to change drastically, however, once the Germans occupied Hungary that March. In a matter of days, Sighet's Jews had to deal with quarantines, expropriations of their property, and the yellow stars that targeted them. Then they were ghettoized and deported. Jammed into train cars, destination unknown, the Jews of Sighet—Elie Wiesel, his little sister, Tzipora, and their parents among them—eventually crossed the Polish frontier and arrived at Auschwitz-Birkenau.

Emerging from their train-car prisons into midnight air fouled by burning flesh, the Jews of Sighet were separated by the secret police: men to the left, women to the right. Wiesel lost sight of his mother and little sister, not fully aware that the parting was forever. Father and son stuck together. Spared the fate of Wiesel's mother and sister, they were not "selected" for the gas chambers but for slave labor instead. From late May, 1944, until mid-January, 1945, Wiesel and his father endured Auschwitz's brutal regimen. As the Red Army approached the camp, the two were evacuated to Germany. Severely weakened by the death march to Buchenwald, Wiesel's father perished there, but the son was liberated on April 11, 1945.

Night details these events, but it is much more than a chronological narrative. The power of this memoir emerges especially from the anguished questions that Wiesel's Holocaust experiences will not put to rest. Before he entered Auschwitz, Wiesel "believed profoundly." Yet on that fateful night, and in the days that followed, his world changed forever. Optimism about humankind, trust in the world, confidence in God—Auschwitz radically threatened, if it did not destroy, so many reasons for hope.

This point is illustrated especially well by what is arguably the most unforgettable moment in the book. Wiesel describes the hanging of three Auschwitz prisoners—one of them a child. As the prisoners watched the child die, Wiesel heard a voice asking: "Where is God now?" Wiesel writes that "I heard a voice within me answer him: 'Where is He? Here He is—He is hanging here on this gallows.' "

Death's reign in the Kingdom of Night was so pervasive that Wiesel ends *Night* by reporting that a corpse stared back at him when he saw his own reflection in a mirror for the first time after liberation. Yet *Night* does not give death—God or humanity's—the last word. By breaking silence, by telling a story that is full of reasons for despair, Wiesel protests against the wasting of life and testifies for the mending of the world by humankind and God alike.

THE ACCIDENT

First published: *Le Jour*, 1961 (English translation, 1962)
Type of Work: Novel

Eliezer, a young Holocaust survivor, wrestles with his past in a struggle to decide whether life is worth living.

The Accident is the third part of a trilogy that begins with *Night*. Originally titled "Le Jour" (the day), it comes after *L'Aube* (1960; *Dawn*, 1961), a novel in which Wiesel explores the ambiguous legacy of *Night* by describing how Elisha, another young Holocaust survivor, confronts the uneasy responsibility of killing to help establish a post-Holocaust homeland for Jews in Israel. The setting for *The Accident* is very different, but this novel also probes Holocaust survival and finds its meaning unsettled and unsettling. Both *Night* and *Dawn* reveal that the swords of politics and history cut many ways. Once one has experienced that kind of destruction, *The Accident* asks whether life is worth living at all.

His present and future overwhelmed by what he has witnessed in the past, Eliezer doubts that he can endure his Holocaust survival. The world will not be changed, it seems, and the dead cannot be brought back to life. Nevertheless, they haunt the living too much, creating feelings of guilt, frustration, anger, and rebellion that make joy and happiness all but impossible. In spite of the fact that he has friends and even a woman who loves him, the young man's life is "the tragic fate of those who came back, left over, living-dead." Thus, not only because he feels that "I am my past," but also because he knows that his inability to move beyond makes others suffer, Eliezer senses that life will force him to lie in ways that he has neither the desire nor the strength to sustain.

Not feeling well, exhausted by the heat and a reporting job that seems of no consequence, Eliezer still manages to keep his date with Kathleen. They decide on a film, *The Brothers Karamazov*. Then, crossing a busy New York street, the young man is struck and dragged by a car: *Le Jour*, rendered in English, becomes *The Accident*. "On the fifth day I at last regained consciousness," Eliezer reports. "I felt alone, abandoned. . . . That I was still alive had left me indifferent, or nearly so."

Hope dawns in the "nearly so." Undeniably, the discovery that he can still speak sparks a choice for life, however faint, that cannot be hidden. Then, nurtured by friends, continuing under the care of a doctor who takes death as his personal enemy, life returns to be chosen again, although not without memory of the Holocaust's ashes. Eliezer is alive in the hospital at the end of *The Accident*, and the reader does not know entirely what will become of him. This much, however, is clear: He has decided to tell his story, to share it with others, and in that action a rejection of death and an affirmation of life can be found.

In a 1985 preface to this novel, Wiesel acknowledged that *The Accident*'s protagonist "has lived through some of my experiences, but I have not lived through his." To that remark Wiesel added a suggestion: "[I]n the end, all works of literature, even despairing ones, constitute an appeal to life." Thus, it is also noteworthy that this novel is dedicated to Paul Braunstein, the skilled physician who restored Wiesel's health after the accident that nearly took the life that Wiesel finds so important.

Summary

"It is given to man to transform divine injustice into human justice and compassion," Elie Wiesel says in *Célébration biblique* (1975; *Messengers of God: Biblical Portraits and Legends*, 1976), his recounting of Bible stories about Abraham, Isaac, Jacob, and many more. Like Wiesel himself, these biblical messengers understood that thought and action have abused the freedom to choose that makes life human. They also wrestled with the fact that human existence neither accounts for, nor completely sustains, itself. Their dearly earned reckoning with that reality led them to a profound restiveness. It revealed, in turn, the awesome injunction that God intends for humankind to endure hard, even impossible, moral work until and through death.

One may not see life the way Wiesel's biblical messengers saw it. Whatever one's choices in that regard, it is nevertheless as hard as it is inhuman to deny that injustice too often reigns and that moral work is indeed given to humanity. Wiesel presumes neither to identify that work in detail for everyone nor to insist, in particular, where or how one should do it. Those questions, however, remain the right ones to ask. All of Wiesel's writings urge people to explore them with the care that they deserve.

Bibliography

Berenbaum, Michael. *The Vision of the Void: Theological Reflections on the Works of Elie Wiesel*. Middletown, Conn.: Wesleyan University Press, 1979.

Berger, Alan L. *Crisis and Covenant: The Holocaust in American Jewish Fiction*. Albany: State University of New York Press, 1985.

Brown, Robert McAfee. *Elie Wiesel: Messenger to All Humanity*. Rev. ed. Notre Dame, Ind.: University of Notre Dame Press, 1989.

Cargas, Harry James. *Harry James Cargas in Conversation with Elie Wiesel*. New York: Paulist Press, 1976.

Estess, Ted L. *Elie Wiesel*. New York: Frederick Ungar, 1980.

Ezrahi, Sidra DeKoven. *By Words Alone: The Holocaust in Literature*. Chicago: University of Chicago Press, 1980.

Fine, Ellen S. *Legacy of Night: The Literary Universe of Elie Wiesel*. Albany: State University of New York Press, 1982.

Rittner, Carol, ed. *Elie Wiesel: Between Memory and Hope*. New York: New York University Press, 1990.

Rosenfeld, Alvin H., and Irving Greenberg, eds. *Confronting the Holocaust: The Impact of Elie Wiesel*. Bloomington: Indiana University Press, 1978.

Roth, John K. *A Consuming Fire: Encounters with Elie Wiesel and the Holocaust*. Atlanta: John Knox Press, 1979.

Stern, Ellen Norman. *Elie Wiesel: Witness for Life*. New York: Ktav, 1982.

John K. Roth

OSCAR WILDE

Born: Dublin, Ireland
October 15, 1854
Died: Paris, France
November 30, 1900

Principal Literary Achievement

A brilliant epigrammist and sparkling social satirist, Wilde was an innovator in art, particularly drama. His single-minded devotion to aestheticism set him apart.

Biography

Born in Dublin, Ireland, on October 16, 1854, into a respected family, Oscar Fingal O'Flahertie Wills Wilde was the second son of Sir William Robert Wills Wilde and his wife, Lady Jane Francesca Elgee Wilde. The father, a noted ear and eye surgeon, wrote some twenty books in his lifetime, including *Practical Observations on Aural Surgery, and the Nature and Treatment of Diseases of the Ear* (1853), a standard textbook. Lady Wilde, under the pseudonym "Speranza," wrote inflammatory articles about Irish nationalism and women's rights. She gained celebrity in 1848 when she admitted writing an article in *Nation* that caused the head of the Young Ireland Party to be tried for high treason. She told the court that she alone was the culprit, thereby becoming the heroine of the movement. She published poems, essays, stories, and folklore.

Wilde was a bright youngster who took prizes in religious and classical studies at Portora Royal School, which he and his older brother Willie (born in 1852) attended. In 1871, Oscar entered Trinity College, Dublin, and gained sufficient recognition in classical studies that, in 1874, he won the Classical Demyship to Magdalen College, Oxford. John Mahaffy, who taught ancient history at Trinity College, greatly influenced Wilde. He supported him for the Oxford scholarship. Wilde spent the summer of 1874 helping Mahaffy, a uniquely skilled conversationalist, revise his *Social Life in Greece from Homer to Menander* (1874). He spent two summers traveling with Mahaffy and others through Italy and Greece.

Wilde blossomed at Oxford, where his witty conversation made him popular. His long poem, *Ravenna* (1878), won him the Newdigate Prize, which included the publication of the poem as a pamphlet. He received his bachelor's degree from Oxford in 1878, but his demyship was extended, enabling him to study further. He was par-

ticularly affected by Walter Pater, a Fellow at Brasenose College, and John Ruskin, Slade Professor of Art, both of whom promoted aestheticism. Ruskin differed from Pater in believing that art should have a high moral purpose. Pater promoted art for art's sake, a doctrine that became Wilde's credo.

Wilde, sharing rooms in London with Frank Miles in 1879, created an aesthetic environment built around white lilies, *objets d'art*, and peacock feathers—many peacock feathers. At their digs gathered artists, aesthetes, and people in theater, including Lillie Langtry, who was fast becoming famous through Miles's drawings of her. Wilde and Miles were magnets that attracted the beautiful people with whom they preferred to surround themselves.

By 1880, Wilde's mother came to London and established herself in Chelsea, where she lived with her son, Willie. Lady Wilde entertained some of the most interesting people in London, and Wilde attended her salons, exposing himself further to the people of privilege about whom he was eventually to write. Renowned for his outlandish dress and for the green carnation or sunflower that he perpetually wore in his lapel, Wilde was best known for his outrageous banter.

The British musical theater team of W. S. Gilbert and Arthur Sullivan made Wilde a character, Reginald Bunthorne, in *Patience: Or, Bunthorne's Bride* (1881), their opera about the aesthetic movement. When the opera completed its successful London run and was scheduled for a September, 1882, opening in New York, followed by an American tour, its promoters decided that Wilde could do an effective job promoting it. In January, 1882, they sent him to the United States for a lecture tour on aestheticism and other topics. He spent a year abroad, giving some 125 lectures throughout the United States and Canada. Wilde's outrageous dress, quick wit, and quotable epigrams attracted large audiences.

Meanwhile, Wilde had published at his own expense a collection, *Poems* (1881), which, despite the refusal of London publishers to accept his manuscript, sold out five editions by 1883. He was also working on a play, *Vera: Or, The Nihilists* (1880), taking it abroad with him and hoping to interest someone in an American production. When he returned to England, Wilde went to France for three months; he then returned and began to establish himself as a man of some importance in London. He became engaged to Constance Lloyd, whom he married in 1883. They had two sons, Cyril, born in 1885, and Vyvyan, born in 1886.

By 1887, Wilde was editor of *The Woman's World,* but he became bored and left the magazine in 1889. Needing money for his growing family, Wilde lectured and wrote reviews. He began to publish prolifically after he left *The Woman's World,* producing *The Happy Prince and Other Tales* (1888), *The Picture of Dorian Gray* (1891), *Lord Arthur Savile's Crime* (1891), *A House of Pomegranates* (1891), and *Intentions* (1891). The range of this writing, which included a novel, critical essays, short stories, and children's stories, was impressive, but brought little money.

His fiction, however, established him as a serious writer. When he turned to drama, which remunerated him generously, he was already well known and respected. In three years, he wrote four popular plays—*Lady Windermere's Fan* (1892), *A Woman of No Importance* (1893), *An Ideal Husband* (1895), and *The Importance of Being Earnest: A Trivial Comedy for Serious People* (1895)—that spread his fame and made him affluent. Wilde then went to France to write *Salomé* (pb. 1893) in French. Sarah Bernhardt agreed to play the lead. Those plans, however, were scuttled by the Office of the Lord Chamberlain, which banned the play. In 1896, *Salomé* was finally produced in French in Paris. By this time, however, Wilde was in prison.

In 1895, the Marquis of Queensberry left a card at Wilde's club accusing him of sodomy. Wilde had maintained a homosexual relationship with Lord Alfred Douglas, son of the marquis. Wilde sued the marquis for libel but ultimately was countersued for his homosexual activities and, after two trials, found guilty and sentenced to two years in prison, where he wrote *De Profundis* (1905), one of his most moving works. Released from prison, ruined financially, socially, and personally, he returned to France, never to see England again. He lived on what his writing now brought him, on a small allowance from Constance, who died in 1898, and on handouts from friends. He died in Paris on November 30, 1900, as a result of syphilitic encephalitis triggered by an ear infection.

Analysis

It is perhaps ironic that Wilde is best remembered as a dramatist, and particularly that the plays for which he is remembered are those that he called potboilers, *Lady Windermere's Fan, A Woman of No Importance,* and *An Ideal Husband.* Only *The Importance of Being Earnest* really delighted him.

Wilde wrote a total of seven plays and clearly considered *Salomé,* which served as the basis for several operas, including the famous one by Richard Strauss, his best. The play had been in rehearsal in London for two weeks with Sarah Bernhardt as Salomé when the licenser of plays banned it, citing a law on the books since the Reformation that prohibited from the British stage plays with biblical characters in them. The reason for this prohibition originally was to prevent Catholic mystery plays from being staged, but the law was the law, and *Salomé* was not performed.

Wilde's nondramatic writing, his critical essays, his children's stories, his short stories, and his novel, *The Picture of Dorian Gray,* were, in their author's eyes, much better works than his social dramas. His poetry, particularly *The Ballad of Reading Gaol* (1898), was important but is ignored by most of Wilde's modern readers. *De Profundis,* written while Wilde was in prison, is perhaps his most personal statement. Its posthumous publication in 1905 enhanced Wilde's tarnished reputation considerably.

Wilde liked his less familiar plays better than those that brought him fame and a fleeting period of economic security. *Vera,* written when he was twenty-five, is a flawed play about revolutionary politics in Russia. It is psychologically unconvincing and painfully melodramatic. It had opened in New York in August, 1883, but closed after seven performances that evoked scathing reviews. *The Duchess of Padua* (pb. 1883), a verse drama, is imitative and tedious. Despite some appealing lines—found to some degree in everything that Wilde wrote—the play is overblown, more suited to the seventeenth century than the nineteenth century stage.

Salomé, however, is an artistic triumph. Wilde's dramatization of the well-known biblical story is serious drama well executed. The directions for the staging capitalize on every dramatic possibility. The notable personality differences between Herod and Herodias are extremely well presented by deft use of dialogue. Both are evil, but they are evil in markedly different ways, and Wilde projects both convincingly within their individual spheres of evil. In this play, Wilde is at the height of his remarkable ability to reveal his characters through conversation without letting the dialogue degenerate into tedium. Although Herod is *Salomé's* main character, Wilde's psychological penetration of Salomé's personality was good enough to make Bernhardt consent to play her.

In his more popular plays, Wilde borrows heavily from the melodrama of his day, but he does so without descending into melodramatic presentation. Rather, his social dramas reflect an art-for-art's-sake attitude. He permits contradictions in his characters' lines and lives because art can accommodate contradictions. Drama is not supposed to be truth in a narrow sense, but, inevitably, like all the other arts, represents Truth in a broader, philosophical sense.

Perhaps to understand some of what Wilde is attempting in his social dramas, one has to consider what the French Impressionist artists painting around the same time were trying to achieve. In eschewing photographic realism, they invented a new, profound, and honest, if somewhat stylized, realism. One must remember that Wilde, unlike the French Impressionists, was producing satire within the staid confines of Victorian England.

The staging of Wilde's plays, considered quite difficult by modern standards, reflects the busyness and crowdedness of Victorian decoration. The pink shades that Wilde loves obscured nature's cruelties, its harsh realities. The verbal superficialities in plays such as *Lady Windermere's Fan* and *The Importance of Being Earnest* became the satirical weapons that Wilde used against the falseness and hypocrisy rampant in *fin de siècle* England.

It was Wilde's whimsical contention, quite in keeping with Walter Pater's aestheticism, of which he had imbibed so heavily at Oxford, that nature imitates art rather than the reverse. In his collection of critical essays, *Intentions*—particularly in its two most important essays, "The Critic as Artist" and "The Decay of Lying"—Wilde made the case for criticism as an art form and for nature's imitating art.

In the year that *Intentions* was published, Wilde's novel, *The Picture of Dorian Gray,* first printed in abbreviated form in the June issue of *Lippincott's Magazine* in 1890, came out in expanded form. In many ways a classic Gothic novel, it was regarded by many as the quintessence of Decadence, an effect that Wilde strove strenuously to achieve. In this novel, Wilde distorts the conventional *Doppelgänger* motif in an outrageously bizarre and Faustian way.

Dorian Gray, having had his portrait painted by Basil Hallward, expresses his wish that the portrait age while he remain as he is. Gray gets his wish. The portrait not only ages but also shows the effect of an existence that becomes increasingly depraved and reckless. Gray, no longer able to display the painting, locks it away in the attic, where it gradually turns into a frightening picture of a depraved man made increasingly hideous by the secret activities in his life. Every flaw of Gray's personality is reflected in the picture. Its subject eventually shows the portrait to Basil Hallward, its creator, but then must kill him to protect his dark secret. The portrait evolves into that of a murderer.

In this book, Wilde stands conventional morality on its head, as he often did in his writing and living. If contemporary critics called *The Picture of Dorian Gray* immoral, as many did, Wilde could respond with impunity that a book is neither moral or immoral; it is merely well written or badly written. Few could deny that this novel is well written.

LADY WINDERMERE'S FAN

First produced: 1892 (first published, 1893)
Type of work: Play

Lady Windermere is forced to reconsider her harsh judgments of Mrs. Erlynne (unbeknownst to her, her own mother) when the latter saves Lady Windermere from disgrace.

Lady Windermere's Fan, the first of Wilde's social comedies, opened on February 20, 1892, in London to lukewarm reviews. A four-act play that employs what are often regarded in drama as cheap tricks—mistaken identity, the lost child restored to the rightful parent, the conversation overheard while hidden, and the romantic triangle—this play ultimately succeeds because it twists the clichés with which it is working. The mistaken identity remains mistaken, the lost child (Lady Windermere) never knows that Mrs. Erlynne is her true mother, and the romantic triangle is really not a romantic triangle, but only appears to be.

The play revolves around Lady Windermere's twenty-first birthday. Her husband is giving a ball in honor of the occasion. Lady Windermere, trusting and innocent, receives information that "poor, dear Windermere" has been seeing another woman and has apparently set her up in style. At first, Lady Windermere does not believe the reports, but the seed of suspicion has been sown.

Hoping to prove her husband innocent, she goes to his desk and looks into his checkbook, finding nothing untoward. Her mind is relieved, but then she notices a second checkbook, this one locked. She breaks the lock, opens the checkbook, and, to her horror, finds that Windermere has written large and regular checks to Mrs. Erlynne, a woman with a past.

When she confronts her husband with this information, he is horrified that she has broken into his checkbook and defends Mrs. Erlynne, who is, as only Windermere knows, Lady Windermere's real mother. Not only does he defend this fallen woman, but he insists that Lady Windermere invite her to the birthday ball to give her a chance to regain some of her squandered social stature. When Lady Windermere refuses, Windermere himself delivers an invitation to Mrs. Erlynne. Lady Windermere threatens to strike Mrs. Erlynne with her fan, a birthday gift from Windermere, if she comes to the ball.

In the next scene, the ball is underway. The butler announces the guests as they enter. He recites a string of names, at the end of which is Mrs. Erlynne's, her isolation heightened by the fact that all the names that he recites are those of pairs of titled people, but Mrs. Erlynne is unaccompanied and untitled. Confronted by this scarlet woman, Lady Windermere drops her fan and bows mechanically. When she overhears Mrs. Erlynne asking Windermere for a large sum of money, she flees from the room.

She writes a letter to her husband announcing that she is going to run away with Lord Darlington, a Beau Brummel type who has rooms nearby. Mrs. Erlynne finds the letter and reads it. She rushes to Lord Darlington's rooms to try to convince her daughter to reconsider, attempting to prevent her from making the sort of mistake that she herself made some years before.

As they talk, they hear voices in the hall, those of Windermere and Lord Darlington. Lady Windermere panics, but the resolute Mrs. Erlynne stashes her behind a curtain so that she will not be discovered. In her haste to hide, Lady Windermere leaves her fan behind. Her husband spots it and demands to know of Darlington what his wife's fan is doing in Darlington's quarters.

Mrs. Erlynne makes her self-sacrifice at this point, coming into the room and saying casually that she took the wrong fan at the party. Lady Windermere's reputation is saved, but at great cost to Mrs. Erlynne. Now it is Lord Windermere's turn to reject Mrs. Erlynne, whom he presumes has left her fan in Darlington's drawing room because they are having a liaison.

The next day, it is Lady Windermere who is charitable toward Mrs. Erlynne; Lord Windermere is condemnatory. Yet the day is saved when Mrs. Erlynne comes by to announce that she is leaving London, and that she is going to marry an elderly, titled admirer.

This play is clearly about appearances and about the kinds of moral judgments that Victorian standards encouraged. Its epigrams are spirited, memorable, and profuse. Lady Windermere, who has been accepting of these standards, is now forced to reconsider her stand. Mrs. Erlynne makes her realize that one cannot divide humanity into those who are good and those who are bad.

In this play, Wilde pits his art against the philistinism of the materialistic Victorian age, and he does so with sufficient wit that he avoids the pitfall of lapsing into moral diatribe. He makes a great deal in one bit of dialogue of the word "trivial." Lord Darlington considers it trivial to talk seriously about anything. He contends that to be understood is to be found out.

Obviously, this emphasis is an example of how Wilde frequently sets conventional morality on its head and causes people to rethink their bland acceptance of the status quo. By never revealing to Lady Windermere that Mrs. Erlynne is her mother, Wilde rises above the major cliché that he uses in the play.

THE IMPORTANCE OF BEING EARNEST

First produced: 1895 (first published, 1899)
Type of work: Play

Jack Worthing discovers that his real name is Ernest, making him acceptable to Gwendolen, his lady love, who cannot love anyone who is not named Ernest.

In the entire Wilde canon, no play better exemplifies the author's art-for-art's-sake stand than *The Importance of Being Earnest: A Trivial Comedy for Serious People.* The play is completely trivial, revolving around the fact that Jack Worthing, who loves Gwendolen Fairfax, cannot marry her, initially because Algernon Moncrieff, her cousin, refuses to sanction the marriage until Worthing resolves the mystery of Cecily, about whom Algernon knows because of an inscription on Worthing's cigarette case.

Worthing reveals that Mr. Cardew, who adopted him after he had been found in a handbag in the parcel room at Victoria Station, appointed him guardian of Cardew's granddaughter, Cecily Cardew, who always knew him as Uncle Jack. For Cecily's benefit, Jack has maintained an air of moral restraint in her presence. To escape from this atmosphere, he has assumed, during his frequent visits to London, the name and generally reprobate behavior of an imaginary brother named Ernest. Worthing's love for Gwendolen is complicated by the fact that Gwendolen cannot love any man who is not named Ernest.

In an often bewildering plot, in which identities are often difficult to follow, Lady Bracknell refuses to acknowledge Jack's engagement to Gwendolen because she learns that Jack was found as an infant in a handbag in Victoria Station. Meanwhile, both Jack and Algernon are individually consorting with Dr. Chasuble to have their names changed to "Ernest." Algernon, too, is in love—with Cecily, who has also revealed a desire to love someone named Ernest.

In the course of the play, the name of Cecily's tutor, Miss Prism, is introduced. Lady Bracknell knows the name and insists that Miss Prism be brought to her. It is revealed that, years before, Miss Prism had been nurse to a family to which Lady Bracknell was connected. One day, Miss Prism, in a state of confusion, thoughtlessly placed the manuscript of a book that she had written in the bassinet of the baby in her care and absent-mindedly placed the baby in the handbag that should have held the manuscript.

She deposited the handbag in the parcel room of Victoria Station, and the baby was never restored to its rightful family. Jack, now thinking that Miss Prism is his mother, embraces her, but Lady Bracknell reveals that Jack's mother was really her sister, Algernon's mother, Mrs. Moncrieff. Algernon and Jack are brothers, but better still, Jack's real name is Ernest. The play ends with Algernon and Cecily and Jack/Ernest and Gwendolen poised on the brink of happy lives together, in what is really a mock-Dickensian ending.

The play, which opened in London on St. Valentine's Day, 1895, evoked incessant laughter from the first-night audience and lavish reviews from most critics. A few, such as George Bernard Shaw, found it wanting in meaning and castigated Wilde for the play's triviality. Yet triviality of the sort that Wilde discussed in "Criticism as Art" was precisely what he sought to achieve in this production.

The Importance of Being Earnest succeeded, not in spite of its unbelievable characters, its improbable situations, its stilted dialogue, and its trivial ideas, but because of them. In this play, Wilde accomplished par excellence what he interpreted as Walter Pater's credo, denying at the same time that part of John Ruskin's credo that placed upon art a moral responsibility.

This play has been the most enduring of Wilde's dramas, still delighting audiences with the sort of childlike unreality found in the stories that constitute *The Happy Prince and Other Tales* (1888). There is a real kinship between the two works despite their obvious differences and the differences of their intended audiences.

THE PICTURE OF DORIAN GRAY

First published: 1891
Type of work: Novel

Dorian Gray, wishing never to age, wants his portrait to age for him and gets his wish.

Dorian Gray, the title character of *The Picture of Dorian Gray,* is a decadent dandy of the Victorian era. Concerned with little but appearances, he lives a reckless, nonproductive existence. A crucial event in his life comes when Dorian meets Lord Henry Wotton in the studio of Basil Hallward, an artist, who has painted a portrait of the breathtakingly beautiful Dorian, now in his early twenties. Lord Wotton intrigues Dorian with his talk of the New Hedonism, which is reflected in the novel by Lord Henry's giving Dorian a copy of Joris-Karl Huysmans' *À rebours* (1884), a novel that articulates this philosophy, the basis of which is the achievement of a complete realization of one's nature.

Dorian now utters a Faust-like proposition. He expresses a willingness to surrender his soul if he can maintain his youth and physical beauty and have his portrait age in his place. Dorian hardly expects to have his wish granted and thinks little more of it. He is busy courting Sybil Vane, a talented young actress, who falls in love with him.

Ironically, Sybil's being in love with Dorian robs her of her ability to act. In time, the very ability that first drew Dorian to Sybil has disappeared, and he rejects her unfeelingly. Having lost Dorian and her acting ability simultaneously, Sybil kills herself. Lord Henry, Dorian's Mephistopheles, convinces Dorian that, in line with the New Hedonism, Sybil's suicide is an experience that will help him to feel life more intensely and that it can be viewed as nothing but a source of personal growth.

When all of this happens, Dorian notices subtle changes in the portrait, which is still on display in his residence. A hint of cruelty, a line near the mouth, forms, but Dorian thinks little of it. Meanwhile, Lord Henry leads Dorian into all kinds of arcane activities that, in the tradition of the Gothic novel, are suggested but never revealed explicitly, making them seem, perhaps, more horrible than they actually are.

By the time Dorian is thirty-eight years old—still looking twenty—the portrait has changed so drastically that it must be hidden under lock and key. Basil, the artist, alarmed at Dorian's dissolute ways, urges him to change, to reform. Dorian shows Basil the portrait, now hideous, reflecting all the corruption of Dorian's past years. Then he turns on Basil and stabs him. To conceal the crime, Dorian forces a chemist whom he has ruined to use his knowledge of chemistry to destroy the body. Finally, weeks later, shaken by what he has become, Dorian tells Lord Henry that he is going to reform. On returning home, he looks at the portrait and, seeing further deterioration in the visage before him, grabs the knife that he has plunged into Basil and sinks it into the grotesque portrait. A cry and a crash are heard. Servants rush to the locked room, forcing open the door. Inside, they find a portrait of an exquisite youth, and on the floor beside it, the body of a hideous, loathsome old man in evening dress, a knife through his heart.

Wilde's novel provoked considerable outrage when it was published. The tenets of the New Hedonism expressed in the book flew in the face of conventional morality to the point that readers were profoundly shocked. Despite these objections, the novel succeeded artistically and attracted many readers.

The book presents Lord Henry's credo within its first few pages, and the rest of the narrative is devoted to Dorian's acting out of that credo. In a sense, Dorian Gray was born with the creation of Basil Hallward's portrait. Readers are not introduced to Dorian Gray, the child. The Dorian that Wilde springs on his readers does not exist until the portrait exists.

According to a letter that Wilde wrote in 1894, he said that he saw in this novel three sides of himself. In Basil Hallward, he creates what he believes is a true perception of himself. In Lord Henry, he projects the person whom the world believes him to be. In Dorian, he presents the self whom he would like to be in some other age. How seriously one can take this assessment remains a matter of scholarly speculation.

The Lord Henry that Wilde projects is, in accordance with Wilde's expressed philosophy, the ultimate artist. He molds raw material (Dorian), shaping it with sure hands into what he wills it to be. In this sense, he is a Pygmalion as much as he is a Mephistopheles.

THE BALLAD OF READING GAOL

First published: 1898
Type of work: Poem

This long poem is about the imprisonment and hanging of a young trooper in the Royal Horse Guards who murdered his wife in a fit of jealousy.

The Ballad of Reading Gaol is the only major work that Wilde produced after his release from prison on May 19, 1897. By mid-October, he had finished this poem, consisting of 654 lines, 109 six-line verses. It was first published the following February. Wilde's name did not appear on the title page. Rather, the number of his prison cell at Reading Gaol—C.3.3.—was the designation by which the book was identified. By writing in six-line stanzas rather than the four-line stanzas typically found in ballads, Wilde was able to add reflective statements to each verse. Using the term that Ezra Pound later made famous, Wilde divided his poem into six "cantos."

The Ballad of Reading Gaol is unique among Wilde's work because it deals with the harsh realities of prison and with the even harsher reality of an execution, the taking of a human life, through legal means, by fellow humans. The world depicted in this poem is light years away from the affluent drawing rooms in which his social comedies are set. It is equally distant from the fantasy worlds of his other poetry and his fairy tales.

The poem's first canto provides the introduction of the murderer into the prison community and the speculation of the other prisoners about him. The canto reflects a softening as it considers the crimes that all individuals commit, commenting on how all people at times kill with a "bitter look" or in some other covert but socially acceptable way. Finally, the prisoners realize that they all have a connection with the condemned man, that, in their own ways, they are all guilty with him. He becomes a sort of Christ figure expiating the universal sins of humankind.

The second canto relates the condemned man's final moments, but it also emphasizes the identification that the other prisoners feel with him as he faces execution. Canto 3 reflects on the days before the execution and on how the prisoners develop a kinship with the unfortunate prisoner. The next canto presents the psychological impact of the execution on the other prisoners.

Structurally, the poem ends with the fourth canto. Wilde chose to continue it beyond that because he wanted to propagandize for prison reform, and it is in this forum that he can best do that. He castigates the legal and prison systems of his time, pointing out that all that is good in humans withers in prison. Despite his recent bitter experience with the legal and prison systems, Wilde remains remarkably detached and objective in his presentation.

This poem is not Victorian. It represents a new direction for Wilde, but one that he did not have the vitality to pursue further after the publication of this poem. *The Ballad of Reading Gaol* is a poem more in the tradition of A. E. Housman's *A Shropshire Lad* (1896), which Wilde had read, than of the Victorian poets, whose work is more like Wilde's earlier poetry.

Summary

Oscar Wilde's life was an outrageously interesting one that grew wholly sensational toward its close. Wilde lived a philosophy that perhaps was not meant for living, but he appears to have believed in it and to have accepted it fully. Art for art's sake remained his credo even after his imprisonment, although it is not reflected in *The Ballad of Reading Gaol,* which is his maverick work. *De Profundis,* written in prison, leaves little doubt about what Wilde really accepted philosophically.

Although the comparisons of Wilde to William Shakespeare abroad when his plays were running in the West End are gross exaggerations, one cannot deny that Wilde was a remarkably able playwright who, by defying social and dramatic conventions simultaneously, created plays that articulated well the aestheticism espoused by Walter Pater. Wilde's often neglected essays on criticism are also significant and deserve further study and consideration. In these essays are articulated the maxims by which Wilde tried to live and write.

Bibliography

Chamberlin, J. E. *Ripe Was the Drowsy Hour: The Age of Oscar Wilde*. New York: Seabury, 1977.

Ellmann, Richard. *Oscar Wilde*. New York: Alfred A. Knopf, 1988.

Ericksen, Donald H. *Oscar Wilde*. Boston: Twayne, 1977.

Hyde, H. Montgomery. *Oscar Wilde: A Biography*. New York: Farrar, Straus, 1975.

_____. *Oscar Wilde: The Aftermath*. New York: Farrar, Straus, 1963.

_____. *The Trials of Oscar Wilde*. New York: Dover, 1973.

Mikhail, E. H. *Oscar Wilde: An Annotated Bibliography of Criticism*. Totowa, N.J.: Roman & Littlefield, 1978.

Murray, Isobel, ed. *Oscar Wilde*. New York: Oxford University Press, 1989.

San Juan, Epifanio, Jr. *The Art of Oscar Wilde*. Princeton, N.J.: Princeton University Press, 1967.

Shewan, Rodney. *Oscar Wilde: Art and Egoism*. New York: Barnes & Noble Books, 1977.

R. Baird Shuman

P. G. WODEHOUSE

Born: Guildford, Surrey, England
October 15, 1881
Died: Long Island, New York
February 14, 1975

Principal Literary Achievement

Regarded as one of the premier humorists in English literature, Wodehouse was a distinctively original comic stylist.

Biography

Pelham Grenville Wodehouse was born October 15, 1881, in Guildford, Surrey, England, the third of four sons of Henry Ernest and Eleanor Deane Wodehouse. His father spent his career in the Hong Kong Civil Service, rising to a judgeship. Wodehouse lived only one year in Hong Kong, spending the remainder of his childhood in England with friends and relatives, when not in school. This upbringing accounts for the inordinately large number of aunts and uncles in his fiction.

Wodehouse, known lifelong to his friends as "Plum," followed his brother Armine to school at Dulwich and distinguished himself in Latin and Greek composition, football, and cricket and by writing comic verses for the school magazine, of which he was editor. Wodehouse's school days were perhaps his happiest, the camaraderie of school being celebrated often in his fiction, where "old boys" never let each other down. Seven of his first dozen books are school novels inspired by his Dulwich experiences, most notably *Mike: A Public School Story* (1909; also known as *Enter Psmith*, *Mike at Wrykyn*, *Mike and Psmith*), which examines the disadvantages of joining an older brother at school. More important, at Dulwich, Wodehouse discovered writers, such as Charles Dickens, W. S. Gilbert, Rudyard Kipling, and Arthur Conan Doyle, who profoundly influenced his development as a literary artist.

Wodehouse had planned to continue his education at Oxford, but his father's financial setbacks forced him to join the London office of the Hong Kong and Shanghai Bank. In several Wodehouse novels, the possibility of having to work in a bank seems grim to the protagonists, and the author himself hated the routine of his job and was determined to leave the bank before being sent to a position in the Far East. After two years as a bank clerk, he was hired by the *Globe*, a London newspaper, through a former master at Dulwich, and he soon inherited the master's column. During this period, he began publishing school novels as serials in boys' magazines

and more sophisticated stories in such magazines as *Strand*. The school serials were also published as books, beginning with *The Pothunters* (1902).

On a trip to the United States in 1909, Wodehouse sold stories to *Cosmopolitan* and *Collier's* for much more than he had received in England. He resigned from the *Globe*, settled in Greenwich Village, and tested the American market further, writing detective stories for pulp magazines and serving as drama critic for *Vanity Fair*. In 1914, *The Saturday Evening Post* bought *Something Fresh* (1915; also known as *Something New*), the first of the series of novels set at Blandings Castle, and went on to publish twenty-one of his novels as serials. Also in 1914, he married Ethel Newton Rowley, a widow. Wodehouse later adopted Ethel's daughter, Leonora.

Wodehouse, unable to serve in the British army during World War I because of bad eyesight, spent the war in America and began working in musical comedy in 1915 by collaborating, as lyricist, with composer Jerome Kern and playwright Guy Bolton. At one point, they had five shows running on Broadway and another twelve productions on the road. Wodehouse also wrote lyrics for such composers as George Gershwin, Cole Porter, Victor Herbert, and Sigmund Romberg. His best-known song is "Bill," with music by Kern, originally written for *Oh, Lady! Lady!* (1918) and incorporated in 1927 into *Show Boat*. Wodehouse also wrote plays with Bolton, adapted foreign plays, and dramatized his novels. His stories and novels, such as *A Damsel in Distress* (1919), often draw upon his theatrical experiences.

The Wodehouses and their numerous pets spent the 1920's traveling between the United States, England, and France. Because of British and American income taxes and British quarantine laws that prevented them from taking their dogs in and out of England, the Wodehouses decided to settle in France. In 1934, they bought a country house in Le Touquet, where they entertained aristocrats, national leaders, and writers such as Arnold Bennett and H. G. Wells. Wodehouse himself made little impression on these dignitaries. Winston Churchill met him six or seven times and always forgot who he was. Evelyn Waugh, an intense admirer of Wodehouse's fiction, described him as the dullest man he had ever met. Wodehouse apparently lived entirely for his work and was comfortable discussing nothing else. He also struck some as eccentric for leaving his own parties to walk his dogs.

Like most popular writers of his time, Wodehouse was called to Hollywood. He spent 1930-1931 at Metro-Goldwyn-Mayer, which used nothing that he wrote. He returned with better results in 1936, adapting *A Damsel in Distress* into a George and Ira Gershwin musical starring Fred Astaire. Wodehouse did not enjoy writing screenplays, however, because he had too many novels that he was eager to create. The quality and popularity of his fiction resulted in his being awarded, in 1939, a doctorate of letters by the University of Oxford.

Wodehouse's life was relatively uneventful until World War II. The Wodehouses stayed in France despite the threat of German occupation, and the author was arrested in June, 1940, and eventually interned at a camp at Tost in Upper Silesia. The following June, he was transferred to a hotel in Berlin and gave five broadcasts over German radio. British politicians and newspapers branded him a traitor, some British libraries withdrew his books, and, worst of all, his beloved Dulwich removed his name from its rolls. Wodehouse's most damaging comment during these broadcasts was that he did not mind being a prisoner as long as he was given materials with which to write. A minority praised Wodehouse's courage for candidly discussing the way Germany treated its prisoners. With "In Defense of P. G. Wodehouse," George Orwell painted the writer as being merely politically naïve in not recognizing the implications of broadcasting over enemy radio.

Wodehouse returned to France in 1943, only to be arrested by the French shortly before Paris was liberated and charged with collaboration and treason. After questioning by British officials, he was released. The Wodehouses continued living in France until 1947, when they moved permanently to the United States. (Wodehouse never returned to England after 1939.) As the passions of the war dissipated, Wodehouse's critics were felt to have overreacted. Dulwich restored his name to its rolls in 1946, and in 1961 the British Broadcasting Company broadcast an apology to Wodehouse, "An Act of Homage and Reparation," by Evelyn Waugh.

The Wodehouses spent their last years in Remsenburg, Long Island, and became American citizens in 1955. Wodehouse continued writing until the end of his long life, devoting little time to anything other than his dogs and cats. He was knighted in January, 1975, but could not go to London for the ceremony because of declining health. He died shortly afterward on Valentine's Day in 1975, in Long Island, New York. Lady Wodehouse lived on at Remsenburg until her death in 1984 at ninety-nine.

Analysis

Between 1902 and 1974, Wodehouse published ninety books—novels, collections of stories, memoirs—and two more books appeared posthumously. This fiction, set mostly in London and the country houses of England with frequent excursions to America, bears little resemblance to real life in any place or time. Wodehouse creates a unique comic universe crammed with aristocrats, servants, secretaries, clerks, clergy, poets, police officers, judges, thieves, and, significantly, musical comedy performers.

With the emphasis on plot and two-dimensional characters, Wodehouse's fiction resembles nothing so much, as the writer himself observed, as musical comedy without the music. The stories and novels concern chiefly romantic and financial difficulties, with all problems resolved by the conclusion.

The only occurrence of anything resembling political commentary is the portrait of Roderick Spode as the founder of a fascist organization ludicrously known as the Black Shorts in *The Code of the Woosters* (1938). Wodehouse ridicules Spode further by making him a secret designer of ladies' underwear. Such episodes seem to place Wodehouse's fiction in a particular time, since foreign and domestic fascism was a threat to Great Britain in the 1930's, but most of Wodehouse's characters and events seem drawn from an England that has changed little since the start of the twentieth century. His characters are slightly modified Edwardians. Anachronisms abound in the later novels and are fitting since they add to the comic absurdity.

More than half of Wodehouse's fiction deals with continuing characters: Uncle Fred, Mr. Mulliner, Ukridge, Psmith, Lord Emsworth, Jeeves, and Bertie Wooster. The most significant of these are the last four. Psmith becomes Wodehouse's first notable adult character. He is rich in *Psmith in the City: A Sequel to "Mike"* (1910) and *Psmith Journalist* (1915), poor in *Leave It to Psmith* (1923), but regardless of his economic circumstances, he is bored by ordinary life and longs to take risks. These chances, from operating a New York newspaper and running into gangsters to posing as a Canadian poet, lead to typically complicated Wodehouse plots. Psmith is a smarter version of Bertie Wooster, a fast-thinking swindler who talks himself both into and out of trouble. Throwing himself rashly into situations with little regard for the consequences, his sole purpose seems to be to start something.

Ronald Eustace Psmith prefigures later characters in frequently quoting poetry and in speaking in characteristic metaphors. Tea is never simply tea but "a cup of the steaming." Rather than resort to a cliché like "in the soup" to indicate trouble, Psmith uses phrases such as "consommé splashing about the ankles" or "knee-deep in the bouillon." Such verbal silliness is indicative of P. G. Wodehouse's style at its best.

Wodehouse writes about Lord Emsworth and the goings-on at Blandings Castle in ten novels from *Something Fresh* to *A Pelican at Blandings* (1969; also known as *No Nudes Is Good Nudes*). These farces feature dotty Lord Emsworth devoting as much time as possible to his flowers or pigs, his sister Lady Constance trying to run his life for him, and assorted ninnies such as his brother Galahad Threepwood. Everything at Blandings Castle appears to be in flux, with numerous characters running down corridors or across terraces in pursuit of or in flight from mischief. Lord Emsworth keeps firing his secretary Rupert Baxter, and Lady Constance constantly rehires him. Baxter longs to impose order on the chaos of Blandings.

Wodehouse's greatest triumph is Jeeves and Bertie Wooster, who appear in eleven novels and more than fifty stories published between 1917 and 1974. The basic plot involves Bertie getting into trouble, making matters worse by trying to extricate himself, and finally relying upon his valet Jeeves to resolve the situation. The problems are often created by Bertie's stern Aunt Agatha or his blustery Aunt Dahlia, by such friends as Bingo Little or Tuppy Glossop, or by someone to whom Bertie is engaged and who is determined to reform him. Through all of these misadventures, Bertie remains cheerfully optimistic.

Having Bertie narrate the stories and novels is a stroke of genius by Wodehouse. Bertie is an ironic narrator who never realizes the ramifications of the events that he is describing. Unusual for a first-person narrator, Bertie is not merely an observer but the central participant, since he influences almost all that happens. Jeeves narrates one Bertie story and one non-Bertie novel, and the effect is not the same. One of the virtues of Bertie as narrator is his use—or misuse—of the language. Combining jargon, slang, clichés, and mangled quotations from literary giants with his absent-minded eccentricity, Bertie speaks in a style all his own:

It is pretty generally recognized in the circles in which he moves that Bertram Wooster is not a man who lightly throws in the towel and admits defeat. Beneath the thingummies of what-d'you-call-it, his head, wind and weather permitting, is as a rule bloody but unbowed, and if the slings and arrows of outrageous fortune want to crush his proud spirit, they have to pull their socks up and make a special effort.

Bertie is Dr. Watson to Jeeves's Sherlock Holmes, for the only rival of this gentleman's gentleman for intellect in fiction is Arthur Conan Doyle's detective. Bertie explains his admiration for Jeeves: "The man's a genius. From the collar upward he stands alone. I gave up trying to run my own affairs within a week of his coming to me." Jeeves is the godlike force who miraculously engineers the denouements of the Bertie stories and novels. Because Bertie has to have a problem to be solved and then compounds matters by attempting to deal with it himself, Jeeves's powers of ingenuity are supremely tested in the best of the fiction, such as the novels *Thank You, Jeeves* (1934), *Right Ho, Jeeves* (1934; also known as *Brinkley Manor: A Novel About Jeeves*), *The Code of the Woosters*, and *Joy in the Morning* (1946), and such stories as "The Rummy Affair of Old Biffy," "Jeeves and the Impending Doom," "Jeeves and the Song of Songs," and "Indian Summer of an Uncle." Because numerous obstacles must be placed in Jeeves's way, Wodehouse also tests himself by making the plots as convoluted as possible. The pieces often fit together with almost mathematical precision.

THE INIMITABLE JEEVES

First published: 1923
Type of work: Novel

Bertie Wooster and Jeeves attempt to assist in the love life of Bingo Little with comic consequences.

Four Bertie and Jeeves stories are included in *My Man Jeeves* (1919), but *The Inimitable Jeeves* is the first book completely about these characters as Wodehouse weaves eleven previously published stories together to create a mostly unified narrative. The first true novel in the series is *Thank You, Jeeves* (1934).

Many of the loose strands of *The Inimitable Jeeves* are held together by the romantic travails of Bertie's friend Bingo Little. Bingo is forever falling in love, and Bertie, with Jeeves's assistance, either promotes the romance or attempts to prevent it, depending on the suitability of the young woman. At the beginning of the book, Bingo is infatuated with a waitress and wants Bertie to make his uncle, Lord Bittlesham, the source of Bingo's income, receptive to Bingo's marrying someone from the working class. Jeeves suggests having Bingo read the uncle such Rosie M. Banks novels as "Only a Factory Girl," in which marriage to someone of lesser social status is advocated. As a result, Lord Bittlesham marries his cook.

Bingo next falls for Honoria Glossop, but Bertie's domineering Aunt Agatha wants her nephew to marry Honoria. Attempting to resolve the problem without Jeeves's help, Bertie pushes Honoria's young brother into a pond so that Bingo can save the boy and appear heroic, but on his way to the pond, fickle Bingo discovers someone else. Bertie becomes engaged to Honoria, who says he must get rid of Jeeves. The valet saves his master by creating an elaborate plot to convince Honoria's father, Sir Roderick, a prominent psychiatrist, that Bertie is crazy.

After Jeeves saves Bertie's friend from two more ill-considered romances, Bingo falls in love with another waitress, who forces him to marry her without his uncle's consent. When presented to Lord Bittlesham, she reveals herself to be Rosie M. Banks, having been working as a waitress to research her next book.

In addition to his superior intelligence, Jeeves must be privy to sources of information denied the other characters, adding ironic distance to Bertie's perception of reality. Jeeves is the all-knowing force manipulating the others as if they were chess pieces. Jeeves even resorts to lying and bribery to achieve his ends. He is everything the naïve Bertie is not.

Though mentally inferior to his servant, Bertie is intelligent enough to rely on Jeeves's judgment in most matters. Bertie also possesses enough self-awareness to recognize his limitations. He is truly an admirable character whose behavior derives from a strict code of conduct. While this code is that of the privileged late Victorian schoolboy, it allows Bertie to be modest, gracious, and magnanimous. He is always willing to devote time and money to assist his friends. When he hesitates over helping Bingo out of a scrape, all his friend need do is remind him that they were at school together.

The Inimitable Jeeves is significant in the Wodehouse canon for introducing numerous stock Bertie/Jeeves elements. These include the pattern of Bertie getting into trouble, Jeeves getting him out, and the young master having to sacrifice an article of clothing that the valet finds offensive: purple socks, loud cummerbund, spats in Old Etonian colors. Others are Aunt Agatha's efforts to have Bertie wed, only for him to escape narrowly, and Sir Roderick Glossop's conviction that Bertie is mad. *The Inimitable Jeeves* also displays Wodehouse's comic style at its best.

LEAVE IT TO PSMITH

First published: 1923
Type of work: Novel

Psmith poses as a Canadian poet to be near the woman he loves and to help steal a diamond necklace in a good cause.

Leave It to Psmith is both a Psmith novel and a Lord Emsworth/Blandings Castle tale. It opens with Rupert Baxter, the overly efficient secretary, completely in charge of Blandings because of Lord Emsworth's obsession with his garden. Lord Emsworth also dares not diminish Baxter's power for fear of annoying Lady Constance, the sister who dominates him. Joseph Keeble, Lady Constance's husband, is also intimidated by her, even allowing her complete control of his money. His beloved stepdaughter Phyllis has recently married the poor Mike Jackson, and he longs to help them get started. Freddie Threepwood, Lord Emsworth's flighty son, suggests that they steal Lady Constance's diamond necklace, give Phyllis the money she needs from what his wife gives Joe to buy a new necklace, and replace it with a reset version of itself.

Ronald Eustace Psmith, broke since the death of his father, has placed an advertisement claiming he will perform any task, legal or illegal, for a fee. Freddie goes to London to attempt to hire Psmith, who is not interested until he discovers that the lovely Eve Halliday is going to Blandings to catalog the library. When Lord Emsworth mistakes Psmith for the Canadian poet Ralston McTodd, whom Lady Constance has invited to Blandings, Psmith is given the means to be near Eve.

Psmith knows nothing about poetry and is not even remotely artistic but is such a charmingly convincing liar that he fools everyone—with the notable exception of the always-suspicious Baxter—at Blandings, even Miss Peavey, another poet. The already complicated plot becomes even more so because Freddie is in love with Eve, because Eve cannot return Psmith/McTodd's affection since the real McTodd is separated from one of her best friends, because Miss Peavey is also a thief after the necklace, and because Eddie Cootes, Miss Peavey's gun-toting former colleague in confidence games, shows up unexpectedly knowing that Psmith is not McTodd. A typically Wodehousian farcical scene results when Baxter, wearing only pajamas, is locked out in the middle of the night and hysterically resorts to throwing flowerpots through Lord Emsworth's bedroom window.

Psmith's prediction to Freddie midway in the novel eventually comes true: "All will doubtless come right in the future." Since Eve agrees to marry Psmith, he becomes, as a married man, disqualified from being a Wodehouse hero and never appears again except in revised versions of earlier novels.

Leave It to Psmith is a typical Blandings Castle novel full of the usual eccentric characters one finds in musical comedies, but it is even more typically a tale dominated by Psmith, whose verbal skills are seen at their best as he double-talks his way through discussions of poetry. Psmith's appeal as a fictional character is illustrated by his willingness to let events take their course. He allows Lord Emsworth to think that he is the Canadian poet even before he knows of the connection to Eve or the necklace because of "some innate defect in his character. He was essentially a young man who took life as it came, and the more inconsequently it came the better he liked it." Psmith's delight in the confusion he creates is infectious.

Summary

While the books that P. G. Wodehouse produced over his last decade do not match the earlier ones in vitality, his fiction was amazingly consistent in quality over much of his uniquely long career. Working so many variations on the same types of characters and situations is truly a remarkable achievement. Even if such an England as he presents never existed, Wodehouse convinces his readers that it should have. His is the sublimest of escapist literature.

Bibliography

Donaldson, Frances. *P. G. Wodehouse: A Biography*. New York: Alfred A. Knopf, 1982.

Edwards, Owen Dudley. *P. G. Wodehouse*. London: M. Brian & O'Keeffe, 1977.

Green, Benny. *P. G. Wodehouse: A Literary Biography*. New York: Rutledge Press, 1981.

Hall, Robert A., Jr. *The Comic Style of P. G. Wodehouse*. Hamden, Conn.: Archon Books, 1974.

Jasen, David. *P. G. Wodehouse: A Portrait of a Master*. Rev. ed. New York: Continuum, 1981.

Morris, J. H. C. *Thank You, Wodehouse*. New York: St. Martin's Press, 1981.

Murphy, Norman. *In Search of Blandings: The Facts Behind the Wodehouse Fiction*. London: Secker & Warburg, 1986.

Sproat, Iain. *Wodehouse at War*. New York: Ticknor & Fields, 1981.

Usborne, Richard. *The Penguin Wodehouse Companion*. New York: Viking Penguin, 1988.

Voorhees, Richard J. *P. G. Wodehouse*. New York: Twayne, 1966.

Michael Adams

VIRGINIA WOOLF

Born: London, England
January 25, 1882
Died: Rodmell, Sussex, England
March 28, 1941

Principal Literary Achievement

Internationally acclaimed as a major novelist of the twentieth century, Woolf made extensive advances in the conception and development of experimental forms in fiction.

Biography

Born into a family in which literary concerns and artistic pursuits were enthusiastically encouraged, Virginia Woolf was predisposed as a child for a writing career. She was born in London, England, on January 25, 1882. Her father, Sir Leslie Stephen, achieved academic fame as the editor of the *Dictionary of National Biography* between 1882 and his retirement in 1891. Her mother, Julia Duckworth, who died when Virginia was thirteen, came from a family with aristocratic connections and artistic sensibilities that sometimes inclined toward the frivolous. Virginia's parents brought to their union (March 26, 1878) children from previous marriages, besides producing four of their own, of whom Virginia was the third. Vanessa, the eldest, who was later to become an important artist, was extremely close to her younger sister; two boys, Thoby and Adrian, completed this very close family group.

Virginia Woolf matured in an intellectual and artistic milieu stimulating to the spirit. Although she envied her brothers' going away to school and resented the exclusion of women from the then-male province of education to the end of her life, she received instruction hardly to be bettered, studying mathematics, literature, history, and foreign languages (both Latin and Greek) privately with her parents or with selected tutors. By age fifteen she enjoyed free access to her father's library and directed her own reading program with a voracious appetite, discussing many works she read with her father.

Her writing career began at the age of nine when she created almost single-handedly a weekly family newspaper, which she continued to produce for more than four years, publishing in this way her own earliest stories. At fifteen she began keeping a diary. Her first professional publication was an unsigned review in *The Guardian* in 1904. *The Voyage Out,* her first novel, begun in 1907 but not completed until

1913 because of illness, was published in 1915. After that, books flowed regularly from her pen in a constant stream, interrupted only by periods of poor health or mental instability. She wrote novels, stories, literary criticism, biographies, and occasional pieces for various periodicals. More than thirty-eight hundred of her letters have been preserved and printed, and the five published volumes of her diary (1915-1941) shed much light not only upon her private life and her circle of friends but also upon the troubled years in which she lived.

Virginia and Vanessa became friends with students whom Thoby met at Cambridge—Lytton Strachey, Saxon Sydney-Turner, Leonard Woolf, and Clive Bell; they remained lifelong friends, with the latter two eventually marrying Virginia and Vanessa, respectively. Shortly after their father's death, showing an independence rare in 1905, the children gave up the large family home to establish a more modest household of their own, where there was generally much talk of intellectual matters. Virginia's marriage to Leonard Woolf proved salutary for her; he provided a firm base of emotional stability upon which she could rely and provided a free intellectual atmosphere that fostered the growth of her aesthetic ideas. Through their joint direction of the Hogarth Press, which they founded in 1917, they came into contact with men and women of letters who often became their close personal friends. Vanessa's career as an artist and her marriage to Clive Bell, who was soon to become an important art critic, brought the Woolf's into frequent friendly relations with such artists as Duncan Grant and Roger Fry. These companions, as well as the novelist E. M. Forster and the economist John Maynard Keynes, are often referred to as the Bloomsbury Group since most of them lived near each other in the Bloomsbury neighborhood of London.

Virginia Woolf was an interesting photographic subject; among the photographs of her that are often printed in biographies, there are three that reveal contrasting aspects of her character. The first, taken by Marianne Beck for *Vogue* in 1926, shows her seated at a table, her hands resting together, gazing pleasantly to the side. She is wearing a dress of her mother's, with puffed sleeves and lace cuffs. She radiates the tranquil loveliness of a young and innocent Victorian woman looking wistfully toward adulthood, but she was actually forty-four years old and had already survived the horrors of World War I and several serious mental breakdowns.

Another photo, taken about a year later by Man Ray, reflects a quite different person. Seated again at a table, wearing a simple dark jacket with a scarf, her hair austerely pulled back, she looks into the lens of the camera in an honest and friendly way, inviting sincere and open communication. One wishes to speak to her. Gisèle Freund's 1939 photograph reveals still another facet of her being. Seated before a modern painting, a book in one hand and a cigarette in the other, she gazes, troubled perhaps by thoughts of madness, death, and disaster, into a distant void beyond her. Physical and mental illnesses dogged her steps and another war seemed imminent, but in spite of internal and external threats, she directed her being toward the perfection of her art.

These three different images reveal the complexity that constitutes the totality of

Virginia Woolf as woman and as artist: the joyful, sweet loveliness masking anxiety and awful dread; the simple, candid honesty and sincerity with which she faced the world; and the distressed resignation with which she accepted the inevitable arrival of the destruction of all that mattered to her. Overwhelmed by the horrors of war and fearing the onset of yet another serious mental breakdown from which she might not recover, she took her own life on March 28, 1941, in Rodmell, Sussex, England.

Analysis

Anyone unfamiliar with the work of Woolf will doubtless be perplexed and confused by the apparent incoherence of her novels. She provides little background for the narrative situation, major characters are often difficult to distinguish from minor ones, and there is usually no important romantic interest. Instead of a story with a beginning, middle, and end consisting of events arranged in chronological order with occasional flashbacks and leading to a satisfying climax, Woolf presents instead an exploration of minds that perceive subtle variations among almost insignificant details (which themselves seem to flow at random), occasionally interrupted by essay-like commentaries. Her nine novels include *Jacob's Room* (1922), *Mrs. Dalloway* (1925), *To the Lighthouse* (1927), *The Waves* (1931), and *The Years* (1937). Many of her excellent essays are to be found in *The Common Reader: First Series* (1925), *The Common Reader: Second Series* (1932), and *The Death of the Moth and Other Essays* (1942).

Though her aesthetic roots are firmly established in the European literary tradition, her genius lies in exploring the inner world of her characters, leading her to elaborate a psychological complexity without parallel in the literature of the past. She invents new methods that permit her to explore this inner world of her characters by allowing them to express their abstract thoughts and feelings in mental monologues that externalize the hidden and secret by means of metaphors, poetic images, and symbols. Thus her novels fall into the realm of psychological studies rather than the adventure stories written by authors she referred to as "materialist writers." She deals primarily with the spiritual side of humanity, not its activities and adventures, by presenting a synthesis of an individual's total response to life and reality, for these responses, colored by the emotions of the character, are never static. The inner world of her characters is constantly shifting and changing, for them as well as for the reader, since their inner life approximates our own. Moreover, an individual is not the same from one moment to the next—his or her identity is unstable and changes as his or her perceptions change. Reality becomes a series of momentary fragments that ebb and flow; the reader must mentally arrange them into a story. A reader is not a passive spectator of events in Woolf's novels but must become actively involved emotionally in the character's thoughts, feelings, and senses.

Woolf's preoccupation with the representation of this reality made up of fleeting moments (the "incessant shower of innumerable atoms," as she put it) leads her to deal extensively with the passing of time and the changes that measure it, whether that duration is only one day or many years. Since the mind is capable of mingling past, present, and future simultaneously, a few seconds of present experience can include variable patterns of memories and fantasies. For example, a woman simply walking down the street may be thinking primarily about her destination, but thousands of other conflicting and divergent thoughts and sensations may flash through her mind in only a few seconds. This stream of thoughts, sometimes tranquil and sometimes troubled, constitutes the true subject matter of all Virginia Woolf's novels.

If thoughts tumble so helter-skelter through the mind, reflecting different atoms of reality moment by moment, then often they will be incomplete, interrupted by others before they can be finished. These fragments of thoughts and feelings are certainly related to one another—one thought or sensation has suggested or inspired another— but the connections are not particularly logical. Or rather, the logic is one of suggestion, or of association of ideas, perceptions, feelings, or emotions. Woolf enters into this process and reveals these fragmentary, interrupted thoughts while they are occurring by developing a kind of "mental speech" with which to express them. Her characters talk to themselves, explain to themselves, question themselves; this technique is generally called interior monologue or stream of consciousness. It requires some effort on the part of the reader to determine what kind of pattern makes a particular sequence logical, what sort of logic it possesses, and the direction of the flow of the stream.

If this complexity of consciousness were rendered literally, Woolf's novels would be extremely difficult to read, but her style is simple and direct, clear and lucid, making few syntactic demands on the reader, who is guided through a story that demands absolute attention and concentration. The vocabulary is simple and words are generally used with their primary meanings. Sentences tend to be rather short and concise, never overwhelming in their volume. The sentence structure is masterly and clear, seldom demanding that the reader ponder the essential meaning. There is nothing flashy or tricky about her writing; the content is highlighted by her invisible style.

To understand and appreciate a novel by Virginia Woolf fully, one should be willing to read it several times, first determining the overall design, then later connecting details and linking images into patterns that gradually become clearer and acquire deeper meanings. A reader discovers the world expressed in a novel by Woolf in a way that is similar to comprehending a great symphonic work through repeated hearings: One is always attentive to slight variations in the melodies, changes in harmony and rhythm, contrasts of key and tempo, and instrumental coloring. Like a great composer, Woolf plots the design of her fictional compositions, orchestrating them with words that form complex patterns and images and creating intricate designs. Her works, accessible to the average reader, nonetheless demand attentiveness and patience. The rewards to be gathered enrich a spirit seeking truth.

MRS. DALLOWAY

First published: 1925
Type of work: Novel

A fashionable, middle-aged woman gives an elegant party for a number of social and professional acquaintances.

Mrs. Dalloway, Virginia Woolf's fourth novel, is the first in which she attained the design she would characteristically impose upon her works of fiction. Rejecting an organization centered on conventional story lines, she focuses upon Clarissa Dalloway, a lady of London high society who is planning a party for her husband's acquaintances. The action takes place on a Wednesday in June, 1923, between 10:00 A.M. and approximately 3:00 A.M. the next day. In the morning, Clarissa goes out to buy flowers and gives final instructions to her staff. In the afternoon, she receives an unexpected visit from a former suitor named Peter Walsh, talks with her husband, who has brought her flowers, and then takes a nap. In the evening, she entertains her guests as a perfect hostess should. The activities and thoughts of Clarissa during the day provide the core of unity in the book. Other characters and their situations appear when they touch or reflect, ever so slightly or symbolically, Clarissa's life and its meaning. The reader observes the behavior of her husband Richard at lunch, watches her teenage daughter Elizabeth with her history tutor Miss Kilman (whom Mrs. Dalloway hates), and accompanies Clarissa on a bus ride through London. The reader catches glimpses of unknown strangers who cross Clarissa's path during the day, among whom figures Septimus Warren Smith, a shell-shocked war veteran who is suffering an episode of insanity.

Clarissa Dalloway represents a rational attitude toward life: She functions well on a day-to-day basis, tends to that which requires attention, and meets the demands made upon her in her situation. She regrets somewhat her marriage to Richard (Peter Walsh seemed to suggest a less predictable and more exciting life) and now realizes that she has lost the sense of individuality she possessed as a young woman, for her identity has been absorbed by her husband's. Clarissa is also distressed because Elizabeth seems to be too strongly influenced by Miss Kilman, an unattractive but educated woman who has recently converted to religion and seeks a recruit in Elizabeth. The book contains a scathing denunciation of those who, intolerant of diversity, seek to destroy the intellectual liberty of others. Though saddened by life, Clarissa seeks to maintain an inner core of joyfulness while fulfilling her various obligations. An unhappy person deep within, Clarissa is nonetheless filled with a great love for life, a zest for living, and a capacity for temporary but intense joy in her daily experiences.

Beginning work on *Mrs. Dalloway,* Woolf noted in her diary (October 14, 1922) that she wanted to show the world as seen by the sane and the insane side by side. If

Clarissa reflects the sanity of adjustments to reality, Septimus Smith reflects the re-jection of rational compromise with life. Though he married a gentle Italian woman (Lucrezia, or Rezia) immediately after the war, their relationship has done little to rescue him from the abyss of terror that madness creates within him. At noon he consults Sir William Bradshaw, a noted medical authority who believes that mental illness is caused by a lack of a "sense of proportion" that can be restored by solitude, rest, and silence. The fate of Septimus now seems sealed: Diagnosed immediately as an advanced case of total breakdown, he is to be committed to an institution later that same day. Septimus, however, prefers death to life on someone else's terms and kills himself by jumping from a window. Learning during the party of this stranger's death, Clarissa withdraws to meditate alone. Feeling a kinship with the dead man, she acknowledges that she herself lives close to death, often feeling the terror, an awful fear of being, and draws courage to continue from the simple presence of her husband. She is recalled from reverie by her social obligations and, putting aside these painful thoughts, returns to her guests.

The conviction that a happy life cannot be lived on another's terms is an important theme of the book. Clarissa lost an important part of herself by marrying Richard and allowing his life to control hers. Peter came to nothing through his failure to choose for himself, longing instead for domination by Clarissa. Mrs. Bradshaw gave her will over in submission to her husband, as did the majority of the doctor's pa-tients who acquiesced to his judgments concerning "proper proportions" in life. Cla-rissa fears that her daughter will dedicate her will to God through religious conver-sion promoted by Miss Kilman, who has already abandoned her own will to a force outside herself that she imagines to be superior.

TO THE LIGHTHOUSE

First published: 1927
Type of work: Novel

A vacationing family cancels its projected excursion to a nearby lighthouse because of bad weather. Ten years later, some family members finally visit it together.

Most critics regard *To the Lighthouse* as Virginia Woolf's finest achievement, and she herself shared this view. Woolf perfected her method in this book, developing a highly individual technique in which structure, form, content, and meaning are ex-tremely complex as they are used to develop individual characters, their relationships to one another, to life itself, and to the most profound problems of human existence, love, art, and death. Her method consists in elaborating a multiple point of view presenting both past and present through her characters' eyes as well as through those of an omniscient writer. She thus reveals to the reader in manifold perspective the extraordinary range of emotional and mental processes that make up human experience for her characters.

The structure of the novel resembles that of a two-act play with an interlude between the acts. In the first and by far the longest part, "The Window," Mr. and Mrs. Ramsay (unmistakably based on her own parents) with their eight children are vacationing at their summer home on an island off the coast of Scotland; some friends are spending a weekend with them. Their six-year-old son James wants to visit the nearby lighthouse the next day; his mother agrees, but his father is certain that the weather will not be fine. The guests intermingle; the artist Lily Briscoe works on a painting. In the evening they all enjoy a meal of *bœuf en daube* and experience a sense of unity and happiness in the perfection of this moment that, like an artist, Mrs. Ramsay has created by controlling the elements that united to produce it. Most of these events are narrated through interior monologues with numerous flashbacks and shifting points of view.

In a second, very brief part, "Time Passes," the events of the next decade are poetically related by the omniscient writer or by the house itself. The house has stood unused for many years and has deteriorated outside and inside; weeds proliferate, and ghostly airs inhabit the empty shell. The reader discovers the destinies of the house and its former residents. Mrs. Ramsay soon died, her oldest son Andrew was killed in the war, her daughter Prue expired during childbirth, a would-be poet became famous. After ten years, two cleaning ladies arrive to restore and prepare the place to receive guests once again. This section of the book constitutes a beautiful prose poem on the devastation time brings to human matters and must be ranked high among the finest pages Virginia Woolf ever wrote.

In the third part, "The Lighthouse," Mr. Ramsay returns with his two youngest children, James (age sixteen) and Cam (age fifteen), to make—after ten years and the intrusions of time, change, and death—the promised excursion to the lighthouse. They are joined by several others, including Lily Briscoe, who hopes to complete the painting begun years earlier. The hostility of the children to their father, obvious all along, is transformed into compassion when, upon reaching the lighthouse, Mr. Ramsay praises his son for steering the boat skillfully. The young people, alienated from their father since childhood because of his dominating and repressive ways, suddenly see him as a suffering human being, lost without his wife, seeking love and understanding in his awkward and insensitive way. Meanwhile, Lily Briscoe, back on shore, has discovered the stroke necessary to complete her painting perfectly. She says, laying down her brush in extreme fatigue, "I have had my vision." It is an ordered vision of successful artistic creation, which Virginia Woolf has also fulfilled in this book.

Interpretations of this novel are as numerous as its commentators. Some admire the representation of ideal Victorian family life just before its demise, while others criticize a male-dominated marriage. Mrs. Ramsay may be an all-embracing principle of universal love in her role as wife and mother. The lighthouse can represent masculine power and supremacy, or the conjunction of the lighthouse with the sea (a female symbol) may symbolize ideal marriage, a mutual cooperation between inseparable partners. Mrs. Ramsay had found the light it projects to be a source of serenity and strength. The child James saw it colored by secret joy, but the maturing James sees it merely as a stark tower on a bare rock. Whatever meaning readers may find, the lighthouse stands as a permanent source of order and light, cutting through the darkness.

THE WAVES

First published: 1931
Type of work: Novel

Six lifelong friends (three men and three women) speak in soliloquies of their childhood, education, and adult experiences of life as they mature and age together.

After the relaxation of a satiric romp through English literary history in the novel *Orlando: A Biography* (1928), Woolf began the composition of the most intricate and complex of all her fictional constructions, *The Waves*. It could be called an "abstract novel" for, like many modern paintings, it is virtually nonrepresentational. Its mirror does not reflect easily recognizable objects or provide familiar images. Dispensing with conventional story line and fully drawn characters, the novel distills human reality and experience. Its six characters are essences without form. The reader has no idea what they look like, how they dress or move or smile. All that is known are their consciousnesses as they contemplate their passage through various stages of life from youth to old age, experiencing various changes as they grow older.

The six characters, who are about the same age and are given no surnames, have grown up together and have continued to keep track of one another as their lives took them in very different directions. Jinny and Susan balance each other as opposites, for Jinny is an urban woman, proud of her body, sensual and passionate with men, while Susan is from the country, where she eventually returns to marry a farmer and rear a family. Neville and Louis also balance as opposites, for Neville is intellectual, homosexual, and assured in the academic world, while Louis, ashamed of his Australian origin, counteracts feelings of inferiority by forcing his way to success in the business world. Rhoda is always a misfit; feeling ugly and alone, she never belongs anywhere and alienation finally drives her to commit suicide. The others continue to exhibit the basic personality traits they acquired as young children and never change internally in any significant way. The child of six remains intact in the adult of sixty. Only Bernard, who loves words and longs to be a writer, shows signs of spiritual growth near the end of the book, but this suggestion of change (he eventually abandons his notebook) seems open to question.

The novel is divided into nine unnumbered and untitled sections composed of fragmented interior monologues that cut back and forth between different speakers.

The six rarely meet or engage in conversation. Instead, their isolated voices speak ("said" is the only verb of speech or thought used in the entire book) into an empty void to no imagined companion or listener in the universe. The language (vocabulary, syntax, sentence length) does not particularize any individual. They all speak with the same voice as if they were one person—as indeed they may be, for they can be understood as six facets of the same personality.

The nine sections of the book reveal the six as children in nursing school, secondary school, and college (the men) or entering social life (the women). They join together for dinner to send their friend Percival, whom they all admire and love, off to India. They later mourn his accidental death as they continue to pursue their separate lives. As each acknowledges the approach of age, they meet once again for dinner to reaffirm their sense of unity. Bernard summarizes the essence of their lives in a long, final speech, attempting to discover what it has all meant, but he sees only inscrutable shadows in a room flooded with light. Truth and meaning seem ultimately to be unknowable.

Each section of the narrative is introduced by an italicized passage tracing the movement of the sun across the sky from dawn to dark, the first describing the sunrise, the last the sunset. The course of the sun's journey parallels the maturation of the six characters. Woolf draws attention to the passage of time with descriptions of the changing patterns of light on the surface of the sea as the waves break on the shore, as well as to the effects of light and shadow on the sand and grass, the behavior of the birds, and the appearance of flowers. In creating verbal landscapes not unlike those of the great Impressionist and Postimpressionist painters, Woolf achieves an extraordinarily high level of "word painting." The language used for the images involving light and water is more intense than that used in the soliloquies, more condensed, compact, and complex. This language of nature seems somehow alien to humankind, however—lofty and remote, inhuman and insensitive to pain, coldly indifferent to human fate.

A ROOM OF ONE'S OWN

First published: 1929
Type of work: Essay

The right to earn an adequate living and to enjoy personal privacy is considered essential to the development of the independence of women.

Woolf's concern about the difficulties women face in a male-dominated world is expressed with force and vigor in her extended essay *A Room of One's Own*. Elaborating on her talks on "Women in Fiction," which she had given at two British women's colleges in 1928, she seeks to present certain facts about the treatment of women through the centuries and to show how patterns established long ago still prevail in modern times. Children, housework, and family obligations have deprived women of privacy and prevented them from earning a living, while social attitudes have approved their continued dependence on men for material necessities and their acceptance of roles as household servants. Though freedom and equality for women have increased considerably since 1929 in both England and America, the ideas Woolf promotes here, fundamental to modern feminist thinking, were radical—even shocking to some—at the time the book was written.

Retaining the tone and style of a casual lecturer, Woolf intends neither to preach nor to scold but to discuss some of her observations, exploring their implications at length. Her position can be stated quite briefly: In order to achieve an adequate sense of personal identity and the fulfillment of her intellectual potential with dignity and joy, a woman must command sufficient financial resources (money) to support herself and adequate privacy (a room with a lock on the door) to permit and promote mental activity. These two keys to spiritual freedom—material security and personal privacy—have been regularly denied to women through the ages. In the first chapter of the essay, Woolf imagines the rude treatment a woman receives if she (in contrast to a man) dares to walk on the grass or use the library of a men's college. She contrasts a luncheon served to college men (five elaborate dishes, with elegant dessert and wine) with a dinner in the women's dining hall (simple fare with prunes and custard, water liberally replacing wine). These examples forcefully illustrate how women are regarded as inferior and how they are expected to welcome their lot without protest.

After a bold and humorous elaboration of the implications of this twofold statement, Woolf goes on in the following five chapters to examine the position of women historically and to focus attention upon several writers who struggled, without total success, against their oppressed condition. Though she surveys only authors, her observations relate also to those women seeking any sort of professional career, for the obstacles blocking advancement in one field also obstruct the way in others. To illustrate her point historically, Woolf invents Judith Shakespeare, younger sister to William, a woman as brilliant and talented as her brother, and speculates about her destiny. The little fiction ends, after episodes of humiliation and failure brought upon Judith by male attitudes and responses, with the young woman's suicide.

Woolf finds the eighteenth century somewhat kinder to women like Jane Austen, willing to stay in her traditional place, writing casually as a pastime. Nineteenth century writers like the Brontë sisters suffered from a lack of exposure to the world, writing within the confines of a limited perspective on life. Charlotte Brontë, frustrated and angered by restrictions, sometimes turned away from her artistic purpose to vent her bitterness. Woolf believes that artistic creativity cannot be attained when thought is deformed and twisted by anger and frustration; she invokes William Shakespeare as one who, entirely purged of resentments, achieved a state of mental brilliance she calls "incandescence." Artists must rise above anger to create works unflawed by personal hostilities. Women, she believes, are learning to do this, but many decades will pass before bitterness is replaced by comprehension.

Summary

Respecting the literary tradition that she inherited, Virginia Woolf nevertheless felt compelled to forsake its influence by inventing fictional techniques to explore even more deeply the minds and hearts of people. Like many modern painters and musicians who were her contemporaries, she sought new ways to render the realities of thought and feeling in her novels. By holding up her mirror of fiction at a different angle, she attempted to help readers see themselves in a more revealing light. Readers, troubled by the reflected images, feel moved to contemplate the meaning of their lives.

Bibliography

Bell, Quentin. *Virginia Woolf.* New York: Harcourt Brace Jovanovich, 1972.

Fleishman, Avrom. *Virginia Woolf: A Critical Reading.* Baltimore: The Johns Hopkins University Press, 1975.

Gorsky, Susan Rubinow. *Virginia Woolf.* Boston: Twayne, 1978.

Leaska, Mitchell A. *Virginia Woolf's Lighthouse: A Study in Critical Method.* New York: Columbia University Press, 1970.

Lehmann, John. *Virginia Woolf and Her World.* New York: Harcourt Brace Jovanovich, 1975.

Marder, Herbert. *Feminism and Art: A Study of Virginia Woolf.* Chicago: University of Chicago Press, 1968.

Richter, Harvena. *Virginia Woolf: The Inward Voyage.* Princeton, N.J.: Princeton University Press, 1970.

Rosenblatt, Aaron. *Virginia Woolf for Beginners.* New York: Writers and Readers Publishing, 1987.

Rosenthal, Michael. *Virginia Woolf.* New York: Columbia University Press, 1979.

Raymond M. Archer

WILLIAM WORDSWORTH

Born: Cockermouth, England
April 7, 1770
Died: Rydal Mount, England
April 23, 1850

Principal Literary Achievement
Wordsworth was a revolutionary poet celebrating nature in experimental verse forms. With his theory of lyrical ballads and his social/psychological themes of humble life, he was a founder of the Romantic literary tradition.

Biography
William Wordsworth was born at Cockermouth, in Cumberland, England, on April 7, 1770, the son of John and Ann Wordsworth. He had an elder brother, Richard, a younger sister, Dorothy, and two younger brothers, John and Christopher. His mother died when William was eight, and he and his brothers were separated from their sister to be reared by grandparents. William's father died when William was thirteen. William first began writing poetry soon after.

When he was seventeen, Wordsworth entered Cambridge and was graduated in 1791. While at the university, he went with a friend on a walking tour of France during the beginnings of its revolution. After leaving the university, he returned to France, where he found himself in the midst of bloody violence in 1792. He met and planned to marry Annette Vallon, but he was forced to return to England and could not marry her, although the relationship produced a daughter.

Uncertain of his future, distraught over events in France, and heartsick about his separation from Annette, he went on a walking tour of Wales in 1793 and then joyfully reunited with his sister, Dorothy, and made plans to settle with her until he could marry Annette. Meanwhile, he met the poet Samuel Taylor Coleridge in 1797 in Dorset. By now, Wordsworth believed that his destiny was to become a poet, and he was encouraged by Dorothy and Coleridge. To finance a trip to Germany, Wordsworth and Coleridge wrote their famous collection of poems, *Lyrical Ballads*, in 1798. One of the poems, "Lines Composed a Few Miles Above Tintern Abbey," was composed after a walking trip that Wordsworth took with Dorothy to visit the ruins of a famous abbey on the Welsh border.

In 1798-1799, the two poets and Dorothy went to Germany, but Wordsworth and his sister returned shortly afterward to England, leaving Coleridge behind. Wordsworth

WILLIAM WORDSWORTH

wrote more poems, which would be included in the second edition of *Lyrical Ballads* in 1800, and he composed his prose essay on his theory of poetry as a preface for the collection. He also began to write long sections in blank verse of his autobiographical poem, to be called *The Prelude: Or, The Growth of a Poet's Mind* (1850), which he had probably begun in Germany. When Coleridge returned to England, he often visited William and Dorothy and soon moved to live near them in the Lake District of north England, where Wordsworth was born.

By this time, Wordsworth and Annette were no longer interested in marrying, and so he married Mary Hutchinson in 1802. The famous "Ode: Intimations of Immortality from Recollections of Early Childhood" has its origins partly in Wordsworth's feelings immediately before he got married; the poem is also a reaction to Coleridge's "Dejection: An Ode," lamenting Coleridge's loss of imagination. Wordsworth, however, was increasing his own powers as a poet, and he began to compose many great sonnets at this time, especially some in response to the wars with Napoleon I in Europe. He was also working hard at his long autobiographical poem, completing the first version in 1805.

By then, he had suffered another painful loss in his family because his favorite brother, John, had died in a shipwreck at sea. His beloved daughter, Dora, was born in 1804, however, and he gave increasing attention to his growing family. His relationship with Coleridge began to weaken after Coleridge left to take a diplomatic post in Malta in 1804. One of Wordsworth's most important collections of poetry was published in 1807 as *Poems in Two Volumes*. It contains, among other great poems, the "Ode to Duty," the "Elegiac Stanzas Suggested by a Picture of Peele Castle," and "Ode: Intimations of Immortality from Recollections of Early Childhood."

Some believe that Wordsworth's poetry began to decline in quality from about this time, but he continued to write much. Some of this work was very important, such as his revisions and additions to the autobiographical poem, which he did not want to publish yet. Wordsworth believed that he had to complete the poem on his life as a preface for a grand philosophical poem to be called "The Recluse" (published in 1888 as *The Recluse*). This ambitious project was never completed, but one of its parts, *The Excursion*, was published in 1814. It is, like *The Prelude*, a long poem in blank verse, but it is organized in nine books around the dramatic monologues of several characters, including the main ones of a Peddler, a Poet, a Solitary, and a Pastor. While this poem is not, at present, highly praised, it was very much noticed by readers of the time, including John Keats, who thought that it was one of the greatest things ever written in modern poetry.

As Wordsworth's family grew, and as he helped to care for Coleridge's family and other friends, he needed more financial resources than his poetry sales could provide. He was appointed by the government to be a collector of taxes from postage rates, a position that caused some critics, such as young Percy Bysshe Shelley, to attack him as a traitor to libertarian causes. His poetry began to show some of his increasingly conservative themes, such as in the *Ecclesiastical Sketches* published in 1822 to describe the history of the Christian church in England. It was not as religious a poem as the subject and title suggest, and Wordsworth did not entirely abandon his poetry of celebrating nature. His *The River Duddon* in 1820 expresses his mature reflections on childhood scenes of nature, and in many of the poems that he composed during tours of Europe, from 1820 to 1837, he occasionally recovers his enthusiasm for pagan-like feelings of nature.

When his friend and neighbor, the poet Robert Southey, died in 1843, Wordsworth succeeded him and became the poet laureate of Great Britain. He had not published *The Prelude*, but he had made many changes and additions to it since starting it years before. In fact, he had produced at least three versions of that great poem. It was never published during his lifetime. He died on April 23, 1850, in Rydal Mount, England, leaving the manuscript of the poem as a part of his estate for his family. It was published in July, 1850, a posthumous memorial to Wordsworth's lifetime of achievements as one of the greatest of English poets.

Analysis

The styles of Wordsworth's poetry are many, although his most famous experiment in style was to compose "lyrical ballads" in simple language and simple meter to express the universal experience of common people in rural settings. These poems treat common incidents as if they are extraordinary; in other words, the lyrical quality of feeling gives importance to the traditional ballad tale. Sometimes these lyrical ballads are spoken by the poet, as in "Lines Written in Early Spring." At other times, they are spoken by characters of Wordsworth's imagination, as in "The Thorn." Although the emotions of these people are common and universal, the incidents of their experiences are unusual and abnormal or undesirable. Thus, the poems are often treatments of outcasts from society, as in "The Female Vagrant," or psychologically abnormal people, as in "The Idiot Boy."

The first edition of the *Lyrical Ballads* contains poems of family affection and warm cordiality, as in "We Are Seven" and "The Last of the Flock." It also contains humorous poems, including "Expostulation and Reply" and its companion, "The Tables Turned." These poems consistently develop a special theme of Wordsworth's enduring interest, that a special bonding occurs in the close relationship of a child reared close to nature. While the bond must be broken when the child has matured, it should neither be prematurely broken nor denied or repressed by too much emphasis on reason and social formulas. The therapy of recalling childhood's passions in association with familiar landscapes is developed in "Lines Composed a Few Miles Above Tintern Abbey," which is included in the *Lyrical Ballads* of 1798. This poem should be recalled as an exception to the rule of those poems, since it is a blank-verse monologue, not a rhyming, narrative "lyrical ballad."

The same notice should be given to the inclusion of the blank-verse narrative of "Michael: A Pastoral Poem" in the second edition of *Lyrical Ballads*. This poem exemplifies a favorite stylistic approach that Wordsworth held throughout his life: to tell a story of rural people, sometimes shepherds, in strong, unrhymed iambic pentameter. It is the style of "Nutting," "The Brothers," and, later, many of the parts of

The Excursion, the only section of *The Recluse* that Wordsworth finished to his satisfaction. The second edition of *Lyrical Ballads* also contains some poems that are truly lyrical ballads but differ from the tone and subjects of those in the first edition: These are the poems known as the "Lucy" poems, and a group that could be called the "Matthew" poems. The striking feature common to these two groups is a deepening interest in the experience of death, of grieving the deaths of loved ones who can never be replaced in one's affections.

A similar feature appears to mark many of Wordsworth's new poems included in his two volumes published in 1807. The great "Ode: Intimations of Immortality from Recollections of Early Childhood" is a major achievement of style in the treatment of a profoundly important theme, whether it is seen as one of growing old, maturity of vision, psychological development, or philosophical transition. Wordsworth made a permanently admirable use of the irregular ode, and he continued to have interest in the ode form, though without such success. He also sustained an interest in the sonnet, mainly in the English or Miltonic version; throughout his career, Wordsworth wrote sonnets and sometimes put them into sequences, as in *The River Duddon*. While his later poems fail to acquire the force of his earlier ones, Wordsworth's continuing style is to balance simplicity of natural themes with the discipline of sophisticated art.

TINTERN ABBEY

First published: 1798
Type of work: Poem

A speaker revisits a scene first observed five years earlier; differences arise from changes in the speaker's own mind more than from the landscape.

"Tintern Abbey" is a shortened version of the poem's full title, "Lines Composed a Few Miles Above Tintern Abbey, on Revisiting the Banks of the Wye During a Tour, July 13, 1798." This full title more accurately locates the situation of the poem and anchors the experience of the poem in a particular place and time. In 160 lines of blank verse, the poet describes what he hears and sees again five years after he last visited this scene along the Wye River in Wales, near the ruins of an ancient abbey.

The poet first notices cliffs, trees, hedges, and farmhouses. Then, he imagines that someone might be camping amid the woods. What he cannot see becomes important, and he lets his imagination go. Then, he recalls how he has recently left a city, where he lived during some of the time since visiting the Wye River. He believes that his spirit was sustained by his memories of this natural scenery through a time of difficulty while in the city. The feelings attached to remembered scenes of nature became sources of imaginative power when detached from actual observation of those scenes.

The poet recalls his attention to the immediate scene before him again, and he compares his present feelings with those that he had had when first visiting this spot. At that time, he was young and thoughtless, unaware of his differences from other animal life; now, however, he feels more burdened by the responsibilities of being human, of having a heart that sympathizes with the sufferings of other human beings. The feelings of youth have been revived by this revisit, and those feelings have energized his moral imagination to universal proportions.

Suddenly, the poet addresses his sister. She seems to be standing beside him, observing this same scene with him. This visit, however, is her first, and he imagines the future, when her memories of this scene will work for her as his do for him at this time. He utters a prayer that nature will supply his sister with the same restorative power of feeling in the future. In this way, each will be a "worshipper of Nature."

PREFACE TO LYRICAL BALLADS (1800)

First published: 1800
Type of work: Essay

Lyrical Ballads experimented in expressing common emotions through the simple language of "humble and rustic" people to please readers of popular ballads.

The preface to *Lyrical Ballads* was written to explain the theory of poetry guiding Wordsworth's composition of the poems. Wordsworth defends the unusual style and subjects of the poems (some of which are actually composed by Samuel Taylor Coleridge) as experiments to see how far popular poetry could be used to convey profound feeling.

There are three general reasons guiding the composition of the lyrical ballads. The first is in the choice of subject matter, which is limited to experiences of common life in the country. There, people use a simple language and directly express deep feeling. Their habit of speaking comes from associating feelings with the permanent forms of nature, such as mountains, rivers, and clouds. The challenge for the poet is to make these ordinary experiences interesting to readers; in other words, the poems attempt to take ordinary subjects and treat them in extraordinary ways. Doing so would cause readers to recognize fundamental truths of universal human experience.

The second reason guiding his poems is Wordsworth's goal of emphasizing the purpose of poetry as art. This purpose is not a moralistic one; indeed, poetry comes from a "spontaneous overflow of powerful feelings," but it is disciplined by remembering those feelings in moods of peaceful meditation. The combination of feeling and meditation produces artful poetry with purpose. Specifically, the lyrical ballads have the purposes of enlightening readers' understanding of basic human feeling, enhancing readers' emotions, and helping readers to enjoy the common things of life. That is important, Wordsworth believes, because too many people seem to have a difficult time enjoying life. They need to search for the unusual, the strange, and the fantastic; they are missing the beauty of the world around them. People need to have more faith in their own imagination to provide the beauty and emotion that they are overlooking in the environment.

Moreover, Wordsworth believes that the style of the poems is important to capture and keep readers' attention, or the other two reasons will fail. Wordsworth thought tricks of personification and artistic diction had dulled people's feelings, and so he wanted to refresh poetry by eliminating ornamentation to return to basics. The strengths of good prose should also be the strengths of good poetry, he writes, and so poetry should be written as the language of a person who speaks directly to other people with the same basic feelings and experiences of all human beings. To this, meter can be added in order to control emotional excitement, as reflection can restrain spontaneous emotion.

Readers are urged to be thoughtful in judging the poems. They should judge with genuine feelings that have been educated by thought and long habits of reading from many good pieces of literature. Wordsworth ends by expressing his faith that such readers will recognize the success of his experiments in the poems that he calls lyrical ballads: poems that express a domination of feeling (lyrical) over form (ballads).

ODE: INTIMATIONS OF IMMORTALITY

First published: 1807
Type of work: Poem

Something is missing from adulthood that once was present in childhood's vision of life and nature, but there are compensations of wisdom and moral sensitivity.

"Ode: Intimations of Immortality from Recollections of Early Childhood" is a personal poem in a traditionally impersonal, formal verse form of eleven stanzas that vary in length and metrical design. Wordsworth uses the ancient Greek Pindaric ode, which had celebrated the virtues of athletic heroes, to examine the strangely compelling process of growing up from childhood to adult maturity. The hero is a child, but the victory is won by the adult who reflects upon childhood's losses.

The epigraph of the poem states the paradox that childhood experiences provide the background and source of the adult's identity, as if a child could be the parent of the adult who develops from childhood. The poet, recognizing that this is so, wishes therefore to be naturally faithful to his past, to build his maturity upon a continuous line of connections with his youth.

The first four stanzas express the poet's strange experience of feeling wonderful on a lovely spring morning in May, when all nature celebrates a rebirth of vegetable and animal life. The poet sees and hears the signs of this rebirth, and he can even feel a stirring of sympathetic identification with the vitality all around him. Yet he also feels a disturbing emotion that shadows the bright landscape. He feels that there is something missing in his own being, that the natural scene does not have the same glorious promise that it had when he looked at it as a child. The rest of the poem is an attempt to identify what is missing and to recover it if possible.

Stanzas 5 through 8 recall childhood as if it were like the dawn of a new day, when the sun peers upon the earth through glowing clouds. The meaning behind the comparison is that a child comes from darkness and awakens to life with a vision still colored by its origins in eternity. Like the sun, a child moves from an exciting, hopeful dawn of life, rises toward the common light of midday's adulthood, and casts shadows that, like a prison, seem to surround a person and block the vision of glorious origins. Human life is also compared to a foster child who is under the care of Mother Nature until it is time for the child to leave home and be independent of the fostering environment. Real parents teach their children games of role playing, which prepare them for adult responsibilities, but those same games (which later concern marrying, working, and dying) drive children farther away from their infant experience of immortality and omnipotence. Finally, the process of growing up is compared to putting layer after layer of ice over a glowing, energetic fire.

The last section of the poem, stanzas 9 through 11, turns from the desolation that ends stanza 8, where the poet sinks beneath the frigid thought of a buried vitality. Suddenly, he realizes that there is something still burning beneath the ice of experience and mortality; he feels an ember of energy remaining from childhood's vitality. Ironically, the feeling of something missing from his joy at the opening of the poem has become a feeling of something present beneath his dejection in the middle of the poem. The question that he poses for himself is to wonder what this is that still lives deep inside him, what this is that refuses to die. There is the reason for the title of the poem: a hint of immortality remaining in the adult from his memory of childhood's experiences.

Stanza 9 recalls the things of childhood that cannot be the source of this feeling of immortality. It is not the animal delight or the irresponsibility of childhood; it is not the unreflecting optimism, either. Instead, it is something more alien to ordinary adult experience: The reason to celebrate what remains from childhood is that childhood was a time when the mind refused to accept natural limitations, when the human creature did not yet feel that it was only a natural being. Babies and children have enormous egos, not yet shaped by an environment that makes them retreat from questioning all sensation and asserting subjective idealism as more real than objective nature. Such a defiant subjectivity and faith in oneself is more real than the world into which the child is born. That buried feeling is what rescues the adult from the dejection of maturity into a posture of power over nature. Maturity is a position from which the adult can look back and recover childhood faith, like a traveller who can look back from an inland mountain to see children playing by the sea and recall that as the place from where he also came.

Thus, the poet celebrates in the last two stanzas his recovery of imaginative power, because he pays tribute to the ember of childhood idealism still glowing beneath his mortality. The loveliness of natural life is paradoxically more lovely now, because the poet's experience of mortality has taught him the lesson of loss, and that makes nature more precious to the mind of a person who knows that spiritual immortality will survive the natural beauty that fosters human growth.

THE PRELUDE

First published: 1850
Type of work: Poem

The hero of a modern epic explores his memory of events, propelling him to undertake the great mission that nature has assigned to him.

The Prelude is a long, blank-verse poem with a complicated history. It was begun as early as 1798-1799. Then it may have been conceived as a short autobiographical poem, before it was expanded to thirteen books by 1805. The poem was never published while Wordsworth lived, but when it was, soon after his death in 1850, *The Prelude* had been revised extensively and expanded to fourteen books. There are significant differences among the three versions of the poem. For convenience, the poem published in 1850 may be assumed for discussion.

The subject of the poem is a review by the poet of his life to explain the growth of his mind as a poet; it examines his past for evidence to account for the growth of his imagination and to justify his calling as a poet. Because Samuel Taylor Coleridge strongly urged Wordsworth to believe in himself as a poet and to use his talent to compose a modern epic poem, Coleridge is given credit for causing Wordsworth to write *The Prelude*. What Coleridge wanted from Wordsworth was not a poem about his own life, however, but rather a poem about the modern state of philosophy and science, as in the *Aeneid* (c. 29-19 B.C.), *La divina commedia* (c. 1320; *The Divine Comedy*), and *Paradise Lost* (1667, 1674). Wordsworth planned to write such an epic, but he could not make progress on it until after he wrote a poem in which he justified his decision to be a poet of any kind. This self-justification would be a prefatory explanation, appearing as the "prelude" for the main movement that would be called "The Recluse."

The prefatory poem, however, became so important that it became the main poem itself, and Wordsworth worked at it for most of his long life. *The Prelude* is more important, and nearer to completion, than *The Recluse* (1888), for which it was intended as an introduction. There are many epic features, nevertheless, in the style and structure of *The Prelude* itself. Epic similes appear in various places, allusions to epic stories recur, and the structure of the poem is loosely modeled upon the classical epic design that begins *in medias res* (in the middle of things).

The first book of *The Prelude* opens with a celebration of freedom, as the poet decides to visit his childhood and leave behind a city and a life of frustration and uncertainty. He composes aloud some verses of happiness as he strides confidently into the countryside, but suddenly he is unable to compose and begins to doubt his ability to continue. He believes that he is intended by nature to be a poet, but he is beginning to doubt himself and his judgment because he is experiencing "writer's block."

In this state of mind, he begins to review his life to see if he has correctly interpreted his vocation. The poem is a search of the poet's past for evidence that the man is intended by nature to be a poet at all. The remainder of the first book is a short summary of the poet's earliest years of boyhood, when he grew up in the Lake District of northern England. In four seasonal episodes, Wordsworth's poem recalls experiences of seedlike origins for his growth of imagination.

The first is an autumn scene of taking woodcocks from other people's traps and then feeling that the hills pursued him to punish him. The second is a springtime experience of robbing birds' nests and then feeling that the wind accused him of being a violator. The third episode is a summer one of borrowing a boat without permission, rowing out onto a lake alone, and then feeling that the mountains rose in condemnation. The final scene is one of winter ice skating at night on frozen lakes; he had stayed out later than he ought, and in a guilty state of mind he would skate alone, feeling nature alive with motion.

Such memories are exercises that raise the poet's imaginative energies to feel regeneration and renewed confidence in himself. Book 2 contains memories of his mother's death and his way of dealing with the threat of alienation it caused in his life; he substituted nature for his lost mother, and he nourished his imagination with lonely wanderings through the hills and among the lakes. That continued until he was old enough to be sent to the university in Cambridge, far from home and as threatening as had been the death of his mother.

Book 3 describes how Cambridge was a vast confusion at first, with its swirl of events and temptations. Gradually, it also nourished Wordsworth's active imagination, both with learning and with urban scenery. Book 4 describes the joyful summer vacations when he revisited youthful scenes and revived his depressed spirits. He renewed social contacts and danced until dawn, when nature summoned him home with morning glory of bright sunrise. The next two books describe how the young undergraduate left England for a walking tour of France and the Alps, where he realized again that his imagination is more important than the natural scenery that nourishes it. Book 7 is a return to England, where the poet finished his education at Cambridge and moved to London.

The books on Wordsworth's residence in France describe his introduction to the French patriot Michel Beaupuy in book 9 and the influence that Beaupuy had on the poet's increasing sympathy for the revolutionaries. Book 10, however, narrates the intensifying pressure on Wordsworth to leave France for safety back in London, where the poet despaired at prospects for a peaceful recovery of freedom in France. Book 11 analyzes the spiritual depression that Wordsworth experienced over his loss of faith that the French Revolution could be conducted in a civilized way, combined with his disgust that Britain should have united to oppose Frenchmen fighting for freedom.

By the end of book 12, Wordsworth is back where the poem began, when he decided to leave London and return to his home in the Lake District. There, he revisited scenes of his childhood and youth, recovered his emotional energies, and realized that his imagination needed to be revived by recovering forgotten experiences. These are the "spots of time" that Wordsworth uses to illustrate his recovery of imaginative power. Book 12 ends with descriptions of two of these spots of time.

The final books are celebrations of restored imagination. Book 13 praises the gifts of nature and childhood for emotion and calm. Book 14 is dominated by a long description of the poet's ascent of Mount Snowdon. On that occasion, the poet realized that his imagination is like the moonlight penetrating the mist that surrounded the mountain top. The last book then ends with expressions of gratitude to Wordsworth's sister, Dorothy, and to Coleridge's friendship. They have inspired the poem by supporting the poet's faith in himself.

Summary

From ballad experiments to innovations of epic, William Wordsworth maintained a total commitment to poetry. He turned his personal experience into public statement, and he modified public genres of writing with personal testimony. He departed from classic ideals of regularity and abstract diction, and he established the Romantic taste for the irregular experience rendered in concrete language.

Life in the solitude of the Lake District provided him with subjects of rustic living, but his education in sophisticated cities added richness of self-reflection and self-discipline. His writing drew from all dimensions of his experience.

Bibliography

Ferry, David. *Limits of Mortality: An Essay on Wordsworth's Major Poems.* Middletown, Conn.: Wesleyan University Press, 1959.

Hartman, Geoffrey H. *Wordsworth's Poetry, 1787-1814.* New Haven, Conn.: Yale University Press, 1964 and 1971.

Heffernan, James A. W. *Wordsworth's Theory of Poetry: The Transforming Imagination.* Ithaca, N.Y.: Cornell University Press, 1969.

Johnston, Kenneth R. *Wordsworth and "The Recluse."* New Haven, Conn.: Yale University Press, 1984.

Lindenberger, Herbert. *On Wordsworth's "Prelude."* Princeton, N.J.: Princeton University Press, 1963.

Moorman, Mary. *William Wordsworth: A Biography.* 2 vols. Oxford, England: Clarendon Press, 1965.

Onorato, Richard J. *The Character of The Poet: Wordsworth in "The Prelude."* Princeton, N.J.: Princeton University Press, 1971.

Perkins, David. *Wordsworth and the Poetry of Sincerity.* Cambridge, Mass.: The Belknap Press of Harvard University Press, 1964.

Wordsworth, Jonathan. *William Wordsworth: The Borders of Vision.* Oxford, England: Clarendon Press, 1982.

Richard D. McGhee

WILLIAM BUTLER YEATS

Born: Sandymount, near Dublin, Ireland
June 13, 1865
Died: Cap Martin, France
January 28, 1939

Principal Literary Achievement

Yeats is one of the leading poets of the twentieth century, as well as a writer who contributed through plays and essays to the institution of modern Irish literature.

Biography

William Butler Pollexfen Yeats was born on June 13, 1865, in Sandymount, a middle-class Dublin suburb, in Ireland. He was the eldest of a family of five, among whom should be noted his brother, the painter Jack B. Yeats. Yeats's father, John Butler Yeats, came from a solid Anglo-Irish background and had originally intended to be a lawyer. Instead, however, he turned to painting. Much financial hardship for his family followed. His wife, Susan Pollexfen, was a native of Sligo in the west of Ireland and came from merchant stock. Because of difficult family circumstances, the poet as a child spent extended periods with his mother's family in Sligo. These stays away from the family home, which was by this time in London, were a formative influence. It is from these that Yeats derived his interest in Irish folklore, the phenomenon of racial memory, and the love of nature, all of which are to be found throughout his poetry.

At the same time, although Yeats was for the most part very unhappy in London, the city also had its influence on him. Through his father, he became acquainted with many of the leading cultural figures of the day, including William Morris and Oscar Wilde. Yeats's dual allegiance to Ireland and London became one of the many sources of the creative tension that animates his mature poetry. It was in Ireland, however, that Yeats made his initial mark as a writer. The family returned to Dublin in 1880, where the poet's lackluster efforts at school continued. After an abortive attempt to study art, and being unable to meet university entrance requirements, Yeats abandoned formal education in 1886 to devote himself to writing.

Two important influences emerged early in the poet's career. One was his attachment to the cause of Irish nationality, which enabled him to establish a distinctive cultural identity. The other was the development of his interest in Theosophy and

spiritualism, which contributed to the growth of the poet's spiritual self. Both these orientations were idealist and symbolic in character, and they form the aesthetic and metaphysical foundation for Yeats's poetry. Yeats's early verse adapts his cultural and spiritual interests to the main poetic current of the time. This current owed much to French poetry, which relied on mood and color rather than on narrative and event. In 1891, Yeats formed the Rhymers Club with some English practitioners of this style.

Yeats's increasing technical mastery, his fresh perception of the possibilities of lyric poetry under the influence of the Rhymers, and his use of pre-Christian Celtic material as distinctive poetic subject matter contributed to the creation of the Celtic Twilight. This school of writing, whose title is borrowed from a collection of folklore produced by Yeats in 1893, projected an Irish mystique. A significant contribution to the growth of Irish literature resulted, with important implications for Irish culture and politics.

A number of other events took place early in Yeats's career that had a lasting effect on his life. One was his meeting Maud Gonne in 1889, with whom he fell in love and who is the subject not only of numerous love poems but also of the poet's more enduring fascination with physical energy and physical beauty. In 1896, Yeats first met Lady Augusta Gregory. She provided his art with financial and moral support and introduced him to Anglo-Irish aristocratic life. This way of life was to be a major source of Yeats's vision of cultural unity.

Through Lady Gregory, Yeats became committed to the establishment of an Irish National Theater, a commitment that culminated in the founding of the Abbey Theatre, in Dublin, in 1904. As a result of his involvement with the theater, Yeats not only developed into a powerful playwright but also developed the strong dramatic undertones of his verse. The success of the Abbey and the growing maturity of his own poetry gave Yeats an increasingly prominent profile in the English-speaking world. To some extent, however, events in Ireland made him a marginal figure in his own country. The rebellion of Easter, 1916, which Yeats memorably commemorated, inspired a more populist conception of Irish destiny than Yeats's art envisaged. The Irish war of independence (1919 to 1921), and the Civil War that almost immediately followed it, also gave rise to some of Yeats's greatest verse. At the same time, however, the poet withdrew from public life, establishing residence in Thoor Ballylee, a tower dating from Norman times, in the west of Ireland.

This withdrawal from Irish public life was not merely a response to the changing political climate in the country. Yeats had acquired alternative bases for identity to those of his youth. In 1917, he married Georgie Hyde-Lees, and the couple soon became parents. In 1923, his international reputation was secured by his being awarded the Nobel Prize in Literature. Other honors followed, notably a doctorate in letters from the University of Oxford in 1931. In 1922, he was nominated to the senate of the Irish Free State, a symbolic political honor, though his record as a senator is one of valuable activity and outspokenness. In addition, his thought had evolved from being primarily preoccupied with Irish matters to concern with the cosmic themes that underlie much of his later verse. These themes address the possibility of unity, which had long been one of the poet's ideals. Yet historical developments not merely in Ireland but also in the West generally seemed determined to frustrate this ideal. Pursuit of his vision of unity led the poet to envision in a mythological light the significant attainments of his generation and to support some of the international political strongmen of the 1930's.

Poor health necessitated long periods away from Ireland after the conclusion of his senate term in 1928. He continued to produce poetry of great vitality and deep thought until his death in Cap Martin, in the south of France, on January 28, 1939. Because of World War II, Yeats's remains were not removed to Ireland until 1948. He was buried in Drumcliff, in the county of Sligo.

Analysis

The main preoccupation of Yeats's imagination throughout his long career is contained in a statement made at the beginning of his career: "Hammer your thoughts into unity." These words suggest the varied nature of Yeats's perception of his poetry's raw materials. They also point to the sense of totality that he wished to derive from those materials. Yeats's raw materials include personal history, family history, cultural history, Irish history both ancient and modern, friendship, mysticism, and philosophy both personal and academic. There is no denying the complexity of some of Yeats's poetry. Some of its difficulty is necessary because it is a means of challenging the reader to become better acquainted with the Irish cultural emphases that Yeats strove to make relevant. Some of the difficulty is necessary because it is a means of reminding the reader of the lengths to which the poet would go in order to create a comprehensive model of unity.

The range of Yeats's poetic resources is also comprehensive. His work covers the gamut of possibilities provided by lyric poetry. Beginning with ballads and songs that are almost naïve in their expression of simplicity, Yeats's verse displays a variety of tones. The allusive symbolism of his third book, *The Wind Among the Reeds* (1899), for example, has by the time of his fifth book, *The Green Helmet and Other Poems* (1910), given way to a more explicit, personal tone, drawing on more obviously autobiographical material. This tone, in turn, becomes more assertive and public in the first Yeats collection of major importance, *Responsibilities* (1914). The increasingly distinctive character of Yeats's verse can be seen also in his poetry's progressively more flexible use of verse structure, rhyme, and, particularly, rhythm.

In addition, Yeats's development is also noteworthy for its reinvigorating effect on certain poetic forms. These forms, particularly the elegy and the dramatic lyric, had received extensive attention from both Romantic and Victorian poets. The elegy was a form renewed particularly by Percy Bysshe Shelley, who was an important influence on the youthful Yeats, as was William Blake, whose reformulation of lyric in terms of spirit and dream made a deep impression on Yeats's early efforts to establish a poetic identity. Yeats's dramatic lyrics intensify that particular form's possibilities in a manner not envisaged by its chief exponent, Robert Browning. Again from a formal standpoint, Yeats's attempts to reproduce in somewhat condensed form the epic ambitions of Alfred, Lord Tennyson, and William Morris reveal his often over-looked interest in form. His use of Irish materials in the elegy and the dramatic lyric is an important example of continuity and change in literary history.

Despite the range and importance of Yeats's renewal of some of the forms of English nineteenth century verse, it would be misleading to consider him an experimental poet. His traditional qualities may be perceived by comparing his work with that of his two most important modernist contemporaries, T. S. Eliot and Ezra Pound. Yeats's use of form expresses a sense of radical continuity. This concept reveals the poet's understanding of tradition, an understanding that is a major souce of duality in Yeats's thinking. In poetry, however, duality can be hammered into unity by reconciling content to form. In addition, emphasizing the formal aspect of his work draws attention not only to the forms themselves but also to the restlessness that their renewal contains. It is this restlessness, this excitation of psychic energy, that is the driving force of Yeats's verse.

This sense of restlessness, of ardor, intensity, longing, and continuity comes to the poet from an awareness of loss. Many of Yeats's most significant experiences are associated with loss. He grew up in a period when loss of faith in organized religion was widespread. The political and economic rule of the landowning class with which Yeats identified was dismantled in the course of his lifetime. As his career evolved, he lost his original audience and adopted a critical posture toward the Ireland that his verse had, in part, inspired. His experience of love is rendered in verse as one of loss, also. Moreover, many of his most important poems are elegies. Yet, while duly admitting the pain of pain, and frequently expressing its effects in terms of violence and apocalypse, Yeats attempts to compensate for its impact. It is from this commitment that his imaginative rage for unity derives.

The reader of Yeats is usually presented with a creative tension between dual elements. These elements occur in various guises. Vagaries of personality find compensation in the stability of masks. The destructive work of time is offset by the constructive work of art. The force of an individual personality can overcome the energies of the general public. The peasant can be reconciled to the aristocrat. The sting of defeat is healed by contemplating the commitment of the hero. Out of such conflicts, Yeats produces what is essentially a poetry of possibility. This poetry expresses both a desire for unity and peace together with an acknowledgment of the remoteness of those ends. Such a realization is sounded in the note of "tragic joy" for which Yeats's verse is celebrated. Aware of the fragmentary nature of modern experience, conscious of the mortal nature of the human condition, suspicious of his age's increasingly democratic trends, Yeats's poetry attempts to stare down such facts of life, achieving greatness through commitment rather than by argument.

ADAM'S CURSE

First published: 1902
Type of work: Poem

This poem is an important early example of Yeats's use of autobiographical materials for poetic ends.

"Adam's Curse" was first published in the *Monthly Review* of December, 1902, and first collected in *In the Seven Woods*, Yeats's fourth book of verse, published in 1904. The poem is an important example of Yeats's mature style in the making. The subject matter of Yeats's early poetry tended to deal with abstractions such as love, truth, and beauty. Missing from these early poems is a sense of the poet dealing with actual experiences of the actual world. Even the early verse's conception of Ireland is extremely romantic.

While in "Adam's Curse" Yeats continues to acknowledge the power of romance, his attitude toward that power is now considerably changed. First, the poem draws on Yeats's own direct experience. The three people mentioned in the poem are real. The basis for the poem is a conversation that Yeats had with "that beautiful mild woman" and is addressed to a third person who was also present at the time. This third person, the "you" of the poem, is Maud Gonne. The "mild woman" is her sister, Mrs. Kathleen Pilcher. Emphasizing the autobiographical origins of "Adam's Curse" should not be understood to mean that Yeats lost interest in the Irish mythological figures that feature so prominently in his early work. This interest was never abandoned. At the same time, however, the presence of intimate acquaintances in a private setting, and the reconstruction of their after-dinner conversation, represents a breakthrough in candor and immediacy for Yeats.

Second, "Adam's Curse" is significant because of the manner in which the poet uses his new materials. His altered attitude to romance is expressed in his critical treatment of the subject. This criticism forms the closing lines of the poem. Yet these lines do not have a dramatic or climactic effect. On the contrary, they reveal the poet's weariness of romantic love, leaving the reader with a sense of his isolation and lack of fulfillment. This strong suggestion of personal loss comes from the realization that love will not conquer all. Love, too, is subject to change, and so are lovers. This thought brings the poet depressingly down to earth.

In addition, Yeats's technique is more sophisticated in "Adam's Curse" than it is in many of his earlier poems. The decision to open the poem with what appear to be direct quotes from the remembered conversation greatly adds to the reader's sense of the immediacy, directness, spontaneity, and candor of actual experience. The informal character of conversation is conveyed by letting the lines run into each other. The first part of the poem reads more as though it is written in sentences than in poetic lines. The poet draws attention to this effect by the poem's form, which consists of one long stanza and two shorter ones. Because of this arrangement, the poem can be described as having, in effect, two parts, even though Yeats does not number or identify those parts.

There is a deliberate sense of disproportion between the parts, which is intended to suggest in one more additional way the problem of duality, which is the poem's theme. Seeing the poem in two parts also draws attention to how Yeats has separated speech from silence, exposition from reflection, and the conversational interlude from the larger emotional context. This strategy of separation underlines the variety of ways in which "Adam's Curse" concentrates on the dual character of human enterprises. The overall effect of the verbal and technical accomplishments of "Adam's Curse" is to make the poet's concerns more accessible. The poem's theme is still basically abstract, but its abstract nature is brought closer to the reader.

The theme, broadly speaking, addresses the discrepancy between appearance and reality. The poet, says Yeats, in the first conversational extract, can slave to perfect a line of poetry yet be considered an idler by the world at large. Similarly, says Mrs. Pilcher, to appear beautiful is the result of hard work. These facts of life are, to the poet, a version of Adam's curse, a reference to the fact that Adam was not only expelled from the ideal existence of paradise but also condemned to earn his bread by the sweat of his brow. Even love requires deliberate effort. Yet that thought reminds the poet that, try as he might, he has failed to perfect his love for Maud Gonne. The reality of life lies in commitment rather than in achievement, though such a realization dampens the spirit of idealism.

EASTER 1916

First published: 1920
Type of work: Poem

A commemoration in verse of the Easter, 1916, Irish rebellion against English rule, this is Yeats's best-known poem.

Although written within a few months of the event that it commemorates, and privately printed later in the year of its composition, "Easter 1916" did not receive general publication until 1920. It was first collected in the volume *Michael Robartes and the Dancer* (1920). It is Yeats's best-known poem. Its title refers to the Irish rebellion of Easter, 1916, when a small group of rebels in Dublin unexpectedly proclaimed the establishment of an Irish Republic. The rebellion was in defiance of British rule under which Ireland was then governed.

The refrain of "Easter 1916" has frequently been thought to refer to the new political arrangements initiated by the rebels. Yet such a reading is not necessarily what Yeats had in mind, as awareness of the poem's publication history will confirm. "Easter 1916" is not a political poem in the sense that it takes one side or the other in the rebellion. Nevertheless, the poem's renown is, to some extent, the result of a narrow, one-sided interpretation of the line "A terrible beauty is born." It is important to note, however, that Yeats carefully refrains from providing a facile understanding of the momentous event in Irish history that has taken place. On the contrary, the poem is notable for the questioning manner in which it expresses awe and bewilderment at the rebels. The difficulty in reaching an immediate understanding of what "A terrible beauty is born" means crystallizes the poet's own stunned reaction to the rebellion. In the first place, therefore, the most striking feature of "Easter 1916" is its honesty.

The basis for the poet's reaction is contained in the poem's opening stanza. The reader is informed that, although the poet and his cronies were aware that republican militants existed, nobody took them seriously. They were unassuming, had little social status, and provided occasions of trivial conversation. In addition, the anonymous "them," which the poet later names, were considered laughingstocks by their social superiors. The poet includes himself among those superiors, members of the "club." Yet social superiority in itself is said to count for nothing, since both the ridiculers and the ridiculed live in a land fit for clowns ("motley" being a reference to the traditional dress of the jester). The suggestion is that the rebel's subsequent heroism and self-sacrifice were unimaginable.

The second stanza presents some of the rebels in a different light. All but the first of those mentioned were executed for their part in the rebellion. Two of those mentioned were well known to the poet. "That woman" is Constance Markievicz, born Constance Gore-Booth, an Anglo-Irish aristocrat whose involvement with the rebels Yeats views as a fall from grace. The other person with whom Yeats was acquainted is Major John MacBride, "A drunken, vainglorious lout" and the estranged husband of Maud Gonne. Yet even he can no longer be considered simply a clown. Mention of these two personal associations, neither of them particularly attractive, provides a frame within which Yeats portrays two of the rebel leaders. "This man" is Patrick Pearse, a poet and teacher who led the rebellion. "This other" is Thomas MacDonough, poet and academic. Although Yeats was not very well acquainted with either of them, he presents them in a favorable light. The effect of doing so is to adjust the force of "motley" in the opening stanza.

The first two stanzas' emphasis on personality and society is replaced in the third stanza. There, a more fundamental conception of life, the natural order, is considered. According to this conception, life may be compared to a stream: Living things continually change as they grow and mature. The rebels differ from this order in the way that a stone is the opposite of a stream. Not only is a stone the stream's opposite; it also deflects or "troubles" the stream's free and direct flow. Similarly, there seems to be something unnatural about those who do not participate spontaneously and naturally in life. Yet, by the opening of the fourth stanza, this view of the rebels is itself challenged, just as the original view of them as clowns was both acknowledged and corrected in the opening two stanzas.

It is impossible, the poem argues, to know how much must be given in the name of a cause. One's human nature, "the heart," may turn to stone, but only a higher power, "Heaven's part," can determine how great a sacrifice is necessary in order to redeem a given situation, in this case the Irish nation. Meanwhile, all that can be done is to ensure that the magnitude of the sacrifice is recognized for what it is. Yeats conveys this sentiment through an appeal to language. Poetic fancy, such as the metaphor of mother and child, is inadequate to register what has taken place, as the stark, "No, no, not night but death" makes clear. Even the fact that "England may keep faith" does not diminish the rebels' impact.

England is mentioned because a version of Irish independence had been passed into law in 1914. Its application was suspended, however, until the end of World War I. According to Yeats, though, one must bear in mind that, not only did the rebels take action; their doing so also cost them their lives. This inescapable and shocking fact is the poem's inspiration and the birth of what it calls "a terrible beauty." The rebels' sacrifice is that terrible beauty, an act as awe-inspiring and overwhelming as the greatest art.

THE SECOND COMING

First published: 1920
Type of work: Poem

This work is Yeats's fullest artistic statement of his apocalyptic theory of history.

The continual broadening of Yeats's scope as a poet and thinker is demonstrated by "The Second Coming." This poem was first published in what was one of the most important literary magazines of the day, *The Dial*, in November, 1920, and first appeared in book form the same year in *Michael Robartes and the Dancer.*

Some technical knowledge is required in order to understand the opening line of the poem. The "widening gyre" (pronounced with a hard *g*) describes not only the circular, ever-widening course of the falcon's flight. It also refers to an important aspect of Yeats's theory of history. Influenced by Giambattista Vico and Friedrich Wilhelm Nietzsche's philosophies of eternal recurrence, Yeats sees history as a cycle of declines and regenerations. Each historical era is replaced by its opposite. Gyres describe the interacting and conflicting eras.

In "The Second Coming," the end of the Christian era is thought to be at hand. The poem's title is intended, first, to bring to mind the Second Coming of Christ. Yet this association, with its promises of salvation, gives way to the monstrous image of the "rough beast," suggesting barbarism. In the New Testament, the Second Coming rescues the faithful from the dreadful conditions that accompany the end of the world. In the poem, the second coming means being condemned to those dreadful conditions. The fact that the "rough beast" is to be born in Bethlehem underlines the enormous changes that the poet believes to be on the way.

Yeats was not the only early twentieth century poet who believed that the historical events of his day suggested profound and disturbing change. The impact of World War I was still being felt in every aspect of public and cultural life at the time "The Second Coming" was written. In addition, conditions in Ireland were deteriorating at a rapid rate. Old political and social forces in the country were giving way to the will of the people. Also, the victory of the Bolsheviks in Russia came as a shocking reminder of the vulnerability of certain social classes in the rest of Europe. Although none of these conditions is mentioned by name in "The Second Coming," the poem's themes of violence and disruption are reinforced by its historical context.

The opening two lines of the poem provide an image of cultural breakdown. The falcon represents those forces that function productively only when disciplined. By as early as the fourth line of the poem, the consequences of this breakdown are being described in violent terms. The word "mere" in this line is not used in its familiar sense and should be understood in its original meaning of "nothing but." Everything that makes life valuable is being drenched in blood. "The ceremony of innocence" refers not to one particular ceremony but is intended to suggest the grace and order of civilized society. Moreover, there is nobody to fight "the blood-dimmed tide."

Such conditions can only mean that the end of the world is imminent. In keeping with the violent imagery of the first stanza, a nightmarish embodiment of what is occurring reveals itself to the poet. The image comes from "Spiritus Mundi." This phrase refers to a belief that individual minds are connected to a collective mind, and that the images that occur in one's imagination are reflections of that greater consciousness. One effect of this reference is that it shows the poet himself to be vulnerable. The admission of this vulnerability gives "The Second Coming" an urgent, dramatic force, which is most clearly felt in the last line. By concluding with a question, Yeats not only crystallizes the sense of doubt and dread that fills "The Second Coming." He also draws attention to the dangerous and unresolved contemporary historical conditions. Yeats makes a powerful case for the relevance of poetry as a means of addressing pressing public issues and of preserving historical awareness.

UNDER BEN BULBEN

First published: 1939
Type of work: Poem

Yeats surveys his artistic origins and influences and makes his poetic last will and testament.

"Under Ben Bulben" was first published in three of Ireland's national daily newspapers within a week of Yeats's death and first appeared in book form in *Last Poems and Plays* (1940). Its newspaper publication was a mark of respect to the dead poet and a call for public recognition of his contribution to Irish life and literature. A similar, less self-centered call is what "Under Ben Bulben" itself communicates. As a result, the poem has long been considered Yeats's last will and poetic testament.

The poem's title refers to the table mountain that overlooks the town of Sligo. If "Under Ben Bulben" may be read as the poet's will, part of his bequest is that he be interred in the landscape of his childhood. Doing so would achieve a long-sought unity, not only with his ancestors but also with much that inspired his poetry. The location and character of the poet's final resting place are given a privileged position at the end of the poem. This position argues for the significance that Yeats attached to being at one with the enduring presences of place and family. It is by its concluding lines, therefore, that "Under Ben Bulben" most resembles a will, since these arrange the terms and conditions of both the poet's death and his legacy.

Yet these lines constitute a relatively small part of what Yeats wants to hand down. The emphasis on landscape and lineage must be seen as the end product of the poem's various other significant emphases. "Under Ben Bulben" ranges far and wide over a large number of Yeats's interests. The poem amounts to a condensed version of the poet's intellectual autobiography. Yet rather than view the poem as a series of six interlinked episodes, it is more appropriate to note how different the parts are from one another and then to notice what they have in common.

The poem opens, as Yeats's poetic career began, with allusions to pre-Christian deities and forces. The interpretation of what these forces represent is what the poem then undertakes. The Witch of Atlas, renowned in mythology for her beauty, and "That pale, long visaged company" of Irish gods and heroes have been identified as agents of vision and passion. These two qualities Yeats then claims as constants that make both the individual existence and the history of Western civilization valuable. The connection between intensity of feeling, even violence, and liberating insight is asserted in the third part of the poem. The link between artistic accomplishment and passionate involvement is made in part 4, though Yeats regrets that this connection has not endured since the middle of the nineteenth century, when the last-mentioned artist, Samuel Palmer, lived. Yeats's message to the Irish poets who follow him is, likewise, a wish that they combine spiritedness and a sense of form. Again, as throughout "Under Ben Bulben" as a whole, the persistent thought is of the unification of different and opposed elements. As part 5 affirms, "Porter-drinkers' randy laughter" is as important as "the holiness of monks."

In form, meter, and language, "Under Ben Bulben" has the flexibility, directness, and verve of Yeats at his best. At the same time, the poem's range of allusions and complexity of thought also make it typical of Yeats's intellectual ambition. Yet it is this combination of complex thought and simple method that gives the reader a direct experience of the poet's struggle for unity. The combination also confirms what the poet himself realized: that art, not life, is the means of attaining this unity.

Summary

There are a number of reasons for considering William Butler Yeats as a major poet. One is his comprehensive growth. Virtually all of his books of poetry represent a development and refinement of his thought. Taken as a whole, therefore, his output represents a major act of witnessing the historical events and cultural tendencies of his time. In addition, Yeats's desire to create meaningful relationships between such different phenomena as love and art, history and poetry, Christianity and apocalypse, and passion and vision remains a striking example of his mind's range. The fact that he produced poems that unify some of these phenomena is commonly accepted as one of the twentieth century's monuments to the power and potential of art.

Bibliography

Bradley, Anthony. *William Butler Yeats*. New York: Ungar, 1979.

Donoghue, Denis. *Yeats*. London: Fontana, 1971.

Ellmann, Richard. *The Identity of Yeats*. London: Macmillan, 1954.

_____. *W. B. Yeats: The Man and the Masks*. London: Macmillan, 1948.

Jeffares, A. N. *A New Commentary on the Poems of W. B. Yeats*. London: Macmillan, 1984.

_____. *W. B. Yeats*. London: Hutchinson, 1988.

McCormack, W. J. *Ascendancy and Tradition in Anglo-Irish Literary History from 1789 to 1939*. Oxford, England: Clarendon Press, 1985.

MacLiammoir, Michael, and Eavan Boland. *W. B. Yeats and His World*. New York: Viking Press, 1972.

Malins, Edward. *A Preface to Yeats*. New York: Charles Scribner's Sons, 1974.

Stallworthy, Jon, ed. *Yeats's Last Poems: A Casebook*. London: Macmillan, 1968.

George O'Brien

YEVGENY YEVTUSHENKO

Born: Zima Junction, Soviet Union
July 18, 1933

Principal Literary Achievement

Appearing at the height of anti-Stalinist activism, Yevtushenko was one of several young poets whose influence led to a decisive change in Russian poetry, as well as in Soviet politics.

Biography

Yevgeny Alexandrovich Yevtushenko was born on July 18, 1933, at Zima Junction, a small Siberian junction near Lake Baikal, in the Soviet Union. Some of his ancestors had been deported to Siberia from Ukraine at the end of the nineteenth century for political activities. Other relatives came from Latvia. "Revolution was the religion in our family," Yevtushenko says in his autobiography. He spent his childhood amid the serene beauty of Siberian nature but also troubled by political uncertainty: Both of his grandfathers were swept away during the purges ordered by Joseph Stalin in the late 1930's. His parents studied geology in Moscow, married, and were divorced before World War II. His mother took Yevgeny to Moscow, but he was evacuated to Zima during the war, where he spent three years.

Back in Moscow, growing up in postwar hardship, he was belligerent and was even thrown out of one school. He surmounted the difficulties, however, and even began to write poetry. For a while, he joined his father in a geological expedition in Kazakhstan and later almost became a professional soccer player. After publishing his first poem in 1949, appropriately in *Soviet Sport*, he concentrated on literature and entered the famous Gorky Literary Institute in Moscow. From the beginning of the 1950's, he published his poems with increasing success. The publication of his first book, *Razvedchicki gryadushchego* (1952; prospectors of the future), decided his fate: He devoted his life to poetry and published numerous books with regularity.

The emotional appeal of his poetry and his innate boldness made him a leader among the new Russian poets eager to assert themselves. Together with other rising poets, most notably Andrei Voznesensky, they were known as "the angry young men" of Russian letters. The age-old generational conflict became acute, and even the very notion of revolution, or the purification of it, was brought into question. During the increasing campaign against Stalin, Yevtushenko contributed several fiery poems of protest and rebellion, "Babiy Yar" ("Babii Yar"), "Nasledniki Stalina" ("Stalin's

Heirs"), and "Miortvaia ruka" ("The Dead Hand of the Past") being the most explosive, making him even more popular with young readers. He was able to publish almost without restriction, including an autobiography in Paris in 1962, *Autobiographie précoce* (published in London in the Russian language as *Avtobiografia*, 1964; *A Precocious Autobiography*, 1973), which appeared without permission from the authorities back home. He was also free to travel abroad and visited the United States many times. His star was rising steadily.

In the changing political climate in the Soviet Union, however, he would soon get into trouble with authorities for his outspoken, inflammatory views. He was chastised, kept in check, even exiled for a short while in the beautiful Caucasus, which he did not find overly punitive. He retreated to Zima for a while, as if to replenish his strength and resolve in his native place, where he wrote a large number of poems. Somehow, Yevtushenko was able to weather this and many other storms and to regain the good graces of the authorities. After several months of official silence, he was allowed to publish again, toning down his virulent attacks somewhat but remaining unbending in his opposition to the suppression of free speech. The situation continued: Periods of freedom were replaced by periods of restriction, until the Mikhail Gorbachev era.

In the 1980's, in addition to publishing poetry, Yevtushenko branched out into politics and filmmaking. He became very active in supporting the establishment of a democratic system. He wrote film scenarios and directed and even acted in movies. Poetry, however, remained his main avocation. He is considered one of the leading Russian poets in the second half of the twentieth century.

Analysis

The beginnings of Yevtushenko's literary activities passed in the spirit of youthful rebelliousness and of the Russian poetic tradition. That tradition, however, was not so much the classical one of Alexander Pushkin, Aleksandr Blok, even Boris Pasternak, with their heavily rhymed and regulated poetry; it was, rather, the tradition of modern, free-verse poetry, which was, by and large, absent from Russian poetry until the middle of the twentieth century. The notable exception was Vladimir Mayakovsky, with whom Yevtushenko has much in common, including the powerful, dramatic way of publicly reading one's poetry.

From the very beginning, Yevtushenko believed that he was bringing something new to Russian poetry. It was not so much the dissatisfaction with the existing state and the ensuing rebelliousness as it was his belief that the torch had been passed and that the new generation should be taking its rightful place. Imbued with the age-old conviction that poets hold a special position in Russian society, he asserted himself forcefully even in his very first poems. In one of his earliest, "Prolog" ("Prologue"), for example, he declares in the very first verse, "I am different," speaking not only for himself but for the entire generation. His early poems also express his love and respect for nature, faith in his people and love for his land, a strong belief in himself, and a confirmation of his faith in the original aims of the revolution, which have been corrupted and are in need of reconstitution. A strong lyrical bent and a desire to experiment with poetic devices, including rhyme, complete the picture of the young Yevtushenko.

As he matured in the course of only a few years during the changes in the Soviet Union after Stalin's death, Yevtushenko turned to wider themes and concerns. His political activism became more prominent, as evidenced in poems such as "Stantsiya Zima" ("Zima Junction"), "Babii Yar," "Stalin's Heirs," and "Conversations with an American Writer." He displayed a willingness to state his position openly and courageously and to fight for his beliefs. By becoming a fighter for his ideals, he identified with one of the oldest traditions of Russian poets—to speak out as the conscience of the people in the absence of other democratic institutions. This attitude, however, had its price: Yevtushenko has often been labeled a topical poet lending his talent to social causes that came to his attention, as illustrated by a poem that he wrote on the spot upon visiting the bombed office of political activists in New York. It is difficult, therefore, to ignore the fact that his political activism and opposition to Soviet authorities contributed heavily to his popularity at home and abroad. His critics, however, accused him of flirting with the authorities and defending the revolution.

Yevtushenko has expressed his resentment over being labeled primarily a political or topical poet. He has frequently pointed out his faith in poetry as a noble endeavor and in the integrity of poets, who should be interested in social issues but should also express high emotions and pursue lofty aesthetic goals. Indeed, in a great number of his poems, he pursues exactly such goals. He conducts a running dialogue with Russian and foreign poets about the mission of poetry. He registers his poetic reactions to sights and sounds on his numerous world travels. He writes poems about everyday life, such as about women burdened with life's miseries, as in "Ne ponimaiu" ("I Don't Understand") and "A Tie Salesgirl"; his mother's contribution in shaping his character, as in "Ia pozdravliaiu vas, mamma" ("I Congratulate You, Momma"); the vagaries of love, as in "Zrelost liubvi!" ("Love's Maturity?"); the simple joys of life, in "Berry-Picking"; or an absent-minded old professor whose wife has left him, in "Okno vykhodit v belye derevia" ("Schoolmaster"). His variety of themes is one of Yevtushenko's most appealing characteristics. As he states in "Prologue," "I want art to be/ as diverse as myself."

In another poem ("Poetry"), he says of poets, "They slander him from left/ and right,/ but he looks down on the liars with contempt." His courage has stood him in good stead throughout his career.

PROLOGUE

First published: "Prolog," 1957 (English translation, 1965)
Type of work: Poem

"Prologue" can be seen as an explanation of Yevtushenko's approach to life and literature and is an introduction to his entire poetic career.

Writing "Prologue" at the very beginning of his poetic career, Yevtushenko felt the need to identify himself. This self-identification, present in many of his poems, voices some of his basic concerns: the need to be different; a realization that somehow he does not fit in; the restrictive nature of his surroundings; and the lack of total freedom to express himself as an artist. As he explains at the end of the poem, he likes to defy the enemy standing in the way of the joy of living. That he sees as the highest purpose of his life.

The difference of which Yevtushenko speaks refers not so much to himself as to each successive generation of poets. The old has ruled Russian poetry for almost four decades; the new, represented best by Yevtushenko and Andrei Voznesensky, has come on the heels of the changes after Joseph Stalin's death. The fact that he feels constrained in his efforts to express himself freely, justifies his eagerness to see these changes made as quickly as possible. The best way to effect the change is by boldness and courage. Only then will he and others experience the full joy of life that he believes is their inalienable right.

The autobiographical nature of the poem is somewhat misleading, because, as stated, Yevtushenko does not plead the case for himself alone. In this sense, the poem has a universal meaning transcending the poet's own predicament, and even that of his generation. It can apply to all generations replacing one another. Supporting this argument is the fact that Yevtushenko is somewhat coy in his allusions to the powers that be (perhaps in order to see his poem in print), despite his well-known boldness. Moreover, some of the attitudes described—a defiant statement of being different, the ebullience of youth, a thirst for life and the joy of living, contradictory forces within oneself—can indeed be applied universally.

Yevtushenko also refers to two poets, Sergei Yesenin, a leading Russian poet in the first quarter of the twentieth century, and Walt Whitman. All three poets are known for their closeness to nature, through which they express their yearning for freedom and determination to be free.

"Prologue" is a manifesto poem, setting a course for future sailings, to which Yevtushenko has remained remarkably faithful.

BABII YAR

First published: "Babiy Yar," 1961 (English translation, 1965)
Type of work: Poem

This poem is a powerful castigation of the latent anti-Semitism in the Soviet Union, which allowed Nazi crimes against the Jews in the Ukraine to be ignored.

"Babii Yar" is Yevtushenko's best-known poem. The poem is about a ravine in the Ukraine where thousands of Jews were slaughtered by the Nazis, yet there is no monument to honor the dead. It is a poem with a thesis, the thesis being that anti-Semitism still exists in the Soviet Union as it has for centuries. What intensifies this accusation is the professed internationalism of the Soviets that was supposed to eliminate all injustices, including the racial persecution. "Babii Yar" is also one of the most political of Yevtushenko's poems and one of the most enduring, requiring and receiving no retraction.

In a series of metaphors, the poet establishes his references. After stating in the first line that there is no monument at Babii Yar, the poet immediately identifies with Jewish people, going back to ancient Egypt and to the agony of crucifixion on the cross, subtly reminding the reader of the common origin of Christ and the Jews. He refers to Dreyfus, a celebrated victim of persecution in France; to a boy in the Byelorussian town of Belostok as an illustration of pogroms; and finally to Anne Frank, the ultimate symbol of the suffering of the young and innocent as a result of racial injustice. When he returns to the victims of Babii Yar, Yevtushenko declares his solidarity with them exactly because he is a Russian, who, as he says, are "international to the core." His final statement is that of a defiance and lack of fear that he will be hated by anti-Semites.

"Babii Yar" is more than a political statement. It is an outcry against all the injustices of the world and a warning that it may not be limited to the Soviet Union, thus lending the poem a universal appeal. The skillful use of metaphors and symbols adds to the overall beauty of the poem, making it one of the most eloquent combinations of message and poetic execution.

"YES" AND "NO"

First published: " 'Da' i 'Net,' " 1965 (English translation, 1968)
Type of work: Poem

In this work, the poet is shuttling between the cities of "Yes" and "No," symbolizing the basic dichotomy in which he is forced to live.

Like many of Yevtushenko's poems, " 'Yes' and 'No' " is in the form of a dramatic monologue. It represents his dilemma in having to shuttle like a train between two cities, "Yes" and "No," causing his nerves to be strained like telegraph wires. The city of No is loveless and without help, inhabited by ghosts and scowling objects. In contrast, the city of Yes is like a bird's song; there are no walls, and even the stars are begging to be friends, the lips offer themselves to be kissed, and the cows provide free milk. At the end, however, the poet tires of this land of plenty, unable to appreciate things given to him gratis. He would rather continue to shuttle between the two cities.

" 'Yes' and 'No' " is a simple poem on the surface, but it harbors some allegories. The poem is subtitled "From the Verses About Love," and this subtitle offers a possible explanation of the allegory of unrequited love in the city of No and the allure of fulfilled love in the city of Yes. The poet uses apt images to characterize the difference between the two emotional states. The decision not to opt for the logical choice of happiness and bliss and to travel between the two instead corresponds to a choice that is made by heart and not by reason. Another possible allegory is of a political nature, the city of No representing the bleak state of affairs in the poet's country and the city of Yes the promise of a better life elsewhere. In this connection, the inability to travel abroad is of particular relevance.

The fact that Yevtushenko remained a man of politics, as well as a man of letters, supports this basic dichotomy, allowing for various interpretations of his works. What should not be ignored, however, is that his first love and avocation was always literature and that his poems are, first, works of art.

Summary

Yevgeny Yevtushenko started his poetic career in a modern idiom, aware that he was helping to bring something new to Russian poetry and that the torch had been passed to a new generation. As he matured, he became increasingly involved in political matters or matters that he believed deserved personal commitment. In this, he played the traditional role of a Russian poet as the conscience of the nation. At the same time, he never compromised his artistic standards to the point of becoming a spokesman for nonliterary causes, of which he has often been accused. It is indeed his artistic qualities that have made him a leading poet in contemporary Russian literature.

Bibliography

Alexandrova, Vera. "Evgeny Evtushenko." In *A History of Soviet Literature*, translated by Mirra Ginsburg. Garden City, N.Y.: Doubleday, 1963.

Babenko, Vickie A. "Women in Evtushenko's Poetry." *Russian Review* 36 (1977): 320-333.

Forgues, P. "The Young Poets." *Survey*, January, 1963, 40-44.

Millner-Gullard, R. R. "Introduction to Yevgeny Yevtushenko." In *Selected Poetry*.

New York: E. P. Dutton, 1962.

Reavey, George. "Yevgeny Yevtushenko: Man and Poet." In *The Poetry of Yevgeny Yevtushenko, 1953-1965*. New York: October House, 1965.

Vasa D. Mihailovich

ÉMILE ZOLA

Born: Paris, France
April 2, 1840
Died: Paris, France
September 29, 1902

Principal Literary Achievement

Zola was the most important author of the naturalist school and an influence upon writers in Europe and the Americas.

Biography

Émile Zola was born in Paris, France, on April 2, 1840, the son of a French mother, Émilie, and an Italian-born father, Francesco Zola, a civil engineer. When the senior Zola's canal project was approved by the government, he and his family moved in 1843 to Aix-en-Provence in southern France. Four years later, he died of pneumonia, leaving his widow and child in difficult circumstances. After grammar school, Émile entered secondary school in 1852, where, thanks to hard work, he became an excellent student, especially in French literature. It was then that he formed a lifelong friendship with Paul Cézanne, who was to become a great Impressionist painter. Taking long walks in the Provençal hills, the two companions talked of art and Romantic poetry, especially that of Victor Hugo and Alfred de Musset.

As the family situation worsened, Mme Zola and her son were forced to return to Paris in the hope of obtaining assistance from her late husband's friends. In 1858, Émile enrolled at the Lycée Saint-Louis. The following year, perhaps because of a long illness, constant worries over the family's livelihood, and homesickness, he failed the qualifying *baccalauréat* examinations. Now living on his own in abject poverty, he began to write poems and stories while looking for a job and rereading the French classics. Hired in 1862 as shipping clerk at Hachette, a publishing house, Zola ultimately rose to head its advertising department. There, the owner advised him to abandon poetry and devote himself to prose instead.

Outside his working hours, Zola continued to read, from the novelists of his generation (Stendhal, Gustave Flaubert, Honoré de Balzac, the Goncourt brothers) to the theoretical writings of Hippolyte-Adolphe Taine and Claude Bernard. In 1864, he published his first book, *Contes à Ninon* (1894; *Stories for Ninon*, 1895), a collection that already sketches certain favorite themes and images. At the same time, newspapers published his literary and artistic reviews, many of which were gathered in a

volume entitled *Mes haines* (1866; *My Hates*, 1893).

Financially more secure, Zola left Hachette in early 1866 and became a free-lance book and art critic for a number of important newspapers. It was in their pages that he eloquently defended the paintings of Édouard Manet and the Impressionists against tradition-bound academicians. He continued to explore human relations in novels such as *Thérèse Raquin* (1867; English translation, 1881) and *Madeleine Férat* (1868; English translation, 1880).

Shortly after the publication of *Madeleine Férat*, Zola signed a contract for *Les Rougon-Macquart* (1871-1893; *The Rougon-Macquart Novels*, 1895-1907), a twenty-volume series depicting the "natural and social history of a family under the Second Empire." The first novel, *La Fortune des Rougon* (1871; *The Rougon-Macquart Family*, 1879), appeared in 1871 and received a warm accolade from Flaubert. Thereafter, a new volume would appear almost every year until 1893, when *Le Docteur Pascal* (1893; *Doctor Pascal* 1893) brought the saga to its conclusion. Zola also wrote political and literary articles, plays, and short stories. In private life, during 1870 he married Gabrielle Meley, whom he had known since 1863, and established close friendships with writers such as Ivan Turgenev, Guy de Maupassant, and Joris-Karl Huysmans.

The year 1877 was important in Zola's career, for it brought him the triumph of *L'Assommoir* (1876; English translation, 1879), the money to purchase a country home in Médan, near Paris, and a reputation as one of the great novelists of the nineteenth century. Three years later, *Nana* (1880; English translation, 1880) was even more successful, in part because of its scandalous subject; it was followed by *Germinal* (1885; English translation, 1885), the thirteenth novel in the series, considered by most critics as his masterpiece. In addition, he exposed his naturalist ideas in nonfictional essays: *Le Roman expérimental* (1880; *The Experimental Novel*, 1964), *Les Romanciers naturalistes* (1881; *The Naturalist Novel*, 1964), and *Le Naturalisme au théâtre* (*Naturalism on the Stage*, 1893). These ideas were being strongly challenged by the summer of 1887, although that same year André Antoine still applied them in his Théâtre Libre productions.

As soon as Zola had completed his magnum opus, he composed *Les Trois Villes* (1894-1898; *The Three Cities*, 1894-1898), a trilogy of lesser merit, while increasingly concerning himself with social and political questions. He became involved in the case of Captain Alfred Dreyfus, who had been unjustly condemned for treason in 1894 and on whose behalf Zola waged a newspaper campaign, culminating in the eloquent—even provocative—open letter published in the January 13, 1898, issue of *L'Aurore* under the title "J'accuse . . . !" ("I Accuse . . . !," 1898).

Sentenced to a heavy fine and a year in prison for this article, Zola fled to England to continue his fight. Returning to Paris in June, 1899, where he saw Dreyfus pardoned by President Émile-François Loubet (full exoneration did not come until 1906), he supervised the publication of the first volume of *Les Quatre Évangiles* (1899-1903; *The Four Evangelists*, 1900-1903). Volume 4, on Justice, remained in the project stage.

On September 29, 1902, Zola died at his Paris apartment of carbon monoxide poisoning caused by a defective chimney, leaving behind his wife, a daughter (Denise) and a son (Jacques), both born of his affair with Jeanne Rozerot. Six years after a public funeral attended by some fifty thousand people, his remains were transferred to the Panthéon and placed near those of Victor Hugo, another great defender of the innocent and the downtrodden.

Analysis

Zola viewed his century as predominantly scientific and saw literature as the best means of observing and studying human forces at work (although he never completely rejected his early Romantic writings). He had been influenced not only by Bernard's *Introduction à l'étude de la médecine expérimentale* (1865; *Introduction to the Study of Experimental Medicine*, 1927), which dealt with biological determinism and the pathological functioning of the organism, but also by the questionable principles propounded by Dr. Prosper Lucas and Jules Michelet regarding hereditary laws. By placing his theory of human conduct in a scientific context, he showed himself to be much more interested in physiology than in character analysis. Indeed, at a congress held in 1866, Zola declared, "The novel is a treatise of moral anatomy, a compilation of human facts, an experimental philosophy of the passions. Its object is . . . to portray mankind and nature as they really are."

In the plan submitted to his publisher in 1869, concerning the writing of *The Rougon-Macquart Novels*, Zola expressed his desire to demonstrate the reciprocal effect of the environment on various family members, with their special temperaments and genetic baggage, during a particular and well-delineated historical period. Into the almost twenty years that constitute Emperor Napoleon III's reign are crammed the lives of the descendants of these two families united by marriage. All suffer to a greater or lesser extent from the original "lesion" passed to future generations by Adélaïde Rougon, the matriarch. (A complete genealogy was later included.)

Fortunately, by manipulating outside influences, Zola makes it possible to escape one's environment as well as, through innateness, one's heredity. Despair would prevail otherwise, since no redemption could be envisioned. Despite the conclusion reached by the 105-year-old Adélaïde that she has raised a pack of wolves, the last volume (*Doctor Pascal*) reveals a glimpse of hope in an infant's arm lifted "very straight, like a flag summoning life."

In addition, Zola wished to present protagonists in different personal or professional situations, such as the unchecked greed of *La Curée* (1872; *The Kill*, 1886); the ravages of alcoholism in *L'Assommoir*; the world of politics in *Son Excellence Eugène Rougon* (1876; *Clorinda*, 1880); the world of art in *L'Œuvre* (1886; *The Masterpiece*, 1946); or the field of high finance in *L'Argent* (1891; *Money*, 1891). To achieve his goal, he read books and archives on the subject at hand, consulted experts and practitioners, and even made on-site inspections, as in the case of his tour of the coal district in northern France and his descent in an actual mine pit in preparation for *Germinal*. He also mentioned in his notes, along with general and chapter outlines, the cast of characters with their outstanding features and, if belonging to the central family, their hereditary traits.

Such detailed research does not lead, however, to an uninspired, quasi-mechanical presentation of facts and actions that reads like the objective, scientific texts he admired and used; on the contrary, many of the series' novels were defined by Zola himself as "poems": for example, "the poem of modern activity" (*Au bonheur des dames*, 1883; *The Ladies' Paradise*, 1883) or "the living poem of the land" (*La Terre*, 1887; *Earth*, 1954). This means that the accumulated documentation often served to fulfill and corroborate an idea already conceived in his mind or to elaborate it. Besides, he remained fundamentally a poet and an artist. That he proved again and again when he described lush or barren landscapes, gigantic crowds in motion, and singular objects endowed with awesome anthropomorphic, even mythic, qualities (whether a locomotive, a greenhouse, or a still).

Sex, too, is an important, omnipresent theme in Zola. Indeed, his contemporaries constantly criticized him not only for his apparent pandering to humanity's prurient instincts but also for removing all sentimental connotations from the sex act. His response was always that nothing natural or human can be excluded from a naturalistic work, that the dichotomy between nature and morality is an unscientific—hence, unacceptable—premise, and that desire is as much a part of a human being as other physiological drives.

As was already evident in Zola's early fiction, his vision of the world was basically dark, and the more he observed and dissected human behavior the more pessimistic he became. Yet at the same time he was fascinated by his characters' pleasure-seeking selfishness and corruption, perhaps because he considered vice more interesting than virtue (to paraphrase Balzac). This fascination explains why so many of his heroes and heroines are, first, embodiments of depravity who may ultimately be punished with death or madness but who remain unrepentant nonetheless. Second, they symbolize the complete rottenness at the core of France in the 1850's and 1860's in general and the very evil of the emperor's regime in particular, on which they are sometimes able to take a sweet revenge (such as in *Nana*). Smartly avoiding the pitfalls of moralistic preaching, Zola conveyed to his readers the warning that capitalism was being undermined by greed and poverty and that the people would, in the end, rise up in just revolt; he was thereby echoing the socialistic doctrines of Charles Fourier, Pierre-Joseph Proudhon, and Karl Marx.

The next two novel series reprise these doctrines. In *The Three Cities*, Zola relates the progress accomplished by Pierre Froment as he travels to miraculous Lourdes, to Catholic Rome, and back to modern Paris, where he discovers a renewed hope in a form of scientific humanitarianism. "The great future harvest of truth and justice," promised at the end of *Paris*, finds its utopian realization in what can be considered a sequel. There, Froment's four sons—Matthew, Luke, Mark, and John—each represent the four values ("gospels" in the series title's literal translation) on which the father's new happiness and "religion" will be built, that is, on "fruitfulness," "work," "truth," and "justice."

THÉRÈSE RAQUIN

First published: 1867 (English translation, 1881)
Type of work: Novel

After murdering her husband, Thérèse and her lover are tormented by their consciences and driven to suicide.

Thérèse Raquin is a gruesome fictional implementation of the scientific theories that influenced Zola. Allying himself with "the group of naturalist writers" (his first mention of the term), he declared in the preface to the second edition (1868) that, much as a surgeon would dissect a corpse, he would attempt the objective study of two different temperaments brought together by circumstances. This novel is also a very good horror story in the vein of Edgar Allan Poe and Nathaniel Hawthorne.

Mme Raquin is aunt to the the orphaned Thérèse and has reared her along with her own son, Camille. Even if not particularly suited for each other, for the young girl is sensual and vibrant and her cousin frail and weak, they nevertheless marry. The three characters then move to a seedy Parisian neighborhood, where mother and daughter-in-law open a dry-goods shop and Camille becomes a railroad clerk. Life is so monotonous and marriage so boring that, when one night Camille brings home a colleague from the office, Thérèse finds herself "thrilled" by the newcomer's robust physical animality.

The lusty Laurent and the unsatisfied Thérèse are soon involved in a highly charged affair. Wanting to be free of Camille (divorce is impossible) and unable to control their sexual needs, they drown him in an apparent boating accident, but not before he bites Laurent's neck and leaves an indelible scar not unlike the mark of Cain. That at times Thérèse fantasizes about tearing it off with her teeth, so as to diminish her disgust and reach a new level of erotic pleasure, is indicative of a certain sadistic cruelty. In their increasingly unstable and guilty minds, the family cat seems to glare at the two murderers with a suspicious eye, while the victim's ghost now lies between them in bed and prohibits their usually passionate sex and their sleep.

Close to a nervous breakdown, horrified by their remorse, and feverish from abstinence, Thérèse and Laurent can consider but one recourse: They take poison and at last find some consolation in their double death, although in Thérèse's fall her mouth hits Laurent's stigmatic scar. Paradoxically, this conclusion shows that far from being mere physiological temperaments, the two lovers made concrete moral—if wrong—choices by deciding how they would live in reaction to their nature; moreover, it shows that there is a moral law after all, in spite of Zola's professed adherence to the axiom of Hippolyte-Adolphe Taine ("Vice and virtue are products like vitriol and sugar"), which he uses as an epigraph to the novel.

GERMINAL

First published: 1885 (English translation, 1885)
Type of work: Novel

Coal miners strike unsuccessfully for better pay and better working conditions but will someday overcome their harsh situations.

Germinal takes its title, first, from the Revolutionary calendar's spring event of 12 Germinal 1795, when the starving populace invaded the National Assembly and demanded bread. Similarly, the miners and their womenfolk act accordingly in one of the novel's most famous and most stirring passages (part 5, chapter 5). Second, by continuing nature's cycle, spring is also symbolic of rebirth and fecundity after months of sterility and death.

Dismissed from his position as a mechanic because of his socialistic ideas, Étienne Lantier (of the Macquart line) arrives in the bleak March landscape of the coal-mining district to start work in the pits, despite his lack of underground experience. Zola masterfully uses Étienne's naïveté regarding his new milieu to educate him and the reader about this forsaken world and people. Since their wages are so low, the miners, regardless of age or gender, have traditionally eked out a miserable existence. Now, however, because of overproduction and the subsequent drop in coal prices, the company wants to impose an even lower tonnage fee. Lantier convinces his coworkers to strike rather than capitulate as they have often done in the past. For its part, the company expects to crush the strike through hunger.

When violence and sabotage occur, the army arrives to restore order, resulting in numerous deaths and acts of revenge. The food provider Maigrat is savagely mutilated, a soldier is murdered by a young boy, and the mine installation is flooded by a Russian anarchist, thus causing additional fatalities. In the end, vanquished by the repressive government forces and by starvation, the miners return to work, while Lantier leaves to militate on behalf of social justice.

Though obviously on the miners' side, Zola does not portray either group in black and white terms. The workers, limited by their environment and devoid of free will, are reduced to the level of animals in their constant search for food. The Grégoires are a local stockholding family who show charitable impulses toward the miners but are ultimately too insensitive to wish to improve their plight; their young daughter, who becomes a symbol of capitalism, will later be cruelly stripped and strangled. Hennebeau, the resident manager, is as much a tool and prisoner of the company as the workers. Zola mythifies the mine pit into a voracious monster, aptly named "le Voreux," feeding on human flesh; even when flooded, it soon returns to its normal state in expectant ambush for the next cargo of miners.

Failure and death aside, the novel closes optimistically, under the glorious April sun. Étienne now hears the hammering sounds of his comrades underground and imagines, in a suffusing prophecy of resurrection, that an "avenging army was slowly germinating in the furrows, sprouting for the harvests of the coming century. And soon this germination would sunder the earth." The promise of the title has been fully realized.

Summary

Émile Zola's novels are object lessons that follow the scientific and socialist evolution of its author and seem to mirror a Dantesque model as well. *The Rougon-Macquart Novels* especially depicts the Inferno with its decadent, corrupt society, whereas *The Three Cities*, as Purgatory, offers hope and rebirth, in turn achieved in the Paradise of *The Four Evangelists*.

Zola's characters, rather than being controlled by fatality, as in Greek tragedy, or by original sin, as in modern literature, are physiologically and sociologically determined. Yet Zola the reformer provides a necessary escape from this vicious circle of heredity and environment, and Zola the prophet envisions a just world and a glorious tomorrow.

Bibliography

Baguley, David, ed. *Critical Essays on Émile Zola*. Boston: G. K. Hall, 1986.

Grant, Elliott M. *Émile Zola*. Boston: Twayne, 1966.

_____. *Zola's "Germinal": A Critical and Historical Study*. Leicester, England: Leicester University Press, 1962.

Hemmings, F. W. J. *Émile Zola*. Rev. ed. Oxford, England: Clarendon Press, 1966.

Knapp, Bettina L. *Émile Zola*. New York: Ungar, 1980.

Lapp, John C. *Zola Before the "Rougon-Macquart."* Toronto: University of Toronto Press, 1964.

Nelson, Brian. *Émile Zola. A Selective Analytical Bibliography*. London: Grant & Cutler, 1982.

Walker, Philip. *Zola*. London: Routledge & Kegan Paul, 1985.

Wilson, Angus. *Émile Zola: An Introductory Study of His Novels*. Rev. ed. London: Martin Secker & Warburg, 1965.

Pierre L. Horn

MAGILL'S
SURVEY
OF
WORLD
LITERATURE

GLOSSARY

Aesthetics: The branch of philosophy that studies the beautiful in nature and art, including how beauty is recognized in a work of art and how people respond to it. In literature, the aesthetic approach can be distinguished from the moral or utilitarian approach; it was most fully embodied in the movement known as aestheticism in the late nineteenth century.

Alienation: The German dramatist Bertolt Brecht developed the theory of alienation in his epic theater. Brecht sought to create an audience that was intellectually alert rather than emotionally involved in a play by using alienating techniques such as minimizing the illusion of reality onstage and interrupting the action with songs and visual aids.

Allegory: A literary mode in which characters in a narrative personify abstract ideas or qualities and so give a second level of meaning to the work, in addition to the surface narrative. Two famous examples of allegory are Edmund Spenser's *The Faerie Queene* (1590, 1596) and John Bunyan's *The Pilgrim's Progress* (1678). For modern examples, see the stories and novels of Franz Kafka.

Alliteration: A poetic technique in which consonant repetition is focused at the beginning of syllables, as in "Large mannered motions of his mythy mind." Alliteration is used when the poet wishes to focus on the details of a sequence of words and to show the relationships between words in a line.

Angry young men: The term used to describe a group of English novelists and playwrights in the 1950's and 1960's, whose work stridently attacked what it saw as the outmoded political and social structures (particularly the class structure) of post-World War II Britain. John Osborne's play *Look Back in Anger* (1956) and Kingsley Amis' *Lucky Jim* (1954) are typical examples.

Angst: A pervasive feeling of anxiety and depression often associated with the moral and spiritual uncertainties of the twentieth century, as expressed in the existentialism of writers such as Jean-Paul Sartre and Albert Camus.

Antagonist: A character in fiction who stands in opposition or rivalry to the protagonist. In William Shakespeare's *Hamlet* (c. 1600-1601), for example, King Claudius is the antagonist of Hamlet.

Anthropomorphism: The ascription of human characteristics and feelings to animals, inanimate objects, or gods. The gods of Homer's epics are anthropomorphic, for example. Anthropomorphism occurs in beast fables, such as George Orwell's *Animal Farm* (1945). The term "pathetic fallacy" carries the same meaning: Natural objects are invested with human feelings. *See also* Pathetic fallacy.

Antihero: A modern fictional figure who tries to define himself and establish his own codes, or a protagonist who simply lacks traditional heroic qualities, such as Jim Dixon in Kingsley Amis' *Lucky Jim* (1954).

Aphorism: A short, concise statement that states an opinion, precept, or general truth, such as Alexander Pope's "Hope springs eternal in the human breast."

Apostrophe: A direct address to a person (usually absent), inanimate entity, or abstract quality.

Archetype: The term was used by psychologist Carl Jung to describe what he called "primordial images" that exist in the "collective unconscious" of humankind and are manifested in myths, religion, literature, and dreams. Now used broadly in literary criticism to refer to character types, motifs, images, symbols, and plot patterns recurring in many different literary forms and works. The embodiment of archetypes in a work of literature can make a powerful impression on the reader.

Aristotelian unities: A set of rules for proper dramatic construction formulated by Italian and French critics during the Renaissance, purported to be derived from the *De poetica* (c. 334-323 B.C.; *Poetics*) of Aristotle. According to the "three unities," a play should have no scenes irrelevant to the main action, should not cover a period of more than twenty-four hours, and should not occur in more than one place or locale. In fact, Aristotle insists only on unity of action in a tragedy.

Assonance: A term for the association of words with identical vowel sounds but different consonants: "stars," "arms," and "park," for example, all contain identical *a* (and *ar*) sounds.

***Auto sacramental*:** A Renaissance development of the medieval open-air Corpus Christi pageant in Spain. A dramatic, allegorical depiction of a sinful soul wavering and transgressing until the intervention of Divine Grace restores order. During a period of prohibition of all secular drama in Spain, from 1598 to 1600, even Lope de Vega Carpio adopted this form.

Autobiography: A form of nonfiction writing in which the author narrates events of his or her own life. Autobiography differs from memoir in that the latter focuses on prominent people the author has known and great events that he has witnessed, rather than on his own life.

Ballad: Popular ballads are songs or verse that tell dramatic, usually impersonal, tales. Supernatural events, courage, and love are frequent themes, but any experience that appeals to ordinary people is acceptable material. Literary ballads—narrative poems based on the popular ballads—have frequently been in vogue in English literature, particularly during the Romantic period. One of the most famous is Samuel Taylor Coleridge's *The Rime of the Ancient Mariner* (1798).

Baroque: The term was first used in the eighteenth century to describe an elaborate and grandiose type of architecture. It is now also used to refer to certain stylistic features of Metaphysical poetry, particularly the poetry of Richard Crashaw. The term can also refer to post-Renaissance literature, 1580-1680.

***Bildungsroman*:** Sometimes called the "novel of education," or "apprenticeship novel," the *Bildungsroman* focuses on the growth of a young protagonist who is learning about the world and finding his place in life; a typical example is James Joyce's *A Portrait of the Artist as a Young Man* (1916).

Blank verse: A term for unrhymed iambic pentameter, blank verse first appeared in drama in Thomas Norton and Thomas Sackville's *Gorboduc*, performed in 1561, and later became the standard form of Elizabethan drama. It has also commonly been used in long narrative or philosophical poems, such as John Milton's *Paradise Lost* (1667, 1674).

Bourgeois novel: A novel in which the values, the preoccupations, and the accoutrements of middle-class or bourgeois life are given particular prominence. The heyday of the genre was the nineteenth century, when novelists as varied as Jane Austen, Honoré de Balzac, and Anthony Trollope both criticized and unreflectingly transmitted the assumptions of the rising middle class.

Burlesque: A work that by imitating attitudes, styles, institutions, and people aims to amuse. Burlesque differs from satire in that it aims to ridicule simply for the sake of amusement rather than for political or social change.

Capa y espada: Spanish for "cloak and sword." A term referring to the Spanish theater of the sixteenth and seventeenth centuries dealing with love and intrigue among the aristocracy. The greatest practitioners were Lope de Vega Carpio and Pedro Calderón de la Barca. The term *comedia de ingenio* is also used.

Catharsis: A term from Aristotle's *De poetica* (c. 334-323 B.C.; *Poetics*) referring to the purgation of the emotions of pity and fear in the spectator aroused by the actions of the tragic hero. The meaning and the operation of the concept have been a source of great, and unresolved, critical debate.

Celtic romance: Gaelic Celts invaded Ireland in about 350 B.C.; their epic stories and romances date from this period until about A.D. 450. The romances are marked by a strong sense of the Otherworld and of supernatural happenings. The Celtic romance tradition influenced the poetry of William Butler Yeats.

Celtic Twilight: Sometimes used synonymously with the term Irish Renaissance, which was a movement beginning in the late nineteenth century which attempted to build a national literature by drawing on Ireland's literary and cultural history. The term, however, which is taken from a book by William Butler Yeats titled *The Celtic Twilight* (1893), sometimes has a negative connotation. It is used to refer to some early volumes by Yeats, which have been called self-indulgent. The poet Algernon Charles Swinburne said that the Celtic Twilight manner "puts fever and fancy in the place of reason and imagination."

Chamber plays: Refers to four plays written in 1907 by the Swedish dramatist August Strindberg. The plays are modeled on the form of chamber music, consisting of motif and variations, to evoke a mood or atmosphere (in these cases, a very sombre one). There is no protagonist but a small group of equally important characters.

Character: A personage appearing in any literary or dramatic work. Characters can be presented with the depth and complexity of real people (sometimes called "round" characters) or as stylized functions of the plot ("flat" characters).

Chorus: Originally a group of singers and dancers in religious festivals, the chorus evolved into the dramatic element that reflected the opinions of the masses or commented on the action in Greek drama. In its most developed form, the chorus consisted of fifteen members: seven reciting the strophe, seven reciting the antistrophe, and the leader interacting with the actors. The chorus has been used in all periods of drama, including the modern period.

Classicism: A literary stance or value system consciously based on the example of classical Greek and Roman literature. While the term is applied to an enormous diversity of artists in many different periods and in many different national literatures, it generally denotes a cluster of values including formal discipline, restrained expression, reverence of tradition, and an objective, rather than subjective, orientation. Often contrasted with Romanticism. *See also* Romanticism.

Comédie-Française: The first state theater of France, composed of the company of actors established by Molière in 1658. The company took the name *Comédie-Française* in 1680. Today, it is officially known as the *Theatre Français* (*Salle Richelieu*).

Comedy: Generally, a lighter form of drama (as contrasted with tragedy) that aims chiefly to amuse and ends happily. The comic effect typically arises from the recognition of some incongruity of speech, action, or character development. The comic range extends from coarse, physical humor (called low comedy) to a more subtle, intellectual humor (called high comedy).

Comedy of manners: A form of comedy that arose during the seventeenth century, dealing with the intrigues (particularly the amorous intrigues) of sophisticated, witty members of the upper classes. The appeal of these plays is primarily intellectual, depending as they do on quick-witted dialogue and clever language. For examples, see the plays of Restoration dramatists William Congreve, Sir George Etherege, and William Wycherley. *See also* Restoration comedy/drama.

Commedia dell'arte: Dramatic comedy performed by troupes of professional actors, which became popular in the mid-sixteenth century in Italy. The troupes were rather small, consisting of perhaps a dozen actors who performed stock roles in mask and improvised on skeletal scenarios. The tradition of the *commedia*, or masked comedy, was influential into the seventeenth century and still exerts some influence.

Conceit: A type of metaphor, the conceit is used for comparisons that are highly intellectualized. When T. S. Eliot, for example, says that winding streets are like a tedious argument of insidious intent, there is no clear connection between the two, so the reader must apply abstract logic to fill in the missing links.

Conversation poem: Conversation poems are chiefly associated with the poetry of Samuel Taylor Coleridge. These poems all display a relaxed, informal style, quiet settings, and a circular structure—the poem returns to where it began, after an intervening meditation has yielded some insight into the speaker's situation.

Cubism: A term borrowed from Cubist painters. In literature, cubism is a style of poetry, such as that of E. E. Cummings, Kenneth Rexroth, and Archibald MacLeish, which first fragments an experience, then rearranges its elements into some new artistic entity.

Dactyl: The dactylic foot, or dactyl, is formed of a stress followed by two unstressed syllables, as in the words "Washington" and "manikin." "After the pangs of a desperate lover" is an example of a dactylic line.

Dadaism: Dadaism arose in France during World War I as a radical protest in art and literature against traditional institutions and values. Part of its strategy was the use of infantile, nonsensical language. After World War I, when Dadaism was combined with the ideas of Sigmund Freud, it gave rise to the Surrealist movement.

Decadence: The period of decline that heralds the ending of a great age. The period in English dramatic history immediately following William Shakespeare is said to be decadent, and the term "Decadents" is applied to a group of late-nineteenth and early twentieth century writers who searched for new literary and artistic forms as the Victorian Age came to a close.

Detective story: The "classic" detective story (or "mystery") is a highly formalized and logically structured mode of fiction in which the focus is on a crime solved by a detective through interpretation of evidence and clever reasoning. Many modern practitioners of the genre, however, such as Raymond Chandler, Patricia Highsmith, and Ross Macdonald, have placed less emphasis on the puzzlelike qualities of the detective story and have focused instead on characterization, theme, and other elements of mainstream fiction. The form was first developed in short fiction by Edgar Allan Poe; Jorge Luis Borges has also used the convention in short stories.

Dialectic: A philosophical term meaning the art of examining opinions or ideas logically. The dialectic method of Georg Wilhelm Friedrich Hegel and Karl Marx was based on a contradiction of opposites (thesis and antithesis) and their resolution (synthesis). In literary criticism, the term has sometimes been used by Marxist critics to refer to the structure and dynamics of a literary work in its sociological context.

Dialogue: Speech exchanged between characters, or even, in a looser sense, the thoughts of a single character. Dialogue serves to characterize, to further the plot, to establish conflict, and to express thematic ideas.

***Doppelgänger*:** A double or counterpart of a person, sometimes endowed with ghostly qualities. A fictional *Doppelgänger* often reflects a suppressed side of his personality, as in Fyodor Dostoevski's novella *Dvoynik* (1846; *The Double*, 1917) and the short stories of E. T. A. Hoffmann. Isaac Bashevis Singer and Jorge Luis Borges, among other modern writers, have also employed the *Doppelgänger* with striking effect.

Drama: Generally speaking, any work designed to be represented on a stage by actors (Aristotle defined drama as "the imitation of an action"). More specifically, the term has come to signify a play of a serious nature and intent that may end either happily (comedy) or unhappily (tragedy).

Dramatic irony: A situation in a play or a narrative in which the audience knows something that the character does not. The irony lies in the different meaning that the character's words or actions have for himself and for the audience. A common device in classical Greek drama. Sophocles' *Oidipous Tyrannos* (429 B.C.; *Oedipus Tyrannus*) is an example of extended dramatic irony.

Dramatic monologue: In dramatic monologue, the narrator addresses a persona who never speaks but whose presence greatly influences what the narrator tells the reader. The principal reason for writing in dramatic monologue is to control the speech of the major persona by the implied reaction of the silent one. The effect is one of continuing change and often surprise. The technique is especially useful for revealing characters slowly and for involving the reader as another silent participant.

Dramatic verse: Poetry that employs dramatic form or technique, such as dialogue or conflict, to achieve its effects. The term is used to refer to dramatic monologue, drama written in verse, and closet dramas.

Dramatis personae: The characters in a play. Often, a printed listing defining the characters and specifying their relationships.

Dream vision: An allegorical form common in the Middle Ages, in which the narrator or a character falls asleep and dreams a dream that becomes the actual framed story.

Dystopian/Utopian novel: A dystopian novel takes some existing trend or theory in present-day society and extends it into a fictional world of the future, where the trend has become more fully manifested, with unpleasant results. Aldous Huxley's *Brave New World* (1932) is an example. The utopian novel is the opposite: It presents an ideal society. The first utopian novel was Sir Thomas More's *Utopia* (1516).

Elegy: A long, rhymed, formal poem whose subject is meditation upon death or a lamentable theme. The pastoral elegy uses a pastoral scene to express grief at the loss of a friend or important person. *See also* Pastoral.

Elizabethan Age: Of or referring to the reign of Queen Elizabeth I of England, lasting from 1558 to 1603, a period of important developments and achievements in the arts in England, particularly in poetry and drama. The era included such literary figures as Edmund Spenser, Christopher Marlowe, William Shakespeare, and Ben Jonson. Sometimes referred to as the English Renaissance.

English novel: The first fully realized English novel was Samuel Richardson's *Pamela* (1740-1741). The genre took firm hold in the second half of the eighteenth century, with the work of Daniel Defoe, Henry Fielding, and Tobias Smollett, and reached its full flowering in the nineteenth century, in which great novelists such as Jane Austen, Charles Dickens, William Makepeace Thackeray, Anthony

Trollope, Thomas Hardy, and George Eliot produced sweeping portraits of the whole range of English life in the period.

Enlightenment: A period in Western European cultural history that began in the seventeenth century and culminated in the eighteenth. The chief characteristic of Enlightenment thinkers was their belief in the virtue of human reason, which they believed was banishing former superstitious and ignorant ways and leading to an ideal condition of human life. The Enlightenment coincides with the rise of the scientific method.

Epic: Although this term usually refers to a long narrative poem that presents the exploits of a central figure of high position, the term is also used to designate a long novel that has the style or structure usually associated with an epic. In this sense, for example, Herman Melville's *Moby Dick* (1851) and James Joyce's *Ulysses* (1922) may be called epics.

Epigram: Originally meaning an inscription, an epigram is a short, pointed poem, often expressing humor and satire. In English literature, the form flourished from the Renaissance through the eighteenth century, in the work of poets such as John Donne, Ben Jonson, and Alexander Pope. The term also refers to a concise and witty expression in prose, as in the plays of Oscar Wilde.

Epiphany: Literally, an epiphany is an appearance of a god or supernatural being. The term is used in literary criticism to signify any moment of heightened awareness, or flash of transcendental insight, when an ordinary object or scene is suddenly transformed into something that possesses eternal significance. Especially noteworthy examples are found in the works of James Joyce.

Epistle: The word means "letter," but epistle is used to refer to a literary form rather than a private composition, usually written in dignified style and addressed to a group. The most famous examples are the epistles in the New Testament.

Epistolary novel: A work of fiction in which the narrative is carried forward by means of letters written by the characters. Epistolary novels were especially popular in the eighteenth century. Examples include Samuel Richardson's *Pamela* (1740-1741) and *Clarissa* (1747-1748).

Epithet: An adjective or adjectival phrase that expresses a special characteristic of a person or thing. "Hideous night," "devouring time," and "sweet silent thought" are epithets that appear in William Shakespeare's sonnets.

Essay: A brief prose work, usually on a single topic, that expresses the personal point of view of the author. The essay is usually addressed to a general audience and attempts to persuade the reader to accept the author's ideas.

Everyman: The central character in the work by the same name, the most famous of the English medieval morality plays. It tells of how Everyman is summoned by Death and of the parts played in his journey by characters named Fellowship, Cousin, Kindred, Goods, Knowledge, Confession, Beauty, Strength, Discretion, Five Wits, and Good Deeds. Everyman has proved lastingly popular; there have been many productions even in the twentieth century. More generally, the term means the typical, ordinary person.

Existentialism: A philosophy or attitude of mind that has gained wide currency in religious and artistic thought since the end of World War II. Typical concerns of existential writers are humankind's estrangement from society, its awareness that the world is meaningless, and its recognition that one must turn from external props to the self. The works of Jean-Paul Sartre and Franz Kafka provide examples of existentialist beliefs.

Experimental novel: The term is associated with novelists such as Dorothy Richardson, Virginia Woolf, and James Joyce in England, who experimented with the form of the novel, using in particular the stream-of-consciousness technique.

Expressionism: Beginning in German theater at the start of the twentieth century, expressionism became the dominant movement in the decade following World War I. It abandoned realism and relied on a conscious distortion of external reality in order to portray the world as it is "viewed emotionally." The movement spread to fiction and poetry. Expressionism influenced the novels of Franz Kafka and James Joyce.

Fable: One of the oldest narrative forms, usually taking the form of an analogy in which animals or inanimate objects speak to illustrate a moral lesson. The most famous examples are the fables of Aesop, who used the form orally in 600 B.C.

Fabliau: A short narrative poem, popular in medieval French literature and during the English Middle Ages. Fabliaux were usually realistic in subject matter and bawdy; they made a point of satirizing the weaknesses and foibles of human beings. Perhaps the most famous are Geoffrey Chaucer's "The Miller's Tale" and "The Reeve's Tale."

Fairy tale: A form of folktale in which supernatural events or characters are prominent. Fairy tales usually depict a realm of reality beyond that of the natural world in which the laws of the natural world are suspended.

Fantasy: A literary form that makes a deliberate break with reality. Fantasy literature may use supernatural or fairy-tale events in which the ordinary commonsense laws of the everyday world do not operate. The setting may be unreal. J. R. R. Tolkien's fantasy trilogy, *The Lord of the Rings* (1955), is one of the best-known examples of the genre.

Farce: From the Latin *farcire*, meaning "to stuff." Originally an insertion into established Church liturgy in the Middle Ages, farce later became the term for specifically comic scenes inserted into early liturgical drama. The term has come to refer to any play that evokes laughter by such low-comedy devices as physical humor, rough wit, and ridiculous and improbable situations and characters.

Femme fatale: The "fatal woman" is an archetype that appears in myth, folklore, religion, and literature. Often she is presented as a temptress or a witch who ensnares, and attempts to destroy, her male victim. A very common figure in Romanticism, the fatal woman often appears in twentieth century American literature.

Figurative language: Any use of language that departs from the usual or ordinary meaning to gain a poetic or otherwise special effect. Figurative language embodies various figures of speech, such as irony, metaphor, simile.

First person: A point of view in which the narrator of a story or poem addresses the reader directly, often using the pronoun "I," thereby allowing the reader direct access to the narrator's thoughts.

Folklore: The traditions, customs, and beliefs of a people expressed in nonliterary form. Folklore includes myths, legends, fairy tales, riddles, proverbs, charms, spells, and ballads and is usually transmitted through word of mouth. Many literary works contain motifs that can be traced to folklore.

Foreshadowing: A device used to create suspense or dramatic irony by indicating through suggestion what will take place in the future. The aim is to prepare the reader for the action that follows.

Frame story: A story that provides a framework for another story (or stories) told within it. The form is ancient and is used by Geoffrey Chaucer in *The Canterbury Tales* (1387-1400). In modern literature, the technique has been used by Henry James in *The Turn of the Screw* (1898), Joseph Conrad in *Heart of Darkness* (serial, 1899; book, 1902), and John Barth in *Lost in the Funhouse* (1968).

Free verse: Verse that does not conform to any traditional convention, such as meter, rhyme, or form. All poetry must have some pattern of some kind, however, and there is rhythm in free verse, but it does not follow the strict rules of meter. Often the pattern relies on repetition and parallel construction.

Genre: A type or category of literature, such as tragedy, novel, memoir, poem, or essay; a genre has a particular set of conventions and expectations.

German Romanticism: Germany was the first European country in which the Romantic movement took firm grip. Poets Novalis and Ludwig Tieck, philosopher Friedrich Wilhelm Joseph Schelling, and literary theorists Friedrich and August Wilhelm Schlegel were well established in Jena from about 1797, and they were followed, in the second decade of the nineteenth century, by the Heidelberg group, including novelist and short-story writer E. T. A. Hoffmann and poet Heinrich Heine.

Gnomic: Aphoristic poetry, such as the wisdom literature of the Bible, which deals with ethical questions. The term "gnomic poets" is applied to a group of Greek poets of the sixth and seventh century B.C.

Gothic novel: A form of fiction developed in the late eighteenth century that focuses on horror and the supernatural. An example is Mary Shelley's *Frankenstein* (1818). In modern literature, the gothic genre can be found in the fiction of Truman Capote.

Grand Tour: Fashionable during the eighteenth century in England, the Grand Tour was a two- to three-year journey through Europe during which the young aristocracy and prosperous, educated middle classes of England deepened their knowledge of the origins and centers of Western civilization. The tour took a standard route; Rome and Naples were usually considered the highlights.

Grotesque: Characterized by a breakup of the everyday world by mysterious forces, the form differs from fantasy in that the reader is not sure whether to react with humor or with horror. Examples include the stories of E. T. A. Hoffmann and Franz Kafka.

Hagiography: Strictly defined, hagiography refers to the lives of the saints (the Greek word *hagios* means "sacred"), but the term is also used in a more popular sense, to describe any biography that grossly overpraises its subject and ignores his or her faults.

Heroic couplet: A pair of rhyming iambic pentameter lines traditionally used in epic poetry; a heroic couplet often serves as a self-contained witticism or pithy observation.

Historical fiction: A novel that depicts past historical events, usually public in nature, and that features real, as well as fictional, people. Sir Walter Scott's Waverley novels established the basic type, but the relationship between fiction and history in the form varies greatly depending on the practitioner.

Hubris: Greek term for "insolence" or "pride," the characteristic or emotion in the tragic hero of ancient Greek drama that causes the reversal of his fortune, leading him to transgress moral codes or ignore warnings.

Humanism: A human-centered, rather than God-centered, view of the universe. In the Renaissance, Humanism devoted itself to the revival of classical culture. A reaction against medieval Scholasticism, Humanism oriented itself toward secular concerns and applied classical ideas to theology, government, literature, and education. In literature, the main virtues were seen to be restraint, form, and imitation of the classics. *See also* Renaissance.

Iambic pentameter: A metrical line consisting of five feet, each foot consisting of one unstressed syllable followed by one stressed syllable: "So long as men can breathe or eyes can see." Iambic pentameter is one of the commonest forms of English poetry.

Imagery: Often defined as the verbal stimulation of sensory perception. Although the word betrays a visual bias, imagery, in fact, calls on all five senses. In its simplest form, imagery re-creates a physical sensation in a clear, literal manner; it becomes more complex when a poet employs metaphor and other figures of speech to re-create experience.

Impressionism: A late nineteenth century movement composed of a group of painters including Paul Cézanne, Édouard Manet, Claude Monet, and Pierre-Auguste Renoir, who aimed in their work to suggest the impression made on the artist by a scene rather than to reproduce it objectively. The term has also been applied to French Symbolist poets such as Paul Verlaine and Stéphane Mallarmé, and to writers who use the stream-of-consciousness technique, such as James Joyce and Virginia Woolf.

Irony: Recognition of the difference between real and apparent meaning. Verbal irony is a rhetorical trope wherein *x* is uttered and "not *x*" is meant. In the New Criticism, irony, the poet's recognition of incongruities, was thought to be the master trope in that it was essential to the production of paradox, complexity, and ambiguity.

Jacobean: Of or pertaining to the reign of James I of England, who ruled from 1603 to 1623, the period immediately following the death of Elizabeth I, which saw tremendous literary activity in poetry and drama. Many writers who achieved fame during the Elizabethan Age, such as William Shakespeare, Ben Jonson, and John Donne, were still active. Other dramatists, such as John Webster and Cyril Tourneur, achieved success almost entirely during the Jacobean era.

Jungian psychoanalysis: Refers to the analytical psychology of the Swiss psychiatrist Carl Jung. Jung's significance for literature is that, through his concept of the collective unconscious, he identified many archetypes and archetypal patterns that recur in myth, fairy tale, and literature and are also experienced in dreams.

Kafkaesque: Refers to any grotesque or nightmare world in which an isolated individual, surrounded by an unfeeling and alien world, feels himself to be caught up in an endless maze that is dragging him down to destruction. The term is a reference to the works of Austrian novelist and short-story writer Franz Kafka.

Leitmotif: From the German, meaning "leading motif." Any repetition—of a word, phrase, situation, or idea—that occurs within a single work or group of related works.

Limerick: A comic five-line poem employing an anapestic base and rhyming *aabba*, in which the third and fourth lines are shorter (usually five syllables each) than the first, second, and last lines, which are usually eight syllables each.

Linear plot: A plot that has unity of action and proceeds from beginning to middle to end without flashbacks or subplots, thus satisfying Aristotle's criterion that a plot should be a continuous sequence.

Literary criticism: The study and evaluation of works of literature. Theoretical criticism sets forth general principles for interpretation. Practical criticism offers interpretations of particular works or authors.

Lyric poetry: Lyric poetry developed when music was accompanied by words, and although the "lyrics" were later separated from the music, the characteristics of lyric poetry have been shaped by the constraints of music. Lyric poems are short, more adaptable to metrical variation, and usually personal compared with the cultural functions of narrative poetry. Lyric poetry sings of the self; it explores deeply personal feelings about life.

Magical Realism: Imaginary or fantastic scenes and occurrences presented in a meticulously realistic style. The term has been applied to the fiction of Gabriel

García Márquez, Jorge Luis Borges, Günter Grass, John Fowles, and Salman Rushdie.

Masque: A courtly entertainment popular during the first half of the seventeenth century in England. It was a sumptuous spectacle including music, dance, and lavish costumes and scenery. Masques often dealt with mythological or pastoral subjects, and the dramatic action often took second place to pure spectacle.

Melodrama: Originally a drama with music (*melos* is Greek for "song"). By the early nineteenth century, it had come to mean a play in which characters are clearly either virtuous or evil and are pitted against one another in suspenseful, often sensational situations. The term took on a pejorative meaning, which it retains: any dramatic work characterized by stereotyped characters and sensational, improbable situations.

Metafiction: Refers to fiction that manifests a reflexive tendency, such as Vladimir Nabokov's *Pale Fire* (1962), and John Fowles's *The French Lieutenant's Woman* (1969). The emphasis is on the loosening of the work's illusion of reality to expose the reality of its illusion. Such terms as "irrealism," "postmodernist fiction," and "antifiction" are also used to refer to this type of fiction. *See also* Postmodernism.

Metaphor: A figure of speech in which two dissimilar objects are imaginatively identified (rather than merely compared) on the assumption that they share one or more qualities. The term is often used in modern criticism in a wider sense, to identify analogies of all kinds in literature, painting, and film.

Metaphysical poetry: A type of poetry that stresses the intellectual over the emotional; it is marked by irony, paradox, and striking comparisons of dissimilar things, the latter frequently being farfetched to the point of eccentricity. Usually used to designate a group of seventeenth century English poets, including John Donne, George Herbert, Andrew Marvell, and Thomas Traherne.

Meter: Meter is the pattern of language when it is forced into a line of poetry. All language has rhythm, but when that rhythm is organized and regulated in the line so as to affect the meaning and emotional response to the words, then the rhythm has been refined into meter. The meter is determined by the number of syllables in a line and by the relationship between them.

Mock epic: A literary form that burlesques the epic by taking a trivial subject and treating it in a grand style, using all the conventions of epic, such as invocation to the deity, long and boastful speeches of the heroes, and supernatural machinery. Alexander Pope's *The Rape of the Lock* (1712, 1714) is probably the finest example in English literature. The term is synonymous with mock heroic. *See also* Mock hero.

Mock hero: The hero of a mock epic. *See also* Mock epic.

Modernism: A term used to describe the characteristic aspects of literature and art between World War I and World War II. Influenced by Friedrich Nietzsche, Karl Marx, and Sigmund Freud, modernism embodied a lack of faith in Western civilization and culture. In poetry, fragmentation, discontinuity, and irony were common; in fiction, chronological disruption, linguistic innovation, and the stream-of-consciousness technique; in theater, expressionism and Surrealism.

Morality play: A dramatic form in the late Middle Ages and the Renaissance containing allegorical figures (most often virtues and vices) that are typically involved in the struggle over a person's soul. The anonymously written *Everyman* (1508) is one of the most famous medieval examples of this form.

Motif: An incident, situation, or device that occurs frequently in literature. Motif can also refer to particular words, images, and phrases that are repeated frequently in a single work. In this sense, motif is the same as leitmotif. Motif is similar to theme, although the latter is usually more abstract.

Myth: An anonymous traditional story, often involving supernatural beings, or the interaction between gods and humans, and dealing with the basic questions of how the world and human society came to be. Myth is an important term in contemporary literary criticism. The critic Northrop Frye, for example, has said that "the typical forms of myth become the conventions and genres of literature." He means that the genres of comedy, romance, tragedy, and irony (satire) correspond to seasonal myths of spring, summer, autumn, and winter.

Narrative: An account in prose or verse of an event or series of events, whether real or imagined.

Narrator: The character who recounts the narrative. There are many different types of narrator. The first-person narrator is a character in the story and can be recognized by his use of "I"; third-person narrators may be limited or omniscient. In the former, the narrator confines himself to knowledge of the minds and emotions of one or at most a few characters. In the latter, the narrator knows everything, seeing into the minds of all the characters. Rarely, second-person narration may be used (an example can be found in Edna O'Brien's *A Pagan Place*, published in 1970).

Naturalism: The application of the principles of scientific determinism to fiction. Although it usually refers more to the choice of subject matter than to technical conventions, conventions associated with the movement center on the author's attempt to be precise and objective in description and detail, regardless of whether the events described are sordid or shocking. Naturalism flourished in England, France, and America in the late nineteenth and early twentieth centuries.

Neoclassicism: A term used to describe the classicism that dominated English literature from the Restoration to the late eighteenth century. Modeling itself on the literature of ancient Greece and Rome, neoclassicism exalted the virtues of proportion, unity, harmony, grace, decorum, taste, manners, and restraint. It valued realism and reason over imagination and emotion. *See also* Rationalism, Realism.

Neorealism: A movement in modern Italian literature, extending from about 1930 to 1955. Neorealism was shaped by opposition to Fascism, and by World War II and the Resistance. Neorealist literature therefore exhibited a strong concern with social issues and was marked by pessimism regarding the human condition. Its practitioners sought to overcome the gap between literature and the masses, and its subject matter was frequently drawn from lower-class life. Neorealism is associated preeminently with the work of Italo Calvino.

Nonsense literature/verse: Nonsense verse, such as that written by Edward Lear and Lewis Carroll, makes use of invented words that have no meaning, portmanteau words, and so-called macaroni verse, in which words from different languages are mingled. The verse holds the attention because of its strong rhythms, appealing sounds, and, occasionally, the mysterious atmosphere that it creates.

Novel of education: See *Bildungsroman*.

Novel of ideas: A novel in which the characters, plot, and dialogue serve to develop some controlling idea or to present the clash of ideas. Aldous Huxley's *Eyeless in Gaza* (1936) is a good example.

Novel of manners: The classic example of the form might be the novels of Jane Austen, wherein the customs and conventions of a social group of a particular time and place are realistically, and often satirically, portrayed.

Novella: An Italian term meaning "a little new thing" that now refers to that form of fiction longer than a short story and shorter than a novel.

Objective correlative: A key concept in modern formalist criticism, coined by T. S. Eliot in *The Sacred Wood* (1920). An objective correlative is a situation, an event, or an object that, when presented or described in a literary work, expresses a particular emotion and serves as a precise formula by which the same emotion can be evoked in the reader.

Ode: The ode is a lyric poem that treats a unified subject with elevated emotion, usually ending with a satisfactory resolution. There is no set form for the ode, but it must be long enough to build intense emotional response. Often the ode will address itself to some omnipotent source and will assume a spiritual hue.

Oxford Movement: A reform movement in the Church of England that began in 1833, led by John Henry (later Cardinal) Newman. The Oxford Movement aimed to combat liberalism and the decline of the role of faith in the Church and to restore it to its former ideals. It was attacked for advocating what some saw as Catholic doctrines; as a result, Newman left the Church of England and became a Roman Catholic in 1845.

Panegyric: A formal speech or writing in praise of a particular person or achievement; a eulogy. The form dates back to classical times; the term is now often used in a derogatory sense.

Parable: A short, simple, and usually allegorical story that teaches a moral lesson. In the West, the most famous parables are those told in the Gospels by Christ.

Parody: A literary work that imitates or burlesques another work or author, for the purpose of ridicule. Twentieth century parodists include E. B. White and James Thurber.

Pastoral: The term derives from the Latin "pastor," meaning "shepherd." Pastoral is a literary mode that depicts the country life in an idealized way; it originated in classical literature and was a popular form in English literature from 1550 to 1750. Notable pastoral poems include John Milton's "Lycidas" and Percy Bysshe Shelley's *Adonais*.

Pathetic fallacy: The ascribing of human characteristics or feelings to inanimate objects. The term was coined by John Ruskin in 1856, who disapproved of it, but it is now used without any pejorative sense.

Persona: *Persona* means literally "mask": It is the self created by the author and through whom the narrative is told. The persona is not to be identified with the author, even when the two may seem to resemble each other. The narrative persona in Lord Byron's *Don Juan* (1819-1824, 1826), for example, may express many sentiments of which Byron would have approved, but he is nonetheless a fictional creation who is distinct from the author.

Personification: A figure of speech that ascribes human qualities to abstractions or inanimate objects.

Petrarchan sonnet: Named after Petrarch, a fourteenth century Italian poet, who perfected the form, which is also known as the Italian sonnet. It is divided into an octave, in which the subject matter, which may be a problem, a doubt, a reflection, or some other issue, is raised and elaborated, and a sestet, in which the problem is resolved. The rhyme scheme is usually *abba abba ced cde*, *cdc cdc*, or *cde dce*.

Philosophical dualism: A theory that the universe is explicable in terms of two basic, conflicting entities, such as good and evil, mind and matter, or the physical and the spiritual.

Picaresque: A form of fiction that revolves around a central rogue figure, or picaro, who usually tells his own story. The plot structure of a picaresque novel is usually episodic, and the episodes usually focus on how the picaro lives by his wits. The classic example is Henry Fielding's *The History of Tom Jones, a Foundling* (1749).

Pindaric ode: Odes that imitate the form of those composed by the ancient Greek poet Pindar. A Pindaric ode consists of a strophe, followed by an antistrophe of the same structure, followed by an epode. This pattern may be repeated several times in the ode. In English poetry, Thomas Gray's "The Bard" is an example of a Pindaric ode.

Play: A literary work that is written to be performed by actors who speak the dialogue, impersonate the characters, and perform the appropriate actions. Usually, a play is performed on a stage, and an audience witnesses it.

Play-within-the-play: A play or dramatic fragment performed as a scene or scenes within a larger drama, typically performed or viewed by the characters of the larger drama.

Plot: Plot refers to how the author arranges the material not only to create the sequence of events in a play or story but also to suggest how those events are connected in a cause-and-effect relationship. There are a great variety of plot patterns, each of which is designed to create a particular effect.

Poem: A unified composition that uses the rhythms and sounds of language, as well as devices such as metaphor, to communicate emotions and experiences to the reader.

Poet laureate: The official poet of England, appointed for life by the English sovereign and expected to compose poems for various public occasions. The first official laureate was John Dryden in the seventeenth century. In the eighteenth century, the laureateship was given to a succession of mediocrities, but since the appointment of William Wordsworth in 1843, the office has generally been regarded as a substantial honor.

Polemic: A work that forcefully argues an opinion, usually on a controversial religious, political, or economic issue, in opposition to other opinions. John Milton's *Areopagitica* (1644) is one of the best known examples in English literature.

Postmodernism: The term is loosely applied to various artistic movements that have succeeded modernism, particularly since 1965. Postmodernist literature is experimental in form and reflects a fragmented world in which order and meaning are absent.

Pre-Raphaelitism: Refers to a group of nineteenth century English painters and writers, including Dante Gabriel Rossetti, Christina Rossetti, and William Morris. The Pre-Raphaelites were so called because they rebelled against conventional methods of painting and wanted to revert to what they regarded as the simple spirit of painting that existed before Raphael, particularly in its adherence to nature; they rejected all artificial embellishments. Pre-Raphaelite poetry made much use of symbolism and sensuousness, and showed an interest in the medieval and the supernatural.

Prose poem: A type of poem ranging in length from a few lines to three or four pages; most occupy a page or less. The distinguishing feature of the prose poem is its typography: it appears on the page like prose, with no line breaks. Many prose poems employ rhythmic repetition and other poetic devices not found in prose, but others do not; there is enormous variety in the genre.

Protagonist: Originally, in the Greek drama, the "first actor," who played the leading role. The term has come to signify the most important character in a drama or story. It is not unusual for there to be more than one protagonist in a work.

Proverb: A wise and pithy saying, authorship unknown, that reflects some observation about life. Proverbs are usually passed on through word of mouth, although they may also be written, as for example, the Book of Proverbs in the Bible.

Psychological novel: Once described as an interpretation of "the invisible life," the psychological novel is a form of fiction in which character, especially the inner life of characters, is the primary focus, rather than action. The form has characterized much of the work of Henry James, James Joyce, Virginia Woolf, and William Faulkner. *See also* Psychological realism.

Psychological realism: A type of realism that tries to reproduce the complex psychological motivations behind human behavior; writers in the late nineteenth century and early twentieth century were particularly influenced by Sigmund Freud's theories. *See also* Psychological novel.

Pun: A pun occurs when words with similar pronunciations have entirely different meanings. The result may be a surprise recognition of an unusual or striking connection, or, more often, a humorously accidental connection.

Quest: An archetypal theme identified by mythologist Joseph Campbell and found in many literary works. Campbell describes the heroic quest in three fundamental stages: departure (leaving the familiar world), initiation (encountering adventures and obstacles), and return (bringing home a boon to transform society).

Rabelaisian: The term is a reference to the sixteenth century French satirist and humorist François Rabelais. "Rabelaisian" is now used to refer to any humorous or satirical writing that is bawdy, coarse, or very down to earth.

Rationalism: A system of thought that seeks truth through the exercise of reason rather than by means of emotional response or revelation, or traditional authority. In literature, rationalism is associated with eighteenth century neoclassicism. *See also* Neoclassicism.

Realism: A literary technique in which the primary convention is to render an illusion of fidelity to external reality. Realism is often identified as the primary method of the novel form; the realist movement in the late nineteenth century coincided with the full development of the novel form.

Renaissance: The term means "rebirth" and refers to a period in European cultural history from the fourteenth to the early seventeenth century, although dates differ widely from country to country. The Renaissance produced an unprecedented flowering of the arts of painting, sculpture, architecture, and literature. The period is often said to mark the transition from the Middle Ages to the modern world. The questing, individualistic spirit that characterized the age was stimulated by an increase in classical learning by scholars known as Humanists, by the Protestant Reformation, by the development of printing, which created a wide market for books, by new theories of astronomy, and by the development of other sciences that saw natural laws at work where the Middle Ages had seen occult forces. *See also* Humanism.

Restoration comedy/drama: The restoration of the Stuart dynasty brought Charles II to the English throne in 1660. In literature, the Restoration period extends from 1660 to 1700. Restoration comedy is a comedy of manners, which centers around complicated plots full of the amorous intrigues of the fashionable upper classes. The humor is witty, but the view of human nature is cynical. Restoration dramatists include William Congreve, Sir George Etherege, and William Wycherley. In serious, or heroic, drama, the leading playwright was John Dryden. *See also* Comedy of manners.

Roman à clef: A fiction wherein actual persons, often celebrities of some sort, are thinly disguised. Lady Caroline Lamb's *Glenarvon* (1816), for example, contains a thinly veiled portrait of Lord Byron, and the character Mark Rampion in Aldous Huxley's *Point Counter Point* (1928) strongly resembles D. H. Lawrence.

Romance: Originally, any work written in Old French. In the Middle Ages, romances were about knights and their adventures. In modern times, the term has also been used to describe a type of prose fiction in which, unlike the novel, realism plays little part. Prose romances often give expression to the quest for transcendent truths.

Romanticism: A movement of the late eighteenth century and the nineteenth century that exalted individualism over collectivism, revolution over conservatism, innovation over tradition, imagination over reason, and spontaneity over restraint. Romanticism regarded art as self-expression; it strove to heal the cleavage between object and subject and expressed a longing for the infinite in all things. It stressed the innate goodness of human beings and the evils of the institutions that would stultify human creativity. The major English Romantic poets are William Blake, Lord Byron, Samuel Taylor Coleridge, John Keats, Percy Bysshe Shelley, and William Wordsworth.

Satire: A form of literature that employs the comedic devices of wit, irony, and exaggeration to expose, ridicule, and condemn human folly, vice, and stupidity. Justifying satire, Alexander Pope wrote that "nothing moves strongly but satire, and those who are ashamed of nothing else are so of being ridiculous."

Scene: A division of action within an act (some plays are divided only into scenes instead of acts). Sometimes, scene division indicates a change of setting or locale; sometimes, it simply indicates the entrances and exits of characters.

Science fiction: Fiction in which real or imagined scientific developments or certain givens (such as physical laws, psychological principles, or social conditions) form the basis of an imaginative projection, frequently into the future. Classic examples are the works of H. G. Wells and Jules Verne.

Sentimental novel: A form of fiction popular in the eighteenth century in which emotionalism and optimism are the primary characteristics. The best-known examples are Samuel Richardson's *Pamela* (1740-1741) and Oliver Goldsmith's *The Vicar of Wakefield* (1766).

Shakespearean sonnet: So named because William Shakespeare was the greatest English sonneteer, whose ranks also included the earl of Surrey and Thomas Wyatt. The Shakespearean sonnet consists of three quatrains and a concluding couplet, rhyming *abab cdcd efef gg*. The beginning of the third quatrain marks a turn in the argument.

Short story: A concise work of fiction, shorter than a novella, that is usually more concerned with mood, effect, or a single event than with plot or extensive characterization.

Simile: A type of metaphor in which two things are compared. It can usually be recognized by the use of the words "like," "as," "appears," or "seems."

Skaz: A term used in Russian criticism to describe a narrative technique that presents an oral narrative of a lowbrow speaker.

Soliloquy: An extended speech delivered by a character alone on stage, unheard by other characters. Soliloquy is a form of monologue, and it typically reveals the intimate thoughts and emotions of the speaker.

Song: A lyric poem, usually short, simple, and with rhymed stanzas, set to music.

Sonnet: A traditional poetic form that is almost always composed of fourteen lines of rhymed iambic pentameter; a turning point usually divides the poem into two parts, with the first part (octave) presenting a situation and the second part (sestet) reflecting on it. The main sonnet forms are the Petrarchan sonnet and the English (sometimes called Shakespearean) sonnet.

Stanza: When lines of poetry are meant to be taken as a unit, and the unit recurs throughout the poem, that unit is called a stanza; a four-line unit, a quatrain, is one common stanza. Others include couplet, *ottava rima*, and the Spenserian stanza.

Story line: The story line of a work of fiction differs from the plot. Story is merely the events that happen; plot is how those events are arranged by the author to suggest a cause-and-effect relationship. *See also* Plot.

Stream of consciousness: A narrative technique used in modern fiction by which an author tries to embody the total range of consciousness of a character, without any authorial comment or explanation. Sensations, thoughts, memories, and associations pour forth in an uninterrupted, prerational, and prelogical flow. For examples, see James Joyce's *Ulysses* (1922), Virginia Woolf's *To the Lighthouse* (1927), and William Faulkner's *The Sound and the Fury* (1929).

Sturm und Drang: A dramatic and literary movement in Germany during the late eighteenth century. Translated as "Storm and Stress," the movement was a reaction against classicism and a forerunner of Romanticism, characterized by extravagantly emotional language and sensational subject matter.

Surrealism: A revolutionary approach to artistic and literary creation, Surrealism argued for complete artistic freedom: The artist should relinquish all conscious control, responding to the irrational urges of the unconscious mind. Hence the bizarre, dreamlike, and nightmarish quality of Surrealistic writing. In the 1920's and 1930's, Surrealism flourished in France, Spain, and Latin America. (After World War II, it influenced such American writers as Frank O'Hara, John Ashberry, and Nathanael West.)

Symbol: A literary symbol is an image that stands for something else; it may evoke a cluster of meanings rather than a single specific meaning.

Symbolism: A literary movement encompassing the work of a group of French writers in the latter half of the nineteenth century, a group that included Charles Baudelaire, Stéphane Mallarmé, and Paul Verlaine. According to Symbolism, there is a mystical correspondence between the natural and spiritual worlds.

Theater of Cruelty: A term, coined by French playwright Antonin Artaud, which signifies a vision in which theater becomes an arena for shock therapy. The characters undergo such intense physical and psychic extremities that the audience cannot ignore the cathartic effect in which its preconceptions, fears, and hostilities are brought to the surface and, ideally, purged.

Theater of the Absurd: Refers to a group of plays that share a basic belief that life is illogical, irrational, formless, and contradictory, and that humanity is without meaning or purpose. Practitioners, who include Eugène Ionesco, Samuel Beckett, Jean Genet, Harold Pinter, Edward Albee, and Arthur Kopit, abandoned traditional theatrical forms and coherent dialogue.

***Théâtre d'avant-garde*:** A movement in late nineteenth century drama in France, which challenged the conventions of realistic drama by using Symbolist poetry and nonobjective scenery.

Third person: Third-person narration occurs when the narrator has not been part of the event or affected it and is not probing his own relationship to it but is only describing what happened. He does not allow the intrusion of the word *I*. Third-person narration establishes a distance between reader and subject, gives credibility to a large expanse of narration that would be impossible for one person to experience, and allows the narrative to include a number of characters who can comment on one another as well as be the subjects of commentary by the participating narrator.

Tragedy: A form of drama that is serious in action and intent and that involves disastrous events and death; classical Greek drama observed specific guidelines for tragedy, but the term is now sometimes applied to a range of dramatic or fictional situations.

Travel literature: Writing that emphasizes the author's subjective response to places visited, especially faraway, exotic, and culturally different locales.

Trilogy: A novel or play written in three parts, each of which is a self-contained work, such as William Shakespeare's *Henry VI* (*Part I*, 1592; *Part II*, c. 1590-1591; *Part III*, c. 1590-1591). Modern examples include C. S. Lewis' Space Trilogy (1938-1945) and William Golding's Sea Trilogy (1980-1989).

Trope: Trope means literally "turn" or "conversion"; it is a figure of speech in which a word or phrase is used in a way that deviates from the normal or literal sense.

***Verismo*:** Refers to a type of Italian literature that deals with the lower classes and presents them realistically using language that they would use. Called *verismo* because it is true to life, and, from the writer's point of view, impersonal.

Verse: Verse is a generic name for poetry. Verse also refers in a narrower sense to poetry that is humorous or merely superficial, as in "greeting-card verse." Finally, English critics sometimes use "verse" to mean "stanza," or, more often, to mean "line."

Verse drama: Verse drama was the prevailing form for Western drama throughout most of its history, comprising all the drama of classical Greece and continuing to dominate the stage through the Renaissance, when it was best exemplified by the blank verse of Elizabethan drama. In the seventeenth century, however, prose comedies became popular, and in the nineteenth and twentieth centuries verse drama became the exception rather than the rule.

Victorian novel: Although the Victorian period extended from 1837 to 1901, the term "Victorian novel" does not include works from the later decades of Queen Victoria's reign. The term loosely refers to the sprawling works of novelists such as Charles Dickens and William Makepeace Thackeray, which are characterized by a broad social canvas.

Villanelle: A French verse form assimilated by English prosody. It is usually composed of nineteen lines divided into five tercets and a quatrain, rhyming *aba*, *bba*, *aba*, *aba*, *abaa*. The third line is repeated in the ninth and fifteenth lines. Dylan Thomas' "Do Not Go Gentle into That Good Night" is a modern example of a successful villanelle.

Well-made play: From the French term *pièce bien faite*, a type of play constructed according to a "formula" that originated in nineteenth century France. The plot often revolves around a secret known only to some of the characters, which is revealed at the climax and leads to catastrophe for the villain and vindication or triumph for the hero. The well-made play influenced later dramatists such as Henrik Ibsen and George Bernard Shaw.

Weltanschauung: A German term translated as "worldview," by which is meant a comprehensive set of beliefs or assumptions by means of which one interprets what goes on in the world.

Zeitgeist: A German term meaning the spirit of the times, the moral or intellectual atmosphere of any age or period. The *Zeitgeist* of the Romantic Age, for example, might be described as revolutionary, restless, individualistic, and innovative.

AUTHOR INDEX

TITLE INDEX

AUTHOR BY COUNTRY INDEX

AUTHOR BY COUNTRY INDEX